GHANA AND NIGERIA 1957-70
A STUDY IN INTER-AFRICAN DISCORD

Ghana and Nigeria 1957-70

A STUDY IN INTER-AFRICAN DISCORD

OLAJIDE ALUKO

BOOKS
10 East 53d St. New York 10022
(a division of Harper & Row Publishers, Inc.)

First published by Rex Collings Ltd
69 Marylebone High Street   London   W1

Published in the USA 1976 by
Harper & Row Publishers Inc
Barnes & Noble Import Division

© Rex Collings Ltd 1976

ISBN 0-06-490163-7

Library of Congress Catalog Card Number 75-1614 6/17/82

Typesetting by Malvern Typesetting Services
Printed in Great Britain
by Billings & Sons Ltd
Guildford, London and Worcester

087042

Contents

Acknowledgements

In preparing this study I have been particularly dependent on the forbearance, co-operation, and assistance of others. I wish to express my thanks to all the staff of the libraries of the following places: University of Ghana, Legon, University of Ibadan, Institute of Administration, University of Ife, and the National Archives, Ibadan.

My field work would have been fruitless and futile but for the active support and enthusiasm of all the ex-politicians and the top government officials I interviewed in Ghana and Nigeria. To all of them I am especially grateful. Many of those who have gladly assisted with this book have done so on the understanding that they would remain anonymous. To these people I can only make my general grateful acknowledgements. However, I wish to record my debt of gratitude to the following people for their comments and advice: Chief Kola Balogun, the first Nigerian High Commissioner in Ghana (1959–61); Mr Victor Adegoroye, the Nigerian High Commissioner in Ghana (1967–71); Mr Peter Afolabi, the present Nigerian High Commissioner in Canada; Mr B. A. Clark, the former Deputy Permanent Secretary, Ministry of External Affairs, Lagos; Mr G. O. Ijewere, the former head of Africa Division, Ministry of External Affairs, and now Nigerian High Commissioner in Ghana. I am also grateful to the following for their helpful assistance while on field trips in Ghana: Mr F. Boateng, then the Principal Secretary, Ministry of Foreign Affairs, Accra; Mr Harry Amonoo, the former Principal Secretary of the same Ministry, and later the Ghanaian Ambassador to Ethiopia; Mr E. N. Omaboe, the former Chief Government Statistician, and the Commissioner for Economic Affairs under the National Liberation Council; Mr. James Nti, Director, Institute of Management and Public Administration, Accra; Mr K. A. Karikari, the head of the Special Action Unit of the National Redemption Council Secretariat. I should also thank Professor Dennis Austin of Manchester University, Professor F. S. Northedge, and Mr J. B. L. Mayall, both of the London School of Economics, for their suggestions and comments on this work. To Mr Samson Adedotun Alli whose diligence matched his skill in typing out the first draft I am particularly thankful. I am also especially grateful to Mr Yekini Onaolapo Oyeleke whose patience and skill were nearly over-stretched in getting the final draft out within record time. Finally, I wish to express my appreciation to my wife, Mrs Ekundayo Monilola Aluko, for her patience, tolerance, and encouragement which stood me in good stead during the sleepless nights spent on this work.

Principal Abbreviations

AAPC — All African People's Conference
AG — Action Group
ANC — Armie Nationale Congolaise
EEC — European Economic Community
CPP — Convention People's Party
GAOR — General Assembly Official Records
MNC — Mouvement Nationale Congolais
NCNC — National Council of Nigerian Citizens
NLC — National Liberation Council
NLM — National Liberation Movement
NPC — Northern People's Congress
NRC — National Redemption Council
OAU — Organization of African Unity
ONUC — Organisation des Nations Unies au Congo
SCOR — Security Council Official Records

*DEDICATED TO MY LATE
FATHER MR THOMAS ALUKO*

Introduction

Relations between Ghana and Nigeria are of long standing rooted in their history as colonies of the same imperial Power. In March 1957 when Ghana became independent the two countries shared many institutions and other interests in common. Apart from this they inherited from the United Kingdom a common official language, and common legal, administrative and educational systems. In addition, both of them joined the Commonwealth on their independence.

All these tended to make people assume at the time that they would continue to strengthen their links which are of vital importance for unity not only among the Commonwealth African countries, but also for the whole of Africa. This is mainly because between them they constitute in size and population a large part of Africa. For instance, over ninety-five per cent of the total population of the former British West Africa in 1965 were living in the two countries; and this percentage represented then over twenty-six per cent[1] of the total population of Africa. In size, Ghana and Nigeria cover over ninety-seven per cent of the total area of the former British West Africa. In natural and mineral resources the two countries put together are a giant in Africa.

In these circumstances the case for close co-operation between the two countries for the purposes of improving the living conditions of their peoples and of promoting pan-African objectives can scarcely be overstated. The leaders of the two countries seemed to recognize the importance of this. Thus on the attainment of independence by the Gold Coast on 6 March 1957, Alhaji Abubakar Tafawa Balewa who later became the Nigerian Prime Minister expressed the hope that the traditional bonds and links between his country and the newly independent Ghana would continue to grow stronger.[2] During his visit to Nigeria very early in 1959, Dr Kwame Nkrumah assured the Nigerians that once their country was independent his government would take prompt measures to 're-establish our connections . . . with Nigeria through the various interterritorial institutions such as the West African Airways'[3] etc. from which Ghana had withdrawn since March 1957 because of her new status as a sovereign independent state.[4] Shortly after independence the Nigerian Federal Government in November 1960 warmly accepted an Opposition motion calling for the resuscitation of 'the interterritorial organizations which have been dissolved, and the promotion of others in the economic, technical, and cultural spheres as a primary step towards the ultimate objective of a Union of West African states.'[5]

Furthermore, some of the leaders of both countries believed that if their countries co-operated extensively their capacity to influence matters abroad would be greater. Thus during the visit of Mr Kojo Botsio, then the Ghanaian Foreign Minister, to Lagos in September 1963 Sir Abubakar told him that if the two countries worked together they would be in a position 'to influence a lot of things not only in Africa but also in the whole world.'[6] In reply, Mr Kojo Botsio said it had always been the view of the Ghanaian government that close co-operation between Accra and Lagos was crucial to the projection of what he called 'the African personality' abroad.[7]

In spite of all these declarations, very little co-operation did really take place between the two countries between March 1957 and 1970. Instead of co-operation, the two countries actually began progressively from the time of Ghana's independence, and even a little earlier, to move apart. By the end of 1970 both had virtually dismissed the hope of co-operating with each other. That year, which saw the signing of the Ghana-Ivory Coast Friendship Treaty[8] under which the Busia government formally committed the country into a sort of an alliance with the Ivory Coast, also witnessed the placing of a premium by Nigeria on her relations with her Francophone neighbours rather than with Ghana. Indeed, the central facts about the Ghanaian-Nigerian relationships during the period under study were those ranging from mutual apathy and suspicion, to violent antagonism and outright hostility. Although there were brief intervals of a relaxed relationship between Accra and Lagos, such as the immediate months following the formation of the Organization of African Unity (OAU) in May 1963, the main feature of their relationship was one of discord. Not only were almost all the common interterritorial organizations between them dissolved by the end of 1962, but no serious efforts were made during this period to establish new ones commensurate with their new status as sovereign independent states. For instance, on 28 March 1964 the Nigerian National Shipping Line and Ghana's Black Star Line agreed in principle to form a Conference Line to control the north-bound trade of the two countries,[9] but because of the political difficulties between the two countries nothing concrete came out of this agreement.

Why was this so? What were the main sources of disharmony in the Ghanaian-Nigerian relationships? Were they caused by 'the dark forces of imperialism' as Mr Kojo Botsio told reporters at the Ikeja airport while in Lagos at the head of a twelve-man Ghanaian government delegation in September 1963?[10] Or were they merely due to 'the activities of mischief makers' as Sir Abubakar told Mr Owusu-Ansah, then the Ghanaian High Commissioner, who had gone to bid him farewell as he was about to leave the country for good in October 1965?[11] Or were the sources of discord more fundamental? And if so what are they? How could they be explained? What are the future prospects of their relations now that the Busia government has been overthrown? These are the main questions that form the subject of this book. We are not so much concerned with passing judgements as with analysing and explaining the factors making for disharmony in their relations. However, judgement, being part of human nature, cannot be entirely avoided in this type of study. But when this is done it is done as much as possible on the basis of available material.

Although the focus of this study is confined to the period between March 1957 and the end of 1970, an attempt is made to extend it as much as possible to the time when the Progress Government was unseated by a coup on 13 January 1972. And as already indicated, we shall try to say something, however tentatively, about the likely pattern of the Ghanaian-Nigerian relationship after the Busia period.

Any account of inter-state relationship as this, written shortly after the events with which it deals, cannot but suffer to some extent some limitations. The most important of these include the lack of access to diplomatic despatches and other official papers; and the fact that the study will lack historical perspective. While recognizing these limitations, one can say that they are not so serious as to make this study unrewarding. This is mainly because most of the centrally important facts about the relationships between Ghana and Nigeria are sufficiently accessible in published sources for the student to understand why certain decisions and not others were taken. Another important factor was that the Nkrumah government, unlike most, frequently published the text of its despatches to other governments. Moreover, the author had access to some unpublished official material during the course of the research that led to this book. Because of all this, the sources used are as far as possible official documents rather than second-hand accounts, though newspapers and magazines like 'West Africa' and 'Africa Research Bulletin' are also used. Finally the yearly visits of the author to Ghana between 1969 and 1972 for the purposes of research for this study, and his frequent discussions with top-ranking officials and former politicians of both countries, put him in a better position to comprehend the different mental attitudes that conditioned the behaviour of the two countries to each other.

Method and Plan

The approach adopted in this study is largely narrative. Since the year 1966 represented a sort of watershed in the internal and external policies of both countries all the themes dealt with in most of the chapters are divided into two sections. The first section deals with the period before the coups of early 1966 in both countries, and the second with the post-1966 period.

Chapter I is intended to set the context — in terms of domestic and external environment — in which the Ghanaian-Nigerian relationship had to operate. Chapter II considers the various types of links, associations, and co-operation between the Gold Coast people and the Nigerians during the colonial era, and also the various types of interterritorial institutions linking the two countries prior to Ghana's independence. It also tries to give reasons for the break-up of most of these links after independence. Chapters III-VII examine the major sources of discord between the two countries. Chapter III deals with their competition over the leadership role in Black Africa by considering such questions as anti-colonialism, anti-neo-colonialism, and African unity. Chapter IV examines their different attitudes to the OAU by dealing with such questions as the OAU Liberation Committee, an African High Command, an African Common Market. Chapter V deals with their attitudes to the Congo crisis, and attempts to offer some explanation for the attitude taken by each country. Chapter VI examines their attitudes to the Great Powers by considering their attitudes to Britain, the Super Powers, and the European Economic Community; and some explanations are also offered for these attitudes. In Chapter VII we give a brief account of Ghana's role in the Nigerian civil war, and some reasons are put forward to explain Ghana's stand. Finally Chapter VIII attempts to look ahead to the future prospects of the Ghanaian-Nigerian relations after the overthrow of Dr Busia's government.

1. *A Survey of Economic Conditions in Africa, 1969*, Addis Ababa, Economic Commission for Africa, 1971 *Doc.. E/CN.14/480/Rev.* Part I, p. 4.
2. *House of Representatives Debates 1955–66*, 5 March 1957, cols. 199-200.

3. *Visit to Nigeria by the Prime Minister of Ghana Dr Kwame Nkrumah*, Accra, Government Printer, 1959, p. 10.
4. Ibid.
6. *Africa Diary*, 28 September–4 October 1963, p. 1366.
7. Ibid.
8. For the text of this Friendship Treaty see *Political Africa*, Vol. 1 No. 6, Accra June 1970, pp. 3–5.
9. *Africa Diary*, 9–15 March 1964, p. 1741.
10. *Africa Diary*, 28 September–4 October 1963, p. 1366.
11. *Africa Research Bulletin*, October 1965, p. 380.

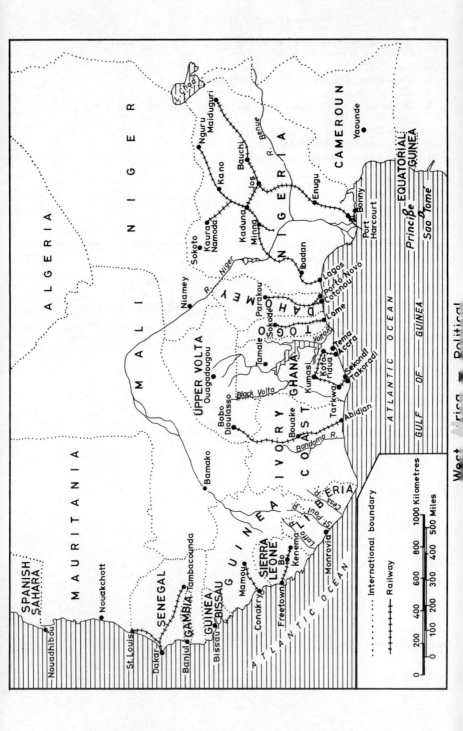

West Africa — Political

CHAPTER I
Post-independence Setting

When Ghana and Nigeria obtained independence on 6 March 1957 and 1 October 1960 respectively, they faced similar and in some ways dissimilar problems in their internal and external environment. It is these environmental factors with which this chapter deals. For these not merely set the context in which their post-independence relationship operated, but also help to explain much of their external behaviour,[1] especially their bilateral relationships. Since these factors, especially the domestic ones, did not remain constant throughout the 1957–70 period, we shall deal briefly with the great changes that occurred in the second half of the sixties in both countries, mainly because these have had profound effects on their external policies.[2] In both countries, however, as in many other developing countries, the leaders enjoyed greater freedom of action in foreign policy matters than their counterparts in the older established nations. Because of this we shall say something briefly about the background, experience, and outlook of the political leaders of both countries on independence, and the type of parties they led.

(i) GHANA ON INDEPENDENCE:

(a) *Domestic Setting*
Ghana achieved independence in March 1957 under a unitary constitution which left the central government strong under the Convention People's Party (CPP) which had won a decisive and resounding victory over the Opposition parties in the July 1956 general elections. But to strengthen further the position of the CPP government, Dr Nkrumah soon after independence took a number of far-reaching measures such as the abolition of the interim regional assemblies, the removal of the entrenched constitutional safeguards for the opposition, and the enactment of the Preventive Detention Act. All the opposition parties that regrouped to form the United Party (UP) soon crumbled under the weight of the CPP. With the

introduction of the Republican Constitution in July 1960, and the frequent and unscrupulous use of the Preventive Detention Act and other powers, the CPP government had by mid-1961 silenced all the voices of dissent in Ghana. By 1964 Ghana which since late 1961 had to all intents and purposes become a 'de facto' single party state became a 'de jure' one.[3]

One of the main consequences of all this development was the emergence of the CPP government as the unchallenged master of the country, and the sole decider of its fate. But in actual fact the CPP government, especially from the Kulungugu bomb episode of 1 August 1962,[4] increasingly degenerated into personal rule till the coup d'état of 24 February 1966.[5]

However, it has to be said that Dr Nkrumah on independence in March 1957 was regarded as a national hero among the bulk of the Ghanaians. His party, the CPP, which was a mass party,[6] enjoyed popular support from its formation in June 1949 till independence, and even for the period immediately following independence. It was the CPP which, by a policy of confrontation with the Colonial Power through the proclamation of a 'Positive Action'[7] policy on 8 January 1950, had hastened the process of decolonizing the Gold Coast. This the CPP—being a nationalist commoners' party—did against the alliance of the traditional chiefs and the intellectuals.[8]

The CPP leadership was made up of the 'verandah boys', 'the elementary school leavers'[9] without the advantage of noble birth or wealth behind them. So they had little or nothing to lose in adopting radical tactics towards the Colonial Government. As a result of their radical and revolutionary tactics, nearly all the top leaders of the CPP including Nkrumah, the party's chairman, and K. A. Gbedemah, the Vice-Chairman, went to jail between September 1949 and early 1951.[10]

Dr Kwame Nkrumah, the chairman of the CPP and later its general secretary, played such a predominant role in the CPP and its government[11] that we should say something about him. Born on 21 September 1909 of humble parentage in Nkroful village in Nzima in the extreme south-west of the Gold Coast, Nkrumah was brought up as a Roman Catholic. He was educated at Achimota College, and later in Lincoln University, Pennsylvania, where by February 1943 he had got two Master's degrees, in Philosophy and Education.[12] After ten years in the United States, he went to Britain in June 1945 where he spent most of his student days searching for 'a formula by which the whole colonial question, and the problem of imperialism could be solved'. He said he read the works of Hegel, Karl Marx, Engels,

Lenin and Mazzini in the process, and that his revolutionary ideas and activities were greatly influenced by the writings of Karl Marx and Lenin.[13] Against this background, his description of himself as 'a Marxist socialist' could easily be understood.[14] Dr Nkrumah said his enthusiasm was fired by the 'Philosophy and Opinions of Marcus Garvey', published in 1923, more than by any other work. He was highly impressed by Marcus Garvey's slogan of 'Africa for the Africans', and his 'Back to Africa' movement.

With all these varied experiences Nkrumah became violently anti-colonial. While in London, he and George Padmore had acted as the joint secretaries of the Organization Committee that made arrangements for the fifth Pan-African Congress in Manchester in October 1945, which endorsed the right of Africans to self-government and also the doctrine of African socialism based on the tactics of positive action without violence.[15] In 1946, Nkrumah became the secretary of the West African National secretariat set up in London with the main purpose of stimulating African nationalism and West African unity. In pursuit of this, Nkrumah visited Paris to meet the African members of the French National Assembly such as Sourou Apithy, Léopold Senghor, Lamine Guèye, Houphouet-Boigny and others.

Socially Ghana was, on independence, different from Nigeria in many ways. Although there were many tribes in Ghana,[16] there was some great underlying similarity between them in language, social customs and religion, as noted by Cardinall as early as 1931.[17] For instance, about seventy per cent of the whole population spoke one of the Kwa family of languages, while the Akan language though still far from becoming a *lingua franca* was not only the language of over half of the people, but also widely spoken all over Ghana.[18] In spite of the fact that there were three main religions in the country, namely, Islam to which twelve per cent of the population belonged in 1960, traditional Koranic lines.[20] There was nothing like the existence of there was no religious intolerance or fanaticism in the country.

Unlike the practice in the Northern Nigerian emirates the Muslims in Ghana established schools conducted on Western instead of the traditional Koranic lines.[20] There was nothing like the existence of Muslim courts and laws for Ghanaian Muslims as in Northern Nigeria.

The level of literacy in Ghana on independence was about thirty per cent higher than that of Nigeria in 1960, partly because of the introduction of free primary schooling by the CPP government in 1951 and partly because the Colonial Administration had spent more on education in the Gold Coast than in Nigeria,[21] though it has to be said that until the fifties the Western form of education was resisted in Northern Nigeria. Because of Western education and economic development in Ghana, there was greater urbanization in Ghana in 1957 than in Nigeria on its independence.

Ghana's economy was buoyant at the time of independence. The foreign reserve assets of the country in March 1957 amounted to about £200 million. The finances of the country were so good that it was able to finance on its own much of the development that took place between 1951 and 1957. For instance, while the government spent £124 million out of its own resources for development between 1951 and 1957, it received a grant of only £3½ million during the same period from the United Kingdom.[22] The national debt, much of which was internal at the time of independence, amounted to about £20 million.[23] The income per capita in 1957 was put at about £50 by Dr Nkrumah, who said this was about two and a half times that of Nigeria. It was all this that made *The Economist* say later that in March 1957 Ghana was 'the richest-looking West African country'.[24]

Although 'richest-looking' the economy was fragile, being largely dependent on the export of a single crop, cocoa, whose prices were subject to wild fluctuation in world markets beyond Ghana's control.[25] In 1957 cocoa accounted for sixty-six per cent of total export earnings. Although Ghana had other export commodities such as timber, manganese, bauxite and gold, they all accounted for less than thirty per cent of the total value of exports in 1957.

Another problem facing the economy was poor agricultural productivity, in spite of the fact that about sixty-two per cent of the working population was engaged in it by 1960. The Lewis Report of 1953 about the poor performance of agriculture was more true in 1957 apart from the increase in world prices of cocoa. In the latter year, Ghana spent £17,400,000 or about thirty per cent of the total import bill on food.[26]

One other problem facing the country was that the economy like that of many of the newly independent states was a colonial one based on the export of primary products in exchange for manufactured goods. As a result of this the country's external trade was mainly with the developed countries of the West, which in 1957 accounted for over ninety-eight per cent and ninety-six per cent of its imports and exports respectively. On the other hand, its trade with other African countries was very small. For example in 1957 Ghana's trade with her West African neighbours was less than 0.5 per cent of the total. Her exports to and imports from Nigeria, her best customer in West

Africa, amounted in 1957 to only £286,000 and £1,413,000 respectively.[27] Ghana's dependence on the export of raw commodities meant that she had to face the difficulties of the worsening terms of trade that had, since the mid-fifties, beset the primary producers of the developing world.

One last point that has to be mentioned about Ghana's economy was the size and population of the country. In size and population Ghana was a small country covering an area of about 92,100 square miles and numbering 6,726,800 in 1960, according to that year's census figures. This smallness of size and population placed a serious limitation on the domestic market and the level of economic activities in the country, in an age when only countries with economies of scale could easily develop rapidly.[28]

In spite of all these, however, the growth of the economy was somehow impressive until 1960. Yet the economy was highly vulnerable,[29] and perhaps no one realized this more than Dr Nkrumah. From independence, and even before,[30] he had wanted to diversify the economy, in order to reduce its dependence on cocoa, by a policy of industrialization and modernization of agriculture. To carry out this policy Ghana, like most of the developing countries, required capital investment and technical know-how from abroad.

On independence Ghana was of no military consequence. Its army, which was formerly part of the Royal West African Frontier Force (RWAFF), was very small in size and poorly equipped. Even in 1964, nearly seven years after independence, the size of the armed forces was still very small, consisting of 9,000 men; and only about 2.2 per cent ($35 million) of the Gross National Product was spent on the armed forces during the same year.[31]

The army was officered largely by the British, who formed three-quarters of the officer corps in 1957. Indeed, on independence, there was no Ghanaian with a higher rank that that of a Major in the army.[32] The complete Ghananization of the army did not take place until 22 September 1961 when Dr Nkrumah sacked all the British army officers, including the British army Chief of Staff, General Alexander.

In 1957, Ghana had a very small and weak navy which was almost entirely officered by the British. It had no air force, and one was not established until September 1959. The force was poorly equipped too, having no jet fighters until 1964. Although from early 1960 onwards Dr Nkrumah for a variety of reasons made strenuous efforts to build up a large modern army, the country's armed forces till the end of his regime remained—mainly because of lack of money and technical know-how—relatively small, and poorly equipped by Western standards. The implication of this was that the armed forces were not viable enough to back up effectively Ghana's foreign policy goals, even in West Africa. For instance Dr Nkrumah's attempt in 1960, through a show of force at the border with Togo, to overawe the government of Sylvanus Olympio in order to secure his compliance with his terms over the integration of Togo with Ghana failed dismally.[33]

(b) *Ghana's External Environment*
In March 1957 when Ghana became independent she found herself a lone shining star in Black Africa. She was surrounded by colonial territories all over West Africa. Furthermore, there was very little intercolonial contact, especially between the Anglophone and Francophone Africans. This situation was serious from Nkrumah's point of view[34] mainly because the Nzimas, his tribesmen, and the Aowin people were arbitrarily split up by the colonial frontiers between Ghana and the Ivory Coast, while the Ewes too had been equally divided up between Ghana and French Togoland.

It was in this type of environment that Nkrumah's aggressive anti-colonial and radical Pan-African programme was meaningful.[35] His programme was that freedom from colonial rule was to be followed by African unity that would end all the artificial barriers created by the colonial powers, and thereby end any tendency towards irrendentism in Africa.

Outside Africa Ghana was, on independence, faced with a larger world dominated by two antagonistic politico-military oligarchies buttressed by different socio-economic systems. There was also already in existence at the UN a small Afro-Asian group of states led by India who refused to join any of the multilateral defence pacts led by either of the Super Powers, and adopted a policy of 'non-alignment' or 'positive neutralism'. Ghana followed the example of this group of neutralist states by adopting a policy of 'positive neutralism' since Ghana's alignment with either of the Super Powers would, as Nkrumah himself said, make no appreciable difference to the balance between them, and would on the contrary be detrimental to Ghana's national interest.[36] Nkrumah's definition and interpretation of his policy of 'positive neutralism' and Nigeria's attitude to it were to become one of the main sources of Ghanaian-Nigerian conflict.[37]

Given all these external and domestic factors, especially the political stability of the country, its relative racial and cultural homogeneity, the structure of its government, the experiences and the dynamic nature of the CPP leaders, and its relative prosperity on independence, the country was in spite of its military weakness poised for a vigorous foreign policy. This was in accord with the mood of the country that wanted Ghana to play a leading role in Africa and in the world because of her position as the first black African country to achieve independence.

(ii) NIGERIA AT INDEPENDENCE:

(a) *Domestic Setting*

Nigeria on independence, on 1 October 1960, though similar to Ghana in certain respects, was in many ways different from her in the internal factors of her leaders had to cope with. Unlike Ghana she became independent under a federal form of constitution that was awkward in several ways. Firstly, it consisted of only three constituent units. Secondly, one of these units, the North, was in area and population larger than the rest of the Federation. Thirdly, it was dominated by the least developed of the Regions, the North.

Although the Federal government had wide exclusive powers, including defence and external affairs, the three Regional Governments apart from their residual authority had enormous powers over a wide range of subjects, with little Federal control. The three Regional Governments were politically and culturally dominated by separate tribal groups—the Hausa-Fulani dominated the Northern People's Congress in the North, the Ibo dominated the National Council of Nigeria and the Cameroons (NCNC)[38] in the East, and the Yoruba dominated The Action Group (AG) in the West. The Regional Governments were largely financially stable, each being buttressed by one or more of the main export crops, with little or no Federal control. The introduction of the Republican Constitution in October 1963 did not increase the power of the Federal Government mainly because the Regions, especially the North, were jealous of their wide powers which would have been threatened by such an increase.[39]

Politically the Federation was weak. Unlike the pre-independence election of the Gold Coast of July 1956, the Nigerian Federal elections of December 1959 did not result in a majority for any one party. Although the coalition government of the NPC and the NCNC and their allies that was formed after the 1959 Federal election had a large majority in the new Legislature, and increased this with the split of the AG in 1962, it remained weak for two main reasons.

First, the NPC/NCNC coalition was a strange one. Apart from the fact that some of the leaders of both parties had since 1954 been working together at the Federal level, the two parties had ideologically little in common,[40] except a common negative hostility to the AG.[41] No wonder then that, with the virtual disappearance of the AG by late 1962, the NPC and the NCNC turned on each other. The second reason was that the leader of the coalition, the Prime Minister, Sir Abubakar Tafawa Balewa, was only the second in command in the NPC hierarchy. The party's leader was Sir Ahmadu Bello, the Sardauna of Sokoto, then the Northern Nigeria Premier.

Unlike Ghana, where Dr Nkrumah emerged as the national hero on independence, there was no such leader in Nigeria in October 1960. The independence struggle, such as there was, did not thrust forward any nationally acceptable hero, as Chief Awolowo was to lament later.[42] Apart from the brief period of violent nationalist activities by the Zikist Movement between 1947 and early 1950, what struggle there was for independence in Nigeria took the form of peaceful negotiation between the nationalist leaders and the British. The result was that the road to independence was on the whole peaceful, and was achieved in close co-operation with the British rather than against them. None of the national leaders of the country in October 1960 was jailed by the Colonial Administration, as were Dr Nkrumah and most of his lieutenants. As a result of all this the nationalist movement in Nigeria when compared with that of the Gold Coast was 'sedate' as Walter Schwarz[43] has rightly stated.

Apart from the socio-political problems which prevented the emergence of a radical nationalist movement in Nigeria, the leaders of the major nationalist parties were of a different stamp from those of the CCP. For instance, the NPC leaders were conservative men who derived their influence from their association with the traditional forms of government and traditional status in the Northern society. The NCNC and the AG were both led by bourgeois nationalists. Most of them were professional men and men with vast business connections. In 1956, Dr Azikiwe, then the NCNC President and Eastern Nigeria Premier, virtually owned the African Continental Bank and a chain of other limited liability companies.[44] Chief Obafemi Awolowo, then the AG leader and Premier of the Western Region, was already a successful lawyer.

Likewise, the parties these men led to independence were in many ways different from the CPP. Unlike the CPP, which was a national party, all the three main political parties in Nigeria were regionally based, each deriving its main support from one of the Regions.

Indeed, while the AG and the NCNC strove to become national parties, the NPC till the coup in January 1966 refused to become one.[45] The NPC which was the senior partner in the Federal coalition, remained a cadre party.[46] The AG which started as a cadre later became during the late fifties a mass party. The NCNC which was the junior partner in the Federal coalition in 1960 was a mass party. But its organization had always been deficient, largely as a result of internal convulsions such as the 'Zik Must Go' campaign of June 1958, and because of lack of discipline.

In spite of the weakness of the Federal coalition, there was little doubt that Sir Abubakar's pre-eminence in the Federal cabinet remained unchallenged till his death. He was nonetheless hamstrung by Sir Ahmadu Bello, the NPC leader,[47] even in foreign policy matters. It was said that it was Sir Ahmadu that prevented the establishment of a Nigerian diplomatic Mission in Israel[48] in spite of the fact that that country had opened an embassy in Lagos as far back as 1960, and in spite of the vast economic, trade and technical connections between that country and Southern Nigeria.[49]

In spite of this, however, the Prime Minister, Sir Abubakar, could be said to have been largely in control of the country's foreign policy until his death. Between October 1960 and July 1961, when Jaja Wachuku was appointed Foreign Minister, the Prime Minister was his own Foreign Secretary. Similarly, from December 1964 until the coup he held the portfolio of the Foreign Ministry, though assisted by two Senators, Nuhu Bamali and Dan Ibekwe. Even when not directly in charge, Sir Abubakar maintained a tight control over the country's external policy.

To understand Nigeria's foreign policy and attitude to Ghana, especially until the coup in January 1966, it is pertinent to say something about the background and experience of Sir Abubakar Tafawa Balewa and of Sir Ahmadu Bello, who was rightly described by Walter Schwarz as 'Nigeria's most powerful politician'.[50] To begin with the Sardauna, he was born in 1910 at Rabah, near Sokoto. His great-grandfather was Sultan Bello, the son of Shehu Usuman Dan Fodio,[51] who before his death had by 1817 succeeded in establishing the Fulani empire over most of what later became Northern Nigeria. Educated, as most Northern leaders were, at Katsina Teacher Training College, the Sarduana first began to teach at the end of his training in 1931.

In 1934 he joined the administration of the Native Authorities. After a course in Local Government in Britain in 1948, he became the Secretary to the Sokoto Native Authority. In 1949, he became a member of the Northern Regional House of Assembly and the leader of the Northern delegation to the Legislative Council in Lagos. He later became the NPC President and the Premier of Northern Region.

Although the Sardauna started a programme of modernization, his main aim was the preservation of the religion and the traditions of the Northern emirates. His ambition was ultimately to resign from politics,[52] and become the Sultan of Sokoto, the religious head of the North. Towards the end of his life he embarked on what Bryan Sharwood Smith has called 'a campaign of militant proselytism for Islam'.[53] Thus between 1964 and September 1965 the Sardauna claimed to have converted 430,000 people to Islam in the North.[54]

Nonetheless, he was a great politician who spent much of his life striving to preserve and defend the rights of the North and its aristocratic system. He refused to become a Nigerian. Till his death, he took every opportunity of trying 'to put right the mistakes of 1914'. But because of his high birth, his position as the Regional Premier, his devotion to Islamic purity and a gradual modernization policy, he was widely respected in the North.[55]

In contrast to the Sardauna, Sir Abubakar was of humble birth. His father was a nomadic Fulani, while his mother was a Hausa native of Tafawa Balewa. He, too, was educated in Katsina College between 1928 and 1933. Later in 1945-6 he went to England for the Diploma in Education at the University of London. After teaching for nearly sixteen years he became an Education Officer in 1949.[56] Though he had been in politics since 1947, Sir Abubakar did not seem to like or enjoy politics. As late as 1957 when he was being proposed as the Prime Minister he had opposed this, wishing instead to return to his former work in the Education Department.[57] But unlike the Sardauna, Balewa till his death strove to preserve and work for Nigerian unity, while nonetheless maintaining the Northern rights within the Federation unimpaired.

Socially Nigeria was different in many ways from Ghana. Although there were between 300 and 400 different tribes with their separate dialects, there were three large ones, each with a common history, common origins, and a common language, which dominated the political scene till the coup and which, as Walter·Schwarz has properly pointed out, were 'big nations'.[58] These were the Hausa-Fulani, numbering over 20 million according to the 1963 census figures and living roughly to the north of the River Niger and the Benue; the Yorubas in the South-West totalling over 10 million; and the Ibos in the Central and South-East of the country, forming about

7.5 million. While by independence in 1960 many Yorubas and Ibos had imbibed Western education and culture, the Hausa-Fulani remained extremely backward, stewed in Islamic conservatism, the result of the excessive pursuit of the policy of indirect rule designed largely to preserve 'the very special identity of the North'.[59]

Furthermore, they were vastly divided by religion. While the majority of the Yorubas and the Ibos belonged to Christianity, the majority of the Hausa-Fulanis belonged to Islam. Although according to the 1963 census about 71.7 per cent of the Northerners were Muslims, if calculated on the Northern emirates alone the percentage would have been over ninety-five. While a substantial proportion of the Yorubas belonged to Islam,[60] the Yoruba Muslims like their Ghanaian counterparts mixed freely with other Nigerians belonging to other religions, and participated in their religious festivals. But in the Northern emirates, it was different. Indeed one could talk of some religious fanaticism and intolerance there.[61] Anyone who was not a Muslim was regarded in the North as a 'Kaferi' or 'Kafirai' (an unbeliever) to be despised. The Southerners, in turn, because of their acquisition of Western education and skills, despised the Northerners as backward and feudal. Largely as a result of this most of the Southerners who went to the North for employment or trade used to live at separate strangers' quarters called 'Sabon Gari'. Unlike the practice in Ghana, the Northern Muslims established schools that were run largely on Koranic lines.

Even Katsina College, the premier teacher training college in the North, founded by the British in 1922, was to turn out teachers that would have nothing but respect and admiration for the Islamic traditions and institutions in the North.[62] Furthermore, there were alkali courts and Muslim laws applicable to Muslims in the North, neither of which were part of the national judicial or legal system.

The implications of all these great diversities in size, culture and religion were serious for Nigerian unity. Although there had been bitter antagonisms between the Ibos and the Yorubas, such as those of late 1940s which drew a dire warning from Sir John Macpherson, then the Governor,[63] the basic problem that faced Nigeria till the coup was North-South conflict, with the North first not really regarding itself as part of the country, and then trying to dominate the Federation at all costs to preserve the institutions and traditions of the emirates.[64] The level of education on independence was poorer than that of Ghana. Over eighty per cent of the population were illiterate,[65] and the level of illiteracy in the North was much higher than this, mainly because of the resistance of the Northern leaders to the introduction of Western forms of education. Because of this, the level of urbanization in Nigeria was not as high as in Ghana. For instance, in 1963, only about fifteen per cent of the total population were living in urban centres of over 20,000 people.[66]

Financially, Nigeria was in 1960 poorer than Ghana. The total value of her foreign reserves in December 1960 of £172.5 million[67] was much smaller than Ghana's reserves on her independence. The smallness of these reserves becomes more striking when it is remembered that by mid-1960 Nigeria was six times Ghana in population. The poverty of Nigeria was underlined by the fact that while income per capita in 1960 was about £70 in Ghana, it was only about £29 in Nigeria during the same year.[68] Nigeria's poverty vis-a-vis Ghana could further be illustrated by the fact that during the 1951-7 period Ghana received only £1.5 million from the Colonial Development and Welfare Fund for development, while by Nigeria's independence in 1960 she had received over £36 million under the Colonial Development and Welfare Acts.[69]

But in reality, Nigeria's economy was more stable and more relatively buoyant than that of Ghana on independence. Like Ghana, agriculture, in which about seventy-five per cent of the labour was engaged in 1960, formed the mainstay of the economy. But Nigeria had a wider variety of agricultural exports. The most important ones were cocoa, palm oil, palm kernel, groundnuts, benniseed, cotton, timber, logs, sawn timber and rubber. None of these occupied the same position as cocoa in Ghana's exports. In 1960, the value of cocoa exports, which provided the largest single export earning that year, was about £35 million, or about twenty-six per cent of the total.[70] Furthermore, although agriculture was still being carried on along traditional lines, Nigeria unlike Ghana was not only self-sufficient in food, but was until the civil war able to export foodstuffs to neighbouring West African countries such as Ghana, Togo and Dahomey.

Like Ghana, manufacturing industry was in its infancy in Nigeria at the time of independence. Its contribution to the Gross Domestic Product in 1958 was about £40.5 million or roughly four per cent of the total; in 1963 the corresponding percentage was still small, only 5.6 per cent. Though richly endowed with mineral resources, such as mineral oil, tin, columbite, hafnium, gold, tantalum, lead, coal, limestone, iron, lignite, wolfram, molybdenum, and bartytes, their contribution in 1960 to the GDP was small. In 1961 mineral exports contributed only about eleven per cent to the total export earnings. But unlike Ghana where the mining industry had been declining, it developed in Nigeria largely as a result of the petroleum industry, in such a way that by 1965 mineral exports came to account for thirty-six per cent of total export earnings.[71]

The country's external trade was based on the export of primary products and the import of finished goods. Because of this and a colonial heritage, the bulk of the trade was with the Western Powers with very little with the rest of Africa. For instance, in 1960 about forty-two per cent of Nigeria's total imports (£91,416,000 of the total of £215,319,000) came from Britain, while forty-seven per cent of her exports (£78,572,000 of £165,009,000) went to Britain.[72] In the same year less than 0.3 per cent of her imports (£638,000) came from Ghana, her best West African customer, while only about 0.6 per cent (£1,054,000) of her exports went to that country. However, Nigeria's position was better than that of Ghana. First her economy was not largely dependent on external trade as was Ghana's. Exports in 1960 made up only about one-fifth of the country's total production.[73] Being four times Ghana's size, with an area of about 356,000 square miles, and with about seven times her population, Nigeria had a large internal market that could fairly support economies of a scale which was not possible in Ghana. Furthermore, the increase after independence in the petroleum industry made Nigeria less vulnerable to the vagaries of the world commodity market.

As a result of these factors Nigeria's economy showed a steady growth on average of four per cent between 1950 and 1960. In spite of this fact, however, the Nigerian leaders, on independence, were determined to diversify their economy by a policy of industrialization and the modernization of agriculture. But because of a shortage of capital and skills, they wanted to do this by foreign assistance, as was clearly shown in the First National Plan 1962-8 which envisaged foreign aid to the tune of about fifty per cent of total capital investment in the public sector during the plan period.

Militarily, the country was of no account at the time of independence. Its army, which was formerly part of the Royal West African Frontier Force, consisted in 1960 of only 7,500 men.[74] Not only this, it was very poorly equipped, using only Second World War weapons. All the leaders of the three main political parties, including the Sardauna, 'the war prince', were, on independence and after, unanimous in their view not to increase the level of the army unnecessarily.[75] They did not see the military as an instrument of foreign policy. Apart from supporting the police in putting down internal riots, the army's other role was for ceremonial parades and guards of honour. Thus in 1964 Nigeria had fewer men under arms than Ghana (8,000 as against Ghana's 9,000); and spent only about one per cent of her Gross National Product on the armed forces as against Ghana's 2.2 per cent during the same year.[76]

The army was officered mainly by the British in 1960. The process of Africanization of the army was slower than that of Ghana because of the delicate task of maintaining ethnic balance. Until early 1965, the General Officer Commanding the Nigerian army was British, and the complete Nigerianization of the officer corps did not occur until early in 1966.

Although the Federal Government took some steps to establish a navy in 1956,[77] in 1960 the naval force was still extremely feeble, consisting of a few patrol boats designed mainly to prevent smuggling rather than for defence purposes. The country had no air force on independence, and one was not established until 1964. Given the attitude of the Nigerian leaders the armed forces of the country were in January 1966 smaller in size and more poorly equipped than those of Ghana.[78] If Ghana's larger armed forces were of little value in foreign policy matters, Nigeria's own were of still less consequence.

(b) Nigeria's External Environment

On 1 October 1960, when Nigeria achieved independence, she found herself surrounded by independent Francophone states. The only territory not independent in West Africa then was Guinea-Bissau. Although there were other colonial territories in Central and East Africa these were in 1960 fairly remote from the Nigerian leaders. While there were some tribes split between Nigeria and her neighbours by colonial boundaries, such as the Yorubas — part in Dahomey, the Hausa-Fulani part in Niger, and the Kanuri part in Chad — there was no serious effort by the country's leaders to bring all these together within a larger Nigeria, mainly because of the enormous difficulty of uniting even those already within the colonial boundary of Nigeria.

In view of these facts, though other factors were important, it was not surprising that Nigeria's leaders should on independence adopt a moderate anti-colonial, gradualist Pan-African policy.

Outside Africa, Nigeria in 1960 like Ghana on her independence faced a world split into two by the cold war. In relation to this world, Nigeria first adopted a policy of 'neutrality', and later of 'non-alignment'. How this was interpreted and followed by Nigeria was to become one of the bones of contention between Nigeria and Ghana.

Because of the external environment in which the country found itself in October 1960, and the domestic situation with which the leaders had to cope, especially the constant threat to national unity, the social instability and difficult federal structure of the country, its military weakness, and the background and outlook of its leaders, the country adopted a cautious note in foreign policy. Unlike Ghana, the internal political and social difficulties of the country did not indeed allow its leaders to turn to foreign matters until very shortly before independence.[79] In spite of the sporadic student demand for a vigorous foreign policy, the mood of the country on independence did not favour such a policy. The main reason for this was the big question mark then hanging in front of the country's survival as a unit.[80]

(iii) THE COUPS AND THE GREAT CHANGES OF THE SECOND HALF OF THE SIXTIES

During the second half of the sixties great changes occurred in the foreign policy posture of both Ghana and Nigeria, to such a degree as to appear in 1970 that they had exchanged their earlier positions, with Nigeria becoming more radical than Ghana. This owed practically nothing to the external factors, which changed very little between 1960 and 1970,[81] but was mainly due to internal factors. The situation had been brought about largely by the profound changes in the fortunes of the political leaders and parties, the changes in the economic and social life, and the changes in the climate of opinion in both countries.

(a) The Coup and the changes in Ghana

The coup of 24 February 1966 that overthrew the Nkrumah regime brought to power army officers who were extremely conservative, anti-communist, and pro-West. For instance, Colonel (later Lieutenant-General) A. A. Afrifa, one of the key architects of the coup, wrote about his affection for 'the British way of life, its legal system, and its democratic ideas',[82] and accused Dr Nkrumah of having 'sold his country to the Russians'.[83]

The former United Opposition (UP) leaders who were brought to positions of influence[84] by the coup were likewise conservative, anti-communist in outlook, and were ideologically pro-West in their foreign policy orientation. These men, who later formed the core of the Progress Party (PP) led by Dr Kofi Busia, made no substantial change in their foreign policy orientation when they formed the government in October 1969.[85] The leaders of the Progress Party, notably Dr Kofi Busia, the then Prime Minister, and Mr William Ofori-Atta, the then Foreign Minister, who were both prominent leading members of the UGCC and later the UP, had scant commitment to African unity.[86]

Furthermore, the civilian leaders who came to power and to positions of influence after the first coup were of a different stamp from the CPP leaders, who were mostly elementary school leavers. The Busia cabinet consisted of the best type of educated men the country had.[87] Some of the cabinet members had been University teachers, while others had been successful professional men. Furthermore, most of them had a chief's background. Given the background and experiences of these leaders it was not surprising that they were a little more cautious than the CPP leaders.

Shortly after the coup, although power was concentrated at first in the newly formed eight-member National Liberation Council (NLC), the new leaders proceeded to decentralize the administration of the country. Apart from the inclusion of civilian commissioners in their cabinet, various committees, such as a political committee, an external affairs committee, an agricultural committee, an economic committee etc., were set up to advise the NLC.[88] Furthermore, the administrative structure was decentralized. Instead of the practice under Nkrumah, where all Ministries had to take instructions from Flagstaff House, each Ministry was given greater autonomy in making decisions affecting it.[89]

This process of decentralization was carried further by the 1969 Constitution, which was so full of checks and balances that some wondered whether it would work.[90] Instead of one man being the head of state and government, two separate people were to hold these offices, the President and the Prime Minister respectively. The constitution also provided for the establishment of a Council of State whose duty was 'to aid and counsel the President'.[91] Article 54 of the Constitution made provision for the setting up of a National Security Council to collect information and make recommendations about the security problems of the country. Apart from all this, the judiciary was to be entirely independent of the executive, and a judicial review of the government's actions was to be final.[92]

Socially Ghana during the second half of the sixties was different from 1957. The traditional chiefs, relegated to the background by the CPP government, were restored to pre-eminence and to positions of considerable influence in the society. Early in 1971, the government approved the building of a modern N₵3-million palace complex for the Asantehene.[93] This can be explained partly by the family background of chiefs of the new leaders,[94] and partly by the fact that most of the influential members of the post 1966 coup governing élite had worked, especially between 1954 and 1956, in close alliance with the chiefs under the banner of the National Liberation Movement against the CPP, together with importance of traditional chiefs under the 1969 Constitution of Regional Houses of Chiefs, and a National House of Chiefs to deal mainly with chieftaincy matters.

The late sixties saw a sort of tribal recrudescence in Ghana, something which seemed to have been totally overcome during the Nkrumah era. The situation was so bad that some feared during the campaign for the 1969 general elections, and shortly after, that there was a danger of the country slipping into the type of tribal antagonisms of the 1954-6 period. For instance, the result of the elections showed that tribal loyalties were more important than an appeal to national issues. The two main parties for the election, the Progress Party (PP) led by the Akans, and the National Alliance of Liberals (NAL) led by the Ewes did not win a single seat in each other's tribal base, something which the PP leader, Dr Busia, described shortly after the election results were known as 'unfortunate'.[95]

Educationally the country has made much progress. The number of children in primary and middle schools rose from 571,580 in 1957 to 1,480,000 in February 1966. Similarly the number of pupils in government-assisted secondary schools almost quadrupled between 1957 and 1966, rising from 9,860 to 35,000.[96] The number of teachers training colleges rose from forty-six in 1965 to eighty-six by the time the coup occurred. Instead of one university as there was at the time of independnce, there were three by the late 1960s, enrolling about 5,500 students. During the sixties university enrolment continued to show an increase.

During the second half of the sixties, the economy was in many ways worse off. Indeed, by the time the coup occurred in February 1966 the economy had become derelict and chaotic.[97] The foreign reserves had virtually gone, amounting to only ₵12.8 million,[98] or about £5 million at the end of March 1966. The national debt by February 1966 had multiplied by about twenty times amounting to £416,666,666: 13s: 4d.[99] Of this about £300 million were owed to external sources, mostly Western European countries.[100] In spite of the fact that Ghana had on two occasions, in 1966 and in 1968, succeeded in persuading the creditor countries to re-schedule the debts, the country's indebtedness by the end of 1970 was still substantial. Indeed, by July 1971, the external debt stood at about £250 million.[101] The total national debt early in July 1971 had increased to N₵1,155,382,000 or about £465 million.[102]

Although by February 1966, the national income had risen to about £77 million, this was largely owing to inflation. For at that time there was a shortage of essential consumer goods such as salt, sugar, and milk in the country. While the NLC and the PP government succeeded with the assistance of the Western Powers in providing these essential consumer goods, they failed to overcome the problem of inflation.

Another problem plaguing the economy was one of poor agricultural productivity which itself contributed to the inflationary pressures in the country. Between 1966 and 1969, an annual average of sixteen per cent of the total import bill went on food imports.[103] And unlike the immediate post-independence years there was insufficient foreign exchange for large food imports. As a result there was a scarcity of food, which in turn led to higher prices. For instance, in mid-1969, a bag of maize which should not sell above N₵10 was being sold at N₵30 in the Accra market. The poor agricultural productivity extended to the cocoa industry, where Ghana's share of world production declined from 36.8 per cent in 1960-1 to 27.2 per cent in 1969.[104]

The country's balance of payments, which reached its highest record deficit during Dr Nkrumah's last year in office, amounting to N₵227 million[105] showed only little improvement in the second half of the sixties. In 1967, the balance of payments deficit was N₵86.6 million. The corresponding deficit declined to N₵51.5 per cent in 1968, but rose to N₵60.4 per cent in 1969.[106]

Another major problem confronting the country was one of mass unemployment. Shortly after the coup, the NLC and later its successor government started to rationalize and streamline the economy of the country. In this process hundreds of people employed at the public expense in non-viable projects were dismissed. By 1967 there were about 60,000 people without jobs. By mid-1969 the number had risen to over 150,000, becoming 'one of the most intractable problems' facing the NLC.[107] By the end of 1970 about 200,000 people, or about thirty per cent of the total labour force, were out of employment. Although the Progress government was aware of the serious nature of this unemployment problem,[108] it failed to solve it, principally because of the poor finances of the country.

Mainly because of these problems the economy was largely

stagnant between 1965 and 1970.[109] The growth rate was 0.6 per cent in 1965, 0.4 per cent in 1968, and 3.4 per cent in 1969.[110] The economy was far from being diversified, with cocoa beans contributing about fifty-six per cent of the total export earnings in 1970.

The poor finances of the country had repercussions on the size of the army and on military expenditure. Shortly after the coup the NLC cancelled the plan to construct with Soviet aid a big air base at Tamale for the air force, and also the Yugoslav-sponsored expansion of the naval base at Takoradi. In August 1971, the Busia administration successfully persuaded the British Government to take back a £5 million frigate ordered for the Ghana navy by Dr Nkrumah in 1965.[111] As a result of this the armed forces with a strength of about 17,000[112] in February came down to about 12,000 at the end of 1970. To emphasize the reduced position of the armed forces in the country's order of priorities, the PP government cut its military expenditure by N₵5 million during the 1971/2 financial year.[113]

The progressive reduction of the strength of the armed forces was matched by a series of cuts in the country's external commitments. For instance, in February 1966 Ghana had sixty-six diplomatic Missions abroad. By early 1970 this was reduced to forty-four, and to forty-one by mid-1971.[114] Although this owed much to the type of leaders in power in the country, and to the economic strait-jacket in which the country found itself after the coup, it was also in accord with the country's mood during the second half of the sixties. The masses that had been disillusioned and disappointed by the way in which Dr Nkrumah sacrificed their well-being on the altar of Pan-Africanism and foreign adventure now favoured retrenchment in foreign commitments. Indeed, the country's mood was one of retreat, which was in sharp contrast to that of 1957, when many informed opinions believed that Ghana had a historic mission to liberate and unite Africa.

(b) *The Coup and the Changes in Nigeria*
Following the coup d'état of 15 January 1966, there came to power army officers whose outlook and experiences were different from those of Sir Abubakar Tafawa Balewa and of Sir Ahmadu Bello, the Sardauna of Sokoto.[115] Although General Ironsi and the Regional Military Governors that came to power as a result of the coup could not be described as radicals, they were far from being as conservative as the former NPC leaders whose conservatism was squarely based on the Northern aristocracy. Although the young Sandhurst-trained

officers that came to power following the coup of 29 July 1966 were to a certain extent conservative, their conservatism was in some sense different from that of the Sardauna and his lieutenants. For one thing, the Middle-Belt Officers such as Akahan and others who spearheaded the coup had no aristocratic roots. Furthermore, the fight against secessionist rebellion between July 1967 and January 1970, backed by Portugal, South Africa, Rhodesia, and mercenaries from Western Europe, knocked the bottom out of their conservatism. So they became a little more radical.

The majority of the civil commissioners appointed by General Gowon in mid-1967 to the Federal Executive Council were members of the former opposition parties in the House of Representatives.[116] These men, especially Chief Awolowo, Mr Joseph Tarka, Alhaji Aminu Kano, Chief Enahoro, and Wenike Briggs, were, by birth and educational background, outlook and experience, totally different from the NPC leaders such as Sir Ahmadu Bello, Sir Abubakar, Alhaji Inua Wada and Makama Bida. For instance, while Sir Ahmadu had stood for the preservation of Hausa-Fulani aristocracy, Alhaji Aminu Kano, who till the coup in January 1966 had led the Northern Elements Progressive Union (NEPU), stood for social revolution and the overthrow of the Northern aristocracy. Likewise, while the NPC leaders favoured a conservative policy, the AG leaders and their allies since they lost the federal elections of December 1959 had gradually moved to a radical posture, advocating nationalization and socialism at home and militant Pan-Africanism and vigorous positive neutralism abroad.[117]

While these men were unable to translate into action most of their programmes while in opposition, they nonetheless brought some element of radicalism into the Federal administration. It seemed as if the military leaders themselves favoured this development, for the first former NPC leader appointed as Commissioner to the Federal Executive was Alhaji Shettima Ali Monguno, who, though a former Minister of State in the last Balewa Government, was one of the most 'progressive'[118] among the NPC leaders.[119]

Constitutionally the country was in many ways different from the first half of the sixties. Following the coup d'état of 15 January 1966, the legislative and executive powers in the country were by Decree No. 1 of 17 January 1966 vested in the Federal Military Government, comprising a Supreme Military Council and a Federal Executive Council. At the regional level, the same process was carried out, vesting legislative and executive powers in the Military Governors.

The supreme body in the country was the Supreme Military

Council, consisting of all the Military Governors, the Heads of the three branches of the armed forces, and the head of the police force and his deputy. Its chairman was the Head of the Federal Military Government, who was also the Chairman of the Federal Executive Council, made up of top members of the armed forces, the police and civil commissioners. Although the Supreme Military Council was theoretically the supreme authority in the country, it rarely met. Of far more practical importance was the Federal Executive Council, which to all intents and purposes had assumed the role of the Federal Government during the First Republic. This body met once a week to consider domestic and external policies.

Unlike the situation under the Balewa government, the powers of the Federal Military Government towered over those of the states. Although Decree No. 1 of 17 January 1966 tended to limit the functions of the Federal Military Government and those of the Regional Military Government within the areas laid down in the Republican Constitution of 1963, the Federal powers increased vis-a-vis those of the states as a result of a series of decrees and the exigencies of the war.[120]

To emphasize further the growth of the Federal Military Government, between mid-1966 and early 1970 certain functions hitherto performed by the former Regional Governments were taken over. The Local Government police forces of the former Western and Northern Governments were merged with the Nigerian Police Force, thereby bringing them directly under Federal Government control. Likewise, all prisons were brought under Federal control, unlike the past when Regional Governments maintained their own prisons. Furthermore, courts especially in the North, hitherto operating outside the national judicial system, were brought into it by 1969. One of the main consequences of all this was the undermining of the basis of state power.

The split of the country on 27 May 1967 into twelve regions, each too small and too weak to threaten the Federal authority, contributed substantially to the growth of the central authority in Lagos. Similarly, the victory over the forces of secession gave the Federal Military Government greater respectability throughout the country than was ever enjoyed by the Balewa Government. Thus the late sixties saw the emergence of a strong central authority. The authority of General Gowon was, and has been, accepted without question throughout the Federation. He could commit, and has committed, the country at home and abroad without any challenge from any other Nigerian leader. Thus the practice of speaking on foreign policy issues 'with too many voices',[121] common during the Balewa era, has become a thing of the past.[122]

Socially Nigeria in the second half of the sixties was different from the pre-coup days. Though tribal loyalty was still important, the hegemonic position of the three main tribal groups, the Hausa-Fulanis, the Ibos and the Yorubas, whose rivalry and jealousy were the main causes of tension during the First Republic, had been dealt a heavy blow by the splitting of the country into twelve states and also by the ascendancy at the federal level of men from the minority groups since the coup of 29 July 1966. More important socially and politically was the loss of powers by the Northern Emirs while still retaining their prestige, as a result of a series óf reforms initiated by the Military Governor of the former Northern Region who was then Colonel (later General) Hassan Katsina, himself the son of the Emir of Katsina. These reforms which were later described by *West Africa* as the 'North's Silent Revolution'[123] deprived the Emirs of their separate courts, their police force and their prison system, and merged them into the national systems.[124] The logic of these reforms was the steady reduction in the social and political status of the Emirs in the North.

Educationally, the country made remarkable progress. Primary school enrolment which stood at about 2.8 million in 1961 rose to about 3.1 million in 1968.[125] Enrolment in secondary schools rose from 195,000 in 1962 to 215,000 in 1968. In 1961 the enrolment in universities stood at about 3,000. The corresponding figure for 1969 was 9,700, rising to about 11,200 during the 1970-1 academic session with the re-opening of the University of Nigeria, Nsukka.[126]

As a result of the advance in education there was some increase in the percentage of the population who could be said to be literate and this rose to about twenty-nine per cent[127] by 1970. Similarly by the end of the sixties the process of urbanization had gone further.

In spite of the disruption of the civil war between July 1967 and January 1970, the economy showed some marked changes in the second half of the sixties. Though agriculture still remained the mainstay of the economy, its contribution to the Gross Domestic Product (GDP) declined—except during the 1967-8 period when large oil producing areas were under the secessionist con-trol—while that of non-agricultural products increased. For instance, at the time of independence in 1960, agriculture contributed about seventy per cent of the Gross Domestic Product, but the corresponding percentage early in 1970 was fifty-five per cent.[128] Mining, whose share of the Gross Domestic Product was below 0.5 per cent in 1960, had risen to over six per cent in 1970, accounting for twenty-seven per cent of Federal Government revenue and forty-four per cent of all export earnings. The most important product in the mining industry was petroleum. For instance, the export of crude oil which provided the sum of £92 million out of the total export value of £278.7 million in 1960 accounted for the sum of £136 million (or about forty-two per cent) of the total export value of £320.1 million in 1966.[129] After the end of hostilities, the oil industry witnessed an immense boom. As a result of this, by early 1971 Nigeria became the tenth largest oil producing country in the world, producing an average of 1.5 million barrels of crude oil a day. The country benefited immensely both from increased production and from the agreement on increased prices[130] reached with the oil firms in Nigeria in May 1971. It was now estimated that fifty-five per cent of the country's foreign exchange in 1971 would be provided by oil as compared to a corresponding percentage of fifteen per cent in 1964.[131] According to Mr Phillip Asiodu, then the Permanent Secretary of the Ministry of Mines and Power, the government would as a result of the new agreement realize an additional revenue of £120 million, bringing the total revenue from oil to over £800 million during the Four-Year Plan Period.[132] By September 1973 the production of crude oil reached the mark of two million barrels a day, and it was now estimated that oil was providing over seventy-five per cent of the total export earnings.

The share of manufacturing industry in the Gross Domestic Product rose during this period from about four per cent in 1958 to over 8.4 per cent in 1967.[133] Indeed, the civil war and the restriction on imports of the wartime period stimulated local manufacturing to a remarkable degree. For instance, the index of industrial production for the rest of Nigeria outside the three Eastern States in 1969 surpassed by over 24.2 per cent that for the entire country in 1966. By the end of the war the country was virtually self-sufficient in the manufacture of soap and detergents, cotton textiles, footwear, soft drinks, beer and matches. In spite of all this, Nigeria had to depend on the advanced countries for most of her finished goods.

Although the country's financial position was not good enough between 1966 and 1970, it remained on the whole strong. The war was financed at a cost of over £375 million[134] without external borrowing. The country's external reserves, which fell from £98.6 million in December 1965 to £51 million in December 1968, gradually picked up towards and after the end of the war, partly as a result of the return of international confidence in the economy. By the end of March 1970 the reserves rose from £64.8 to £114.1 million in March 1971[135] and to over £225 million in May 1973. Because of this growth in the financial strength of the country and because of the stability of the economy during the war and the phenomenal rise in the oil industry, the Four-Year Development Plan 1970-4, drafted between 1969 and early 1970, expected only twenty per cent of all the capital investments in the public sector during the Plan period to come from abroad, instead of the corresponding percentage of fifty per cent in the First National Plan 1962/8.

Militarily the country during the second half of the sixties was very different. Largely because of the civil war the armed forces saw enormous expansion in men, money and equipment. The army, which numbered 10,500 in January 1966, rose by over 23.8 per cent to 250,000[136] in January 1970. The navy and the air force, each with a force of 1,500 and 1,000[137] respectively in January 1966, were about 6,500 and 7,500 strong at the end of the war in January 1970.

The defence estimates which amounted to only £7,831,030 during the 1965-6 financial year, forming about eight per cent of the Federal Government expenditure for that year, rose to £20.24 million in 1967-8. During the 1968-9 fiscal year the defence expenditure rose by over 145.2 per cent above that of the previous year to £49.65 million,[138] which represented 38.45 per cent of total government expenditure for that year. Although the first budget after the war slightly reduced defence expenditure to £38,906,110,[139] in actual fact the expenditure had increased several times. The actual defence expenditure on the recurrent account rose to £92.4 million[140] during the first nine months of the 1970-1 financial year, while capital expenditure in the defence sector for 1970-1 rose from £15 million provided for under the Four-Year Plan to over £21 million during the same period.

Apart from the 122mm Soviet guns, and a few tanks and heavy artillery, the Nigerian army was equipped with light arms. However, the army chiefs wanted up-to-date equipment and weapons. Thus during the visit of Brigadier (later General) Hassan Katsina, then the Chief of Staff of the Nigerian army, to Paris in June 1971 he said his army was interested in acquiring the new French 120mm mortar, the AMX13 light armoured car, and the AML command vehicle.[141] The navy acquired new frigates and other battle ships. The air force, which in 1966 had no jet fighters, was equipped with Soviet MiG fighters and Ilyushin war planes, and Colonel Ikwue, then the Chief of Staff of the Air Force, announced plans to make Nigeria's air force the best and the most powerful air force in Black Africa.[142]

Indeed, since the end of the civil war, instead of demobilizing the armed forces expanded in material and men, the latter through the regular recruitment of young people with a minimum of the General Certificate of Education (Ordinary Level), together with specialists of all types. The maintenance, and the expansion, of these fairly large armed forces made possible by the growing economic strength of the country was favoured by the new politico-military leaders, who believed that the military had a more positive role to play than mere appearances in ceremonial parades. The military was now to be powerful enough not only to defend the sovereignty and the independence of the country,[143] but also to be able to assist directly, and swiftly, in defending the independence of any other African country attacked by an extra-African Power, such as Portugal's abortive invasion of Guinea in November 1970.[144] Furthermore, many Nigerian leaders now accepted that their armed forces should be physically involved in the struggle to free Guinea-Bissau and Southern Africa.[145]

One of the implications of all this was the pursuit of a vigorous foreign policy, especially in Africa. This was in accord with the mood of the public who, incensed at the assistance given by the white supremacist governments of Southern Africa to the secessionists during the war, and buoyed up by the confidence arising out of victory over the secessionist forces, now wanted a speedy elimination of all these regimes.

From the analysis above, one can easily detect some basic factors that could not but cause difficulties in Ghanaian-Nigerian relations. The vast differences in size and population of the two countries, the different social backgrounds of the governing élite, especially till early 1966, and the differences in the structure of their governments—all led to confusion and misunderstanding. For instance, Dr Nkrumah did not really understand how the federal form of government under Sir Abubakar worked. To him the Nigerian Federation was a 'neo-colonized' one.[146] And following Balewa's death Nkrumah in a nationwide broadcast described him as 'a victim of the neo-colonialist (Federal) system of which he was merely the figurehead'.[147] Likewise, Sir Ahmadu Bello viewed the organization of the CPP throughout Ghana with contempt.[148] Sir Abubakar, too, saw nothing but dictatorship in the Nkrumah government.[149] The differing road to independence of the two countries was a further source of suspicion and conflict. Nigeria achieved independence without having to declare 'Positive Action'. This made her independence bogus as far as Nkrumah was concerned, since no genuine independence could be attained by any colony without 'Positive Action'.[150] Indeed, after the coup in January 1966, Dr Nkrumah accused the Northern ruling classes, who till then had dominated the Federal Government, of a sort of betrayal because they continued after independence 'to look upon British imperial power as the source of their authority; and they considered independence merely as a method of continuing indirect rule over a large area by other means'.[151]

Furthermore, during the second half of the sixties the two countries seemed to be moving in opposite directions in many ways. For instance, while this period saw a remarkable trend towards more centralization within a federal framework in Nigeria it witnessed the progressive decentralization of administration in Ghana.[152] Again while the Ghanaian government restored the influence and the pre-eminence of the tribal chiefs, the Nigerian Government actually reduced the powers and the influence of the Northern emirs, who till early 1966 remained the only group of traditional rulers whose powers, position and prestige were little affected by the development of the parliamentary form of government in the fifties. Furthermore, while the Ghana government during the late sixties made a series of cuts in the size of its armed forces and in the expenditure on them, the Nigerian government increased both several times during the same period. The two countries, moreover, were not militarily or economically interdependent. In fact, they had to compete for the same markets for the sale of their products, and for financial and military aid from the same donor powers.

In spite of all this, however, it was hoped, especially during the immediate post-independence period, that the two countries would work together closely because of their common colonial heritage, and because Britain had left some common interterritorial institutions between the two countries on Ghana's independence in 1957. This hope was further strengthened by the political, economic and social co-operation between the four British West African colonies in pre-independence days. All these factors, namely, colonial heritage, common interterritorial institutions and early co-operation, form the subject of the next chapter.

1. Professor F. S. Northedge has shown in an admirable analysis that the foreign policy of any country is an interplay of domestic and external forces. For further details, see F. S. Northedge ed. *The Foreign Policies of the Powers*, London 1968.

2. For a good account of how Nigeria's foreign policy has been influenced by domestic and external factors, see J. S. Coleman 'The Foreign Policy of Nigeria',

in *Foreign Policies in a World of Change*, ed. by Joseph E. Black and K. W. Thompson, New York 1963, pp. 379–405.

3. For trends towards one-party state in Ghana, see Dennis Austin, *Politics in Ghana 1946-60*, London 1964, pp. 31-9.

4. Kulungugu is a village in Ghana, near the border with Upper Volta, where a major bomb attack was made on Nkrumah's life in August 1962 while returning from Upper Volta.

5. For further details see Henry L. Bretton *The Rise and fall of Kwame Nkrumah: A Study in Personal Rule in Africa*, London 1967.

6. For further details about mass party, see Maurice Duverger *Political Parties*, London 1961, pp. 63-4.

7. 'Positive Action' was defined by Nkrumah as 'legitimate political agitation, newspaper and educational campaigns, and in the last resort, the constitutional application of strikes, boycotts, non-cooperation based on the principle of absolute non-violence'. Kwame Nkrumah *Ghana: The Autobiography*, London 1957, p. 112.

8. Dennis Austin op. cit., p. 29.

9. Ibid. p. 416. Of the first nine members of the Central Committee of the CPP only two of them, Nkrumah and Kojo Botsio, had University degrees. Also p. 167 n.

10. Ibid. pp. 114-15.

11. Jitendra Mohan, formerly of the Department of Political Science, University of Ghana, Legon, wrote though with some exaggeration that Ghana's foreign policy till the coup in February 1966 was largely that of Kwame Nkrumah, and that his successive Foreign Ministers were little more than 'diplomatic couriers' — See Jitendra Mohan' Ghana's Parliament and Foreign Policy 1957-60' in *The Economic Bulletin of Ghana*, Vol. X No. 4, Accra 1966, p. 29.

12. *Ghana: The Autobiography*, op. cit., p. 33.

13. Ibid. p. 45.

14. Ibid. p. 12.

15. *Ghana: The Autobiography*, op. cit. p. 52.

16. Apart from the Akan tribe which formed over half of the population — 2,964,580 of the total indigenous population of 5,899,820 , according to the 1960 census figures — the other important ones were the Ewes, the Nzimas, the Ga-Adangbes, and the Mole-Dagbani.

17. A. W. Cardinall *The Gold Coast*, 1931, p. 74.

18. Because the vast majority of the Ghananians speak Akan the possibility of turning it into the country's lingua franca in place of English was widely discussed in the press and in the National Assembly in mid-1971. But because of the technical and other practical difficulties that would be involved in the change, the Government rejected the proposal for a change at that time. However, the whole National Assembly unanimously passed a motion taking 'note of the need for a common Ghananian language in view of its importance in working for national unity.' See *West Africa* 11 June 1971.

19. Seven per cent of the people said they belonged to no religion, according to the 1960 census figures.

20. C. G. Baeta 'Aspects of Religion' in W. Birmingham, E. N. Omaboe, and I. Neustadt ed. *A Study of Contemporary Ghana*, Vol. II, London 1967, p. 244.

21. For instance, in 1935 the expenditure of the Nigerian Government per child in school was £1. 1s. 2d. compared with the corresponding sum of £3. 10s. 10d. in the Gold Coast. Joan Wheare *The Nigerian Legislative Council*, London 1950, p. 19.

22. Gold Coast *Legislative Assembly Debates 1954-7*, Vol. 4 col. 27, 5 March 1957.

23. *NLC Budget Statement 1966/7*—Supplement to *Ghana Today*, 10 August 1966.

24. *The Economist*, 24 April 1965, p. 394.

25. For the crucial position of cocoa in Ghana's economy see Tony Killick

'Possibilities of Economic Control' in Birmingham, E. N. Omaboe and I. Neustadt, ed. *A Study of Contemporary Ghana*, Vol. I, London 1966.

26. *Economic Survey 1957*, Accra, Government Printer, p. 2.

27. *Annual Abstract of Statistics 1961*, Lagos, Federal Office of Statistics, pp. 58-9.

28. Mr E. N. Omaboe, formerly the Chief Statistician and later Commissioner for Economic Affairs under the NLC, spelt out these limitations in his introduction to *A Study of Contemporary Ghana*, op. cit. Vol. I, p. 18.

29. Several books written after the overthrow of the Nkrumah regime have exaggerated the strength of Ghana's economy on independence. One such book is *Kwame Nkrumah: The Anatomy of an African Dictatorship*, by Peter Omari, London 1970, for example, pages 99-100.

30. The CPP had included the development of the Volta River Project in its manifesto for the 1951 general election which it said must be carried out for the industrialization of the country. See *The Volta River Project—Statement by the Government of Ghana 20 February 1961*, WP No. 1/61, Accra, Government Printer, p. 1.

31. William Gutteridge *The African Military Balance*, Adelphi Paper No. 12; The institute for Strategic Studies, London 1964, p. 13.

32. N. J. Miners *The Nigerian Army 1956-1966*, London 1971, p. 3.

33. E. O. Saffu 'Nkrumah and the Togoland Question' in *The Economic Bulletin of Ghana*, Vol. XII, No. 2/3 1968, p. 39.

34. *Ghana: The Autobiography*, op. cit., p. 4.

35. If on Ghana's independence in 1957 she had found herself surrounded by independent African states Nkrumah's idea that Ghana's independence would be meaningless unless linked with that of all African territories would probably not have arisen, and if it had, would have been bogus.

36. *Foreign Affairs*, October 1958.

37. See Chapter VI.

38. With the withdrawal of Southern Cameroons from Nigeria in 1961 this party changed its name to the National Council of Nigeria Citizens (NCNC).

39. Though no formal increase in the Federal Powers occurred till January 1966, the increasing dependence of the Regions on the Federal Government for economic and financial subsidies and support had the effect of strengthening the Federal Government between 1960 and January 1966. J. P. Mackintosh *Nigerian Government and Politics*, London 1966, p. 85.

40. In December 1959 the NPC was the most conservative party, while the NCNC remained the most radical in Nigeria.

41. For further details, see Frederick A. O. Schwarz Jr — *Nigeria, The Tribes, the Nation, or the Race*, Massachussetts 1965, p. 112; pp. 101 FF.

42. Obafemi Awolowo *Awo, the Autobiography*, London 1960, p. 299.

43. Walter Schwarz *Nigeria*, London 1968, p. 82.

44. *The Foster-Sultan Commission: Proceedings of the Tribunal appointed to inquire into Allegations of Improper Conduct by the Premier of the Eastern Region of Nigeria in connection with the Affairs of the African Continental Bank Ltd., and other Relevant Matters*, Lagos, Government Printer 1957, p. 205.

45. In spite of some pressure from within its ranks especially from 1962 onwards, the Northern leaders refused to change the name of their party from 'Northern' to 'Nigerian' People's Congress.

46. See M. Duverger op. cit., pp. 63-4, for differences between a cadre party and a mass party.

47. According to an ex-NPC Federal Minister, Sir Abubakar could not make the following appointments without the approval of or consultation with the Sardauna: Federal cabinet Ministers, Federal Permanent Secretaries, Chairmen of Federal Boards and Corporations, and Ambassadors.

48. Five years after the Israelis had established an embassy in Lagos the Sardauna in a diatribe against the Israelis described them as enemies, and added that for him an Israeli state did not exist. *Africa Diary*, 18-24 September 1965, p. 2518.

49. Since the coup in January 1966, the Federal Government has not been able to establish an embassy in Israel partly because of lack of funds, and partly because of Israeli Government aid to the secessionist rebels during the civil war. Still another reason has been the refusal of Israel to withdraw from the Arab territories occupied as a result of the 1967 June war.

50. Walter Schwarz op. cit. p. 103.

51. Indeed, the Sardauna traced his descent to the Holy Prophet, Mohammed: Sir Ahmadu Bello *My Life*, London 1962, p. 239.

52. Sir Ahmadu Bello op. cit. p. 83.

53. Bryan Sharwood Smith *But Always As Friends*, London 1969, p. 400.

54. *Africa Diary*, 18-24 September 1965, p. 2518.

55. Bryan Sharwood Smith op. cit. p. 395.

56. For further details see his biographical note in *Nigeria Speaks—Speeches of Alhaji Sir Abubakar Tafawa Balewa*, 1964, p. XIII.

57. Balewa's letter of 10 February 1957 to Sir Bryan Sharwood Smith, then the Northern Nigeria Governor, expressing his desire to quit politics. Bryan Sharwood Smith op. cit. pp. 363-4.

58. Walter Schwarz. op. cit. p. 14.

59. Margery Perham *Native Administration in Nigeria*, London 1937, p. 326.

60. In 1963, 43.4 per cent of the people in the West were Muslims, while the corresponding percentage in the Lagos territory was 44.3 per cent, *Census Report 1963*.

61. Many people complained about the religious intolerance of the Northern Muslims especially towards non-Muslims in the emirates before the Willink Commission in 1958. HMSO *Report of the Commission appointed to enquire into the fear of Minorities and the means of allaying them*, London 1958, pp. 64-6.

62. See extract from the speech of Sir Hugh Clifford, then Governor of Nigeria, at the opening of Katsina College on 5 March 1922 in Ahmadu Bello, op. cit. pp. 28-9.

63. Margery Perham's introduction to Joan Wheare op. cit. p. x.

64. P. C. Lloyd has given a good account of this in his chapter on 'The Ethnic Background to the Nigeria Crisis' in S. K. Panter-Brick ed. *Nigerian Politics and Military Rule: Prelude to the Civil War*, London 1970, pp. 1-13. Another good account of North-South confrontation is given by Frederick Schwarz op. cit. pp. 71-81.

65. The Royal Institute of International Affairs *Nigeria, The Political and Economic Background*, London 1969, p. 3.

66. It is important to note that what was classified as an urban centre in Nigeria was several times larger than what was so called in Ghana.

67. Federal Office of Statistics, *Digest of Statistics*, No. 4, Lagos October 1961, p. 16.

68. W. Birmingham, E. N. Omaboe, and I. Neustadt Vol. I op. cit. p. 18.

69. RIIA — *Nigeria The Political and Economic Background*, London 1960, p. 8.

70. *First National Development Plan 1962/68*, Lagos, Government Printer, p. 11.

71. *Second National Development Plan 1970/74*, Lagos, Government Printer, p. 62.

72. *Annual Abstract of Statistics 1961*, op. cit. pp. 58-9.

73. For a fuller comparison with that of Ghana, see RIIA, *Nigeria The Political and Economic Background*, op. cit. p. 121.

74. N. J. Miners op. cit. p. 2.

75. Sir Ahmadu Bello op. cit. p. 236.

76. William Gutteridge *The African Military Balance*, op. cit. p. 13.

77. *Sessional paper* No. 6, of 1956.

78. For a comparison of the strength of the armed forces of both countries early in 1966 see David Wood *The Armed Forces of African States*, Adelphi paper No. 27, London 1966, pp. 14-16.

79. J. P. Mackintosh op. cit. p. 268.

80. For the mood of the country as expressed by many MPs on the eve of independence, see *H. R. Deb.*, 14 January 1960, cols. 33-48. See also Chief Awolowo's warning and fears about the country's future in the Parliament, *H.F. Deb.*, 1 April 1960, cols. 460-1.

81. Some changes have, however, occurred in their external environment such as the founding of the organization of African Unity (OAU) in May 1963; and the growing *détente* between East and West since the Partial Nuclear Test Ban of August 1963.

82. A. A. Afrifa *The Ghana Coup*, 24 February 1966, London 1966, p. 29.

83. Ibid. p. 15.

84. The political committee set up by the NLC in 1966 to advise it on all political matters was made up of the former UGCC or UP leaders. Its first chairman was Edward Akufo Addo, one of the prominent leaders of the UGCC. Later in 1967, when Akufo Addo was appointed Chief Justice, he was succeeded by Dr Kofi Busia, the former UP leader.

85. *The Manifesto of the Progress Party*, Accra 1969.

86. Earlier in December 1947, Danquah, the then vice-president of the UGCC, had asked Nkrumah how he was able to 'reconcile his active interests in West African Unity with the rather parochial aims of the United Gold Coast Convention'. See *UGCC Minute Book*, 28 December 1947.

87. Mr Eric O. Ayisi has classified the Busia cabinet into three. The first group were the former UGCC and later UP members who did not join the CPP; the second group were those who joined the National Liberation Movement between 1954 and 1957, later joined the CPP, and later still defected from it; and the third were the new breed of politicians. See Eric O. Ayisi 'Ghana and Return to Parliamentary Government' in *The Political Quarterly*, October–December 1970, pp. 438-9.

88. For further details see *A New Era in Ghana*, Accra, Government Printer, 1967, pp. 21-5.

89. For details about administrative decentralization since the coup of February 1966, see D. K. Greenstreet, 'Trends in Decentralization in Ghana', in *The Quarterly Journal of Administration*, January 1971, pp. 167-82.

90. See the editorial 'Political Development' in *The Political Quarterly*, June 1969, by Professor Bernard Crick; 'a constitution is emerging so heavily checked and balanced, so full of divisions of power, so wedded to judicial review, that while it seems likely to prevent the abuse of government power, it may well also prevent its proper use.'

91. *Constitution of the Republic of Ghana*, 1969 Accra, Government Printer, para. 53.

92. However, the Progress Government had within twelve months of its existence refused on three occasions to accept a judicial review of its action as final. The most celebrated one was the Sallah case over which Busia accused the judges of political partisanship. For a critical comment on the confrontation between Busia's Government and the judiciary during his first year in office, see Kwame Afreh, 'The Busia Administration and the Law' in the *Legon Observer*, 25 September 1970, pp. 20-4.

93. *West Africa*, 7 May 1971.

94. For instance, Lt. General A. A. Afrifa comes from a long line of chiefs. His great grand-father, Owusu Sekyere, was a Manpong chief. Dr Kofi Busia was the son of a Wenchi chief; William Ofori-Atta was of the royal family of Akim Abuakwa. Akufo Addo was born into an aristocratic family, and married to the daughter of Nana Sir Ofori-Atta. Even J. H. Mensah's mother's uncle was the late Chief Sampson of Mankessim.

95. *Daily Graphic*, Accra, 2 September 1969.

96. Philip J. Foster *Education and Social Change in Ghana*, London 1965, p. 191.

97. This was due to a number of factors such as mismanagement by the Nkrumah government, low agricultural productivity, poor prices of cocoa in the world market, poor weather, and corruption.

98. In July 1965, Ghana decimalized her currency. The cedi (₵) was then equivalent to 10/- sterling. But with the devaluation of July 1967, and that of sterling in November 1967, the new exchange rate was £1=N₵2.45 till the Busia devaluation of December, 1971.

99. *NLC Budget Statement 1966-67*, p. 2. Supplement to *Ghana Today*, 10 August 1966.

100. According to a correspondent in *The Times*, London, 2 June 1966, £76 million were owed to the UK, £86 million to West Germany, Switzerland £26 million, Netherlands £19 million, USSR £19 million, Japan £12 million, France £12 million, and Yugoslavia £12 million.

101. As a result of the rescheduling agreements, eighty per cent of the debts that fell due between 1 June 1966 and 31 December 1968 were spread over a longer period averaging eight years beginning in 1971. For further details see *NLC Budget Statement 1969/70*, Accra, Government Printer, pp. 19-20.

102. *West Africa*, 3 September 1971.

103. *NLC Budget Statement 1969/70*, op. cit. p. 3.

104. *Economic Survey 1969*, op. cit. p. 58.

105. *Economic Survey 1967*, Accra, Central Bureau of Statistics, 1968, p. 43.

106. *Economic Survey 1969*, op. cit. p. 48.

107. *NLC Budget Statement 1969-70*, op. cit. p. 3.

108. See *West Africa*, 30 July 1971.

109. Mr J. H. Mensah in July 1971 described the 1960-70 decade as 'wasted years' as far as economic development was concerned, see *West Africa*, 13 August 1971.

110. *Economic Survey 1969*, op. cit. p. 39.

111. *West Africa*, 10 September 1971.

112. William Gutteridge, *The Armed Forces of African States*, Adelphi Paper No. 27, London 1966, p. 14.

113. *West Africa*, 13 August 1971.

114. *West Africa*, 6 August 1971.

115. The coup of 15 January 1966 was carried out by a small group of young radical army officers. Though they themselves did not come to power, their radical programmes had some influence on the Ironsi government, especially in foreign policy matters.

116. Five of the seven former politicians appointed to the Federal Executive Council in 1967 belonged to the AG and its allies. The Vice-Chairman of the Councilwas Chief Awolowo, the former opposition leader in the House of Representatives. There were other civil commissioners who were not previously active politicians. They were Dr Dikko and Dr Arikpo, who were both public servants before their appointments, and Dr Adetoro, who was still then a University teacher.

117. Although Chief Awolowo did not succeed in making the Federal Government accept most of his ideas on socialism and radical Pan-Africanism, he continued to advocate these ideas in most of his works since 1966 See *The People's Republic*, London 1968; *Strategy and Tactics of the People's Republic of Nigeria*, London 1970; and *Socialism in the service of the new Nigeria*, London 1970.

118. As an MP Shettima Ali Monguno, unlike most other NPC leaders, advocated a strong federal government and militant foreign policy.

119. Another respected former NPC leader was made a Federal Commissioner later. He was Alhaji Shehu Shagari.

120. For details see Olajide Aluko, 'Federal—State Relationship' in the *Quarterly Journal of Administration*, July 1969, pp. 289-98.

121. See Claude S. Phillips *The Development of Nigerian Foreign Policy*, 1964, pp. 80-5.

122. This development started under the Ironsi regime which abolished all the offices of all the Agents-General maintained by each of the former Regional Governments in London.

123. *West Africa*, 25 June 1971.

124. For further details, see S. K. Panter-Brick and P. F. Dawson, 'The Creation of New States in the North' in S. K. Panter-Brick op. cit. pp. 128-34.

125. *Second National Development Plan 1970-74*, pp. 235-6.

126. Ibid. p. 316.

127. This percentage, which includes those literate in Roman and Arabic script, comes down to something below twenty per cent if we reckon only those with full primary school education as 'permanently literate', as the Second National Development Plan (p. 64) has tried to do.

128. Ibid. p. 103.

129. Ibid. p. 23.

130. Under the agreement the posted price of Nigerian crude oil was increased from $2.36 to $3.21. See *West Africa*, 7 May 1971. Following the devaluation of the dollar in December 1971 Nigeria like other OPEC countries was to receive an increased price for her oil.

131. *West Africa*, 17 September 1971.

132. *Sunday Times*, Lagos, 23 May 1971.

133. *Second National Development Plan 1970-74*, p. 137.

134. *West Africa*, 28 March 1970.

135. *Central Bank of Nigeria, Monthly Report*, May 1971.

136. This figure is given by the Federal Military Government see *Daily Times*, Lagos 11 September 1971.

137. David Wood, *The Armed Forces of African States*, Adelphi paper No. 27, London 1966, p. 16.

138. *Report of the Accountant-General for the year ending 31 March 1969*, p. VII.

139. *Federal Government Estimates* 1970-1, p. 85.

140. See the statement of Mr I. J. Ebon, the Permanent Secretary of the Federal Ministry of Economic Development, *Daily Times*, Lagos 20 July 1971.

141. Brigadier (later General) Hassan Katsina accompanied by four other top army officers also visited Belgrade and London to see various types of modern arms, and equipment. See *West Africa*, 18 June 1971.

142. *West Africa*, 30 July 1970.

143. The provision of the sum of £0.1 million under the Four-Year Plan for the setting up of a Nigerian Institute of Strategic Studies further testified to the greater attention of the Federal Government on defence problems. See *Second National Development Plan 1970-74*, p. 98.

144. The extraordinary meeting of the OAU Council of Ministers held in Lagos in December 1970 following the invasion of Guinea was summoned at the initiative of the Federal Military Government. Nigeria was appointed the chairman of the OAU defence committee set up later to review and make recommendations about the security problems facing independent Africa.

145. More of this will be dealt with later in Chapter III. It is, however, important to note here that Chief Enahoro, the Federal Commissioner for Information and Labour, had spoken of the role of the Nigerian army in the liberation struggle in Southern Africa, see *Daily Times*, Lagos 21 March 1970. Furthermore, a seminar held for over 150 army officers in Lagos between 14 and 16 July 1971 was largely devoted to the role of the army in defending independent Africa, and in liberating colonial areas of Africa.

146. *West Africa*, 16 June 1962.

147. *West Africa*, 29 January 1966.

148. Sir Ahmadu Bello op. cit. p. 200.

149. *H. R. Deb.*, 21 April 1965, col. 1140.

150. Kwame Nkrumah *Consciencism*, London 1964, p. 104.

151. *West Africa*, 29 January 1966.

152. This process is part of what some people have called the 'de-kwamefication' of Ghana.

CHAPTER II

Colonial Heritage, Early Co-operation, and Common Interterritorial Institutions

When Britain terminated her colonial rule in the Gold Coast and in Nigeria in 1957 and 1960 respectively she left them[1] with a considerable common heritage in culture, language and common interterritorial institutions which had previously facilitated co-operation between the two territories and their peoples,[2] and which were expected to be tapped to greater advantage during the post-independence period. The British government left behind in both countries similar patterns of administrative, legal and educational systems. In both countries English was the *lingua franca* and there was a common currency.

Added to all this was the fact that, in spite of the physical distance between the two, the British government attempted to run their administration as a unit in the latter part of the nineteenth century. Thus in 1874 the Lagos dependency was annexed to the Gold Coast though the former retained its own administrator. But in 1883, the post of the administrator was abolished, and the Lagos administration was merged into that of the Gold Coast.[3] Though this arrangement ended in 1886, it must have contributed to the concept of the oneness of British West Africa prevalent among the educated élite of the area towards the turn of the century. While after 1886 no attempt was made to administer the two countries as one, though Sir Alan Burns as Governor of the Gold Coast acted briefly in 1942 as Nigeria's Governor, the British government, especially from the mid-1930s[4] tried to encourage uniform laws to cover a wide range of subjects in both territories and in the rest of British West Africa. After making allowances for local variations, the British government in its colonies in West Africa from the late 1930s to the early fifties tried to ensure uniformity of law in such matters as international conventions, customs duty, import quota, labour relations, sedition, marriage and so on. For instance, in 1938 the Gold Coast government recommended the following Bills to the unofficial members in the Legislative Council in the light of the Nigerian and the Gambian precedent or intention, namely, the Folded Woven Goods Bill, the

Sedition Bill, the Customs Tariff Ordinance (Amendment) Bill, and the Workmen's Compensation Bill.[5] In August 1939, all the four Governors of British West Africa agreed that all the other three colonies should copy Nigeria's immigration laws.[6] The net result of all this was that on independence Ghana and Nigeria had the same types of law governing many subjects, thereby making it appear that their collaboration after independence would be easy.

Furthermore, the laws governing the conditions of service of colonial officers in all the British West African colonies were the same. Likewise, the conditions of service including pensions, of the Africans in the public services were tackled on a uniform basis. These made promotion and transfer of officers from the public service of one colony to another easy.[7] It was this that made it possible during the early period of colonial rule, when sufficient numbers of educated Nigerians were not coming forward, to recruit a large number of educated Gold Coasters to the Nigerian public service,[8] something for which the Ghanaians were later to earn the tribute of Sir Abubakar Tafawa Balewa at a time when his government's relation with the Nkrumah government was sour.[9]

(i) EARLY CO-OPERATION

The effects of having the same colonial overlord as outlined above went beyond the mere recruitment of educated Gold Coasters to the Nigerian public service in the early colonial days. Indeed, as indicated earlier, they extended to the fostering of close political, economic and social co-operation between the two territories and their peoples, especially during the pre-Second World War period. For one thing, up till the early 1930s the educated Africans in Lagos and Accra, and their counterparts in Freetown and Bathurst (now Banjul), had more in common in outlook, experience and aspirations with one another than with the illiterate peasants of their own territories. The fact that Nigerians and Gold Coasters found themselves in familiar legal and administrative environments, using the same currency and the same official language in each other's territories further facilitated their collaboration. Furthermore, the relative ease of east-west coastal communications between Accra and Lagos compared to the laborious task of travelling inland, especially up till the Second World War, made it easy for the educated élite[10] of both territories to meet regularly for consultation and co-operation. Another factor that was important in bringing together the Gold Coasters and the Nigerians was that the growth of political consciousness among the educated Africans up to the 1930s expressed itself in terms of race and colour rather than territory. The fact that they had to confront the same colonial Power also served to draw them together.

(a) Political Platform

Although the concept of a united West Africa could be traced back to the middle of the last century,[11] it was not until 1920 that any serious attempt was made to translate the concept into reality. In March of that year, the inaugural conference of the National Congress of British West Africa, held in Accra, was attended by six representatives from Nigeria, three from Sierra Leone, one from the Gambia, and forty from the Gold Coast. The moving spirit behind the Congress was J. E. Casely Hayford, who between 1914 and 1920 had devoted much of his thought to summoning such a conference. It was Dr R. A. Savage, a Nigerian then editing *The Gold Coast Leader*, who first suggested the holding of such a conference[12] and on his return to Nigeria in 1915, the idea passed into the powerful hands of J. E. Casely Hayford who in 1913 had written:

> One touch of nature has made all West Africa kin. The common danger to our ancestral lands has made us one . . . United we stand, divided we fall.
> United West Africa . . . shall take her true part among the nations of the earth.[13]

The statements quoted above were to form the philosophy of the Congress. After sitting for two weeks, they agreed, among other things, to establish the National Congress of British West Africa as a permanent organization with its headquarters in Sekondi, the home town of Casely Hayford, and to hold the meetings of the Congress in each of the four capitals of British West Africa in rotation. The Congress also decided to send a deputation to the Secretary of State for the Colonies to demand greater autonomy for British West Africa within the British imperial system.

Several resolutions on political, social and economic matters were passed by the Congress. One of the resolutions on economic development to which we shall later refer read:

> . . . the time has come for . . . the formation of a Corporation, to be known as the British West African Co-operative Association . . . to found Banks, promote shipping facilities, establish co-operative Stores, and produce buying centres, in such wise as to inspire and maintain a British West African National Economical development.[14]

To follow up the decisions of the inaugural conference at Accra, the Congress sent a delegation led by J. E. Casely Hayford to see the Colonial Secretary in 1920.[15] They asked him for the following — the establishment of a legislative Council, half of it to be elected, and a 'House of Assembly' containing the legislative council plus six financial members to control revenue and expenditure; municipal corporations with unofficial majorities; the appointment of Africans to judicial offices; and the establishment of a West African unity.[16]

While in England the delegates met several groups, such as the League of Nations Union, sympathetic to their demands. They failed to get the sympathy and the support of the Colonial Secretary, Lord Milner, who denounced them as being unrepresentative of the people, and therefore incapable of speaking for them. Because of this, Lord Milner refused to grant the delegation any interview.[17]

Although between 1921, when the delegates returned to West Africa, and 1930, when the Congress fizzled out following the death of Casely Hayford, the Congress languished, political co-operation nonetheless continued between Nigerians and the Gold Coasters during this period. For instance, the fourth session of the Congress was held in Lagos between December 1929 and January 1930 with the full support and co-operation of the Nigerian National Democratic Party (NNDP.)[18] A year later Mr Winifried Tete-Ansa, a businessman from the Gold Coast, was given the membership of the Nigerian political party, the NNDP.[19]

But of far greater significance from the mid-1920s till after the Second World War was the political co-operation between the students of Nigeria and the Gold Coast in England and in the United States. In 1925 as a result of the initiative of a Nigerian student in London, Mr Ladipo Solanke, the West African Students' Union (WASU) was formed in England. The nucleus of this Union was formed by the merging of the Gold Coast Students' Union and the Nigerian Progress Union in London.[20] Among the ten founder members of the WASU were, from the Gold Coast, Mr J. B. Danquah and E. O. Asafu-Adjaye, who became one of the early Presidents of the Union, and from Nigeria, apart from Ladipo Solanke who from 1932 till his death in 1958 was the warden of the WASU's hostel in London,[21] Kusimo Soluade and Olatunde Vincent.

The objective of the WASU was to discuss all matters affecting West Africa 'educationally, commercially, economically, and politically, and especially to co-operate with the National Congress of British West Africa.'[22] But only in educational and political fields did the WASU really make some impact. In the former field, apart from encouraging their fellow men to take advantage of Western education at home and abroad, they acquired in the early 1930s a hostel in Camden Town, London, for West African students.[23] During the second half of the forties, the Union acquired a second hostel at 69 Warrington Crescent, London W9.[24] In the politcal field, the WASU agitated through public lectures and pamphlets for political, economic and social reforms in West Africa. For instance, two of its leading figures, Ladipo Solanke and J. W. de Graft-Johnson from the Gold Coast, produced *United West Africa (or Africa) at the Bar of the Family of Nations* (1927), and *Towards Nationhood in West Africa* (1928) respectively, both of which had been described by James Coleman as 'the first major literary works of a nationalist character to appear since Blyden's writing in the late nineteenth century.'[25] Both works further stimulated political and racial consciousness among the Nigerian and Gold Coast students in England.

Furthermore, the WASU tried to influence constitutional and political development in Africa, especially West Africa, through protest and petition. Thus in 1935 it set up an Ethiopia Defence Committee to protest at the Italian invasion of Ethiopia.

In 1941 following the publication of the Atlantic Charter, the WASU petitioned Clement Attlee that it should be applied to West Africa.[26] On 6 April 1942, the Union submitted a memorandum to the British Undersecretary of State for the Colonies demanding 'internal self-government now' and complete self-government within five years after the war.[27]

In England in the 1930s and 1940s many Gold Coast and Nigerian students co-operated in such organizations as the League of Coloured Peoples and the Union of African Peoples. Similarly they were prominent in the Fifth Pan-African Congress held at Manchester in 1945 at which Kwame Nkrumah acted as the co-secretary. Other delegates included, from the Gold Coast, J. Annan, who later became Ghana's Secretary of Defence, E. A. Ayekumi, later Dr Nkrumah's financial adviser, and Joe Appiah; and from Nigeria Chief H. O. Davies and Chief S. L. Akintola, who, with the exception of the period May to December 1962, was the Western Nigeria Premier from 1960 until 14 January 1966.

In the United States, too, before the Second World War, the Nigerian and the Gold Coast students worked together on a nationalist front in spite of their small number. Thus at Lincoln University, Pennsylvannia, they launched a monthly organ, the *African*

Interpreter in the late 1930s which carried nationalist articles demanding constitutional, political and economic reforms in West Africa.[28] Although the student campaigns in the United States and the United Kingdom might not have had a substantial effect on developments in West Africa, what was more important was the fact that their organizations and agitations brought together men who were to play important political roles in both countries before and after independence. For instance, the three Nigerians, namely Mbonu Ojike, K. O. Mbadiwe and Nwafor Orizu, and the three Gold Coast students, namely Ako Adjei, H. A. B. Jones-Quartey and Kwame Nkrumah, who co-operated together to launch the *African Interpreter* in Lincoln University in the late 1930s became important leading figures in their own countries. Mbonu Ojike was a respected nationalist leader in Nigeria until his death,[29] K. O. Mbadiwe was a popular nationalist who became the personal adviser of Sir Abubakar on African Affairs during the first two years of independence, and later became one of the senior cabinet members of the Federal coalition till the coup in January 1966. Nwafor Orizu became the President of the Senate, and later the Acting President shortly before the coup. In Ghana, Ako Adjei was a founder member of the CPP, and from 1960 till August 1962 was Ghana's foreign Minister. Kwame Nkrumah became the first Prime Minister of Ghana, and her first President until the coup of February 1966. H. A. B. Jones-Quartey, who did not go directly into active politics, had risen by 1960 to the post of Deputy Director of the Department of Extra-Mural Studies, University of Ghana, Legon.

This was true of the WASU too. David Kimble said in 1963 that almost all Ghanaian politicians of note had been associated one time or the other with the WASU.[30] During his stay in London in the early forties, Kwame Nkrumah was made the Vice-President of the Union.[31] In the late forties, Mr Joe Appiah, who until the 1966 coup was one of the best debaters in the National Assembly, and who was later the Chairman of the banned Opposition Justice Party, became the President of the WASU, while Mr Kola Balogun from Nigeria who later after serving as a Federal cabinet Minister became Nigeria's first High Commissioner in Ghana was then the Vice-President of the Union. Among prominent Nigerian politicians who had been closely associated with the WASU during their student days in London were Chief H. O. Davies, who later became one of the founder members of the Nigerian Youth Movement(NYM), and Chief S. L. Akintola.

Finally, mention has to be made of Dr Nnamdi Azikiwe's political activities in the Gold Coast between 1934 and 1937 when he was deported to Nigeria. On 22 December 1934, the first issue of Dr Azikiwe's newspaper the *African Morning Post* came out in Accra.[32] In this very issue, and in subsequent ones, he made scathing attacks on the British imperial system in Africa. For instance, in an editorial on 2 January 1935, he demanded Dominion status for the Gold Coast.[33] Furthermore, he advocated in his newspaper the establishment of a self-governing federation consisting of all the four British West African territories.[34]

In this political campaign Dr Azikiwe got the support, and co-operation of many educated Gold Coasters. For instance, he later in 1965 referred to how Dr J. B. Danquah had worked closely with him in the 1930s in the Gold Coast in the common struggle against imperialism and colonialism.[35] Indeed, during the short period of his stay in the Gold Coast, Dr Azikiwe did seem to have succeeded in stimulating political awareness among the Gold Coast people, and in creating for himself an image of an indefatigable nationalist fighter viciously victimized by the colonial administration.[36] His deportation from Ghana did not mean the end of political co-operation between him and the Gold Coast nationalists. For in February 1959 Dr Azikiwe recalled with pride how many Gold Coast nationalists in England including Kojo Botsio, who for several years, till late in 1965, was Ghana's Foreign Minister, had come to London to assist him and his colleagues in their secretarial work during the NCNC-led delegation to England in 1947.[37]

(b) Economic Level
Co-operation on an economic level took two main forms. The first was the establishment of limited companies on a West African basis, as contained in the resolution on economic development of the National Congress of British West Africa at its inaugural meeting at Accra in March 1920; and the second was the intercolonial migration for trade and employment.

It was a businessman from the Gold Coast, Mr Winnifried Tete-Ansa, who spearheaded the move to translate the resolution of the Congress on economic development in West Africa into reality. He formed three limited companies. The first was the West African Co-operative Producers Limited inaugurated in Accra in 1925, registered in England in that year and in Nigeria in 1928. Among the directors of the Company were prominent men from the Gold Coast such as P. H. Williams, A. J. Ocansey and R. M. Lamptey, and leading men from Nigeria such as D. T. Sasegbon, a cocoa farmer, Dr C. C. Adeniyi-Jones, T. A. Doherty and Dr J. C. Vaughan, who were all supporters of the aims of the National Congress.[38] This company, which was expected to serve as a co-ordinating body for the numerous farmers' groups in both territories, was said to have by 1930 won the support of forty-five leading farmers' associations in the Gold Coast and Nigeria.[39]

Between 1928 and 1929, Tete-Asa set up another limited company, the Industrial and Commercial Bank Limited, in Nigeria and the Gold Coast. Its directors included A. J. Ocansey, R. M. Lamptey, and other financiers and politicians such as C. da Rocha, and J. B. Danquah — all from the Gold Coast; and A. A. Oshodi from Nigeria.[40] In May 1931, Tete-Ansa established his third limited company, the Nigerian Mercantile Bank Limited. In that same year, the then President of the NNDP, Dr C. C. Adeniyi-Jones, became the chairman of the Mercantile Bank. Other directors of the Bank included T. A. Doherty, Dr A. Maja and Mr H. A. Subair.[41]

All these companies soon faded out mainly because of lack of experience, of managerial skill, of capital, and because of their inability to compete with the giant expatriate firms which received the backing of the colonial administration. Nonetheless, the efforts of Tete-Ansa were appreciated. In 1931 Herbert Macaulay, the founder of the NNDP, had to describe him as the 'Hero in the Commercial Battle'.[42]

As indicated earlier, another form of economic co-operation between the Gold Coast and Nigeria took the form of intercolonial migration for employment and trade in each other's territory. This process was further facilitated by the fact that travellers between the two territories could do so without passports as long as they were in possession of travel certificates showing their identity. But the influx of Nigerians into the Gold Coast for employment and trade was several times higher than that of the Gold Coasters to Nigeria.

The reasons for this were obvious. The Gold Coast (or Ghana since 1957) had been comparatively better off economically than Nigeria. The gap between the two territories in economic terms was further widened by the fact that the modern pattern of economic development, with the government taking an active role, started much earlier, in the 1920s, in the Gold Coast, with the launching of the Ten-Year Development Plan by Governor Guggisberg, the first in British Africa, begun at a time when Nigeria was considered unsuitable for such development.[43] For instance, during the 1936-7 fiscal year the value of investments in the gold mining industry in the Gold Coast was estimated at about £2.7 million as compared to only £156,000 in the mining industry in Nigeria during the same period.[44]

In spite of the fact that Nigeria's population was, according to the 1931 census, about six times that of the Gold Coast, the total amount of official currency in circulation in the former country in 1930 and in 1939, amounting to £6,279,000 and £3,285,000[45] respectively, was much less than that in the Gold Coast during the same years, where it amounted to £6,435,000, and £7,673,000 respectively.[46]

In trade Ghana was ahead of Nigeria. For instance, in 1936 the total value of Ghana's external trade was about £6 per head, while that of Nigeria was about £1. 5s.[47] Indeed, by the 1930s it was estimated that the income per head in the Gold Coast was five times that of Nigeria.[48] All this made the Gold Coast after the Second World War 'the most materially successful of British African colonies'.[49] Till 1960, Ghana maintained this lead in economic development.

Because of all this, rates of pay were higher in Ghana before and after her independence, and there were greater chances of employment and commercial opportunities there than in Nigeria. In the late 1930s when the average weekly wage of a gold miner in the Gold Coast was about ten shillings, a Nigerian tin miner earned between two shillings and six pence, and three shillings and six pence.[50] Although the rate of pay for labourers on cocoa farms in the Gold Coast was not known it must have been several times higher than that in Nigeria. For the gold mines and the cocoa farms were the main lures for Nigerians emigrating to the Gold Coast or Ghana for employment until the late fifties.[51] Similarly several towns in the Gold Coast, such as Accra, Kumasi, Cape Coast and Sekondi were flooded with Nigerian traders, mainly Yorubas, who were eager to exploit the commercial opportunities in the country. There were also many Hausas from Nigeria trading in Northern Ghana, as Sir Ahmadu Bello was to see during his visit there in 1959.[52]

Consequent upon this there grew up from 1930 onwards a fairly large Nigerian population in the Gold Coast. In 1931, there were 67,703 Nigerians there[53] and in 1960 the number had risen to 209,120.[54] By the end of 1969, when the Ghana Government started to expel Nigerians and other aliens without residential permits, the actual number of Nigerians in Ghana was not precisely known. For Dr Kofi Busia, the then Ghanaian Prime Minister, put it at 540,000,[55] while his Minister of the Interior, Mr Dombo, put it at 750,000 during the same period.[56] Although there was some tendency on the part of the Ghanaian Government to inflate the number of Nigerians in their country for propaganda purposes, it seemed probable that the number of Nigerians in Ghana by early December

1969 must have increased to something close to Busia's figure.[57]

While many Nigerians migrated to Ghana, very few Ghanaians went to Nigeria. Since Nigeria was comparatively poorer there was very little economic justification for such migration. Furthermore, there were no compelling social or political reasons to necessitate the immigration of large numbers of Ghanaians into Nigeria. However, some Gold Coasters, especially the educated ones, had come to work as clerks in the Nigerian public service during the early period of colonial rule. This was facilitated, as earlier stated, by the fact that the conditions of service of African staff in all the public services in British West Africa were uniform.[58] Others had been brought into Nigeria as clerical officers, accounting clerks and store-keepers during the same period by foreign firms operating in Nigeria. Still others came as teachers, and a few as businessmen. A few came in the fifties as High Court judges.

As was to be expected the number of people coming into Nigeria was very small. Although the exact number of Gold Coasters in Nigeria before independence was unknown,[59] in 1963, for instance, there were only 7,561 Ghanaians in Nigeria.[60]

(c) Social Plane

On the social plane there was co-operation between the two peoples before and after their independence. They competed yearly in sports, and annual competitions in football between the two countries went back to 1935. There was a regular exchange of visits between the musicians of both territories. The Ghanaian 'high life' music was very popular in Nigeria in the fifties and early sixties.[61] Similarly, some Nigerian musicians were popular in Ghana.

In education, the move towards co-operation was evident. Apart from the fact that the children of Nigerians who had migrated to the Gold Coast were educated there, many Nigerian young men and women who could not find places at the University College, Ibadan, in the fifties went to the University College, Legon. There were some Ghanaian students too in Nigerian secondary schools and higher institutions. Furthermore, there was the regular annual literary debate between the students of the University College, Legon, and their counterparts at Ibadan, dating back to the early 1950s.[62]

(ii) COMMON INTERTERRITORIAL INSTITUTIONS

If much of the co-operative moves dealt with earlier were due to the initiative of the peoples of the two countries, those we shall consider below were largely due to British Government effort through the establishment of interterritorial institutions. Although some of these, such as the West African Currency Board and the West African Court of Appeal, had been established before the Second World War, it was not until during and shortly after the war that the British took effective steps to set up a large number of common interterritorial organizations, both to facilitate their administration and to promote intercolonial contacts in their West African colonies. Thus the period between 1940 and 1956 saw a proliferation of interterritorial institutions covering administrative, military, marketing, transport, currency, research, educational and judicial matters. But because these interterritorial institutions are too numerous to be dealt with in detail here, we shall only consider the most important ones in each of the various fields listed above, though the judicial field must be omitted because of constant change.[63]

(a) Administrative

The first major attempt to set up an interterritorial administrative machinery to co-ordinate the administration of all the British West African colonies was the first West African Governors' Conference held in Lagos from 10 to 18 August 1939. At this conference the Governors discussed how to co-ordinate all matters of common concern such as immigration, subversive propaganda, research programmes, higher education, culture and agriculture. The conference decided that the Governor of Nigeria should be the permanent chairman of the Governors' Conferences, and that Nigeria should be its permanent Secretariat, with an officer of the Nigerian Secretariat as secretary to the Conference. They also agreed to send to one another copies of their despatches to the Colonial Secretary, to ensure as much as possible a similar pattern of development in all the colonies. Finally they agreed to meet frequently for further deliberation and to review administration in their territories.[64] Before they could meet again, the War had begun. Nonetheless, the organization was able at the beginning of the war to co-ordinate the actions of the various governments, especially in their relations with the fighting services.[65]

Their work was somehow revived in the appointment of a Resident Minister for West Africa with his headquarters in Accra in 1942. The Resident Minister, Viscount Swinton, set up a War Council into which the Governor's Conference was absorbed, and which also included the heads of the three services of the armed forces. After the abolition of the post of the Resident Minister in 1945, a West African Council under the chairmanship of the Secretary of State for the Colonies was set up. It included the Governors of the British West

African colonies as members. A permanent secretariat under a Chief Secretary was set up at Accra. The main purpose of the West African Council was to secure the co-ordination of the policies of the four territories in all matters of common concern.[66]

What the Council achieved must have been very small. For it did not meet until 1948, three years after its inauguration. Its composition, consisting of largely expatriate officials under the Colonial Secretary, at a time when demands for political and constitutional reforms in the Gold Coast, Nigeria and to some extent in Sierra Leone were strong and strident, must have been a serious handicap to it. Moreover, it was doubtful whether it was adapted to changes going on in British West Africa in the late forties. Thus the liberal Governor of Nigeria, Sir John Macpherson, later had to refer to the Council as 'a relic of a wartime organization (that) had become out-dated'.[67]

Because of all this the West African Council was replaced in 1951 by the West African Interterritorial Conference with headquarters in Accra. The composition of the new Conference reflected constitutional advance in British West Africa.[68] For apart from the four Governors and top officials of the West African Interterritorial secretariat, it consisted of two Ministers or members of the Executive Council[69] from each of the territories.[70] The Governor of Nigeria was to chair all the meetings of the Conference. Apart from this, a West African Interterritorial Secretariat under a Chief Secretary based in Accra was also set up.

The members of the Conference were to meet annually for consultation among themselves, and with other Commonwealth and non-Commonwealth countries. They were also to take steps to strengthen interterritorial and international harmony, and to review annually the progress made in interterritorial co-operation, in social and economic policy, and in research programmes.

The West African Interterritorial Secretariat was charged with the task of co-ordinating all types of research schemes in all the four colonies. In this task, the Interterritorial Secretariat excelled the West African Interterritorial Conference, which by the mid-fifties had virtually faded away. By recruiting able research experts in various fields the West African Interterritorial Secretariat was able to kindle the interests of the leaders of all the colonies in research. Until 30 September 1962, when the interterritorial research organization in West Africa was abolished, the Chief Secretary of the Interritorial Secretariat in Accra remained the chairman of all the management committees of all West African research institutions, such as the West

African Oil Palm Research Institute (WAIFOR) and the West African Medical Council etc. Perhaps it would not be too much to say that the fact that the interterritorial research organization in West Africa was not abolished until 30 September 1962, in spite of the Nkrumah government's announcement in 1958 of the plan to establish a National Research Council to be in charge of all research programmes in the country,[71] must have owed something to the able administration of the West African Interterritorial Secretariat.[72]

(b) Marketing

At the outbreak of the War in 1939 the British Government assumed responsibility for the purchase and shipping of cocoa from the Gold Coast and Nigeria. And in September 1941 an interterritorial organization, the West African Cocoa Control Board, was set up for the purchase and the sale of cocoa from the two territories on behalf of the British government.[73] In July 1942, the West African Cocoa Control Board was reconstituted as the West African Produce Control Board. This new Board, which comprised the Parliamentary Under-secretary of State for the Colonies as the chairman, members of the Colonial office, the principal merchant interests, and the nominees of the Nigerian and the Gold Coast governments,[74] was responsible for the marketing and the export of the whole of certain agricultural commodities, namely cocoa, palm oil, palm kernels, groundnuts and benniseed.[75]

Producer prices were fixed yearly after consultation between the colonial office and the local governments. The Board also fixed the export quotas of shippers licensed to buy produce. While the merchant firms acted as buying agents of the Board at fixed commissions, each of the British West African government created in its own territory a supply board which took instructions from the West African Produce Control Board, the British Ministry of Supply and the Ministry of Food.

But shortly after the war territorial Cocoa Marketing Boards were created in 1947 in the Gold Coast and in Nigeria, and it was these that took over the function of the West African Produce Control Board in the 1947-8 session.[76]

(c) Military

The history of military co-operation between the Gold Coast and Nigeria went back to 1873 when Sir John Glover led a force of Hausas from Nigeria and local allies from the Volta Region of the Gold Coast against the Ashantis.[77] But an interterritorial organization to promote military co-operation between the two territories was not formally established until 1897 when the West African Frontier Force (WAFF)[78] was formed by the amalgamation of all the various territorial constabularies. Although the actual integration of the Force by the colonies did not occur until 1901,[79] hundreds of Nigerian troops under the WAFF had a year earlier joined their counterparts in the Gold Coast in the final campaign against the Ashantis.

Although the Nigeria Regiment of the WAFF and the Gold Coast Regiment had joined hands in the operation against the German territories in Togo, the Cameroons and East Africa (Tanganyika) during the First World War,[80] they remained essentially territorial armies. After the war they all returned to their separate territories of origin[81] and were run as 'national' forces. Although during this period there was an Inspector-General with the rank of a colonel who was to be in charge of the WAFF (or the RWAFF as it became after 1928) and whose main function was 'to assist in maintaining a satisfactory and uniform standard of efficiency and training and to advise the Governors and Secretary of State (for the Colonies) on military matters.[82] The effective administration of the forces was in the hands of each colonial Governor, who was the Commander-in-Chief of the forces in his territory, and the subordinate military officer directly in charge of such forces at the local level.[83] For one thing the Inspector-General had his headquarters in the Colonial Office in London. Furthermore, the costs of maintaining and equipping the territorial forces of the Royal West African Frontier Force during the inter-war period were met out of the revenue raised by each colonial government. Because of this the composition, organization and strength of such forces were determined by each of the British West African governments, subject to the sanction of the Colonial Secretary.[84]

Much of this changed during the Second World War when it was thought that the Germans would attack West Africa. The War Office in London took over the defence of West Africa by appointing Lt-General G. J. Giffard in July 1940 as the General Officer Commanding West Africa, with his headquarters in Achimota, near Accra.[85] His function was the defence and the co-ordination of the war efforts of all the four territories. The Royal West African Frontier Force was turned into the West Africa Command arm of the British Army, and henceforth it was run essentially as one. Although all the Governors remained the Commanders-in-chief of the forces in their territories, only the General Officer Commanding-in-Charge at the Command Headquarters could give any valid instruction for a military operation. Furthermore, from 1940 until June 1956 when the Command Headquarters in the Gold Coast was closed down,[86] it was the British government that was largely responsible for financing the RWAFF.

Apart from the rapid expansion of the RWAFF to meet the exigencies of the War, a military training school was established at Teshi, near Accra, in 1940 to serve the whole of West Africa. This military school, which was retained at the end of the war, served all the colonies till 31 March 1960 when Nigeria ceased to use it.[87] Though the exact number is unknown, most of the Nigerian officers in the late fifties must have passed through the Teshi training school where candidates selected for regular commissions at the Royal Military Academy (RMA) Sandhurst, and those for short-service commission at the Officer Cadet Training Unit (OCTU) at Aldershot were required to undergo a special preliminary training course of six months.[88]

One of the main effects of all this was the fostering of a sense of oneness within the RWAFF, and the coming together of the Nigerian and the Gold Coast troops, especially their African officers, more closely after the Second World War than during the period before it. The fact that they had fought side by side during the War against the Italians in East Africa and against the Japanese in Burma, where Colonel A. Haywood and Brigadier F. A. S. Clarke said 'the Gold Coast and the Nigerian brigades displayed the same sterling qualities as their forbears',[89] must have contributed to this.

Although all the RWAFF brigades returned to their territories of origin after the War, another organization, the West African Forces Conference, was set up later in the forties to ensure further military co-operation in British West Africa. This organization, which consisted of the Colonial Secretary as its chairman and of the representatives of the War Office, the United Kingdom Treasury, and of the four British West African governments, became the supreme policy-making body on military matters in West Africa.

At its meeting in 1949, the West African Forces Conference decided that the four territories should contribute £1,331,000 out of a total of £3,400,000 annual recurrent military expenditure, while the United Kingdom government was to pay the rest.[90] Nigeria was to pay £750,000 and the Gold Coast £500,000, Sierra Leone £66,000 and the Gambia £15,000. Four years later in 1953 the Conference, which now included some African Ministers,[91] agreed to increase the contribution of the four colonial governments. The annual recurrent expenditure would rise to £5.5 million in 1954, and the total contribution from the four governments would amount to £2,496,500. Nigeria's contribution was to be £1,380,000, that of the Gold Coast £1 million, Sierra Leone £100,000, and the Gambia £16,500.[92]

The Conference made several recommendations. The most important were the following: the consolidation of the Regiment and supporting troops in each territory into a sort of 'national' military force for the immediate defence of the territory; all the forces to continue to work under the close association of the RWAFF; and the establishment of an Army Advisory Council for West Africa to which each of the four British West African governments should send representatives, and of which the GOC-in-chief at the Accra Headquarters should be a member.[93] The Conference decided to meet again in 1958 to review military co-operation in West Africa.[94]

In 1956, all the four colonial governments agreed, though reluctantly by the Gold Coast, that a Lieutenant-General should be appointed to 'assist their governments in the co-ordination of defence'.[95] But this, as other resolutions agreed to in 1953, did not work mainly because each territory wanted control of its own army. The proposed Army Advisory Council failed to get off the ground, while the Forces Conference expected to meet in 1958 could not do so. On 6 March 1959, Ghana formally withdrew from the RWAFF, whose life came to an end finally on 1 August 1960.[96]

(d) *Transport*

To promote air transport between the Gold Coast and Nigeria,[97] the West African Airways Corporation (WAAC) was established by 'The West African Territories (Air Transport) Order in Council 1946' which came into operation on 1 June 1946.[98] The governing body of the Airways Corporation was the West African Air Transport Authority made up of the representatives of all the four West African governments.

The Corporation was entirely financed by the four colonial governments. Thus the capital contribution to it was apportioned between the colonies as follows: Nigeria sixty per cent, the Gold Coast thirty per cent, Sierra Leone eight per cent, and the Gambia two per cent.[99] In March 1957, Dr K. O. Mbadiwe, then the Nigerian Minister of Communication and Aviation, said that Nigeria held 68 per cent of the total shares of the Corporation.[100]

By the early fifties, the Corporation had acquired various types of aircraft such as the 'Doves' and the 'Marathon'[101] for its operations. In 1954, the WAAC operated internal services in the Gold Coast and Nigeria, intercolonial services between Accra and Lagos, and international services between Lagos and Dakar and between Lagos and Khartoum. But after 1955 the Corporation stopped its Lagos-Khartoum service. Very early in 1957, the WAAC acquired a Stratocruiser for its service between Lagos and London, but just when the aircraft was making its maiden flight from London to Lagos in April 1957 came the Ghanaian government's announcement of its intention to withdraw from the West African Airways Corporation.[102]

While nationalist feeling must have been important in Ghana's withdrawal from the WAAC, it has to be said that from the early fifties till 1958, when the Corporation was formally abolished, Nigeria seemed to have derived the greatest benefit from its operation. For instance, while in 1954 only about forty-seven per cent[103] of the services of the Corporation operated in Nigeria, the corresponding percentages in 1955 and 1957 were fifty-nine per cent and sixty per cent respectively.[104]

(e) *Currency*
Co-operation in monetary matters between the Gold Coast and Nigeria went back to 12 November 1912, when the Secretary of State for the Colonies set up the West African Currency Board following the recommendation of the departmental committee under the chairmanship of Lord Emmott.[105] Under the direction of the Board West African silver coins were introduced in that year, and were followed in 1916 by the introduction of notes. In 1920, the Board decided to replace the silver coins by West African alloy coins of the same denominations, namely two shillings, one shilling, sixpence, and threepence.[106]

The Currency Board was more or less another name for the British West African Governments, whose representatives composed it. In each of the territories' capitals the Board was represented by a currency officer. The functions of the Board were limited. According to its 1914 report, these were two. The first was to ensure the proper management of the new silver coinage. The second was to secure the convertibility of the new silver into gold in London.[107]

The last function was carried out by the establishment of one centre in each colony which was bound to issue drafts on the Board, payable in gold in London, in exchange for silver coin paid in at that centre, and by the maintenance of a gold standard reserve in London. But the business of receiving, storing and subsequently issuing the coin tendered in exchange for drafts on London was discharged by the Bank of British West Africa Limited, acting as the agent for the Board.[108]

The Board was, in fact, not a money issuing bank with power to vary the amount of currency at will, but merely a passive money changer which received superior money, that is, sterling, and gave in return token money, the West African currency.[109] For it was an essential feature of the sterling exchange standard currency that the issue and redemption were entirely automatic, that is, the currency authority did not exercise any discretion as to the amount it issued or redeemed. The West African currency was so closely tied to the sterling that when the latter was devalued in 1949, the former had to follow suit.

Furthermore, all the sterling balances of the West African Currency Board were invested in the securities of the governments of any of the British Dominions, or in such other manner as the Secretary of State for the Colonies might approve. However, the interest on such investments was paid, after deducting the expenses of running the currency system, to the four West African governments through their agency, the West African Currency Board.[110]

Although the West African currency system was important in fostering intercolonial cultural and commercial contacts, it was too closely tied to the colonial system for its disruption not to be inevitable with the progressive devolution of power to African political leaders in the fifties. Indeed, unlike the case of many other interterritorial institutions, the first major official demand for the breakup of the West African Currency Board came from the Nigerian Government in 1952, when it set up a Commission under Mr J. L. Fisher to study the possibilities of establishing a Centrral Bank in the country.[111]

(f) Research
In the field of research various types of interterritorial institutions were set up between the early forties and the early fifties. The most important were the West African Institute for Trypanosomiasis, the West African Cocoa Research Institute, the West African Institute for Oil Palm Research, the West African Council for Medical Research, the West African Institute of Social and Economic Research, the West African Stored Products Research Unit[112] and the West African Maize Rust Research Unit. We shall briefly consider all these except the last two, which had ceased to exist long before the dissolution of the West African Interterritorial Research Organization on 30 September 1962.[113] We shall, not however, deal

with the West African Institute of Social and Economic Research
because it was largely a Nigerian institution.[114] In dealing with the
remaining four we shall consider their organization, aims and
objectives,their administration, finances and activities.

The West African Institute for Trypanosomiasis

The West African Institute of Trypanosomiasis was established in
1947, following the report of Professor T. H. Davey of the Liverpool
School of Tropical Medicine who was sent to West Africa in 1945 by
the Tse-tse Fly and Trypanosomiasis Committee set up by the
Secretary of State for the Colonies. The report recommended the
establishment of a regional research organization to serve all the four
British West African colonies. It defined the main function of the new
institute as 'research on all aspects of trypanosomiasis, human,
animal, and entomological,[115]and emphasized the need for basic
studies on trypanosomiasis. Apart from this, the Institute served as a
clearing house for information about trypanosomiasis, as an advisory
bureau, and as a centre for the training of expert technical
personnel.

The Institute was organized in four sections, namely Entomology
and Epidemiology at Kaduna, and Protozoology and Veterinary
trypanosomiasis at Vom, in Nigeria. From 1947 till October 1950,
the Institute was administered by the Nigerian Government. But
from the latter date its administration was vested in its own Statutory
Managing Committee under the chairmanship of the Chief Secretary
of the West African Council (later West African Interterritorial
Secretariat). There were eleven other members of the Committee.
Apart from the Director of the Institute the others were the
representatives of the four West African governments—four from the
Gold Coast (among whom was Dr Kofi Busia, who later became the
Ghanaian Prime Minister from October 1969 till the coup d'etat of 13
January 1972), four from Nigeria, and one each from Sierra Leone
and the Gambia.[116]

Up till its dissolution in 1962, the Institute was financed jointly by
the British government and the four governments in proportion
directly related to the constitutional advance of each territory. For
instance, during the period before 31 March 1951, when there was no
representative government in any of the colonies, the British
government under the Colonial Development and Welfare Scheme
R. 140 (CR & WR) provided about two-thirds or £300,000 of the
estimated capital and recurrent expenditure.[117] After 1 April 1951
the proportion was revised, with the British government paying half

of the recurrent expenditure not exceeding £60,000 a year under the
CD & WR 424, and the four colonial governments paying the other
half. But in the mid-fifties the contribution towards the institution
was made according to the following proportions, Nigeria fifty-three
per cent, the Gold Coast thirty-eight per cent, Sierra Leone eight per
cent, the Gambia one per cent. But the British Government was
responsible for half of the contribution of any colony until its
independence.[118]

The Institute's activities were concentrated more on Nigeria where
there was a wider variety of conditions connected with the tsetse fly
and trypanosomiasis than in any of the other colonies, and where the
animal and human population was highest. For instance, in 1960
about fourteen entomological surveys were carried out in the Western
Region of Nigeria alone. But during the same year, there were only
advisory visits by the Director to Tamale, Wa and Kumasi in Ghana.
Even Sierra Leone and the Gambia made greater use of the Institute
than Ghana.[119]

The Institute had by 1962 achieved some success. Apart from the
regular publication of its research findings, the cheapest and most
effective way of controlling tsetse fly had been discovered.[120] A new
species of forest tsetse fly was discovered by Dr T. A. M. Nash, the
Institute's Director from 1955 to 1959.[121] Furthermore, some progress
had been made towards achieving immunization against the diseases
caused by trypanosomes.

The West African Cocoa Research Institute

The West African Cocoa Research Institute (WACRI) came into
existence on 1 April 1944 following the recommendation of the
Agricultural Adviser to the Secretary of State for the Colonies after a
visit to West Africa in 1943. He advised that the scope of cocoa
research[122] should be extended to meet the growing threat of insect
pests and diseases to the cocoa industry in the Gold Coast and
Nigeria. The functions of the WACRI were, according to Mr J. West,
then its Director, 'to investigate all matters affecting the cultivation of
the (cocoa) crop, and the preparation of the beans for market'.[123]

Owing to the shortage of staff the WACRI had no other station
outside Tafo in the Gold Coast, where it had its headquarters until
1953. In that year, however, a sub-station was opened at Ibadan. The
Institute was administered by a Managing Committee consisting of
the Chief Secretary of the West African Interterritorial Secretariat as
the chairman, four members representing the Gold Coast govern-

ment and four the Nigerian government, and the Director of the Institute.

The Institute was financed by contributions from the two territories. But initially it was the sum of £1.25 million set aside from the West African Produce Control Board that was used to endow the Institute, and to carry out cocoa surveys in the Gold Coast and Nigeria.[124] In 1948, a further £1 million was allocated to the funds of the Institute by the Cocoa Marketing Boards of the two territories.[125] From the early fifties till 1962 when the WACRI was dissolved into national institutions, contributions to it were made according to agreed proportions.[126]

The activities of the WACRI included investigations at the two centres, Tafo, and Ibadan on the swollen shoot disease, and the mealy bug vectors, and on the capsid buds of cocoa. Other lines of work included the methods of establishing and growing cocoa, cocoa breeding and selection, fertiliser trials, and methods of fermentation.[127] In addition to all this, conferences were held frequently between the top officials of the two stations, usually at Tafo, where papers on various aspects of cocoa industry were presented.[128]

The West African Institute for Oil Palm Research

The West African Institute for Oil Palm Research (WAIFOR) came into existence by the enactment of an Ordinance (Nigeria No. 20 of 1951) which took effect on 27 September 1951. However, for all practical purposes its operation began on 1 April 1952. The WAIFOR grew out of the former Oil Palm Research Station established in 1939 as an experimental station by the Department of Agriculture in Nigeria.[129] The Ordinance establishing the WAIFOR said it was 'for the purposes of undertaking research into and investigations of problems and matters relating to the oil palm and its products, and for the provision of information and advice relating to the oil palm.'[130]

The WAIFOR which was to serve the British West African colonies, except the Gambia which had no oil palm to develop, had its headquarters somewhere about twenty miles from Benin in Nigeria. Till late 1954 all the WAIFOR's operations were largely confined to Nigeria, where it had one sub-station and two selection areas, and where it was involved in five stations set up by the Agricultural Department, and in eight farmers' plantations and school plots. The first sub-station of the Institute outside Nigeria was opened in Njala, Sierra Leone, towards the end of 1954.[131] The

WAIFOR had no station in the Gold Coast, mainly because the oil palm industry was not of any major economic significance there, unlike Nigeria where it used to be one of the main foreign exchange earners.[132] However, the two experimental stations at Aiyinasi and Bunsu, set up by the Gold Coast Department of Agriculture during the mid-fifties, relied on the advice of the WAIFOR.

The administration of the Institute was in the hands of a Management Committee with the chief Secretary of the West African Interterritorial Secretariat as its Chairman. The other members were six officers representing the various governments and boards from Nigeria, one from the Gold Coast, one from Sierra Leone, and the Director.[133]

The Institute was financed entirely out of contributions from the three colonies. During the first quinquennial 1952/3 to 1956/7, Nigeria was required yearly to pay £126,000, Sierra Leone £16,000 and the Gold Coast £8,000 towards the cost of the Institute.[134] Early in 1952, the Nigeria Oil Palm Produce Marketing Board set up an endowment fund of £1,100,000 to be expended on the Institute during the ten-year period 1957-8 to 1966-7. Earlier in 1951, the Board had provided the sum of £150,000 to the WAIFOR for capital development.[135] A further sum of £190,000 was provided by the Board early in 1952 to complete its capital development. Although during the 1958/9 fiscal year the Ghana government on appeal from the WAIFOR doubled its annual contribution to £16,000,[136] while the Sierra Leone government increased its contribution to £20,000, the Institute continued to be heavily dependent on Nigeria for its finances. Thus in July 1961, the Federal and the Regional Governments agreed to increase the country's contribution from £126,000 to £230,000 yearly for the following five years.[137]

Between 1952 and 30 September 1962, when the WAIFOR ceased to be an interterritorial organization, it conducted research into problems of crop establishment, problems of breeding, and problems of yield maintenance and improvement. Although shortage of qualified staff handicapped its work, it nonetheless succeeded in publishing the results of some of its research activities before its dissolution.[138]

The West African Council for Medical Research

The West African Council for Medical Research (WACMAR) was instituted in August 1954. On its formation the Council took over three units, namely the Helminthiasis Research Unit at Kumba in Southern Cameroons, the Hot Climate Physiological Research

Unit at Oshodi, Nigeria, and the Virus Research Institute at Yaba, Nigeria. But the Hot Climate Physiological Research Unit at Oshodi was later closed down,[139] and other units were established. These included the Child Health Unit based on the Wesley Guild Hospital Ilesha, Nigeria, the Tuberculosis Research Unit at Kumasi, and later a unit in Bolgatanga, in the Upper Region of Ghana, for research in and work on onchocerciasis, the vector, and simulium.[140]

The West African Council for Medical Research had its administrative headquarters in Yaba. Its administration was vested in a management committee comprising the Chief Secretary of the West African Interterritorial Secretariat as the chairman, the Administrator of the West African Research Office, three nominees of the Ghana government, three of the Nigerian government, two of the Sierra Leone government, and one representing the Gambian government.[141]

The West African Council for Medical Research was financed almost entirely by contributions made by the British government and the four West African governments. Given below is a table showing the contribution of each government during the 1954-5 and 1956-7 fiscal years.[142] Apart from this, the World Health Organization

(All in £)

Fiscal Year	Total (4)	United Kingdom	Nigeria	Gold Coast (Ghana)	Sierra Leone	Gambia
1954-5	52,881	40,987	7,969	3,140	628	157
1956-7	91,600	46,044	23,100	18,480	3,696	280

(WHO) provided WACMAR with grants for research into different types of health problems.

The Council conducted research into all sorts of diseases, child mortality, leprosy, tuberculosis and yaws. The Council met in each of the four British West African capitals in rotation in conferences where various research papers were presented and discussed. These conferences were used as a forum for further co-ordination of information between all the top research workers. In Nigeria, the research staff of the Council frequently worked in collaboration with the staff of the University College Hospital, Ibadan.[143] Like many other research organization, the results of the Council's research activities were regularly published.

(g) *Education*

To further educational co-operation in its West African colonies the British government established in 1953 the West African

Examinations Council (WAEC) with its headquarters in Accra. However, it also had an office in Yaba, Nigeria, but an office was not established in Freetown until the sixties. The main purpose of the Council was to conduct various types of examinations, in co-operation with some British educational and professional bodies to ensure a uniform high standard in education in West Africa.

During the 1954-5 period its office in Yaba received over 10,788 entries, and the Accra office 19,985 for twenty-five different examinations.[144] These included the School Certificate, the Higher School Certificate, the General Certificate of Education, the Gold Coast Sixth Form Bursary Examination, the Gold Coast School Entrance Examination, the Gold Coast Public Service Competition, the City and Guilds of London Institute, the Royal Society of Arts, the Associated Board of the Royal Schools of Music etc. From the late fifties, the Nigerian Governments began to hand over many examinations to the Council. These included the competitive examination to the executive and administrative posts of the public service, the teachers' examination, and the common entrance examination to many secondary schools. Furthermore, the WAEC used to act and has continued to act as the agent of the London University for candidates sitting the external degrees of the University.[145]

The governing board of the WAEC was made up of nominees from all the four governments, and one representative each of the London University and the Cambridge University. During the 1954-5 period there were ten Nigerian nominees on the Board, six from the Gold Coast, four from Sierra Leone, and three from the Gambia.[146]

The Council was, and has continued to be, financed by the four governments. During the fiscal year 1954-5, Nigeria contributed £10,122. 12. 1d towards the cost of recurrent expenditure, while the Gold Coast and Sierra Leone during the same year contributed £7,159. 3. 7d and £1,406. 14. 0d respectively.[147] The contribution towards the capital expenditure of the Councils has continued to be paid according to the following proportions: 50:40:8:2 by Nigeria, Ghana, Sierra Leone and the Gambia respectively.[148]

Unlike the other interterritorial institutions, the West African Examinations Council, described in 1958 as 'probably the most successful interterritorial body' in West Africa,[149] has not merely survived the growth of local nationalism in all the four territories but has since independence continued to expand its activities. Indeed, the Council has started to go beyond the limits of former British West Africa by associating Liberia with its work.

(iii) DECLINE IN CO-OPERATION AND BREAK-UP OF COMMON INSTITUTIONS

Apart from the West African Examinations Council none of the other interterritorial institutions has survived till today.[150] Why has this been so? And why was it that only very little of the earlier co-operation in political, social and economic matters between the Gold Coast and Nigeria in the pre-independence days has remained? These are the questions we shall try to discuss in the rest of this chapter. Broadly speaking, the reasons could be divided into four, namely the growth of local nationalism, the exigencies of independence, jealousy, and post-independence political discord.

If the 1920s saw the growth of West African nationalism, the following decade witnessed the effective beginning of local nationalism in Nigeria and the Gold Coast. The effect was that from the 1930s onwards some Pan-West African organizations began to lose support to local organizations. Thus in 1933 all the Nigerian directors of Nigerian Mercantile Bank Limited, founded in 1931 by Mr Winifried Tete-Ansa from the Gold Coast, resigned to found the National Bank Nigeria Limited to be run by Nigerians and operated in Nigeria for Nigerians only.[151] In the political field the Nigerian Youth Movement, led by Chief H. O. Davies and others who advocated self-government on a territorial basis, displaced Herbert Macaulay's NNDP with its Pan-West African programme by decisively defeating it in the elections to the Legislative Council in 1938, and in the election to the Lagos Town Council that same year. James Coleman said that one important element in the defeat of the NNDP in 1938 was the insistence of its opponents that Nigerian nationalism should be led by Nigerians,[152] and should not include men who thought of themselves primarily as West Africans.[153] In the Gold Coast, too, the pattern was similar. In the late 1930s Dr J. B. Danquah came out strongly in favour of national development in the Gold Coast rather than in West Africa.[154] The United Gold Coast Convention (UGCC) that dominated the Gold Coast politics till June 1949 when the CPP was formed was very parochial in its programme. It has to be remembered that one of the main divisive factors between Kwame Nkrumah and the UGCC leaders was his insistence on West African unity which they found difficult to 'reconcile' with 'the rather parochial aims' of the party.[155] Even with the ascendancy of the CPP in the Gold Coast after 1951, the struggle for independence was, as in Nigeria, fought on a territorial basis.

The exigencies of independence made the dismemberment of some of the common interterritorial institutions inevitable. A country's independence could hardly be meaningful without its control over its own currency and its own army. As we have earlier pointed out the Nigerian Government as far back as 1952 had in anticipation of full self-government set up a Commission to enquire into the possibilities of establishing a Nigerian Central Bank with powers to issue and control its own currency. Though the report of this Commission was in 1953 against the setting up of a Central Bank, the Nigerian government in 1954 set up another Commission to re-examine the question. This Commission reported in favour of establishing a Central Bank in the country.[156] When the proposal to establish the Central Bank was finally accepted by the government it was greeted with joy in the Nigerian House of Representatives. Chief Ayo Rosiji, then one of the AG opposition leaders in the House described the government's acceptance of the proposal as 'a sign of maturity'. He added that it showed that 'we are prepared to shoulder our responsibility ourselves instead of depending all the time on outside support'.[157]

In April 1955, the CPP government in the Gold Coast announced its intention to set up a central bank to issue the country's currency. Mr K. A. Gbedemah, the then Finance Minister, said:

The issue by this country of its own currency will be one of the more significant marks of its own attainment of full nationhood.[158]

This also applied to the dissolution of the Royal West African Frontier Force. Justifying Ghana's withdrawal from the RWAFF in 1959, Mr A. E. Inkumsah, then a Minister of State, said it 'was raised and maintained as a colonial force, and it is from that aspect of it that we wish to dissociate ourselves, so as to emphasize that the Ghana Army is the independent Army of an independent state'.[159] As early as 1953, the Nigerian Government had expressed its wish to have greater control over its own army, and to establish its own military training school instead of depending on the RWAFF training school at Teshie in Ghana.[160] Since 1955, the Nigeria MPs had been advocating the need to have a Nigerian national army. So when Sir James Robertson, then the Governor-General of the federation, announced in Parliament that the government would as from 1 April 1958 take full control of the Nigerian Regiment of the RWAFF, this was greeted with cheers.[161]

Dr Nkrumah later justified his government's decision to pull out of many of the interterritorial institutions as no more than 'a demonstration of our sovereignty'.[162] This contained much truth, even in the Nigerian government's case. However, the Nkrumah government tended to push the question of independence to a ridiculous extent. The existence of some of these common institutions, such as those dealing with co-operation in research and air transport, was not incompatible with independence. Some arrangement could have been worked out for co-operation in air transport, as was shown later by the Ghana-Nigeria Airways Pool Agreement of May 1967,[163] without necessarily destroying completely the West African Airways Corporation. The dissolution of this Corporation was received with 'great regret' by the Federal Government.[164]

There was the question of mutual jealousy between the two countries dating back to pre-independence days. Partly because of Nigeria's bigger size and population, and partly because she contributed the lion's share in maintaining most of the interterritorial institutions, the Nigerian leaders felt that they should have a major voice in any decision affecting them. Thus during the debate on the losses of the West African Airways Corporation (WAAC) in the House of Representatives in April 1955, Chief S. L. Akintola, then the Opposition leader, said that since Nigeria paid twice as much as the Gold Coast to make up for the losses[165] of the WAAC Nigeria's opinion should be decisive in all matters affecting the Corporation.[166] Furthermore, many Nigerians did not like the fact that Accra was made the headquarters of most of the important interterritorial institutions.[167]

The Gold Coast leaders felt superior to the Nigerians for three main reasons. Firstly, the Gold Coast had the advantage of higher education earlier than Nigeria.[168] Secondly, most of the Nigerians trading and working in Ghana till the early fifties were largely uneducated and unskilled labour, and 'farm hands'.[169] Thirdly, the faster rate of the decolonization process in the Gold Coast, which started with the 1946 constitution, made its leaders feel more important than the Nigerians.[170] The result of all this was that the Gold Coast did not want to be in any position subordinate to Nigeria. Thus in the mid-forties the Gold Coast refused to accept the decision of the Secretary of State for the Colonies that only a single University should be established in Nigeria to serve the needs of all the British West African colonies, as recommended by the minority report of the Elliot Commission on Higher Education in West Africa in 1945.[171] Instead the Gold Coast leaders chose to have their own separate university.[172] And to this the Colonial Secretary agreed on the understanding that it would be endowed largely from local resources.

Thus in 1948 two separate universities were established in Ibadan and Achimota.[173]

In spite of all this, however, there was some measure of co-operation between the two territories till Ghana's independence. The fact that they failed to build upon this past co-operation after independence was due mainly to ideological differences and political discord, to bitterness arising out of the struggle for leadership in Africa, to their conflicting views about African unity, the Congo crisis and attitudes to the Great Powers, and to Ghana's attitude to the Nigerian civil war. It is all this that will be dealt with in subsequent chapters.

1. This is true of the other two former British colonies of Sierra Leone and the Gambia in West Africa. But we shall concentrate mainly on the Gold Coast and Nigeria, which form the focus of this study.

2. There were commercial and religious contacts between the two peoples before the colonial era. For instance, the trade in kolanuts, and 'kente' cloth between the Hausas and the Ashantis was said to have preceded the commercial contact between the Hausas and the Southerners in Nigeria See *West Africa*, 9 March 1957. Similarly, there was a steady inflow of Muslim elements from Nigeria to Gonja in the Gold Coast between sixteenth and eighteenth centuries. See C. G. Baeta, 'Aspects of Religion' in W. Birmingham, E. N. Omaboe, and I. Neustadt Vol. II op. cit. p. 243. But colonial rule certainly promoted the contacts between the two peoples, especially the educated classes.

3. Martin Wight, p. 18.

4. From the end of the 19th century until the late 1930s the British government did little to promote inter-colonial contacts in its colonies in West Africa. See Michael Crowder *West Africa Under Colonial Rule*, London 1968, p. 202.

5. Martin Wight op. cit. p. 103.

6. *Report of the Proceedings of the First West African Governors' Conference held in Lagos 10-18 August, 1939*, Lagos, Government Printer, pp. 6-7.

7. I. F. Nicolson, *The Administration of Nigeria, 1900-60*, London 1969, p. 235.

8. Educated Sierra Leoneans were also recruited to the Nigerian public service during this period. See Alan Burns *History of Nigeria*, London 1963, pp. 269-70.

9. *H. R. Deb.*, 21 April 1965, col. 1139.

10. It was all this that made it easy for Dr Edward Blyden to travel to all the four British West African colonies in the nineteenth century; and also for J. E. Casely Hayford to do the same in the 1920s. it made it possible for J. B. Horton to serve in all the four colonies, and Edward Blyden and Dr Obadiah Johnson to work in Nigeria and Sierra Leone. For further details see E. A. Ayandele *Holy Johnson*, London 1970, pp. 12-13.

11. *Michael Crowder* op. cit. p. 202.

12. J. S. Coleman *Nigeria, Background to Nationalism*, Berkeley 1963, p. 192.

13. J. E. Casely-Hayford *The Land Question*, pp. 99 and 112.

14. David Kimble *A Political History, of Ghana 1850-1928*, London 1963, p. 384.

15. Other delegates included from the Gold Coast T. Hutton Mills and H. Van Hien; from Nigeria Chief Oluwa of Lagos and J. Egerton Shyngle; from Sierra Leone Dr H. C. Bankole-Bright and Mr F. W. Dove; and from the Gambia Mr E. F. Small and Mr H. N. Jones.

16. *The Times*, London 16 December 1920.

17. For the way in which the delegation to London was sabotaged by the Gold Coast chiefs and members of the Aborigines' Society, see Martin Wight op. cit. p. 27.

18. David Kimble op. cit. p. 402.

19. A. G. Hopkins, 'Economic Aspects of Political Movements in Nigeria and in the Gold Coast 1918-39' in the *Journal of African History*, Vol. vii, 1, London 1966, p. 145.

20. *West Africa*, 31 October 1925.

21. *West Africa*, 13 September 1958.

22. For further details, see Ladipo Solanke *United West Africa (or Africa) at the Bar of the Family of Nations*, London 1927; and *WASU magazine*, London 1926, no. 1.

23. One of the first residents of the hostel was Adetokunboh Ademola, the First Nigerian Chief Justice.

24. Kola Balogun *Village Boy*, Ibadan 1969, p. 45.

25. J. S. Coleman op. cit. p. 205.

26. Ibid. p. 239.

27. Memorandum from WASU to Under Secretary of State for the Colonies, 6 April 1942.

Ä28. J. S. Coleman op. cit. pp. 242-4.   Ä   Ä

29. For some time now, there has been a nation-wide fund-raising campaign to build a teaching hospital in memory of Mbonu Ojike. At present, his former colleague, Dr K. O. Mbadiwe, is in charge of this plan, and he has recently said he would want the Federal Government to take ovar the building of the teaching hospital.

30. David Kimble op. cit. p. 549.

31. *Ghana, The Autobiography*, op. cit. p. 51.

32. V. C. Ikeotuonye *Zik of New Africa*, London 1961, p. 120.

33. Ibid. p. 121, and pp. 118-27 for Azikiwe's political activities in the Gold Coast in the 1930s.

34. In the issue of 29 September 1936, Dr Azikiwe referred to the formation of a federation of 'Gamsierragolderia' consisting of all the four British West African colonies which would be independent, and whose executive would consist, among others, of Herbert Macaulay from Nigeria as Governor-General, Kojo Thompson and Akilagpa Sawyerr from the Gold Coast as Attorney-General and Secretary General respectively; and Olu Alakija, another Nigerian, as the solicitor-General etc.

35. *Africa Diary*, 27 February-5 March 1965, pp. 2208-9.

36. The memory of Dr Azikiwe's nationalist agitation in the Gold Coast in the 1930s helped to swerve substantial opinion in Ghana behind the 'Biafran' cause during the last civil war, especially before Dr Azikiwe came out openly against secession in August 1969.

37. Nnamdi Azikiwe *Zik—A Selection from the Speeches of Nnamdi Azikiwe*, London 1961, p. 69.

38. A. G. Hopkins in *Journal of African History*, op. cit. p. 138.

39. Ibid. p. 139n.

40. Ibid. pp. 139-40.

41. Ibid. p. 145.

42. *Daily News*, Lagos 29 May 1931.

43. I. F. Nicolson op. cit. p. 218.

44. P. A. Bower, 'The Balance of Payments in 1936' in Margery Perham (ed.) *Mining, Commerce and Finance in Nigeria*, London 1948, p. 304n.

45. J. Mars, 'Extra-Territorial Enterprises' in Margery Perham (ed.) op. cit. p. 180.

46. Ibid.

47. Ibid. p. 298, p. 326.

48. Ibid. p. 167.

49. Martin Wight op. cit. p. 27.

50. J. Mars. 'Extra-Territorial Enterprises' in Margery Perham (ed.) op. cit. p. 116.

51. Most of the Nigerians that went to work in Ghana after 1957 went to towns rather than cocoa farms, and the mines. See W. Birmingham, E. N. Omaboe, and I. Neustadt, Vol. II op. cit. p. 112.

52. Sir Ahmadu Bello op. cit. p. 200.

53. *1971 Census*, Accra, Government Printer.

54. The breakdown of the figures in 1960 was as follows: 109,090 were Yorubas, 61,730 Hausas, 14,050 Ibos and 24,350 other Nigerian tribes. *1960 Census*, Accra, Government Printer.

55. *West Africa*, 31 January 1970.

56. Ibid.

57. Information from the Nigerian High Commission in Accra tended to support Dr Busia's figure.

58. Sir Alan Burns said that during this period educated Gold Coasters, and Sierra Leoneans were given good salaries by the colonial administration to attract them to Nigeria. Sir Alan Burns op. cit. pp. 269–70.

59. In the 1952-3 Nigerian census, all non-Nigerian Africans were simply classified 'African' or 'West African'.

60. *1963 Census*, Lagos, Government Printer.

61. In the late fifties, the Ghanaian 'high life' was so popular in Nigeria that anything different from it was treated with contempt. During this period the slogan 'Ghana Style', that is, a peculiarly Ghanaian way of doing things, was popular among young Nigerian men and women.

62. In spite of poor relations between Ghana and Nigeria later, these social contacts were not seriously disrupted. Thus in June 1971, students of Ibadan University went to meet their counterparts in Legon for debates and for other student activities, at a time when there was a sort of press war between the two countries over the enforcement of the Ghana Aliens Compliance Order.

63. Between 1867, when the West African Court of Appeal (WACA) was first established, and 1874, all appeals from all the British colonies in West Africawere sent to it, and from there final appeals were made to the Privy Council in London. But in the latter year, the WACA was broken into two. One was for Sierra Leone and the Gambia, and the other for the Gold Coast and Lagos, the latter being administered as its Eastern province. For some time before 1928, each of the colonies used to send its appeals direct to the Privy Council. After that date, appeals to the Privy Council lay from the Court of Appeal. But Nigeria did not accept its jurisdiction until 1934. By 1958 the WACA had jurisdiction only in Sierra Leone and the Gambia, while Ghana and Nigeria had their own Supreme Courts from where appeals were made direct to London. But with the assumption of Republican status in Ghana in 1960, and in Nigeria in 1963, an end was put to appeal to the Privy Council. For a brief history of the West African Court of Appeal, See *West Africa*, 4 October 1958.

64. For further details, see *Report of the proceedings of the First West African Governors' Conference*, held in Lagos, 10–18 August 1939, Lagos, Government Printer.

65. Sir Alan Burns op. cit. p. 248.

66. Lord Hailey *African Survey*, Revised 1956, London 1957, p. 1608.

67. *Minutes of the First Meeting of the West African Inter-territorial Conference, held in Accra on 22 and 23 July 1952*.

68. It has to be remembered that in 1951 a semi-representative form of government was introduced in all the four British West African colonies.

69. The Ministers representing Nigeria at the first meeting of the Conference in July 1952 were Shettima Kashim, and Mohammadu Ribabu; and the Gold Coast Ministers present were A. Casely-Hayford and Kojo Botsio.

70. In some real sense, Sir John Macpherson's description of the West African Interterritorial Conference and the Secretariat as 'an African organization responsible only to the four British West African governments' was correct. See *Minutes of the First Meeting of the West African Conference held in Accra on 22 and 23 July 1952*, para. 2.

71. *West Africa*, 14 June 1958.

72. But for the outbreak of intense mutual recriminations and the press war between Ghana and Nigeria in mid-1962, following the Federal government's dismissal of the AG government of Western Nigeria, the interterritorial research organization might probably have had a longer life. The decision to fold up the organization was taken towards the end of June 1962 at the height of mutual abuse. This meant that this strained relationship contributed substantially to the decision, though other factors were certainly involved.

73. There was, however, a subsidiary of the Cocoa Board in the Gold Coast and Nigeria.

74. *Record of Proceedings of the Conference of African Governors held in Convocation Hall, London*, 8–21 November 1947, p. 183.

75. The British Ministry of Supply took powers during the war to purchase hides and skin, rubber and cotton from the colonies.

76. *Record of Proceedings of the Conference of African Governors*, 1947, op. cit. p. 183.

77. Sir Alan Burns op. cit. p. 132n.

78. The prefix 'Royal' was given to it in 1928 by King George V in recognition of its performance during the First World War, and it became RWAFF.

79. Colonel A. Haywood and Brigadier F. A. S. Clarke, *The History of the Royal West African Frontier Force*, Aldershot 1964, p. 38.

80. For further details, see Sir Alan Burns op. cit. pp. 224, and 226–7.

81. The organization which was given in the early 1920s as consisting of the Gold Coast Regiment, the Nigeria Regiment, the Sierra Leone Battalion, and the Gambia Company is a further proof that the WAFF was not really integrated as a single force. See *Regulations for the West African Frontier Force*, London 1923, p. 5.

82. Ibid.

83. The Governor, however, could rarely order any military operation without consulting the military officer in charge at the local level.

84. *The West African Forces Conference 1953 Cmnd 6577*, London HMSO, 1954, p. 3.

85. Colonel A. Haywood and Brigadier F. A. S. Clarke op. cit. p. 364.

86. Ibid. p. 484.

87. *H. R. Deb.*, 18 February 1958, col. 6.

88. Colonel A. Haywood and Brigadier F. A. S. Clarke op. cit. p. 477.

89. Ibid. p. 485.

90. *Report of the West African Forces Conference held in Lagos, 20–24 April 1953*, Lagos, Government Printer, p. 11.

91. For example Sir Abubakar, then the spokenman on the army in the Central Legislature, and at the same time a Minister in Lagos, attended this 1953 Conference.

92. *Report of the West African Forces Conference, 1953*, op. cit. p. 13.

93. Ibid. pp. 2–4.

94. Ibid. p. 15.

95. Colonel A. Haywood and Brigadier F. S. A. Clarke op. cit. p. 484.

96. Ibid.

97. Although the aim was to promote air transport between all the British West African colonies, the West Airways Corporation did not actually operate services to Sierra Leone and the Gambia before its formal dissolution in 1958.

98. *Report of the West African Airways Corporation for the period ending 31 March 1947*, Lagos, Government Printer, p. 1.

99. Ibid. p. 3.

101. *H. R. Deb.*, 2 March 1957, col. 61.

101. *H. R. Deb.*, 7 April 1955, col. 1069.

102.   *West Africa*, 4 May 1957.

103.   *Digest of Statistics*, Vol. 3, No. 2, April 1954, Lagos, Government printer, p. 56.

104.   *Digest of Statistics*, Vol. 7, No. 3, July 1958, Lagos, Government Printer, p. 58.

105.   *Report of the Departmental Committee appointed to enquire into Matters affecting the currency of the British West African Colonies and Protectorate*, London 1912.

106.   This was done mainly to discourage hoarding and melting down, which was the fate of too large a proportion of the silver coinage. See J. Mars, 'The Monetary and Banking System and the Loan Market of Nigeria' in Margery Perham (ed.) op. cit. p. 181.

107.   *Report of the West African Currency Board for period ended 30 June 1914.*

108.   J. Mars, 'The Monetary and Banking System' in Margery Perham (ed.) op. cit. p. 179.

109.   Ibid. p. 186.

110.   For further details about the West African Currency Board, see W. T. Newlyn and D. C. Rowan *Money and Banking in British Colonial Africa*, Oxford 1954.

111.   The Fisher Report of 1953, however, came out against the establishment of the Central Bank. See *H. R. Deb.* 2 March 1957, p. 61.

112.   The West African Stored Products Research Unit was entirely a Nigerian institution. It was financed entirely by Nigeria from its inception in 1948 till its dissolution. See *West African Stored Products Research Unit, Annual Report*, Lagos, Government Printer 1956.

113.   By 1958, it was agreed to dissolve the West African Maize Rust Research Unit, See *H. R. Deb.*, 30 July 1958, col. 75.

114.   The Gold Coast government did not actually make any financial contribution to this Institute for years, and its administration was from the start in the hands of a few top members of staff of the University of Ibadan. For details see *WAISER, Annual Reports 1952-3, 1954-5.*

115.   *The West African Institute for Trypanosomiasis Annual Report*, 1951, p. 1.

116.   Ibid. p. 23.

117.   Ibid. p. 1.

118.   *The West African Institute for Trypanosomiasis Research, Annual Report*, 1959, p. 3.

119.   For further details, see the various annual reports of the Institute from 1951 to 1962.

120.   See *The West African Institute for Trypanosomiasis Research Annual Report*, 1962, pp. iv-ix — for an account of the work of the Institute between 1947 and 1962 given by its Director, Dr K. C. Willett.

121.   Ibid.

122.   A cocoa research station had been established by the Agricultural Department of the Gold Coast in 1939 at Tafo which later became the Headquarters of the WACRI.

123.   *Proceedings of the West African International Cocoa Research Conference held at Tafo, Gold Coast 12-16 December 1953*, p. 2.

124.   Ibid.

125.   Ibid.

126.   Though the proportions were not exactly known, they must have been close to each other. But if based on the principle of benefits derived, which was the main criterion for allocating contributions to each of the West African interterritorial institutions, Ghana might pay more since she was a bigger cocoa producer than Nigeria.

127.   For further details see *Proceedings of the Cocoa Breeding Conference, 1-3 October, 1956.*

128.   Even after the break-up of the WACRI, the top officials of Ghana and the Nigerian Cocoa Research Institutes used to attend research conferences

organized by each national organization. Thus in 1963, Mr R. H. Kenten, the Director of the Nigeria Cocoa Research Institute, and his Deputy, Dr J. K. Opeke, attended the Cocoa Mirid Control Conference organized by the Ghana Cocoa Research Institute at Tafo in August 1963, See *Proceedings of the Cacao Mirid Control Conference, at Tafo, 6-7 August, 1963*, Accra, Government Printer.

129. *The West African institute for Oil Palm Research, Annual Report 1952-53*, p. 13.

130. Ibid.

131. *WAIFOR, Annual Report 1953-54*, p. 15.

132. In Nigeria in 1960 the export of palm oil and palm kernel accounted for about twenty-sevan per cent of total export earnings.

133. *WAIFOR, Annual Report 1952-53*, p. 14.

134. Contributions were based on two criteria, namely the relative importance of oil palm to the territory, and the relative benefits to each territory both as exporters and as consumers of oil palm products. Ibid. p. 15.

135. This was the unspent part of the £530,608 granted by the Board to the Oil Palm Research Station for capital development between 1949-50 and 1951-2. Ibid. p. 16.

136. *WAIFOR, Annual Report 1958-59*, p. 11.

137. *WAIFOR, Annual Report 1961-62*, p. 14.

138. For further details about the activities of the WAIFOR, see the various annual reports, especially from 1954-55 to 1962-63.

139. *The West African Council for Medical Research, Annual Report 1957-58*, p. 1.

140. *The WACMAR, Annual Report 1958-59*, p. 1.

141. *WACMAR, Annual Report 1957-58*, p. 29.

142. Ibid. p. 34.

143. *WACMAR, Annual Report 1958-59*, pp. 1-2.

144. *The West African Examinations Council Annual Report 1954-55*, p. 6.

145. For further details see the various annual reports of the WAEC especially from 1955-6 onwards.

146. *WAEC, Annual Report 1954-5*, pp. 3-4.

147. Gambia did not contribute anything towards the recurrent expenditure in 1954-5. Ibid. p. 23.

148. Ibid. and *Annual Report 1959-60*, p. 59.

149. *West Africa*, 24 May 1958.

150. The WAEC has survived partly because it is not political, and so does not involve matters of national pride and power, and partly because both Ghana and Nigeria have found it useful and convenient to maintain an institution that gives their education some stamp of international standing.

151. A. G. Hopkins in *Journal of African History*, op. cit. p. 146.

152. J. S. Coleman op. cit. p. 225.

153. Most of the NNDP leaders were non-Nigerian Africans without support in Nigeria outside Lagos. For instance, Edward Blyden and John Payne Jackson were Liberians; J. E. Egerton-Shyngle was a Gambian by birth and early education; C. C. Adeniyi-Jones, former president of the party, and J. C. Zizer, for years the editor of *West African Nationhood*, were both Sierra Leoneans; while Herbert Macaulay, the founder of the party, was culturally a Freetown Creole, though he was the grandson of Bishop Crowther from Nigeria. See J. S. Coleman op. cit. p. 211.

154. Dr Danquah called in the 1930s for a national effort to develop 'our country' by which he said he meant 'the Gold Coast', and 'not negroes'. See J. B. Danquah, *Self Help*, p. 18.

155. UGCC, *Minute Book*, entry for 28 December 1947.

156. For details of this report see *Economic Development of Nigeria*, Lagos, Government Printer, 1955. See also *H. R. Deb.*, 2 March 1957, p. 61.

157. *H. R. Deb.*, 2 March 1957, cols. 49-50.

158. *Gold Coast, L. A. Deb.*, 5 April 1955.

159. *N. A. Deb.*, 19 February 1959.

160. *MR PRIME MINISTER, A Selection of Speeches made by Alhaji the Right Honourable Sir Abubakar Tafawa Balewa*, Lagos 1964, p. 133.

161. *H. R. Deb.*, 18 February 1958, col. 6.

162. Kwame Nkrumah's Broadcast 5 March 1959. See also Kwame Nkrumah *Hands Off Africa*, Accra 1960, p. 36.

163. This Agreement was terminated in December 1970.

164. *H. R. Deb.*, 2 March 1957, col. 61.

165. The WAAC's losses were defrayed as follows: Nigeria was to pay £299,467, the Gold Coast £129,916, Sierra Leone £8,806, and the Gambia £2,201. See *H. R. Deb.*, 7 April 1955, p. 1069.

166. Ibid. p. 1070.

167. Chief Ayo Rosiji, one of the top Opposition leaders in the House of Representatives, said in 1957 shortly before the independence of the Gold Coast that the Nigerian leaders felt jealous that the Gold Coast should have its independence before Nigeria because they were not in any way inferior to the Gold Coast people. *H. R. Deb.*, 2 March 1957, col. 50.

168. The certificates awarded by the Achimota College founded in 1927 were superior to those awarded by the Yaba Higher College founded in 1934. This continued until 1948 when the University College, Ibadan, was established.

169. For the extent to which this contributed to the Ghanaian air of superiority over Nigerians, see Chief Kolawole Balogun *Mission to Ghana, Memoir of a Diplomat*, New York 1963, p. 54.

170. More will be said of this in the next chapter. For this attitude did affect their post-independence relationship.

171. *The Elliot Commission of 1945—Report of the Commission on Higher Education in West African Cmnd 6655*, HMSO London 1945.

172. *Lord hailey*, op. cit. p. 1181.

173. The site was later moved to Legon, near Accra.

CHAPTER III

Leadership Role in Africa

The struggle for leadership in Africa, especially in Black Africa, was one of the greatest difficulties in Ghanaian-Nigerian harmony. Apart from sentiment, the qualifications of both countries for the leadership role were not impressive. As earlier shown in chapter one, both were, on independence, militarily and economically weak. However, the Ghanaians and the Nigerians based their claim to leadership on other factors which we shall briefly consider.

The Ghanaians based theirs firstly on the fact that their country was the first to be independent in Black Africa. This they thought gave them a 'unique' opportunity to play a leading role in Africa. Shortly after independence, Dr Nkrumah spoke of the 'historic role' of the Ghanaians 'to lead . . . our brethren who are still struggling to be free.'[1] Later in 1958, Dr Nkrumah declared in the National Assembly that 'whether we like it or not history has assigned to us a great responsibility, and we (must not) fail all the millions on this continent who look to us as a symbol of their hopes in Africa.'[2]

The second was the myth of the new Ghana being the rebirth of the old Ghana Empire. Although there has been no concrete historical evidence to substantiate the assertion that the new Ghana was a direct descendant of the ancient Ghana,[3] the CPP leaders held this to be true, and maintained the myth mainly to justify their country's leadership role in Africa. Thus on the eve of independence, Dr Nkrumah said:

> . . . according to tradition, the peoples of the Gold Coast originally came from the great Empire of Ghana, and that at the University of Sankore of the old Ghana Empire there were teachers . . . from all parts of the Arab world of the Middle Ages, and there was a mingling of the cultures of the peoples from the North and the South of the Sahara . . . it is our earnest hope that the Ghana which is now being reborn will be like the Ghana of the old, a centre to which all the peoples of Africa may come . . .[4]

This myth was kept up in different ways. The title *Ghana Resurgent* given to the book published in 1964 by Mr Michael Dei-Anang, formerly head of the Ministry of External Affairs, and later till the coup in 1966 an Ambassador Extraordinary in charge of the African Affairs Secretariat, was to boost the myth.[5] Some world leaders tried to keep up this myth by flattery. Thus the leader of the British Parliamentary delegation to present a Speaker's chair to the Ghana National Assembly in February 1959, Mr R. H. Turton, flattered the Ghanaians by saying that he hoped that the present Ghana like the Ghana Empire of the Middle Ages would play a leading role in Africa.[6]

Another factor on which the Ghanaian leaders tried to base their claim to leadership in Africa was that on independence their country was by far the more united politically, and was more prosperous than any other British African colony, including Nigeria. Furthermore, the Ghanaian feeling of superiority over the Nigerians, though difficult to justify on the basis of practical achievement, made them believe that their country should lead Africa. Although, as pointed out in chapter two, this Ghanaian air of superiority was due mainly to the fact that most Nigerians in the Gold Coast until the mid-fifties were illiterate traders and labourers.[7] And the fact that it was the NPC leaders that dominated the Federal coalition on independence contributed to this. For one thing, to Nkrumah and his colleagues, the NPC leaders were nothing but feudal lords who had still to come into the twentieth century. Finally the fact that for nearly two and a half years after her independence Ghana was virtually the spokesman for Africa in world affairs convinced the Ghanaians that they should continue in that role.[8]

But once Nigeria became independent in October 1960 she tried to stop Ghana from playing that leadership role in Africa which many Nigerians considered their 'birth-right,' to quote Chief Anthony Enahoro.[9] Even before independence, Alhaji Maitama Sule, the leader of the Nigerian delegation to the Second Conference of Independent African States in Addis Ababa in June 1960, had spoken severely against anyone—evidently referring to Nkrumah—who considered himself 'a Messiah' with 'a mission to lead Africa'.[10] It has to be noted that in January 1960 the Nigerian Prime Minister, Sir Abubakar, had told the House of Representatives that after independence Nigeria would have 'a wonderful opportunity' to speak for Africa at the United Nations.[11]

The Nigerian claim to the leadership role in Africa was based on the country's vast size, population and natural resources. The fact that these vast human and material resources had not been fully developed did not seem to affect their judgement that Nigeria was 'the giant' of Africa, and so had to lead the continent. The pages of Nigerian newspapers and the country's Hansard, especially shortly before and after independence, were full of all sorts of rhetoric about Nigeria's leadership role in Africa. We shall only refer to a few of them here. In 1958 Mr R. A. Fani-Kayode, then an Action Group leader in the Federal Legislature, said that 'Nigeria is destined to lead Africa . . . black Africa as a whole to the total emancipation of all our peoples . . .'[12] Mr Jaja Wachuku who later became the country's first Minister of External Affairs said in January 1960, ' . . . Nigeria . . . is the largest single unit in Africa . . .' and so 'must lead Africa . . . and we are not going to abdicate the (leadership) position in which God Almighty has placed us.'[13] In 1964 at the ceremony to mark the establishment of the Nigerian Institute of International Affairs, Sir Abubakar spoke of the need for Nigeria to take her 'rightful place' in the continent.[14]

This sentiment about Nigeria's importance and her leadership in Africa was encouraged by some world leaders. In 1960, Mr Harold Macmillan, then the British Prime Minister, spoke of Nigeria's great size and population, and of her playing a leading role in Africa and in the Commonwealth.[15] In 1965, Mr Mennen Williams, then the Assistant Secretary of State for African Affairs, referred in Lagos to Nigeria's 'importance, weight, and leadership' in Africa.[16]

Just as Ghana viewed Nigeria as the greatest single obstacle to her dominance in Africa, so also did Nigeria view Ghana. To emphasize that they had a special claim to lead Africa, the Nigerian leaders used to stress, and sometimes overstress, the size and wealth of their country, and to refer to Ghana's size with contempt. Thus in March 1957, Chief S. L. Akintola, then the leader of the AG Opposition in the House of Representatives, declared that Ghana was no more than two of Nigeria's provinces, namely Kano and Katsina. He added that, though independent, Ghana must 'deal with us as an elder brother'.[17] Dr Michael Okpara said in 1962 that to compare Ghana with Nigeria was to compare an ant with an elephant. This same comparison was repeated in April 1965 by Sir Abubakar Tafawa Balewa, who added that in terms of 'size, population and wealth' there was nothing for which Nigeria could envy Ghana.[18]

The struggle for leadership between Ghana and Nigeria centred largely on the question of who should be Africa's spokesman in international affairs on such things as anti-colonialism, anti-racism, neo-colonialism, African unity and African ideology. Since the year 1966 marked a distinct change in the domestic and external policies of the two countries, we shall deal with most of these questions under two separate divisions. The first section will deal with the period before February 1966, and the second with the 1966-70 period.

(i) AN IDEOLOGY FOR AFRICA

Being a revolutionary, Dr Kwame Nkrumah believed that independent Africa required an ideology of its own that would be different from that of the colonial past. As he later wrote:

> With true independence regained, . . . a new harmony that will allow the combined presence of traditional Africa, Islamic Africa, and Euro-Christian Africa, so that this presence is in tune with the original humanist principles underlying African society.[19]

Although Nkrumah had described himself as a Marxist socialist in his autobiography, the name given to his new ideology for Africa was Nkrumaism. Nkrumah, who was later described by Professor Ali Mazrui as 'Africa's Lenin', wanted 'Nkrumaism to assume the same historic, and revolutionary status (in Africa) as Leninism'[20] Much of Nkrumah's energy was directed towards promoting 'Nkrumaism'[21] beyond Ghana's borders, mainly because like Trotsky, though in different circumstances, he did not believe that his new ideology could survive in a single country. It has to be noted that the CPP activists who manned the *Spark* later described Nkrumaism as 'the ideology of the New Africa.'[22]

But the Nigerian leaders, including the AG and the NCNC nationalists who attended the First All-African People's Conference in Accra in December 1958, were, on the basis of their country's diversity and their own experience, not sure that a single ideology could serve the whole of the continent given its diversity in history, geography, culture, language, customs and tradition.[23] The Northern leaders in the Federal Coalition in Lagos and in the former Northern Nigerian Government, who were extremely conservative, would have nothing to do with an African ideology. Indeed, they had found a single ideology acceptable to all Nigerians difficult to evolve, let alone an Africa-wide ideology. The result of this was an ideological conflict between Nigeria and Ghana.

(a) Ideological Conflict: I Nkrumaism versus Pragmatism

Nkrumaism is a term difficult to define precisely. The *Spark*,[24] the most authoritative exponent of the ideology, defined it as follows:

> Nkrumaism is the ideology for the new Africa, independent and absolutely free from imperialism, organized on a continental scale, founded upon the conception of one and united Africa drawing its

strength from modern science and technology and from the traditional belief that the free development of each is the condition for the free development of all.[25]

Mr Kofi Baako, the last defence Minister under Nkrumah, and one of the leading exponents of Nkrumaism, gave some further elucidation. He said: 'Nkrumaism (is) a non-atheist socialist philosophy which seeks to apply the current social, economic, and political ideas to the solution of our problems, be they domestic or international, by adapting these ideals to the realities of our every day life.[26] Nkrumaism' he continued, 'is basically socialism adapted to conditions in Africa and African tradition, and "Nkrumaism" is the same as "African socialism"'.[27] Dr Kwame Nkrumah himself said in his address to the first seminar on ideology at the Ideological Institute, Winneba, Ghana, 'Nkrumaism (is) the term given to the consistent policies followed and taught by Nkrumah.'[28]

From these various definitions, it is extremely difficult to say what Nkrumaism actually is. However, it is clear that it has a domestic and international aspect. From the book entitled *Some Essential Features of Nkrumaism* written by the editors of the *Spark*, one can say that Nkrumaism rather than being a consistent ideology consists of some themes such as anti-colonialism, African unity, socialist development, the role of the party, and the consolidation of people's power.[29] As we shall consider the Nkrumah government's attitude to colonialism and African unity later in this chapter, we shall consider here only the two broad themes which form the core of Nkrumaism on the home front, and which Dr Nkrumah said must be adopted by all national liberation movements after independence in order 'to achieve their objectives[30] of people's political power and socialism'.[31] These were the consolidation of people's power, and socialist development.

Nkrumah's concept of a people's power in which sovereignty was vested in the broad masses of the people was no more than the establishment of a people's republic in Ghana similar to that existing in any of the East European countries. Dr Nkrumah had argued in 1959 that the African society was corporate in nature, and communal in behaviour,[32] and therefore the Western brand of democracy was unsuitable for the Africans. Because of this Nkrumah began shortly after independence to remodel Ghana into a corporate state where there would be no dissent. Thus in his address at the tenth anniversary of the CPP in 1959, Dr Nkrumah said 'the Convention People's Party is Ghana';[33] and that 'the party is the state, and the state is the party'. He proceeded to affiliate all interest groups previously independent of the government with the CPP. By 1960, the Ghana Trade Union Congress, the National Council of Ghana Women, the United Ghana Farmers' Council, the Co-operative Societies, the Youth Movement and the Workers' Brigade had become different wings of the CPP. Similarly by early 1962 the Government had taken over all the newspapers such as the *Daily Graphic* which had been hitherto independent. In November 1964, a censorship committee under the chairmanship of Professor Willie Abraham was set up by Nkrumah to search for and destroy all books and papers from all libraries and bookshops in Ghana whose philosophy was contrary to that of the party.

Furthermore, Dr Nkrumah said the organization of the CPP was based on democratic centralism. The party was to be at the head of the toiling masses. The party was also above the government. For Ministers who were at the same time members of the Central Committee of the party were to take precedence in public and civic function over non-Central Committee Ministers.[34] As we have shown in chapter one, with different constitutional changes the sovereignty of the masses became the sovereignty of the party, and eventually the sovereignty of one man.

Beginning with the introduction of the Preventive Detention Act in 1958, the CPP government moved against the dissenters. By late 1961, all opposition groups had been cowed or driven underground. In 1964, the country formally became a one-party state. Parliamentary elections held last in 1956 under Nkrumah were forgotten; and the one held in June 1965 was a sham election in which all the party nominees were voted in unopposed by over ninety-nine per cent of the voters. The Parliament constituted as a result of these 'elections' was described by Dr Nkrumah as 'the first socialist Parliament of Ghana',[35] and its first session he said marked 'the watershed in our strivings to consolidate the gains we have made since independence'.[36]

The independence of the judiciary was removed by a series of constitutional amendments. With the dismissal of the Chief Justice, Sir Arku Korsah, in December 1963, Dr Nkrumah removed the last shred of independence the judiciary might have had. In a referendum late in January 1964, an amendment to the Constitution which sought to give the President power to remove from office a Judge of the Supreme Court or a Judge of the High Court 'for reasons which appear to him sufficient' was said to have been overwhelmingly voted for by 92.81 per cent of the total 92.89 per cent of the registered voters.[37] As a concomitant of this, Ghana by 1962 had become virtually a police state where people lived under constant fear of the Preventive Detention Act, which continued to be amended from 1958 until the coup in February 1966.

The second theme of Nkrumaism on the domestic front is socialist development, or what Nkrumah called 'economic reconstruction along socialist paths'. Although in his *Autobiography* published in 1957, Dr Nkrumah had stated that 'capitalism is too complicated a system for a newly independent nation', he did not take any decisive step towards adopting a socialist pattern of development until the second half of 1961. In July of that year, all the subsidiaries of the Industrial Development Corporation set up to encourage private enterprise were turned into state-owned limited liability companies.[38] Similarly the Agricultural Development Corporation originally established to provide assistance to private farmers was dissolved. Instead large state-owned farms were set up. Justifying this move late in 1961, Mr Krobo Edusei, then the Minister of Light and Heavy Industries, said it was an attempt 'to embark on the building of a socialist pattern of society' in Ghana.[39] Later a more authoritative version of the government's new economic policy was given by Nkrumah in March 1962. He said

> It's the declared policy of the government to build a society in which the principles of social justice will be paramount. Towards this end, it will maintain its policy of economic planning and increasing participation in the nation's economic activity. Therefore, no sector of the economy will be the exclusive rights of operation in respect of any single person, company or establishment. All enterprises are expected to accept the economic policy of the government as the basis of their activity . . .[40]

He then enumerated five sectors of the economy recognized by his government. These were state enterprises, foreign private enterprises, enterprises owned jointly by the state and foreign private interests, co-operatives and small-scale Ghanaian private enterprises.

These five sectors of the economy were incorporated into the CPP Programme of 'Work and Happiness' adopted by the Party Congress in July 1962, which later formed the basis of the Seven-Year Development Plan 1963-4 to 1969-70. According to the Seven-Year Plan, the five sectors were to exist only during the transitional period in the move to full-blooded socialism. Two things should be noted during this plan period. The first was that the government's ownership and control of the means of production and distribution must continue to increase. Thus the number of state enterprises which was thirty-two in 1965 rose to fifty-two by the time the coup occurred in February 1966.[41] There were also then 105 state farms and thirty-four workers' brigade farms. The second was that large-scale Ghanaian private enterprises must not be allowed to emerge.

Indeed, as far back as September 1960, Dr Nkrumah had expressed his hostility towards the emergence of Ghanaian capitalism.[42] This was mainly because according to him 'capitalism at home is domestic colonialism'.[43]

Other features of Nkrumah's socialist development included the establishment of new institutions and agencies to replace the former colonial institutions promoting economic activity, and the adoption of a new budgetary and fiscal system.[44] Beginning with the tough budget of 7 July 1961, which was hastily prepared on the advice of a Cambridge socialist economist, Mr Nikolas Kaldor,[45] the CPP government introduced different economic and fiscal policies in order to eradicate the colonial structure of the economy. However, when the CPP regime was overturned in February 1966 it had achieved very little in this sphere.

Another important element in Nkrumaism was the setting up of educational institutions to instil into the people's minds the philosophy and the teaching of Dr Nkrumah. For the adults, especially party officials, cabinet Ministers and top civil servants, the Ideological Institute at Winneba was to perform this function. For school boys and girls this was to be done through the Young Pioneers' Movement.[46] Dr Nkrumah himself later stressed the importance of teaching everybody, from primary school to university level, the socialist philosophy in order to ensure the emergence of a truly socialist society in Ghana.[47]

While many Nigerian leaders during the Balewa era were frankly anti-Communist,[48] they nonetheless maintained on the whole a pragmatic attitude to the socio-economic organization of the country. There was a wide measure of agreement between the leaders that Nigeria should continue with the parliamentary form of democracy left by the British. Even the AG opposition party which later supported Dr Nkrumah's brand of militant Pan-Africanism said it was against his dictatorship and favoured instead liberal democracy.[49]

Although between independence in October 1960 and the coup of January 1966, a number of measures, such as the abolition of the Judicial Service Commission in 1963, the declaration of a state of emergency in the former Western Region for six months in 1962, and the subsequent treason trial of some opposition leaders, were taken by the Federal Government, and other actions by the Regional Governments against opposition parties tended to call into question the practice of democracy in Nigeria,[50] visible signs of it and its practice were not totally erased from the country, which remained a multi-party state till the coup in spite of the fact that there was a tendency towards a one-party system at the Regional level.[51] The Fundamental Human Rights guaranteeing individual rights under chapter three of the Republican Constitution were not totally discarded. And in 1962-3 the leaders resisted the suggestion of a Preventive Detention Act against the opposition groups.

Furthermore, the Trade Unions, the farmers' societies, the youth movements, the co-operatives and many other voluntary organizations continued throughout to exist outside the orbit of direct governmental control. Apart from the government-owned newspapers, there were some papers, such as the *Daily Times*, the *Nigerian Tribune*, the *West African Pilot* and the *Daily Express*, which were on the whole free to criticize the government under the law. There were also regular parliamentary elections, even though they were marked by fraudulent practices.

On the economic level, the Nigerian leaders were not dogmatic, as the CPP leaders were, though there was no doubt that they favoured the leaving of the bulk of the economy in the hands of private entrepreneurs. Thus unlike Ghana, there emerged in Nigeria, pre-dating independence a number of indigenous business tycoons such as Dr Bank Anthony in Lagos, the late Sir Odumegu Ojukwu, Chief T. A. Odutola, Chief Festus Okotie-Eboh, Dr Nnamdi Azikiwe, Chief Olatunbosun Shonibare, Dr Akinola Maja, Mr Joseph Ade Tuyo, Chief Henry Fajemirokun and Chief S. B. Bakare, to mention only a few.[52] There were also giant foreign private firms such as Shell-BP, Unilever, A. G. Leventis, the United Trading Company (UTC), the 'Société Commerciale de L'Ouest Africain' (SCOA), the Gulf Oil Company and the Esso, and Agip oil companies, whose interests were not in any way threatened by the Balewa government. Not only was the Balewa government opposed to nationalization, but was also against any threats of nationalizing foreign firms, threats which were common pronouncements at CPP party rallies in Ghana.

Nonetheless, in addition to the public corporations such as Nigerian Railways, the Nigerian Broadcasting Corporation and some others set up prior to independence, the Federal and Regional governments took steps shortly after independence to set up more public corporations and state-owned companies. There was no doctrinaire approach to this development. Some of them were set up in places where private entrepreneurs would not readily move in, while others were set up mainly as a further source of political patronage by the various ruling parties.[53]

In some ways there were similarities between the economic organization in Ghana and Nigeria, but many Nigerian leaders were totally against the socialist philosophy. Thus in March 1965, Chief Okotie-Eboh, then the Federal Finance Minister and the National Treasurer of the NCNC, which had adopted 'pragmatic socialism' as part of its manifesto for the Federal elections of December 1964, made a ringing denunciation of 'socialism' which he described as the 'canker-worm'[54] that could 'surely destroy the economic fabric of the nation'. Later in April 1965 Mallam Ibrahim Gusau, an NPC Minister of State in the Federal Government, said the government would have nothing to do with 'African socialism'.[55] Even the AG opposition that adopted 'socialism' early in 1962 qualified it with the word 'democratic' to distinguish it from the authoritarian socialism of the Communist countries. As indicated above the NCNC which adopted 'socialism' for the Federal elections of December 1964 qualified it with 'pragmatic' to assure people that it was different from a blind application in Nigeria of a foreign-grown ideology.

The fact that Nkrumah's Ghana and Balewa's Nigeria embraced different types of ideology bred mutual suspicion and mistrust. Thus early in 1965, Chief Okotie-Eboh declared that some African countries (clearly referring to Ghana) did not like Nigeria being referred to as 'an example of parliamentary democracy in Africa'.[56] This might contain some truth. For shortly after the coup that resulted in the death of Sir Abubakar, Dr Nkrumah referred with disdain to the Nigerian leaders who after independence 'assumed that they had only to copy the British parliamentary system in every detail to ensure freedom and justice in Nigeria', but who in fact succeeded in transferring 'to the parliamentary stage the underlying contradictions of Nigeria as colonially constituted'.[57] Many Nigerian leaders, on the other hand, viewed with contempt Nkrumah's dictatorship in Ghana. On 27 August 1962 at his monthly press conference, Sir Abubakar deplored the trend towards tyranny in Ghana, but added that he was reluctant to make further comment because it was that country's internal affair.[58] Earlier in 1961 an NCNC MP, Mr V. Iketuonye, had said that Ghana and Nigeria could not be compared because one was a dictatorship and the other a democracy.[59]

A further ideological conflict arose out of Nkrumah's desire to export his brand of socialist philosophy across his country's border to Nigeria, and the frequent press criticism in Nigeria of undemocratic measures of the CPP government. The visit of Chief Awolowo, then the leader of the Opposition in the House of Representatives, to

Ghana in mid-1961 was believed by the government leaders to have had a profound influence on his ideological orientation towards socialism. Leading members of different Nigerian opposition groups were encouraged by Ghana to adopt socialism, while others were given ideological training in the Ideological Institute at Winneba.[60] The Nkrumah government also provided facilities for left wing leaders to operate from Ghana. For instance, in July 1962, a small group of radical Nigerian politicians and trade union leaders formed in Accra a political party called the Nigerian Socialist Group, led by Mr A. B. Bassey and Mr Alex Ukut.[61] This Socialist Group called on all Nigerians to withdraw their support from the Balewa administration because Nigeria required a Lenin, a Mao Tse-Tung, a Fidel Castro and an Nkrumah. Furthermore, many Nigerian students were given scholarships by the Nkrumah government to study in Ghana or in any of the East European countries so that they could in the end return to Nigeria to propagate the 'socialist' ideology. It has to be remembered that Mr Samuel Ikoku, then the AG Secretary-General, who was wanted for treason in Nigeria, became one of the Professors of the Kwame Nkrumah Ideological Institute at Winneba, and till February 1966 remained one of the strong men behind the *Spark*.

All this caused anger in Nigeria. Thus in September 1962 Dr Michael Okpara, then the Premier of the former Eastern Region, accused Dr Nkrumah of subversion through his ideological influence on the 'leftist elements' in Nigeria.[62] In 1965 Chief Festus Okotie-Eboh accused Ghana of trying to spread confusion in Nigeria by exporting into the country what he called 'the dangerous doctrines' of 'socialism'.[63]

The ideological conflict was exacerbated mainly because while the CPP leaders wanted to spread 'Nkrumaism' throughout Africa, most of the Nigerian leaders wanted liberal democracy to survive in all African countries. While not many Nigerian leaders would go all the way with Chief Enahoro, who said that the defence of 'democracy in Africa, even at the expense of being accused of interfering in the internal affairs of neighbouring states' should be the cornerstone of Nigeria's foreign policy because 'the defence of democracy elsewhere in Africa must be recognized as an insurance for democracy in Nigeria,'[64] few would doubt the need to speak for parliamentary democracy in Africa.

Largely because of diplomatic niceties and tact, the Nigerian leaders could not always speak out against authoritarian tendencies in Ghana. This role was taken up mainly by the Nigerian press. Hardly any dictatorial measure could go through in Ghana without scathing criticism from the Nigerian press. Late in 1962, when proposals were being made in the CPP ranks to make Nkrumah life President of Ghana, the Federal Government-owned newspaper, the *Morning Post*, came out with an editorial titled 'Nkrumah's Hard Road' and condemned the proposals, and called instead for the liberalization of the CPP government.[65] Following the security measures taken immediately after the Kulungugu bomb attack on Nkrumah in August 1962, the *Morning Post* in a leader titled 'Fugitive from the . . . Assassin's Bullet' deplored Nkrumah's actions as virtually turning Ghana into 'a three-penny dictatorship'.[66] The *Daily Times* ridiculed the bomb episode as being stage managed by Dr Nkrumah to curb the activities and ambition of Tawia Adamafio,[67] who was considered by Nkrumah as being dangerously close to the presidency.[68] Later the newspaper condemned Nkrumah's strong-arm measures against those suspected in the bomb attack, and warned that Dr Nkrumah should realize he could 'not achieve African socialism by liquidating his colleagues'.[69] The motion passed in the Ghana National Assembly on 11 September 1962 to turn Ghana into a one-party state was deplored in Nigeria as a rape of democracy.[70] So scurrilous were the press criticisms of Ghana in Nigeria that by mid-September 1962 almost all Nigerian newspapers were banned in Ghana. Nonetheless, they continued to condemn the CPP dictatorship at every available opportunity. The dismissal of the Ghana Chief Justice in December 1963 and the death in detention early in 1965 of Dr J. B. Danquah led to further criticism of Ghana in Nigeria. But this time Dr Nnamdi Azikiwe, then the Nigerian President, came out openly against the ugly situation which led to the death of Dr Danquah without being tried.[71] It has to be noted too that during this period, especially during late 1961 and 1962 and 1965, the Ghanaian press and radio were unrelenting in their criticism and abuse of the Nigerian leaders. For instance, the Ghana radio on 16 September 1962 described Mr Jaja Wachuku, then the Nigerian Foreign Minister, as 'a witless popinjay', and condemned other Nigerian leaders whom it called 'mad dogs'.[72] The *Spark* had to engage in verbal sabre-rattling with Dr Azikiwe over his criticism of the death of Dr Danquah in detention.[73]

(b) Ideological Conflict:II

After the overthrow of the Nkrumah regime in February 1966, one could not talk of serious ideological conflicts between Nigeria and Ghana. Nonetheless there were still some ideological differences, especially in the economic sphere. With the coup d'etat of 24 February 1966 went Nkrumaism in Ghana. The National Liberation Council (NLC) government ridiculed socialism, and the CPP's doctrine of 'democratic centralism'. The police state apparatus of the Nkrumah era was dismantled and individual freedom restored. One of the greatest legacies of the NLC was freedom of expression. This was somehow maintained by the Progress Government whose 'goal' was to ensure every individual in Ghana 'a life of dignity in freedom'.[74]

As pointed out in chapter one, under the 1969 Constitution there were provisions for safeguarding individual rights and for preserving the independence of the judiciary. The Constitution formally prohibited the turning of Ghana into a one-party state. With the formation late in 1971 of the Ghana People's Party led by Mr Kwame Jantuah, there were till 13 January 1972 six political parties in the country.[75] Different types of voluntary organizations, trade union movements and youth movements were allowed to a large extent to operate without coming directly under the Government, and they received encouragement from the Centre for Civic Education.[76]

In the economic field, the NLC Government recognized four major sectors, namely the private sector (both foreign and indigenous), the joint private/Government sector, the government sector, and the co-operative sector. But unlike the CPP government, it was the private sector that had to remain the largest sector. Another novel idea was that large-scale Ghanaian private enterprises stifled under the Nkrumah regime were to be encouraged. Furthermore, unlike the past when it was virtually compulsory for foreign private enterprise to accept the government's participation, this was henceforth to be entirely voluntary. As General Ankrah said, 'No private enterprise will be forced to accept government participation.'[77] Henceforth, state participation in economic activities would be limited to 'certain basic and key projects', especially where private capital might not be available. Furthermore, the NLC said it was opposed to nationalization.

In pursuit of this new policy, the Government cut down the number of state enterprises from fifty-two to nineteen and sold the rest to private organizations. The remaining nineteen were reorganized and placed under the control of the Ghana Industrial Holding Corporation (GIHOC) in 1967. Most of the state farms were sold to private concerns, while others which had no chance of viability were abandoned.

The development in Nigeria after 1966 was a little different. Although the country was under military rule after 1966, civil liberties and individual rights were not unnecessarily curtailed, even during the civil war. The press remained on the whole free from censorship. Frequent jibes were made by the newspapers, notably by the Northern-based *New Nigerian*, the *Daily Times* and the *Daily Express*, against government measures considered unwise, despite the fact that after the end of June 1966 the country was technically in a state of emergency.[78] Likewise, the independence of the judiciary has not been seriously tampered with although in one notable incident, the Western State Government versus Lakanmi and others, the Federal Government overruled the judgement of the Supreme Court by Decree 28 of 1970. An example of the continuing independence of the judiciary was the ruling against the Government by an Ibadan High Court in June 1969 in the case of the detention of Mr Mojeed Agbaje, involving the Commissioner of Police, Western State. The Government accepted the court's verdict that Agbaje's detention was unlawful.[79] Moreover, it has to be stressed that the Federal Military Government made the building of 'a free and democratic society' one of the main objectives of its Second National Development Plan.[80]

On the economic level, the Federal Government recognized the existence of mixed economy like the Ghana government. But there were some differences. First, while encouraging private enterprise both foreign and indigenous, the Federal Government was determined to increase its participation in and control over all sectors of the economy hitherto held by foreign private interests. It said that before long all the country's resources, such as land, mineral deposits and other natural endowments had to be owned and controlled by Nigerians.[81] Already in pursuit of this policy Nigeria has taken 33.3 per cent of the shares of the Safrap oil company, Agip, and the Philips oil exploration company, and fifty-one per cent of the shares of Occidental Petrol of Nigeria.[82]

Unlike the Progress Party government in Ghana and its predecessor, the Nigerian government decided to expand the public sector of the economy. Public corporations and state-owned companies were to be increased in number because they were said to be 'crucial in Nigeria's quest for true national economic independence, and self-reliance.'[83] In some ways Nigeria's Four-Year Development Plan was similar to the defunct Seven-Year Plan 1963–4 to 1969–70 of Dr Nkrumah's government, except in the important sense that large-scale Nigerian private enterprises were to be encouraged and assisted during the Plan period.

Although from the above one can say that in socio-economic

organization the two countries came to have many things in common, some conflicts arose because of the fact that between the 1966 coup and the Acheampong coup the Ghanaian government pushed its 'de-Kwamefication' policy to extremes. For instance, the handing over of the two leading Hotels in Accra, the Continental Hotel and the Ambassador Hotel, which were making profits even under the CPP government, to a foreign organization, the Intercontinental Hotels Corporation of New York, to manage[84] was seen in Nigeria as an attempt to sell Ghana out to the 'neo-colonialists'. The Busia government's decision to leave the dominant part of the economy in the hands of some European and American giant firms, while expelling almost all the Africans engaged in small-scale trade, was seen in Nigeria as a betrayal of Africa. Similarly the enactment of laws by the Busia government against those advocating the return of Nkrumah to Ghana and against the TUC for daring to campaign against the PP government over the Development Levy was seen in Nigeria as excessive and undemocratic.[85] Likewise the utterances of a former Ghanaian Minister, Mr Reginald Amponsah, that the Government might enact a law to make it a criminal offence to insult Dr Kofi Busia evoked widespread criticism in Nigeria.[86] Indeed, all this made some Nigerian newspapers wonder whether Dr Busia was not heading for some sort of tyranny worse than that of Dr Nkrumah. As would be expected all these Nigerian press criticisms were met by counter-attacks from the Ghanaian press and radio.

(ii) (a) ANTI-COLONIALISM, ANTI-IMPERIALISM, ANTI-RACISM: I

As far as the elimination of colonialism, imperialism and racism from Africa was concerned there was no difference in objective between Nkrumah's Ghana and Balewa's Nigeria. But there were vast differences between them on these issues in regard to method, timing and style.

The way in which Dr Nkrumah pursued his anti-colonial crusade was direct, aggressively militant and vigorous. There was no question of mincing words about the evils of colonialism, imperialism and racism. At every available opportunity, violent verbal attacks must be made against the 'colonizers,' the imperialists and the fascists of Southern Africa. On the other hand, Balewa's style was much more restrained and, in fact, excessively cautious and apologetic. Sir Abubakar believed that colonial and racial problems like any other problems could be solved through patient and skilful diplomacy rather than by high-flown language. This difference of style on issues such as colonialism and racism, as in other matters was one of the causes of the discord between Ghana and Nigeria prior to 1966.[87] In this case, Balewa's restrained style was seen by Nkrumah as a sign of being 'soft' on colonialism, imperialism and racism.

But greater conflicts arose on methods of ending colonialism, imperialism and racism in Africa. Mainly because Dr Nkrumah was passionately anti-colonial, his government had an elaborate programme of combating colonialism and racism. The Government believed that this could be achieved in five main ways, namely, through political education, diplomatic action in co-operation with other independent African states within and outside the UN, through propaganda, direct bilateral material aid to the nationalists, and through a policy of non-fraternization with the imperialists and the apartheid regime of South Africa.[88] Political education consisted mainly of teaching all African nationalists still struggling for full self-government, irrespective of their different colonial conditions, to adopt the same tactics as those earlier used by the CPP to force the British Government to grant independence to the Gold Coast within eight years of the formation of the party. To do this effectively Nkrumah had to bring various African nationalist leaders to Accra. This was the main motive behind the holding in Accra in December 1958 of the first All-African Peoples' Conference (AAPC) which was attended by representatives of all African nationalist parties except the NPC and the 'Rassemblement Démocratique Africain' (RDA) of Black French Africa.

His main message to the first AAPC was that all nationalists must first work for the achievement of political independence, and that with this other problems could be tackled. As he put it 'Seek ye first the political kingdom and all the rest will be added unto it.' To attain this end, they must organize their peoples, their trade unions, their peasants and their youth societies along a mass line. Furthermore, the nationalists must be ready to take 'positive action' against the colonial Powers in their different territories as the CPP had against the British in January 1950.

All this was further elaborated upon by Dr Nkrumah in subsequent conferences of African nationalists in Accra, especially at the Conference on Positive Action and Security in Africa in April 1960, and at the Conference of African Freedom Fighters in June 1962. At the latter conference. Dr Nkrumah went to great lengths in his attempts at political education. He advised his audience to unite and to organize themselves along mass lines, with the trade unions acting

as 'the active vanguard of all political operations' as it did in the Gold
Coast. Furthermore, the concept of 'positive action'[89] was raised by
Nkrumah to that of a fetish. It was highly recommended to all the
freedom fighters as being unavoidable if genuine independence was
to be won. In his book *Consciencism* published later in 1964, Dr
Nkrumah said that there could be 'no true independence without
positive action.'[90]

But because only little could be achieved by way of political
education in Accra at periodical conferences of African nationalists,
Dr Nkrumah's government founded in 1959 the African Affairs
Centre in Acra[91] to house freedom fighters who might like to stay in
Ghana for longer periods of further education in the strategy and
tactics of the liberation struggle. Till the coup in February 1966,
many African nationalist leaders, especially from South Africa and
the Portuguese African territories, used this centre.

The Nkrumah regime tried to assist the freedom fighters through
propaganda. To this end it established a chain of newspapers and
periodicals to champion their cause (as well as that of African unity)
and to encourage them. Apart from the *Ghanaian Times* and the
Evening News, there were the *Spark* and the *Voice of Africa*, both
of which were edited by Mr Kofi Batsa. Others included *Freedom
Fighters Weekly*, *Pan-Africanist Review*, *African Chronicle*,
L'Etincelle, and the Bulletin on African Affairs published by the
Bureau of African Affairs.[92] To bring home its propaganda role
to the nationalists in Portuguese Africa, the *Spark* began late in 1965
to publish some of its issues in Portuguese. The first edition to be
published in Portuguese appeared on 22 July 1965.[93]

Diplomatic action in co-operation with other independent African
states within and outside the United Nations was taken by the
Nkrumah government to further the cause of those struggling for
independence. One of the main reasons behind Nkrumah's initiative
for the first Conference of Independent African States in Accra in
April 1958 was the acceleration of the decolonization process in
Africa. It has to be remembered that one of the major items discussed
by the Conference was the complete emancipation of Africa from the
colonial yoke.[94] The African permanent machinery set up at the UN
as a result of this Conference served until late 1960 as a valuable focus
for co-operation between the independent African states on questions
of colonialism and racism.

From late in 1960, when African unity at the UN was fractured by
the Congo crisis, the Ghanaian government tried to use the UN, with
or without the support of other African states, to advance the cause of

the nationalists. Thus in September 1960 Dr Nkrumah called on the United Nations 'to face up to its responsibilities, and ask those who would bury their heads like the proverbial ostrich in their imperialist sands to pull their heads out and look at the blazing African sun now travelling across the sky of Africa's redemption . . .'[95] At the Belgrade Conference of the non-aligned Powers in 1961, Dr Nkrumah called on the UN to 'organize plebiscites in all colonial territories based upon universal adult suffrage, one man, one vote . . .'[96] Ghana also actively worked in co-operation with other anti-colonial forces at the UN to get the General Assembly in December 1960 to adopt resolution 1514(XV), known as the Declaration on the Granting of Independence to Non-Self-Governing Territories and Peoples. This resolution, which was later described by Mr Alex Quaison-Sackey, then the Ghanaian Permanent Representative at the United Nations, as the 'Magna Carta of the colonial peoples',[97] was used till the coup by Ghana to harass the colonial Powers and South Africa at the United Nations.

Outside the world body the Ghanaian government continued to speak for the African nationalists. Thus at the Commonwealth Prime Ministers' conferences in 1964 and 1965, Ghana was the most vocal in her defence of the black African majority in Rhodesia and the most critical of the British government's handling of the situation.[98] At other international conferences such as the Second Conference of the non-aligned Powers in Cairo in October 1964, at various African conferences, and at the Afro-Asian People's Solidarity Conference held at Winneba, Ghana, in May 1965,[99] Ghana did not miss any opportunity to speak for the rights of those in colonial Africa and in South Africa.

Apart from action through international organizations, Dr Nkrumah tried to speed up the liberation of the whole of Africa, including South Africa, by offering the nationalists direct material aid. Since independence according to Dr Willard Scott Thompson, Nkrumah had been providing small quantities of aid to some nationalist leaders.[100] Since the aid figures to the nationalists were not usually published only very little could be said about them, but in April 1959, Dr Banda's party was said to have received the sum of £10,000[101] to promote its nationalist campaign in Nyasaland (later Malawi). Another form of aid offered to the colonial peoples in Africa by Nkrumah was scholarships. Thus during the 1963-4 academic session, the Ghanaian government gave 100 scholarships for secondary school and university education to students from various colonial territories in Africa.[102] In addition to this, Ghana was one of the fourteen UN member states providing, by late in 1963, special scholarships for students from Portuguese territories in Africa.[103]

Since the overthrow of the CPP government, it has been possible to say that Ghana under Nkrumah did provide some military aid to the African freedom fighters. As the control by the Portuguese, the South African racist government and the Rhodesian Front regime over the areas under their rule began to increase instead of decline after 1963, Dr Nkrumah began to give serious thought to assisting the freedom fighters in those places with small arms and military training. It is important to note that at the Second Conference of the non-aligned Powers at Cairo in October 1964, Dr Nkrumah for the first time spoke openly of the need to promote armed struggle in order to complete the liberation of Africa.[104] It was probable that it was in that year that Ghana began to give military training to some freedom fighters, for Willard Scott Thompson referred to the attempt of Mr A. K. Barden, then the director of the Bureau of African Affairs, in 1964 to bring to Ghana twenty-five nationalists belonging to the banned African People's Congress (APC) of South Africa for military training.[105] Dr Nkrumah himself later wrote from his exile in Conakry that the training camps exposed to the world press by the NLC as his training ground for subversion in independent African states were, in fact, used only for training freedom fighters[106] from dependent African territories, including South Africa.[107]

The final way in which the Nkrumah government tried to assist the nationalists was through a policy of non-fraternization with those he called 'the oppressors of the African people.' Although for a brief period after independence, Dr Nkrumah attempted to maintain some contact with the South African Government to see whether he could thereby change their attitude about the ability of Africans to govern themselves,[108] the central element in the Ghanaian government's attitude to South Africa and Portugal till the coup was one of boycott, isolation and rejection. Ghana played a dominant role in the anti-South Africa campaign at the 1961 Prime Ministers' Conference which resulted in the withdrawal of South Africa from the Commonwealth. Furthermore, all South African and Portuguese nationals, ships and aircraft were banned from Ghana, and the Ghanaian attacks on the 'fascists' that had replaced imperial Germany in South-West Africa were incessant and violent. Because of all this, in 1961 Dr Verwoerd banned the importation and sale of Nkrumah's book 'I Speak of Freedom' in his Republic. Dr Nkrumah went beyond this. He extended his policy of rejection to the NATO powers who by economic, trade, military and political links continued to prop up South Africa and the Portuguese in Africa.[109]

But the programme of the Balewa government for terminating colonial rule was less elaborate. This was mainly because, unlike Nkrumah, Balewa did not consider the question of colonialism as being central to the problems facing Nigeria and Africa. For instance, in his first major policy statement on 20 August 1960 on his government's foreign policy after independence, he did not anywhere refer to the question of decolonization or apartheid.[110]

Nonetheless, the Balewa government tried to assist those struggling for independence in two main ways as stated by Mr Jaja Wachuku. The first was through diplomatic action at the UN, and the second was through direct but quiet diplomatic contact with the colonial Powers, with a view to persuading them to speed up the decolonization of their African territories.[111] As far the direct bilateral supply of arms to the freedom fighters was concerned the Balewa government would have nothing to do with it,[112] and the Federal government turned down the request of Mr Holden Roberto, then the leader of the Provisional Government of Angola in exile (GRAE), for military aid in May 1962.[113]

However, at the UN, the Federal government tried to champion the cause of the African nationalists even more than it was doing outside.[114] For instance, early in 1962, Nigeria co-sponsored a draft resolution at the United Nations calling on France to grant independence to Algeria by applying the principle of self-determination, and requesting France to recognize the Algerian Provisional Government which the Nigerian government itself did not then recognize.[115] Indeed, on almost all anti-colonial and anti-racist issues at the UN Nigeria and Ghana voted alike.[116]

Apart from the UN, the Nigerian government believed that it could assist the African nationalists through a policy of direct quiet diplomatic contact with the Administering Powers. It was claimed in 1961 by Alhaji Mohammadu Ribadu, then the Federal Minister of Defence, that Sir Abubakar had helped to secure the release of Jomo Kenyatta from detention through 'quiet and tactful contact' with the British Government.[117] Nigeria also maintained contact with other colonial Powers and with the white minority regimes of Southern Africa. Although not independent, the defunct Central African Federation maintained in 1962 a High Commission in Lagos, and late in that year, Southern Rhodesia (now Rhodesia) participated in Nigeria's International Trade Fair.[118] Up till the time of the coup in

January 1966, the Portuguese government maintained a diplomatic post in Lagos, though manned by a very junior official.[119] Although Sir Abubakar played a prominent role in the events that led to the withdrawal of South Africa from the Commonwealth during the Prime Ministers' Conference of March 1961, he believed that contact must be maintained with the apartheid regime. Thus he said in 1962 that he would visit South Africa, if invited, with a view to changing the system of government there.[120] Till the coup in January 1966, South African nationals were allowed into Nigeria. Indeed, by April 1965 according to the NPC Parliamentary Secretary to the Federal Minister of Internal Affairs, Mallam Salihu Abdul, there were twenty-eight white South Africans in the country working as teachers, medical practitioners and as employees of some foreign private firms.[121] All these made Nigeria appear to Ghana as if she were more or less in collusion with the colonialists, the imperialists and the racists.

Another source of conflict was the timing of the complete decolonization of Africa. From its own philosophy, the CPP did not believe that any degree of preparation was required before the granting of independence. It has to be noted that in 1949 the party's slogan was 'Self-Government Now'. The motto of the party's newspaper, the *Evening News*, was 'We prefer Self-Government with danger to servitude in tranquility'.[122] So from independence in 1957, the CPP government had demanded the independence of the rest of Africa within the shortest possible time in order to make Ghana's independence 'meaningful'. At first Dr Nkrumah did not put a time limit to the termination of colonialism in Africa. But with the adoption by the UN General Assembly of resolution 1514(XV) in December 1960, known as the Declaration on the Granting of Independence to Non-Self-Governing Territories and Peoples, Dr Nkrumah said in September 1961 at the Belgrade Conference of the non-aligned Powers that with the strict application of this General Assembly resolution it should be possible to eliminate colonialism and racism from Africa by 1962.[123] After this Conference all the Ghanaian Ambassadors in different world capitals and at the United Nations began to say, and demand, that colonialism and racism in Africa must be eliminated by December 1962.

But the Balewa government would not be hurried about decolonizing the rest of Africa. The Nigerian government believed in a naive way that all colonial Powers, including Portugal and apartheid South Africa, were like the British preparing their colonial peoples for ultimate self-government. So at the time Dr Nkrumah was proclaiming 1962 as the target year for the total liberation of Africa, Mr Jaja Wachuku was busy lecturing his fellow MPs that 'in the light of our own experience . . . (there were) problems that must be tackled by a slow process' before the granting of independence to those still under colonial rule in Africa.[124] He said because of these problems the Nigerian government was in favour of the year 1970 as the final target for ending colonialism and racism in Africa. Similar opinion was expressed by Sir Abubakar later in 1962 that from Nigeria's experience there was need for adequate preparation by the colonial Powers before granting independence.[125] To the Balewa government the Congo (later Zaire) tragedy was primarily due to inadequate preparation for independence, and this situation must not be allowed to occur elsewhere in Africa. So the government set its face against any hasty granting of independence. Indeed, it was doubtful whether Balewa and his Ministers ever believed that all the colonial peoples in Africa would be ripe for independence by 1970.

(b) *Anti-Colonialism, Anti-Imperialism, and Anti-Racism: II*
After the coup in Ghana and in Nigeria early in 1966, there occurred some changes in their attitude to colonial and racist problems in Africa. As shown in chapter one, the police and the army that seized power in Ghana on 24 February 1966 had little or no commitment to decolonization programmes, and neither had the Progress Government that succeeded the NLC government in October 1969. Indeed, throughout his inaugural address at Black Star Square on 1 October 1969, Dr Kofi Busia said nothing about decolonization.[126] The debt burden inherited from the Nkrumah regime and the country's growing economic difficulties in the second half of the sixties further made it extremely difficult for the NLC and its successor, the PP government, to take any strong anti-colonial line.

Because of all this, Ghana's efforts at liberating colonial Africa during the latter part of the sixties were very limited. The campaign in the press and at international conferences for the freedom fighters that was the order of the day during the Nkrumah era stopped. Largely as a result of the initial hostile attitude of the NLC to the freedom fighters, Accra ceased to be their Mecca. Indeed, for some time many of the freedom fighters thought that the NLC government was collaborating with the racist governments in Southern Africa against them.[127] However, the Ghanaian government continued though with less vigour to back anti-colonial draft resolutions at the UN. Apart from this, the only other way in which the Ghanaian government since the coup tried to assist the African nationalists was through contributions to the liberation fund of the Organization of African Unity (OAU) to which we shall refer later in chapter four.

Another novel factor introduced to the Ghanaian anti-colonial and anti-racist programme by the Progress Government was one of dialogue. Dr Busia believed that instead of the Nkrumah policy of rejection and isolation of the white supremacist governments in Southern Africa direct contact should be maintained with them, with the ultimate aim of changing their racist systems. That the Nkrumah government though in a different style had tried this method between March 1957 and early 1960 without avail did not persuade Dr Busia of the futility of dialogue. On the contrary, he passionately believed that dialogue would work. So early in 1971, Dr Busia got the Ghanaian Parliament to vote overwhelmingly in favour of dialogue with South Africa, though within the framework of the Lusaka Manifesto.[128] The PP government proceeded to educate the Ghanaian public critical of dialogue[129] on the virtues of the new policy towards South Africa by publishing booklets and pamphlets about the failure of the past policy and the enormous opportunities presented by the new dialogue policy. The most important of these was 'Apartheid and Its Elimination',[130] which contained excerpts from various speeches by Dr Busia in favour of dialogue.

Although Ghana had voted against the dialogue proposal with the majority of the OAU member states at the meeting of the OAU Council of Ministers in June 1971, Dr Busia later expressed his views that common sense would prevail in the end so that the wisdom of dialogue would be seen by everybody.[131] Furthermore, after the coup white South Africans and Rhodesians were allowed entry into Ghana, while some South African products banned under Nkrumah found their way into the Ghanaian market.[132] Colonial issues also ceased to be a source of conflict between the Western Powers and Ghana.

But the development in Nigeria was in the opposite direction since the coup of January 1966. The reasons for this were not difficult to see. Firstly, the coup swept away leaders and parties that were conservative in their anti-colonial attitude. It has to be remembered that for most of the early fifties the NPC strove to postpone Nigeria's independence. This attitude was later transferred to the African policy of the Federal government after independence. Secondly, the moral and material assistance given to the Biafran secessionists during the civil war brought it home to the new Nigerian leaders that the existence of these white supremacist regimes was a threat to their country's independence and security. Furthermore, even shortly after the end of the war, Dr Okoi Arikpo, the Commissioner for External

Affairs, said that he had reliable information that South Africa was still planning to disrupt Nigeria's unity and independence.[133]

The upshot of all this was a radical change from Nigeria's past attitude to colonialism, imperialism and racism. First, a policy of boycott and confrontation was adopted towards the minority racist regimes in Southern Africa. Shortly after the coup the Ironsi government closed down the Portuguese diplomatic Mission in Lagos. Then the government declared white South Africans and Portuguese prohibited immigrants in Nigeria.[134] Soon after this, on 22 July 1966, General Ironsi in a note through Chief S. O. Adebo, then Nigeria's Permanent Representative at the UN, stated that his government had banned Portuguese ships and aircraft from Nigeria because of 'her (Portugal's) brutal colonial policy in Africa'.[135] After the coup the Nigerian government started to criticize any Western Powers that appeared to be supporting colonialism and racism in Africa. Thus early in February 1966, the Ironsi government protested to the United States government at what it called 'America's apparent collaboration with the Smith rebel regime' which had then recently opened an information office in Washington. The Nigerian Government called for its closure for Nigerian-American amity.[136] The British government's announcement of its intention to sell seven Wasp helicopters to South Africa early in 1971 was severely criticized in Nigeria. General Gowon, then the Head of State, condemned it as 'a total disregard of African opinion',[137] and announced Nigeria's withdrawal from the eight-member Commonwealth committee set up at Singapore in January 1971 to report on the security problems in the Indian Ocean.

Not only did the Nigerian government reject dialogue, which it felt must first begin between the Vorster regime and the black Africans in his Republic, but also, especially since 1968, gave moral and material support directly to all the freedom fighters.[138] The material aid usually took the form of money, military trucks, medical supplies and blankets. Moral support was provided for them by inviting leading freedom fighters to visit Nigeria. Among those that visited Nigeria were Amilcar Cabral, the late leader of the PAIGC (African Independence Party for Guinea and Cape Verde) of Guinea-Bissau, and Oliver Tambo, the president of the banned African National Congress. Some of the freedom fighters started to use Nigeria more or less as their base of operation.

Propaganda in the press on behalf of the freedom fighters was encouraged by the Federal government. Similarly, the rapid growth of left-wing, anti-imperialist groups such as the Nigerian Afro-Asian

Solidarity Organization (NAASO), the Black Renaissance Movement, the Nigerian Youth Movement, the Nigeria-Soviet Friendship Society, the Nigeria-China Friendship Society, especially since 1968 when the Federal Government allowed the Nigerian Trades Union Congress (NTUC) to affiliate with the World Federation of Trades Unions, with its headquarters in Prague, did much to give a greater boost to anti-imperialist campaigns in Nigeria. These left-wing groups used to organize public lectures, symposia and demonstrations on anti-imperialist and anti-racist struggles. In some cases they used to get the Government's tacit support. For instance, in August 1970, the Nigerian Afro-Asian Solidarity Organization (NAASO) organized a two-day campaign to raise money for African freedom fighters. This campaign of the radicals which would have been anathema to the Balewa government received the Federal government's support, and all those intending to make contributions were to do so through the Ministry of External Affairs.[139]

Abroad too, Nigeria was doing some propaganda for the freedom fighters through her diplomatic Missions. Unlike the past, Nigeria was no longer content to participate in a rather passive, penitent way in debates on colonial and racist issues at the UN, the OAU, and other international organizations, but launched herself into an active leading role in all such issues, taking, as Nkrumah's Ghana, an intransigent stand. Thus in an address to the OAU Assembly of Heads of State and Government early in September 1970, General Gowon warned in very strong language 'the enemies of African freedom fighters, particularly Portugal, and the racist minority regimes of South Africa, and Rhodesia with the active collaboration of their military and business allies (who were) striving to check the historical trend towards freedom, and independence for all of Africa.'[140] A month later Dr Arikpo called in the same vein at the UN General Assembly on 'all men who abhor oppression, and exploitation (to join hands) to fight apartheid' and colonialism in Africa.[141]He further called for the establishment of a UN liberation fund, which should be mandatory for all member states, in order to speed up the liquidation of imperialism, colonialism and racism in Africa.

Though the Nigerian leaders wanted the immediate elimination of colonialism, imperialism and racism from Africa, they were realistic enough to know that it was futile to fix a time limit as in the early 1960s. Nonetheless, they wanted a timetable for ending colonialism and racism, as Dr Arikpo demanded from the UN General Assembly on 16 October 1970. But as the General Assembly did not give them any date, the Nigerian government decided to fix one for itself. Thus General Gowon declared at the OAU Summit Conference in June 1971 that at least one colonial territory must be liberated by armed struggle within the next three years in Africa.[142] On the other hand, the Busia government did not seem to have given any consideration to any timetable for completing the liberation of Africa. The preoccupation of Dr Busia and his colleagues with domestic problems were too time-consuming to allow for such a thought.

One of the main consequences of these different approaches by Ghana and Nigeria to solving colonial and racial issues in Africa was the worsening of their relations. While the Nigerian government had been content with describing as unrealistic any dialogue with South Africa, the Nigerian press had been more forthright in their criticism of Dr Busia's Ghana for this. The *Renaissance* said that by advocating dialogue with South Africa, Ghana had joined 'the company of those (African States) that were notoriously pro-West.'[143] The *Daily Times* described Ghana and other African countries advocating dialogue as 'lackeys of the imperialists.'[144] The *Nigerian Observer* described Ghana and other African countries still calling for dialogue even after the OAU had overwhelmingly rejected it as 'traitors' to Africa.[145]

(iii) (a) NEO-COLONIALISM: I

The term 'neo-colonialism', regarded by many writers[146] and statesmen[147] as no more than a myth raised up by the leaders of some Afro-Asian countries to explain their failure to transform economically their countries since independence, was used by Dr Nkrumah in a descriptive sense essentially for a situation in which the pattern of relationships between a former metropolitan Power and its former colony remained unchanged even after the attainment of independence. Although in his book *Neo-colonialism: The Last Stage of Imperialism,*[148] Dr Nkrumah tried to extend the definition of the term to embrace all sorts of Western, especially American, activities in all developing countries, including the wars in Vietnam, the U-2 spy aircraft, to Hollywood shows and the United States Peace Corps, in such a way as to make his definition almost meaningless, there can be no doubt that the essence of Nkrumah's neo-colonialism was the attempt by a foreign (notably Western) Power to control by other means[149] a country already politically independent. As he put it in his work *Consciencism*, 'Any oblique attempt of a foreign power to thwart, balk, corrupt, or otherwise pervert the true independence of a sovereign people is neo-colonialist. It is neo-colonialist because it seeks, notwithstanding the acknowledged sovereignty of a people, to subordinate their interests to those of a foreign power.'[150]

The emotive way in which Dr Nkrumah used the term, 'neo-colonialism', and his growing obsession with it, especially from late 1960 until the coup in 1966, showed that he regarded the anti-neo-colonial crusade as a continuation of the struggle of the pre-independence days.

'The struggle against the imperialist and colonialist forces', he said in 1962, 'does not automatically end with the onset of independence and sovereignty. Rather, experience has shown repeatedly that the achievement of independence by a colonial territory drives the colonial power not to an acceptance of the new relationships, but to a change in tactic and strategy as a means of maintaining the old relationship in disguised form. There is an outward transformation of the apparatus of government. But this is subordinated to a new method which refurbishes the entire economic, political, and military system as well as the very ideology of imperialism. This is the methodology of what I have described as neo-colonialism. It is sinister in its subtle and insinuating infiltrations. For it makes easy . . . the acceptance of client status by states supposedly free but economically dependent upon the ex-colonial Power.'[151]

He continued'. . . we in Africa have to recognize that with independence we begin a new phase of the anti-colonialist struggle in which we face not a single colonial Power, but the total might of collective imperialism and colonialism. For the imperialist and colonialist powers are determined at all costs to maintain their areas of political, and economic influence.'[152]

To Nkrumah, neo-colonialism presented a worse danger to Africa than the old form of colonialism, mainly because of the absence of public accountability for the neo-colonists. He said:

> Neo-colonialism is also the worst form of imperialism. For those who practise it, it means power without responsibility and for those who suffer from it, it means exploitation without redress. In the days of old-fashioned colonialism, the imperial power had at least to explain and justify at home the actions it was taking abroad. In the colony those who served the ruling imperial power could at least look to its protection against any violent move by their opponents. With neo-colonialism neither is the case.[153]

This was one of the major reasons why till the coup Dr Nkrumah made himself the chief spokesman for Africa on the anti-neo-colonial drive to awaken the other African leaders to 'the new dangers' facing them. It has to be noted that his book *Neo-colonialism: The Last Stage of Imperialism* was launched in October 1965 on the eve of the OAU Summit in Accra. He was not only concerned with rousing other African leaders to these 'dangers', but also with eliminating neo-colonialism in Africa.

Before saying something about how he planned to defeat the neo-colonialist manoeuvres in Africa, we may consider briefly what Nkrumah saw as the 'tactics and strategy' of the neo-colonialists. Although his account of these in his book was very elaborate, we shall only deal with what is relevant to Africa. It has to be noted that to Nkrumah the aim of neo-colonialism was the same as that of colonialism, which was economic exploitation. So all its instruments were directed mainly towards that single end. These included the policy of balkanization, the lowering of the living standard of the people in the developing countries, the retention of military bases in former colonies and the signing of military pacts with extra-African Powers, and the maintenance in power through any means including coup d'état of puppet regimes in Africa.

The classic example of the policy of balkanization was the Congo (later Zaire) where 'the imperialists, and the neo-colonialists' had been creating 'confusion, and division' to 'reinforce their profit-yielding zones.'[154] The break-up of former colonial federations into unviable national units after independence, as the French did in Africa, was to set up client states that would look to France for direction. The policy of balkanization was also directed against African unity by the neo-colonialists in order to retain their economic spheres of influence.

The lowering of the standard of living of the people of the developing countries was practised by the neo-colonialists in four main ways. Firstly, by tying the economy of the developing countries closely to that of the developed countries, as with the association of the eighteen African countries with the European Economic Community (EEC), which Nkrumah described as 'collective imperialism' designed 'to retard the industrialization, and therefore, the prosperity' of the African countries associated with it.[155] Secondly, there was the tactic of depressing the prices of primary products while at the same time increasing the prices of manufactured goods. This featured prominently in most of Nkrumah's speeches between 1960 and 1966. For instance, he said that the unhelpful attitude of the developed countries could be seen from the fact that in the fifties the British Government and the British chocolate manufacturers had encouraged Ghana to produce more cocoa on the understanding that on no account would the prices be allowed to slip below £220 and £210 per ton; and that despite this the price fell to about £90 per ton in July of 1965.[156] Thirdly, the granting of loans to developing countries at very high rates of interests, such as those on the loan for the Volta River Project.[157] was regarded by Nkrumah as a deliberate attempt by the neo-colonialists to increase the economic difficulties of such countries.[158] Fourthly, the operation of giant international financial concerns was designed to maximize the economic exploitation of the poor countries and to dictate policies to them, as the Union Miniere did in the Congo.

The maintenance of military bases by the former metropolitan Powers in their former colonies, such as the French bases in many black African countries after independence, and the signing of military pacts between an African country and the ex-colonial Power, such as the one between Nigeria and Britain abrogated in January 1962, were part of the instruments of the neo-colonists. Similarly, the propping up or establishing of puppet regimes by any means, including coup and counter-coup such as the French military intervention in Gabon early in 1964, was an important tactic of the neo-colonialists.

To destroy the 'dangerous flirtations' arising from all these neo-colonialist manoeuvres Nkrumah advocated three main steps. The first was the formation of an all-union government of Africa which he regarded as being 'primary' and 'basic' to the destruction of neo-colonialism.[159] Apart from the security that would follow a united government of Africa it would put Africa in a strong bargaining position for the prices of her products.[160] This mainly accounted for Nkrumah's single-minded advocacy of a united African government pursued with increasing vigour from 1960 onwards. The second was that the public sector of the economy must be expanded to neutralize any neo-colonialist threat. It was said that because Ghana had done this, and because even foreign capital[161] had been tamed through the introduction of the Businessman's Charter of 1961, she had 'withstood all efforts by imperialists and its agents'.[162] The third was the replacement by force of the puppet regimes in Africa by those radical opposition groups who on getting into power could be expected to be tough with the neo-colonialists. To this end, Dr Nkrumah started late in 1962 to train guerrilla groups from different African countries under neo-colonial regimes.[163] In July 1963, after the ratification of the OAU Charter which forbade the armed support by any member state for opposition groups of another state against the regimes in their countries, Dr Nkrumah said as long as puppet regimes existed in Africa he would be ready to assist those fighting to overthrow such regimes.[164]

On the other hand, the term 'neo-colonialism' found little or no expression among the leaders of the Balewa government described in June 1962 as neo-colonial by Mr Tawia Adamafio, then Ghanaian Minister of Information.[165] Indeed, the only instance when Sir Abubakar ever used something near to the term was in relation to association with the EEC under the Yaounde type of agreement which the British Government offered to the Commonwealth African countries between late 1961 and 1962, when it made its first application to join the Community. In actual fact, he carefully avoided using neo-colonialism, and merely said that the Yaounde type of agreement was only good for colonial territories and not independent African states.[166] He further said that the EEC had 'political overtones' that could not make it appeal to the independent African countries. Alhaji Zanna Bukar Dipcharima, then the Nigerian Minister of Commerce and Industry, said in August 1962 in the House of Representatives, in course of a debate on Nigeria's attitude to the EEC, that Nigeria would not enter into any neo-colonial arrangement with the Community as had the African associates.[167] Beyond this, the Balewa government had nothing near the term as used by Nkrumah. Indeed, to many of the Nigerian Government leaders neo-colonialism was used by Nkrumah more as a cover-up for dictatorship at home and failure abroad than as a description of any real danger to the new Africa emanating from the imperialists. The result of this great divergence on neo-colonialism was the further straining of Ghanaian-Nigerian relations.

NEO-COLONIALISM: II

Just as the attitude to colonialism and apartheid changed in Ghana and Nigeria after the coup that occurred in both countries early in 1966 so did those to neo-colonialism. After the coup d'état of 24 February 1966 in Ghana, neo-colonialism disappeared from the political vocabulary. Indeed, from then till 13 January 1972 it became almost impossible to find anything about neo-colonialism on the pages of the Ghanaian newspapers except where it was referred to as a myth used as a scapegoat by some African leaders who had failed their people. For instance, on 12 November 1966, in a comment on President Nyerere, who attributed the series of coups that raged through Africa between late 1965 and early 1966 to neo-colonialist forces bent on disrupting the OAU, the *Daily Graphic*, a government-owned newspaper, ridiculed this statement, and added that the troubles in Africa were not caused by the 'neo-colonialists' but by a few radical African leaders who armed with foreign ideologies wanted to dictate to their fellow African leaders.[168]

None of the leaders of the NLC or the Progress Government ever engaged in any anti-colonial campaign. To most of them neo-colonialism was incomprehensible. It was meaningless. At best it was part of the Communist jargon mouthed by the CPP leaders to hoodwink the people into passive submission to tyranny.[169] But since neo-colonialism did not exist as far as the Progress Government leaders were concerned the question about its elimination did not arise.

But to the Nigerian leaders neo-colonialism had become a real threat to their country, and to Africa, as was never recognized by the Balewa regime. Although none of them had any elaborate definition of neo-colonialism[170] as Dr Nkrumah had, most of them identified it with sinister imperialist forces using the instruments which Nkrumah said were employed by the neo-colonialists. These included balkanization, economic exploitation, the depression of world prices of primary products, and the propping up or establishing of puppet regimes by any means including coup d'état.

To the Nigerian leaders the French government's backing for the Biafran secession, and the neutrality which indicated support for the secessionists of most of the Western Powers during the civil war, was a neo-colonialist design to prevent the emergence of a strong viable state in Black Africa. Shortly after the war, in Algiers, General Gowon referred to all this as part of 'the imperialist conspiracies and threats to the integrity of our fatherland'.[171] By direct extension, the Nigerian Government saw any attempt at secession in Africa, such as in the Sudanese Republic, as being the handiwork of the imperialists. Furthermore, the Nigerian leaders believed that the neo-colonialists would always try to divide the OAU by such tactics as the dialogue proposal, which Dr Arikpo said was initiated from outside Africa by 'the enemies of Africa' to weaken the Organization.[172]

The Nigerian government of General Gowon believed that the neo-colonialists would continue to exploit the economic resources of the developing nations to the latter's disadvantage, and that they would continue to operate international trade in favour of the developed countries. This would widen the gap between the living standards of the developed countries and the less developed ones, and would present the latter with great dangers. Thus Dr Arikpo said at the UN General Assembly in October 1970:

> . . . the greatest threat to world peace and prosperity is the refusal of former colonial powers to recognize the co-relationship between political freedom and economic independence. Consequently the new nations are generally dependent on the former colonial powers in economic matters as the latter refuse to loosen their economic strangle-hold over the former.[173]

At the Lusaka Conference of the Non-aligned Powers in September 1970, Dr Arikpo referred to 'the existing inequitable pattern of international economic pattern',[174] as a result of the refusal of the developed countries to improve the prices paid for the primary products of the developing countries, while at the same time increasing prices of their own manufactured goods.

Finally, the Nigerian rulers believed that the neo-colonialists would do everything possible to maintain or install puppet regimes in Africa. French aid to most of the ex-French colonies in Africa was regarded as serving such a purpose. Although the Nigerian government was one of the first countries to recognize the government of General Amin in Uganda towards the end of February 1971 when the OAU Council of Ministers met in Addis Ababa, doubts persisted among some Nigerian leaders as to whether the coup against Dr Milton Obote was not neo-colonialist inspired especially considering the *volte face* of the Amin government on arms sales to South Africa.[175]

Nigeria saw the struggle against the neo-colonialist forces more or less as a continuation of the colonial struggle. This could be seen from General Gowon's speech at a dinner party arranged in his honour by President Boumédienne in Algiers on 26 August 1970. He said *inter alia* '. . . our fight against the enemies is not yet over. Imperialism has many faces. . . . We must deal a final blow on the external forces which seek to promote unrest, and rebellion in independent African states'.[176]

To this end Nigeria was to discourage any secessionist movement in Africa. Thus during his official visit to the Sudan late in August 1970, General Gowon promised to assist the Sudanese government in its effort to defend the independence and territorial integrity of its country against 'international and imperialist conspiracies'.[177] As a follow-up to this in October 1971, the Sudanese Minister of Information, Mr Musa, announced that the Nigerian government had given his government the sum of £50,000 to combat the secessionist movement in the Southern part of the country.[178]

Another way in which Nigeria wanted to defeat neo-colonialist manoeuvres was through the strengthening of the OAU, which was described by General Gowon and President Kenyatta in a joint communique as having 'an effective role in frustrating the subversive forces which aim to divide the African continent, and pose threats to the political independence and territorial integrity of independent African states.'[179] Nigeria tried to strengthen the OAU in two main ways. First, she increased her own contributions to the ordinary budget of the Organization by about forty-seven per cent between 1968 when it was £78,121, to £150,000 in 1971.[180] Secondly, Nigeria continued to be unrelenting in her efforts to preserve the unity of Africa within the OAU. Instances of this could be seen in her efforts to reconcile the African countries who were in favour and those who were against the seating of the Amin regime's representatives at the OAU conferences during the first part of 1971; and in her efforts to unite the OAU member states on the line of policy to be followed as regards the dialogue with South Africa.

To reduce the economic dependence of some of her neighbours on France, Nigeria signed a series of bilateral trade agreements with all of them.[181] Not only that, she started to grant some technical and capital aid to a number of them. In mid-1971, she agreed to finance the cost of reconstructing the road from Idiroko (the common border between Nigeria and Dahomey) to Porto Novo (about sixteen miles inside Dahomey) with an interest-free loan of one million pounds.[182]

To overcome the dangers of foreign domination and exploitation of the economy and to win the fight for 'economic independence' Dr Arikpo said 'a revolutionary struggle' involving perhaps greater sacrifice than was made in the struggle for political freedom was required.[183] Although Dr Arikpo did not spell out what form this 'revolutionary struggle' would take, one could say it would involve the gradual elimination of the dominant position of foreign interests in the country's economy, as earlier indicated in this chapter and as was abundantly made clear by the Second National Development Plan 1970–4 through a policy of indigenous ownership and control.[184] Furthermore, the Federal government and the state governments would expand the public sector of the economy in order to ensure, to quote the Second National Plan 'the economic independence of the nation, and the defeat of neo-colonialist forces in Africa.'[185]

To overcome the low prices of primary products, the developing countries had to try to diversify their economy through industrialization. But if the developed nations were seriously trying to assist the poorer nations, Dr Arikpo said that they would then have to accept the Algiers Charter drawn up by the group of seventy-seven in 1964.[186] But since the developed nations might not do this, then the developing countries would have to try to adopt the principle of self-reliance.

From the above, we can see that, after 1966, Ghana and Nigeria could be said in many ways to have exchanged their earlier positions on neo-colonialism. Just as the divergences between the two countries prior to 1966 on this issue led to difficulties in their relationship, so also did their differences after 1966 breed mistrust and suspicion.

(iv) AFRICAN UNITY: TWO SETS OF OBJECTIVES AND APPROACHES

Another major source of discord between Ghana and Nigeria especially before 1966 was the question of African unity. As Dr Nkrumah put it in a comment shortly after the coup d'état in Nigeria, 'the Nigeria — Ghana (sic) dispute arose through Ghana's insistence on African unity. The tragedy of Sir Abubakar was that he never realized that for Nigeria the choice was either immediate political unification of Africa or Nigeria's disintegration . . .'[187]

To Dr Nkrumah the objective must be the immediate establishment of a Union Government of Africa. He believed so passionately in this that the Republican Constitution of 1960 made provision for the surrender of Ghana's sovereignty to a union of African States. Any alternative to a union African Government was unacceptable as it would be disastrous to Africa. Thus he said in July 1960, 'We have the choice of three things: to unite, to stand separately and disintegrate, or to sell ourselves to foreign powers.'[188]

In Addis Ababa on 24 May 1963, Dr Nkrumah repeated this view with greater force. 'We have already reached the stage,' he said, 'where we must unite or sink into that condition which made Latin America the unwilling and distressed prey of imperialism after one-and-a half centuries of political independence.'[189]

To Dr Nkrumah a functional approach to African unity was a non-starter. Once the union government was established all the functional activities would follow. 'African unity,' he said, 'is, above all, a political kingdom, which can only be gained by political means. The social and economic development of Africa will come only within the political kingdom, not the other way round.'[190] The formation of an African union government he believed would solve all the problems in the continent such as imperialism, neo-colonialism, racism, poverty, insecurity and instability, and border disputes, and would give Africa a greater voice in world affairs. Regardless of the differences between Africa and vast areas like China, the Soviet Union and the United States, Dr Nkrumah could not see why Africa could not form a single political unit if such vast areas could form single political entities. What Nkrumah wanted, moreover, was not any Union African Government but a Continental 'Union integrated', as he put it, 'by socialism without which our hard-won independence may yet be perverted and negated by a new colonialism'.[191]

Furthermore, Dr Nkrumah wanted an immediate establishment of the Union African Government. For any delay in its formation was dangerous, as it would be disastrous to the whole idea. Thus in an interview with the editor of the Nigerian *Sunday Express* in May 1965 Dr Nkrumah said 'any further delay in the formation of the Union Government would be dangerous since the delay would allow the existing arrangements in Africa to crystallize, thus creating indigenous vested interests around the status quo. Once such interests, supported by imperialism and neo-colonialism become entrenched, the fight for African unity will become much more difficult and even violent.'[192]

But the Balewa government wanted a loose association of African states in which all its members would be equal and sovereign, and in which their relationships would be based strictly on the principle of respect for the sovereignty, independence and territorial integrity of each other and the principle of non-interference in the internal affairs of the others. To the Nigerian leaders there was no question of Nigeria surrendering its sovereignty to any supranational body; and any talk of an African Union Government was 'premature' and 'unrealistic' as put by Alhaji Maitama Sule at the Second Conference of Independent Africa States in Addis Ababa in June 1960.[193] Shortly after independence Sir Abubakar gave three main reasons why a Union African Government was impracticable. These were the diversity of Africa, the personal ambitions of various African leaders, and the absolute unwillingness of any African country once given a seat at the UN to give up its sovereignty.[194] In view of this, Nigeria opted for a loose association of African states. This infuriated Nkrumah who later said at the Cairo Summit of the OAU in July 1964 that any suggestion that a Union African Government was premature was 'to sacrifice Africa on the alter of neo-colonialism'.[195]

Since the Pan-African objectives of Ghana and Nigeria were different, their approaches were necessarily different. Broadly speaking Dr Nkrumah's approach could be divided into bilateral action and action through African conferences of independent States.

At the bilateral level, Nkrumah's Ghana strove to bring about the Union African Government in many ways. These included the signing of union agreements with radical African government leaders, the formation of Pan-African organizations for African trade unions, farmers, women, teachers and students, the formation of the Committee of African Organization (CAO), ideological training, subversion and propaganda. We shall only consider some of the most important of these briefly.

On 23 November 1958 the Ghana-Guinea Union agreement was signed in Accra by Dr Nkrumah and President Ahmed Sekou Touré. In 1960, Mali acceded to this union which in 1961 became the Ghana-Guinea-Mali Union. On 8 August 1960, Dr Nkrumah and Mr Patrice Lumumba signed a 'secret agreement'[196] to establish a union of Ghana and the Congo (later Zaire). Apart from a series of meetings between the leaders of Ghana, Guinea and Mali, nothing substantial came out of this union, and it was buried unceremoniously in 1963. The Ghana-Congo Union never became operational as a result of the Congo crisis and the death of Lumumba.

On the formation of different types of Pan-African organizations only the one set up to bring together all African trade unions called the All-African Trade Union Federation (AATUF) assumed any importance in African politics, and hence it is the only one we shall consider here. The preparatory committee for the formation of the AATUF met in Accra in November 1959. In his address to this committee Dr Nkrumah said the AATUF was to be 'the vanguard of the struggle for political freedom, independence, and unity of our continent.'[197] Furthermore, the AATUF would have no link with any extra-African trade union movement such as the International Conformeration of Free Trade Unions (ICFTU) or the World Federation of Trade Unions (WFTU) and would owe allegiance only to 'Mother Africa'. But the AATUF was not effectively launched until mid-1961 when it appointed John Tettegah, then the Secretary General of the Ghana Trade Union Congress as its first Secretary-General, and chose Accra as its headquarters. But the second conference of the AATUF did not take place until mid-1964 at Bamako. This conference was said to have been attended by representatives of thirty-six national unions.[198] In his opening address to the conference, John Tettegah said that 'a united African trade union movement is indispensable in the building of the Africa of tomorrow . . . free of colonialism, neo-colonialism, and racial segregation . . .'[199] In February 1965, Dr Nkrumah told the Executive Bureau of the AATUF to intensify its efforts at the liberation struggle and its fight for African Union Government, in order to frustrate the attempt of the ICFTU which had become 'a threat to the working people of Africa.'[200]

But in spite of all these efforts, the AATUF[201] made little headway in Africa. It had adherents only in a few countries led by radical politicians.

Another important organization set up to promote the emergence of a Union African Government was the Committee of African Organization (CAO). This organization with its headquarters in London was set up in 1958. Its aim was 'unity for Africa', and 'freedom for all African countries.'[202] Mr Kwesi Armah, who was Ghana's High Commissioner in London in 1962, later became its chairman. This organization which was open to any African was entirely financed by the Ghanaian Government who in 1960 made a grant of £2,000 to the organization.[203]

The meetings of the CAO were usually held in London, but at times they could be held elsewhere, as in 1962 when the organization met in Belgrade.[204] The CAO was radical in their attitude to African affairs. For instance, in 1962 it called for an armed struggle to liberate colonial Africa. In the same year it published a journal entitled *United Africa*, and adopted 'the flag of the continental union drawn . . . on the design described in the Conakry Declaration of 1959'.[205] At its London conference in 1963 it passed a series of resolutions calling *inter alia* for the immediate formation of a Union African Government and the frustration of imperialist and neo-colonialist manoeuvres in Africa.

Since it was a continental socialist union government that Nkrumah wanted, he tried to produce some of its future socialist leaders at his Ideological Institute in Winneba. Part of the aims of the Institute was to 'train Africans in the spirit of Pan-Africanism as a method of making progress towards African union'.[206] The training of some opposition groups in Ghana to overthrow reactionary regimes that were opposed to a Union African Government was also adopted. But very little came out of all this. Nowhere could it be proved on the basis of concrete facts that an African conservative regime had been overturned by opposition socialists previously trained in Ghana.

The Bureau of African Affairs set up in 1960 was mainly to promote the birth of a Continental Union Government through reports on developments in each African country and through propaganda. Various newspapers and periodicals were established for propaganda purposes for the Union of African states. These were not set up for commercial purposes. For instance, an MP, Mr J. D.

Wireko, said in 1965 that the *Ghanaian Times* did not need to make a profit since it was playing 'a vital role in the furtherance of African unity'.[207]

Dr Nkrumah so passionately believed in African unity that he placed much of his country's resources behind it. The Ghana Airways in 1962 had to operate uneconomic routes from Accra to Addis Ababa, to Cairo and to Casablanca in the interests of African unity. A year later, Mr E. K. Bensah, then the Minister of Communications and Works, said that in spite of the losses of Ghana Airways, its services would be extended to East and Central Africa 'in furtherance of the policy of African unity'.[208] Similarly, early in 1965, when the country's finances were in chaos, the Government announced that it would increase the number of its diplomatic missions in Africa from twenty-nine to thirty-four before the end of the year[209] in accordance with its Pan-African policy.[210] Dr Nkrumah tried to justify all this by saying in March 1965 that 'all our efforts and aspirations at home must be geared to one purpose and one grand objective . . . the one mighty continental effort'.[211]

All the various inter-African conferences especially between 1960 and the coup of 24 February 1966 were used by the Ghanaian leaders as a platform for calling for the immediate formation of an African Union Government. Mr Ako Adjei, then the Ghanaian Foreign Minister called for this at the Second Conference of Independent African states at Addis Ababa in June 1960. It was, however, at the Conference of Independent African states in May 1963 at Addis Ababa that Dr Nkrumah made his most far-reaching call for a Union African Government 'now'. There he called on the Heads of State and Government to make 'a formal declaration that all the independent African states here and now agree to the establishment of a Union of African States'.[212] As a second step, an All-Africa Committee of Foreign Ministers should be set up to work out the unification. This committee should establish on behalf of the Heads of State and Government a permanent body of officials, two from each state to work out the Constitution of the Union. A Praesidium of Heads of Government should later meet to adopt a constitution, and other recommendations designed to launch the Union Government of Africa. Several commissions should be set up to work out a continent-wide plan for a unified or common economic and industrial policy, and their task should include proposals for setting up an African Common Market and an African Central Bank. Separate commissions should be set up to plan for common African foreign policy, a common defence system, and for common African citizenship.

Though all these proposals were turned down by the majority members of the African states, Dr Nkrumah persisted in his advocacy of a Union African Government. Thus at the Cairo Summit of the OAU in July 1964, he made another call for the establishment of a Union Government in Africa, though not as elaborate as his proposals in 1963. On this occasion he called on the Assembly of Heads of State and Government of the OAU to establish an African Union Government with a President, an executive council to be led by a Prime Minister, and to have a senate and a House of Representatives. The Senate was to be made up of two representatives from each African state, while the House of Representatives should be composed of members elected on a population basis from independent Africa.[213]

As before the Nkrumah proposals were rejected. But he would not be daunted. Thus at the 1965 OAU Summit in Accra he made another call for a Union African Government but in an attenuated form. He suggested the establishment of a full-time body or Executive Council of the Assembly of Heads of State and Government. The chairman of the Executive Council should be appointed by the Assembly of Heads of State and Government. The Executive Council which would be responsible for implementing the decisions of the Assembly of Heads of State and Government should also initiate policies and recommendations to the same body.[214] Furthermore, the Assembly should elect a Union President and a number of Union Vice-Presidents to meet periodically to review the work of the Executive Council when the Assembly was not in session.[215]

All these approaches by Dr Nkrumah were considered unrealistic in Nigeria. The Nigerian leaders believed that African unity could be best attained through functional co-operation in various fields such as transport, trade, communications, currency, culture, education and science. As Balewa told a meeting of the OAU Council of Ministers in Lagos early in 1964:

> We in Nigeria believe that by taking genuine practical steps in the economic, educational, scientific co-operation, and by trying first to understand ourselves we would get nearer towards the solution of the problem of re-establishing unity and cohesion. Any precipitate or false step would militate against the early attainment of this objective . . . It would be a mistake not to take cognisance of the great diversity in Africa today.[216]

In pursuit of this policy Nigeria had taken many steps. But we shall only consider briefly a few of the most important ones, especially in the field of communications, economics and education.

In the field of communications, Nigeria since independence has spearheaded the efforts to break down the barriers dividing many African countries, starting with her immediate neighbours. Thus on 7 August 1962, the first direct telecommunication between Nigeria and Dahomey was inaugurated.[217] In October of the same year, a similar link with Togo was established.[218] By January 1966, Nigeria had established telecommunication links with over sixteen African countries. At the end of the civil war, in 1970, Nigeria had telegraphic links with twelve African countries, radio-telephonic links with eighteen, and telex links with ten.[219]

In the field of education, Nigeria had tried to work out student exchange programmes between herself and other African countries. For instance, in September 1963, an agreement was signed in Lagos under which Nigeria and Guinea would exchange thirty-six students every year.[220] Mr Jaja Nwachuku, then the Federal Minister of Education, who signed this agreement on behalf of the Government announced that the Federal Government proposed to award in the near future 500 scholarships yearly to other African states tenable in Nigerian institutions of higher learning. In 1963, Mr F. U. Mbakogu, then the Parliamentary Secretary to the Federal Minister of Economic Development, said the government in pursuit of African unity had been voting £2,000 annually since 1961 to train nationals of other African countries in Nigeria.[221] Apart from the Federal Government, the former Regional Governments used to provide scholarships to other African countries. For instance, at the end of President Nyerere's visit to the former Western Nigeria in June 1965, Chief S. L. Akintola, then the Region's Premier and Chancellor of the University of Ife, announced the offer of twelve scholarships to the Tanzanian Government tenable at the University of Ife, Nigeria.[222]

Apart from all this, Nigeria provided technical assistance in the form of lawyers, magistrates and judges to most of the East and Central African countries, including the Congo (later Zaire). The money value of this form of technical assistance could not be determined. But it had to be relatively small since only a few men were involved at a time. For example, during the 1962-3 fiscal year only ten lawyers were recruited by the Federal Government for service under its technical assistance programme.[223]

In the economic field, the government had taken measures to improve its co-operation with other African countries through bilateral and multilateral arrangements. Trade and custom agreements[224] were signed with many African countries. In 1962 Nigeria joined Chad, Niger and the Cameroons to form the Chad

Basin Commission. Although the Commission held its first meeting in November 1962 in Lagos, described by Walter Schwarz as 'a useful beginning to African unity',[225] it did not actually begin to operate from its headquarters in Fort Lamy, Chad, until 1964. By then Nigeria had also joined the following countries to form the River Niger Commission: Cameroons, Chad, Dahomey, Guinea, Ivory Coast, Mali, Niger and Upper Volta. The main aim of these Commissions was to harmonize the development policies[226] of its member countries.[227]

In all the various inter-African conferences after 1960, the Nigerian leaders were often at pains to demonstrate the value of a functional approach to African unity. Furthermore, they tried to show that the process of forging unity in Africa would be slow and would not be achieved overnight as Dr Nkrumah envisaged.

These differences in objective and approach to African unity between Nkrumah's Ghana and Nigeria were at the root of much of the bitterness that marked their relationship till the coup d'état of 24 February 1966 in Ghana. After the dismissal of Nkrumah's government, these differences virtually disappeared, and so ceased to cause difficulties in their relationship, as the NLC government and its successor, the Progress government, rejected both the Nkrumah call for a Union African Government[228] and his methods. Instead they adopted a functional approach to African unity as in Balewa's Nigeria; and their objective was a loose form of association based on the principles of respect for the sovereignty, independence and territorial integrity of each other, and of non-interference in the internal affairs of other states.[229] On the other hand, after the overthrow of the Balewa regime the Nigerian government did not change the basic principles underlying its Pan-African policy which were essentially incorporated into the Charter of the OAU.

1. *N. A. Deb.*, Vol. 2, 15 July 1958, col. 471.
2. *N. A. Deb.* Vol. 12, 12 December 1958, col. 390.
3. Ken Post has shown that the new Ghana, and the old Ghana Empire are not geographically the same. See K. W. Post *The New States of West Africa*, London, Penguin 1964, p. 66.
4. Kwame Nkrumah *Hands Off Africa*, op. cit. p. 14.
5. Mr Michael Dei-Anang did little to show a direct relationship between the new Ghana and the ancient Ghana beyond vague references. Indeed, the book deals mainly with native resistance to European rule in the Gold Coast from the early fifteenth century until independence in 1957. See Michael Dei-Anang *Ghana Resurgent*, Accra 1964.
6. *N. A. Deb.*, Vol. 14, 20 February 1959, col. 17.
7. Until very recently, the ordinary Ghanaian used to refer to Nigerians by the

derogatory name 'Baba Alata', meaning somebody who sells pepper. This was derived from the name given to Nigerians selling pepper in the Gold Coast before 1957.

8. Indeed, it has to be noted that in spite of the depressed economic position of the country since 1966, some Ghanaians still want their country to continue to play a leading role in Africa. See Colin Legum, 'Ghana's Return to Democracy' *The Round Table*, No. 237, January 1970, p. 32.

9. *H. R. Deb.*, 4 September 1961, col. 2813.

10. *RIIA—Documents on International Affairs 1960*, London 1964, p. 364.

11. *H. R. Deb.*, 14 January 1960, col. 33.

12. *H. R. Deb.*, 5 August 1958, col. 2082.

13. *H. R. Deb.*, 16 January 1960, cols. 154-5.

14. *West Africa*, 16 May 1964.

15. *H. R. Deb.*,13 January 1960, col. 20.

16. *Africa Research Bulletin*, October 1965, p. 388.

17. Chief S. L. Akintola was speaking with indignation at the fact that only four official invitation cards, apart from the one to the Governor-General, were sent from Ghana to Nigeria for that Country's independence celebrations whereas many European and American individuals had been invited in their private capacity to attend the celebrations. See *H. R. Deb.*, 5 March 1957, p. 123.

18. *H. R. Deb.*, 21 April 1965, col. 1138.

19. Kwame Nkrumah *Consciencism*, op. cit. p. 70.

20. Ali A. Mazrui *On Heroes and Uhuru Worship*, London 1967, p. 113.

21. After his overthrow, Dr Nkrumah preached the adoption of scientific socialism by all African countries. But till then, it was Nkrumaism which was in some ways different from Scientific Socialism that he advocated.

22. The Editors of *The Spark* (ed.) *Some Essential Features of Nkrumaism*, London 1970, p. 126.

23. *West Africa*, 13 December 1958.

24. From early 1962 until the February 1966 coup all newspapers were owned and rigidly controlled by the CPP government. Furthermore, all the editors were members of the Central Committee of the ruling party. Therefore, the editorials of the most important newspapers in Ghana during this period had to be regarded more or less as official releases, as is the case in totalitarian or Communist states. The most important of these were *The Spark*, the *Ghanaian Times*, the *Daily Graphic* and *The Evening News*.

25. *The Spark*, Accra, 17 March 1964.

26. For further details see Kofi Baako's address on 'Nkrumaism—African Socialism' to the Conference of Ghana Envoys in Accra in January 1962 *Confidential Report of Conference of Ghana Envoys*, Vol. II, Accra, 1962, pp. 118-24.

27. Ibid.

28. *Guide To Party Action*, An address by Osagyefo Dr Kwame Nkrumah to the First Seminar at the Ideological Institute, Winneba, 3 February 1962.

29. *Some Essential Features of Nkrumaism*, op. cit. p. 7.

30. Ibid. p. 29.

31. In his *Towards Colonial Freedom* first published in 1947 and later again in 1962, Dr Nkrumah outlined three objectives for which the national liberation must struggle. The first was political freedom, the second was democratic freedom in which sovereignty was vested in the broad masses of the people, and the third was social reconstruction in which there would be freedom from poverty and economic exploitation. See *Towards Colonial Freedom*, London 1962, p. 43.

32. *Evening News*, Accra, 31 July 1959.

33. Dennis Austin said this was implicit in the objective of the CPP in 1949 in which it said a nationalist party represented the whole State. See Dennis Austin *Politics in Ghana*, op. cit. p. 31n.

34. Ibid.

35. *Blueprint for the Future*, Sessional Address by Osagyefo Dr Kwame Nkrumah at the State Opening of the First Session of the Second Parliament of the Republic of Ghana on 24 August 1965.

36. Ibid.

37. *Ghana Today*, 12 February 1964.

38. *N. A. Deb.*, Vol. 24, 4 July 1961, col. 22.

39. *Ghana Today*, 6 December 1961.

40. *Overseas Capital and Investment in Ghana* — Text of a speech by Osagyefo Dr Kwame Nkrumah at the foundation stone laying ceremony of the Kumasi City Hotel on 24 March 1962, Accra, Government Printer, 1962.

41. *N. A. Deb.*, Vol. 43, 1 February 1966, cols. 8–9.

42. *N. A. Deb.*, Vol. 20, 2 September 1960, col. 1073.

43. Kwame Nkrumah *Consciencism*, op. cit. p. 74.

44. *Some Essential Features of Nkrumaism*, op. cit. pp. 59, 66.

45. Colin Legum, 'Socialism in Ghana' in William H. Friedland and Carl G. Rosberg (ed.) *African Socialism*, 1964, p. 148.

46. David Apter, 'The Politics of Solidarity in Ghana' in J. S. Coleman and Carl G. Rosberg (ed.) *Political Parties and National Integration in Tropical Africa*, Berkeley 1964, pp. 296–7.

47. *Seven-Year Development Plan 1963-4 to 1969-70*, p. x.

48. Chief F. S. Okotie-Eboh, then the Federal Minister of Finance, had in 1958 spoken against communist ideology which he described as being 'wholly alien' to Nigeria. See *H. R. Deb.*, 22 February 1958, col. 229.

49. *H. R. Deb.*, 14 April 1962, col. 1685.

50. For further details see Frederick Schwarz op. cit. pp. 136–9.

51. Ibid. pp. 155–164. ——

52. Walter Schwarz op. cit. pp. 28–30.

53. For details about the development and organization of Nigeria public corporations and state-owned companies, see O. Nwanwene: 'Public Corporation and State-Owned Companies' in the *Quarterly Journal of Administration*, October 1970, pp. 53–75.

54. *H. R. Deb.*, 31 March 1965, col. 303.

55. *H. R. Deb.*, 7 April 1965, col. 910.

56. *H. R. Deb.*, 31 March 1965, col. 300.

57. *West Africa*, 29 January 1966.

58. *Daily Times*, Lagos, 28 August 1962.

59. *H. R. Deb.*, 16 November 1961, col. 2918.

60. See various evidence at the treason trial of 1962-3, and especially the statement of Mr Adeyiga Akinsanya before Justice Sowemimo that several AG opposition members had been to Ghana for ideological (and military) training. See *Daily Times*, Lagos, 6 December 1962.

61. *Daily Times*, Lagos, 6 December 1962.

62. *Daily Times*, Lagos, 22 September 1962.

63. *H. R. Deb.*, 31 March 1965, cols. 304-6.

64. Anthony Enahoro, *Fugitive Offender*, London 1965, p. 380.

65. *Morning Post*, Lagos, 6 September 1962.

66. *Morning post*, Lagos, 10 September 1962.

67. Tawia Adamafio was one of the two CPP Ministers detained and later tried as a result of the Kulungugu episode.

68. *Daily Times*, Lagos, 3 September 1962.

69. *Daily Times*, Lagos, 10 September 1962.

70. *Daily Times*, Lagos, 13 September 1962.

71. *Africa Diary*, 27 February–5 March 1965, pp. 2208-9.

72. *Morning Post*, 18 September 1962.

73. *Africa Diary*, 6-12 March 1965, p. 2218.

74. Speech by Dr K. A. Busia at the Inauguration of the Second Republic on 1 October 1969, Accra, Government Printer.

75. *West Africa*, 8 October 1971.

76. The Centre for Civic Education was set up in 1966 by the NLC to teach the ordinary people their civic rights. The first head of the Centre was Dr Kofi Busia. Since its establishment, the Centre has published many pamphlets on the role of the individual, voluntary organizations etc. in the society.

77. *Rebuilding the National Economy*, Broadcast speech by the Chairman of the NLC on 2 March 1966, Accra, Government Printer 1966.

78. See criticisms of the Nigerian Federal Government by the *New Nigerian* over the public execution of armed robbers, quoted in *West Africa*, 15 October 1971; over African High Command *Daily Times,* and *Daily Express*, 16 and 17 October 1971, and over the Adebo Salary award, *Daily Times*, 27 October 1971.

79. See the judgement of Justice Akinola Aguda in *Mojeed Agbaje versus the Commissioner of Police, Western State, 18 June 1969, Suit No. M/22/69.*

80. *Second National Development Plan 1970/74*, p. 32.

81. Ibid. p. 34.

82. *Daily Times*, Lagos, 20 October, 1971.

83. *Second National Plan 1970/74*, p. 75.

84. *Ghana Today*, 11 January 1967.

85. See *The Renaissance*, Enugu, 19 September 1971; and the *Daily Times*, Lagos, 18 September 1971.

86. *Daily Times*, Lagos, 29 September 1971.

87. J. Mackintosh op. cit. p. 280.

88. For further details about how the Nkrumah government tried to speed up the elimination of colonialism and racism in Africa see *N. A. Deb.*, Vol. II, 3 September 1958, cols. 2086-7.

89. *Step to Freedom, Speech by Osagyefor Dr Kwame Nkrumah at the opening of the Conference of African Freedom Fighters in Accra*, Accra, Government Printer 1962.

90. Kwame Nkrumah *Consciencism*, op. cit. p. 104.

91. Kwame Nkrumah *Dark Days in Ghana*, London 1968, p. 138.

92. Ibid, for the role of these newspapers and periodicals on behalf of the freedom fighters.

93. *Africa Research Bulletin*, July 1965, p. 345.

94. Colin Legum *Pan-Africanism*, New York 1962, p. 141.

95. *GAOR 869th Pl. mtg.*, 23 September 1960, para. 5.

96. *Conference of Heads of State or Government of Non-aligned Countries*, Belgrade 1961, p. 103.

97. *SCOR 104th meeting*, 24 July 1963, para. 77.

98. *West Africa*, 19 March 1966.

99. For details about Ghana's role at the Afro-Asian People's Solidarity Conference see *Africa Research Bulletin*, May 1965, p. 302.

100. W. Scott Thompson, *Ghana's Foreign Policy 1957-66*, Princeton 1969, p. 66.

101. Ibid. p. 67.

102. *Africa Diary*, 28 September-4 October 1963, pp. 1364-5.

103. Ibid.

104. *Africa and World Peace*, Text of an address by Osagyefo Dr Kwame Nkrumah, President of the Republic of Ghana, to the Second Conference of Non-aligned States in Cairo, on 7 October 1964 — Supplement with *Ghana Today*, 21 October 1964.

105. W. Scott Thompson, op. cit. p. 360.

106. Kwame Nkrumah *Dark Days in Ghana*, op. cit. p. 140.

107. It was probable that the camps were used by both nationalists fighting for full self-government and by guerrilla groups working for the overthrow of the puppet regimes in their different countries, for some of those deported shortly after the coup by the NLC came from South Africa, Rhodesia and the Portuguese territories.

108. Dr Nkrumah sent an invitation to the South African government to participate in the first Conference of Independent African states of April 1958 at Accra; but this was turned down by the Pretoria Government because other Administering Powers in Africa were not invited. Even early in 1960, there was a Ghanaian invitation to the South African Foreign Minister, then Sir Eric Louw, to visit Ghana, but this was turned down because it was tied to the establishment of a diplomatic Mission in Pretoria by Ghana which the Verwoerd government opposed because it would then become the headquarters for agitators in the Republic. See Sir Robert Menzies *Afternoon Light: Some Memories of men and events*, London 1967, pp. 206–7.

109. All this affected Ghana's relations with the Western Powers. We shall refer to this in greater detail in chapter six.

110. *H. R. Deb.*, 20 August 1960, cols. 2669–71.

111. *H. R. Deb.*, 31 August 1961, col. 2599 (Oral Answers).

112. *H. R. Deb.*, 5 April 1962, cols. 911–12 (Oral Answers).

113. J. S. Coleman, 'The Foreign Policy of Nigeria' in Joseph E. Black, and Kenneth W. Thompson (ed.) op. cit. p. 404.

114. The reasons for this are unclear. Perhaps it was due to the fact that faced with the stiff attitude of many other Afro-Asian states on colonialism Nigeria did not want to be left behind with the possibility of being accused of being in collusion with the imperialists.

115. For this discrepancy in the government's policy over Algeria, the AG opposition bitterly criticized it. See *H. R. Deb.*, 14 April 1962, col. 1683.

116. For details about the analysis of African voting pattern at the UN, See Thomas Hovet *Africa in the United Nations*, London 1963, pp. 233–61.

117. *H. R. Deb.*, 30 November 1961, col. 3630.

118. *Daily Times*, Lagos, 16 November 1962.

119. In spite of the stiff opposition by many MPs against the existence of this Portuguese post in Lagos, the Balewa government refused to close it down on the grounds that such an act would serve no useful purpose. See *H. R. Deb.*, 6 August 1963, cols. 2633–4.

120. J. S. Coleman, in Joseph E. Black and Kenneth W. Thompson (ed.) op. cit. p. 405.

121. *H. R. Deb.*, 5 April 1965, col. 507 (Oral Answers).

122. Kwame Nkrumah *I speak of Freedom*, London 1961, p. 10.

123. *Conference of Heads of State or Government of Non-aligned Countries*, Belgrade 1961, p. 104.

124. *H. R. Deb.*, 4 September 1961, cols. 2787–8.

125. Sir Abubakar Tafawa Balewa: Nigeria Looks Ahead in *Foreign Affairs*, October 1962.

126. *Speech by Dr K. A. Busia, Prime Minister, at the Inauguration of the Second Republic at Black Star Square in Accra, on 1 October 1969*, Accra, Government Printer.

127. For instance, the exiled Pan-Africanist Congress of South Africa said that the co-operation between Ghana and South Africa against nationalists was so close that Ghana was planning to open a diplomatic Mission in Pretoria. This worried the NLC government to such an extent as to issue a denial. See *Africa Research Bulletin*, 15 September 1957, p. 858.

128. *West Africa*, 2 April 1971.

129. For opposition to dialogue in Ghana, see 'Ghana's Foreign Policy under Busia' *Legon Observer*, 25 September–8 October 1970, and also *West Africa*, 2 April 1971.

130. To emphasize its propaganda intent it was published early in 1971 by the Ghana Public Relations Dept. Accra.

131. *West Africa*, 23 July 1971.

132. *West Africa*, 13 August 1971.

133. *West Africa*, 25 July 1970.

134. *Africa Research Bulletin*, May 1966, p. 528.

135. *Morning Post*, Lagos, 23 July 1966.

136. *Africa Research Bulletin*, February 1966, p. 475.

137. *New Nigerian*, Kaduna, 25 February 1971.

138. This was in addition to Nigeria's contribution to the OAU liberation fund which we shall deal with in the next chapter.

139. *Daily Times*, Lagos, 15 August 1970.

140. Seventh OAU Assembly of Heads of State and Government, Addis Ababa, 1–4 September 1970 — *Long Live African Unity—Statement by His Excellency Major-General Yakubu Gowon, Head of the Federal Military Government, and Commander-in-Chief of the Nigerian Armed Forces.*

141. *Statement By His Excellency Dr Okoi Arikpo, Commissioner for External Affairs to the Fifth Meeting of the Commemorative Session, 16 October 1970, 25th Session of the General Assembly of the UN.*

142. *Morning Post*, Lagos, 25 June 1971.

143. *The Renaissance*, Enugu, 13 December 1970.

144. *Daily Times*, Lagos, 30 March 1970.

145. *The Nigerian Observer*, Benin City, 23 October 1971.

146. See for example T. Jones: 'Neo-colonialism: The Highest Stage of Imperialism' Paper for discussion at a Post-graduate seminar, at the Institute of Commonwealth Studies, London, on 9 March 1966 (mimeo.); and J. D. B. Miller, 'The Instusion of Afro-Asia' in *International Affairs*, London November 1970. But Kenneth J. Twitchett said that 'neo-colonialism' has some meaning though not as all-embracing as Nkrumah's definition. See Kenneth J. Twitchett *Neo-colonialism in Political Studies*, October 1965.

147. Sir Alec Douglas-Home, then the British Prime Minister, told the Nigerian Parliament in March 1964 that 'the word (neo-colonialism) finds no place in the dictionary of our political terms in the United Kingdom. We simply do not know its meaning'. See *H. R. Deb.*, 20 March 1964, cols. 487-8.

148. Kwame Nkrumah *Neo-colonialism: The Last Stage of Imperialism*, London 1965. This title was a conscious attempt to re-echo Lenin's work, *Imperialism: The Highest Stage of capitalism*.

149. It has to be remembered that Nkrumah did not begin to mouth 'neo-colonialism' until the bubble burst in the Congo (now Zaïre) when the Western Powers were supporting the virtual break-up of the Congo. Thus in his address a week after the outbreak of violence in the Congo and 'the imperialist, and colonialist intrigue' there, Dr Nkrumah cited it as example of 'the (new) danger besetting us'. See *Speech by Osagyefo Kwame Nkrumah at the opening of the Conference of Women of Africa*, on 18 July 1960, Accra, Government Printer. The fact that the independence of most of the black French countries later in 1960 did not imply any change in their attitude to France gave an added force to Nkrumah's view that a sinister force was at work.

150. Kwame Nkrumah *Consciencism*, op. cit. p. 102.

151. *N. A. Deb.*, Vol. 29, October 1962, col. 10.

152. Ibid.

153. Kwame Nkrumah, *Neo-colonialism*, op. cit. p. x.

154. *N. A. Deb.*, Vol. 29, 2 October 1962, col. 10.

155. *N. A. Deb.*, Vol. 24, 4 July 1961, col. 8.

156. *Blueprint for the future: Session Address by Osagyefor Dr Kwame Nkrumah at the State opening of the First Session of the Second Parliament of the Republic of Ghana on 24 August 1965.*

157. Except for the US loan of $9,643,000, all the loans for the Volta River project were raised at commercial rates of interest. See *The Volta River Project — the Volta River Authority, and the VALCO*, Vols. I & II; Seven-Year Plan op. cit. p. 204.

158. Kwame Nkrumah *Neo-colonialism*, op. cit. p. 241.

159. Ibid. p. 253.

160. We shall soon say more about union African government below.

161. This contained some exaggeration. For in spite of Dr Nkrumah's efforts to increase state participation in the economy, the bulk of the productive sector of the economy remained till the coup in private hands, private cocoa farmers and private giant foreign firms. Indeed, the Volta Aluminium Company (Valco) formed by two American companies, the Kaiser Aluminium Company and the Reynolds Metals Company, to smelt aluminium at Tema, were under the agreement signed with the Ghanaian government in 1962 exempted from all the exchange regulations introduced in 1961, and they were free from nationalization during their first thirty years of operation. See the *Volta River project Agreements*, Vol. II, Doc. 16.03g.

162. Kwame Nkrumah *Neo-colonialism*, op. cit. p. 253.

163. See NLC — *Nkrumah's Deception of Africa*, Accra, Government Printer 1966, pp. 19-26.

164. *N. A. Deb.*, Vol. 32, 21 June 1963, col. 75.

165. *West Africa*, 16 June 1962.

166. *Daily Times*, Lagos 6 September 1962.

167. *H. R. Deb.*, 21 August 1962, cols. 2484-5.

168. *Daily Graphic*, Accra 12 November 1966.

169. A few Ghanaians, including the members of the Justice Party opposition warned the government of the dangers of neo-colonialism which could result from excessive dependence on the Western Powers . See K. A. Karikari, 'Ghana's External Relations since the coup' in *Legon Observer*, February 17-2 March 1967. See Dr Obed Asamoah's speech in Parliament on Ghana's foreign policy on 2 December 1969, *N. A. Deb.*, 2 December 1969, col. 245.

170. In fact, the Nigerian leaders rarely used the word, neo-colonialism, but preferred to use other descriptive words for a situation which would be described by Nkrumah as neo-colonialist.

171. *Long Live Algeria/Nigeria Fraternal Relations And Cooperation: Text of Speech by His Excellency Major-General Yakubu Gowon, Head of the Federal Military Government, at Dinner Party held in His Honour by President Boumédienne of Algeria* on 26 August 1970, Lagos, Ministry of External Affairs, 1970.

172. OAU Council of Ministers — 17th Session Statement made by Dr Arikpo, the Commissioner for External Affairs on 18 June 1971 in *Nigeria: Bulletin on Foreign Affairs*, Vol. 1 No. 1, Lagos, Nigerian Institute of International Affairs July 1971.

173. *Text of the Speech of His Excellency Dr Okoi Arikpo, the Commissioner for External Affairs, before the UN General Assembly on 16 October 1970.*

174. *Third Summit Conference of Non-aligned Powers, Lusaka 8-10 September 1970: Statement by His Excellency Dr Okoi Arikpo, the Commissioner for External Affairs*, Lagos, Ministry of External Affairs, 1970.

175. The Nigerian government accorded General Amin's regime recognition mainly because it was clear that he was in full control and that the situation was virtually irreversible.

176. *Long Live Algeria/Nigeria Fraternal Relations And Cooperation*, Lagos, Ministry of External Affairs 1970, op. cit.

177. Nigerian-Sudanese Joint Communique issued on 31 August 1970 Lagos, Ministry of External Affairs.

178. *West Africa*, 22 October 1971.

179. See the *Joint Communique* at the end of General Gowon's visit to Kenya, 8-12 May 1971, Lagos, Ministry of External Affairs.

180. *Federal Government Estimates 1970-71.*

181. For further details see Olajide Aluko, 'The Civil War and Nigerian Foreign Policy' in the *Political Quarterly*, April 1971.

182. The top officials of the Nigerian Ministry of External Affairs said that more of such projects were being worked out between Nigeria and her neighbours.

183. See text of Dr Okoi Arikpo's Address to the UN General Assembly on 16 October 1970.

184. *Second National Development Plan 1970-4*, pp. 288-9.

185. Ibid. pp. 32 and 75 where public enterprises are described as 'crucial to Nigeria's quest for true national economic independence, and self-reliance'.

186. See *Dr Okoi Arikpo's Statement to Third Conference of Non-aligned Powers, Lusaka, September 8-10 1970.*

187. *West Africa*, 29 January 1966.

188. *Speech by Osagyefo Kwame Nkrumah at the opening of the Conference of Women of Africa*, on 18 July 1960, Accra, Government Printer.

189. *United We Stand*, Address delivered by Osagyefor Dr. Kwame Nkrumah, President of the Republic of Ghana, at the Conference of African Heads of States and Government, in Addis Ababa, on 24 May 1963, Supplement with *Ghana Today*, 5 June 1963.

190. Ibid.

191. Kwame Nkrumah *Consciencism*, op. cit. p. 118.

192. *Sunday Express*, Lagos, 27 May 1965. See also *Africa Research Bulletin*, May 1965, p. 291.

193. R. *IIA—Documents on International Affairs*, London 1960, p. 363.

194. *H. R. Deb.*, 24 November 1960, col. 370.

195. *Africa Diary*, 22-8 August 1964, pp. 916-17.

196. This agreement was not published until 1967 in Nkrumah's *Challenge of the Congo*, London 1967, pp. 30-1 for the text.

197. Kwame Nkrumah *Hands Off Africa*, op. cit. pp. 52-3.

198. *Ghana Today*, 17 June 1964.

199. Ibid.

200. *Ghana Today,*24 February 1965.

201. After the coup the NLC closed down the AATUF headquarters in Accra; they later moved to Dar es Salaam. The Ghana TUC also broke its ties with it.

202. Kwesi Armah *Africa's Golden Road*, London 1965, p. 7.

203. *Ghana Today*, 3 August 1960.

204. Kwesi Armah op. cit. p. 277.

205. Ibid. p. 24.

206. NLC—*Nkrumah's Subversion in Africa*, 1966, p. 44.

207. *N. A. Deb.*, Vol. 40, 10 September 1965, col. 687.

208. *N. A. Deb.*, Vol. 34, 7 November 1963, cols. 632-3.

209. *Ghana Today*, 24 February 1965.

210. There was provision for Pan-African cooperation in the Seven-Year Development Plan 1963-4 to 1969-70 pp. 15-17.

211. *N. A. Deb.*, Vol. 38, 26 March 1965, col. 1530.

212. Kwame Nkrumah *United We Stand*, op. cit.

213. *Africa Diary*, 22-8 August 1964, pp. 916-17.

214. *OAU Verbatim Records of the Plenary Meeting of the Second Ordinary Session of the Assembly of Heads of State and Government, Accra, 21-6 October 1965*, Addis Ababa 1965, pp. 9-10.

215. Ibid.

216. *Africa Diary*, 4-10 April 1964, p. 1693.

217. *Daily Times*, Lagos, 6 August 1962.

218. *Federal Nigeria*, Vol. 6 No. 2, 1963, p. 9.

219. *Second National Development Plan 1970–4*, p. 89.

220. *Africa Diary*, 28 September–4 October 1963, p. 1366.

221. *H. R. Deb.*, 18 September 1963, Col. 2948.

222. *Africa Research Bulletin*, June 1965, p. 326.

223. *H. R. Deb.*, 11 April 1963, cols. 1133–4.

224. We shall deal with these in some detail in the next chapter.

225. *Daily Times*, 15 November 1962.

226. *Second National Development Plan 1970/4*, p. 82.

227. It is outside the scope of this study to examine the achievements and failures of these Commissions.

228. In the 1969 Constitution there was no provision for surrendering Ghana's sovereignty to any supra-national body as there was in the Constitution of the First Republic.

219. For further details about the Pan-African policy of the Progress Government, see *Sessional Address by Brigadier A. A. Afrifa at the State Opening of the First Session of the First Parliament of the Second Republic in Accra on 2 October 1969*. Accra, Government printer, pp. 9–10.

CHAPTER IV

Ghana, Nigeria and the Organization of African Unity

Another source of discord between Ghana and Nigeria until early 1966 lay in their differing attitudes to the Organization of African Unity. This was understandable. The Charter of the OAU drew little from the Nkrumah proposals about African unity, whereas as rightly pointed out by Mr Jaja Wachuku about ninety per cent of its provisions were found in the Nigeria-sponsored Charter of the Afro-Malagasy Organization.[1] On his return from the OAU inaugural Conference, Sir Abubakar proudly told the nation in a broadcast that 'all the decisions reached (there) accord with the policies of the Federal Government'. He continued '. . . I am happy that our stand has been vindicated'.[2] The upshot of this was that while Dr Nkrumah remained extremely critical of the OAU, which he later said in 1965 was incapable of being 'an effective instrument of achieving African aspirations',[3] the Nigerian leaders held the view that the OAU was the best form of association possible at that time, and should therefore be strengthened.

But after the overthrow of the Nkrumah regime Ghana changed her attitude profoundly by adopting a policy towards the OAU similar to that of Balewa's Nigeria. While there were no fundamental changes in Nigeria's attitude to the OAU as a result of the coup d'état of January 1966, there were some changes of emphasis and of detail in her attitude to the Organization. Because of all this, we shall consider their attitudes to the OAU under two separate sections: the first dealing with the pre-coup days, and the second with the period after.

In dealing with this subject, we shall consider their attitudes to the OAU Liberation Committee, an African High Command and an African Common Market. The reasons for this are not far to seek. The question of liberation was one on which all the African countries were united, and the liberation committee of the OAU occupied a central place in this task. For instance, in June 1971 while a budget of about £1.4 million was approved by the Assembly of Heads of State and Government for the regular budget of the OAU,[4] the approved budget of the liberation committee was about £1 million.[5] The question of an African High Command and of an African Common Market had long been live issues in African politics and with the OAU. The establishment of an African Common Market was prominent in most of the discussions of the Casablanca and the Monrovia Powers between 1961 and May 1963. Although only the Casablanca Powers spoke of an African High Command, the Monrovia Powers discussed various defence arrangements for their own security. Apart from the various OAU Summit conferences, the issue of an African High Command had featured prominently at the meetings of the OAU Defence Commission, while that of an African Common Market had formed the subject of discussions at the meetings of the Economic and Social Commission of the Organization.[6]

(i) (a) LIBERATION COMMITTEE: I

Ghana and Nigeria were united in their support for the aim of the Liberation Committee, which was the co-ordination of all aid to all the freedom fighters in Africa. The disagreement between them arose over such things as the composition, organization and administration of the committee, its policies and its activities, its finances and its banking policy.

When the committee was set up in Addis Ababa in May 1963 it consisted of nine member states, namely Algeria, Congo (Kinshasa) (later the Republic of Zaire), Egypt, Guinea, Ethiopia, Nigeria, Senegal, Tanganyika (later Tanzania) and Uganda.[7] The exclusion of Ghana from this committee was seen by Mr Jaja Wachuku as a defeat for Ghana's brand of anti-colonial policy. Reporting to the Parliament on 1 August 1963, Jaja Wachuku said in an arrogant manner that the Liberation Committee was set up as a result of one of Nigeria's proposals to the Assembly of African Heads of State and Government at Addis Ababa; and added, evidently referring to Ghana though not mentioning her by name, that there were 'a number of countries that used to make a big noise about themselves, but they were not nominated to serve on the Committee of Nine'.[8]

Ghana felt slighted by her exclusion for two main reasons. Firstly, she had been the most consistent spokesman for the nationalists since 1957. Secondly, Dr Nkrumah's proposals at the Addis Ababa Summit where the liberation committee was set up were the most far-reaching. To liberate the whole of Africa now, he said:

It is . . . imperative for us here and now to establish a Liberation bureau for African freedom fighters. The main object of this bureau, to which all our Government should subscribe, should be to accelerate the emancipation of the rest of Africa still under colonial and racialist domination, and oppression. It should be our joint responsibility to finance and support this bureau.[9]

Apart from this Dr Nkrumah thought that the committee should have been made up of radical African countries genuinely committed to the liberation struggle. Therefore, the pro-West countries like the Congo (later Zaire) of Cyrille Adoula, Balewa's Nigeria, Senegal and even Ethiopia ought not to have been members.

Furthermore, Dr Nkrumah did not like the administration of the Liberation Committee. The four top officials of the Liberation Committee's secretariat at Dar es Salaam, namely the executive secretary and the three assistant secretaries, were *de facto* to come from the member states of the committee with Tanzania nominating the executive secretary.[10] Moreover, the secretariat was to work under the general direction of three standing sub-committees of the Committee of Nine, namely General Policy, Defence and Finance.[11] The OAU Secretariat at Addis Ababa and the Assembly of Heads of State and Government had virtually no influence on the executive secretariat at Dar es Salaam. Mr Jaja Wachuku confirmed this by saying that by appointing Nigeria as the Chairman of the General Policy Committee 'the effective determination of the course of action in this matter (of decolonization) is more or less squarely resting on our shoulders'.[12] He added 'when the Committee of Nine is meeting the General Policy Committee is responsible to (sic) direct affairs'.[13] In these circumstances, the chances of Ghana influencing the policies of the Liberation Committee were very slight.

Because of all this Ghana from the start refused to support the Liberation Committee, preferring instead direct assistance to the freedom fighters. Thus while by early July 1963 Nigeria had voluntarily made the largest single contribution, of £110,000,[14] to the special fund of the Committee, in accordance with the decision of the Assembly of Heads of State and Government in Addis Ababa in May 1963 that by 15 July 1963 all African countries should have made voluntary contributions to the liberation fund, Ghana, the darling of the freedom fighters, refused to pay anything to it. At the Cairo Summit of the OAU in July 1964, where a majority of the Heads of State and Government decided in favour of making contributions to the special fund compulsory for all members in the same proportion as their contributions to the regular budget of the OAU, which was based on a UN scale of assessment, the Ghanaian delegates boycotted the discussion.[15]

In spite of this decision by the majority of the African states, Ghana refused to make her contribution. During much of this time the Nigerian Government spokesmen at various OAU Summit meetings continued to appeal to countries who had not paid their contributions to the special fund to do so, thereby trying to hit at Ghana, and a few months before the OAU Summit Conference in Accra in October 1965, Ghana to save herself any diplomatic embarrassment paid up.[16] Had she not done so by the time the conference began, she would have laid herself open to a charge of working against the OAU. This was what Dr Nkrumah wanted to avoid. He wished his government and his newspapers to be free to criticize the work of the Liberation Committee, and this they continued to do before, during and even after the Conference.

Another major source of disagreement between Ghana and Nigeria was over the policies of the Liberation Committee. Dr Nkrumah wanted the Committee to support only African freedom fighters led by radical leaders who were likely to establish a 'socialist' state and who would support his idea of a Union African Government after the attainment of independence. Furthermore, to him any collaboration between the freedom fighters and puppet regimes, or pro-West African governments, would be disastrous to the liberation movement.

On the other hand, the goodwill mission of the Liberation Committee headed by Nigeria to Leopoldville (later Kinshasa) made certain recommendations on 18 July 1963 which were later that month accepted by the OAU Council of Ministers in Dakar, Senegal. The most important of these were the following: all aid to the Angolan freedom fighters should be channelled through the Government of the Congo (later Zaire) with the collaboration of the Liberation Committee; the Angolan National Liberation Front (FLNA) of Holden Roberto should be recognized as the only fighting front in the struggle for Angolan independence; all African governments should offer aid to the FLNA, and not to the other organization claiming to fight for Angolan independence, that is, the Popular Front for the Liberation of Angola led by Dr Augostino Neto; and finally all the OAU countries should recognize the government of Mr Holden Roberto in exile.[17]

All this met with scathing criticism in Ghana. The way was led by the *Spark*. In a front-page editorial the *Spark* condemned the Liberation Committee for exceeding its mandate, which merely provided for giving assistance to the liberation movements and not for running them or for entrusting them to a single neighbouring state.[18] It described the decision of the Committee to give the Adoula government the power to guide the activities of the Angolan freedom fighters as *ultra vires*. The paper further said that the Committee acted contrary to its mandate by recognizing only one nationalist movement in each territory. The decision to recognize the Angolan Provisional Government in exile (GRAE) of Mr Holden Roberto was regarded as an action taken by the Committee because it had 'succumbed to the blackmail of the Adoula Government'. It then went on to say that '. . . there can be no doubt whatever that imperialism has cast its net wide around the Liberation Committee'.[19]

At the OAU Summit Conference in Cairo on 19 July 1964, Dr Nkrumah himself made a ringing denunciation of the Committee of Nine. He said there was 'general dissatisfaction . . . regarding the functioning of this Committee . . .' The choice of the Congo (Leopoldville) as a training base for freedom fighters was a logical one, and there was every reason to accept the offer of the Congolese Government to provide offices and accommodation for the representatives of the Liberation Committee.

What could be the result of entrusting the training of freedom fighters against imperialism into the hands of an imperialist agent? Under the Liberation Committee set up at Addis Ababa, the freedom fighters had no real security, and were not provided with instruments for their struggle, nor were food, clothing, and medicine given for the men in training. Thus, their training scheme collapsed within two months under the eyes of the Liberation Committee, and the freedom fighters became disappointed, disgruntled and frustrated.'[20]

The reasons for the Ghanaian attacks[21] were clear from the *Spark's* criticism earlier referred to. By entrusting the task of guiding the liberation movements in Angola into the hands of the Adoula government the Liberation Committee, as far as Dr Nkrumah was concerned, had betrayed the freedom fighters. For to him the Adoula government was a puppet of the Americans and the Belgians. Furthermore, the influence of the US Central Intelligence Agency (CIA) was then very powerful in Leopoldville (later Kinshasa).[22] By recognizing the Holden Roberto Provisional Government in exile, the Liberation Committee was assisting conservative and anti-socialist forces. It must be remembered that Holden Roberto's FLNA was largely dependent on the Western governments, voluntary organizations and conservative African governments for arms and funds, while the rival party, the MPLA of

Dr Neto, relied largely on the East European countries and the former Casablanca Powers for aid.[23] Indeed, because of this Mr Holden Roberto had accused Dr Neto of being backed by the Communists.[24]

The provision of assistance to the freedom fighters in the former British High Commission territories provided another occasion for conflict between Nigeria and Ghana in 1965. The Nigerian Government wanted the Liberation Committee and other agencies to stop all assistance to the nationalists in the three territories because the British government had already agreed to grant independence to them, and representative governments working for full self-government had been installed in all three places by late 1965.[25] But the Ghanaian Government said aid to the freedom fighters there should continue because the governments installed in the three High Commission territories were puppet regimes imposed by South Africa.[26]

On the eve of the OAU Summit in Accra in October 1965 the *Ghanaian Times* came out with a leader in which it attacked the Liberation Committee for its ineptitude and for acting *ultra vires* by applying rigidly the principle of recognizing only one liberation movement in any one territory.[27] Another reason for the Ghanaian criticism of the Liberation Committee was its use of Barclays Bank DCO as its banker. To the Ghanaian leadership this was fatal to the effectiveness of liberation movements in Africa. As the *Spark* put it as long as the Liberation Committee continued to use Barclays Bank DCO as its banker, it would have no secrets, and all its plans would always be sabotaged by the imperialists.[28]

The Nigerian Government did not see anything wrong in using Barclays Bank DCO. Indeed, most of the Ghanaian attacks against the Liberation Committee were regarded by Nigeria as groundless,[29] and as no more than a sullen reaction by Ghana to her exclusion from the Committee. Nigeria's usual reply to Ghana's criticism was that all countries should pay their contributions to the special fund of the Committee.

(b) African High Command: I
The history of an African High Command can be traced back to the first meeting of the All-African People's Conference in Accra in December 1958. In one of its resolutions it called for the establishment of an African legion to defend 'the freedom of the African people.'[30] Since then Dr Kwame Nkrumah had been advocating the setting up of an African High Command, especially

from late 1960 onwards when the Congo (later Zaire) crisis demonstrated the powerlessness of the African countries to defend their independence.

As conceived by Dr Nkrumah the objectives of an all-embracing African High Command were threefold. The first was the defence of independent African states. Indeed Mr Kofi Baako, then the Ghanaian Defence Minister, extended this point by saying that 'the survival (of Africans) as a race depended upon it' (i.e. an African High Command).[31] Basic to the thinking of the CPP leaders was that no single independent African country could on its own ward off any imperialist aggression. The second was the removal of Africa from the cold war pressure made inevitable as a result of military pacts between some African countries and some Nato Powers. The High Command would make such pacts and foreign bases in Africa unnecessary.[32] The third was to spearhead the liberation of areas under colonial and white supremacist regimes in Africa.

The Balewa government had little or nothing to offer as the objectives of an African High Command. Prior to early 1963 it did not give any serious thought to such a Command.[33] Sir Abubakar did not mention anything about an African High Command in his address to the Assembly of African Heads of State and Government in Addis Ababa on 24 May 1963. When his government was forced to say something about it at the first meeting of the OAU Defence Commission in Accra between 29 October and 2 November 1963, its spokesman there, Mr M. T. Mbu, then the Federal Minister of State in charge of the Navy, said that Africa did not require any High Command to protect independent states. This was because, he argued in a naive way, no external Power would endanger the security of any African state as such an act would be inconsistent with the Charter of the United Nations.[24] Furthermore, he argued that bilateral arrangements had been made between many African countries to defend their independence, sovereignty and territorial integrity to fulfil Article II, 1(c) of the OAU Charter. The only purpose which an African Force could serve according to him was to assist in the liberation of areas under colonial and racist rule; and even then, this did not require the type of High Command advocated by the Ghanaian leaders.

Although Sir Abubakar and his colleagues had nothing but contempt for the idea of an African High Command, it still led to a most critical confrontation between Ghana and Nigeria at the first meeting of the OAU Defence Commission in Accra, late in 1963. Both countries presented separate proposals on the African Defence

Organization to the meeting of the Defence Commission and these were described as 'contradictory' by the Senegalese representative on the Commission, Captain Sarazin.[35]

The Ghanaian proposals contained in document DEF1/Memo.3 addendum which was introduced by Brigadier (later Lt.-General) J. A. Ankrah, later the first Chairman of the NLC after the coup, and ably supported by Brigadier (later Major-General) Barwah, provided for the following: firstly for the establishment of a military organization controlled by one military authority, a Supreme Command Headquarters to be responsible to the Assembly of Heads of State and Government, and secondly for the setting up of the Union Joint Services Supreme Military Command Headquarters and of Regional Command Headquarters. Largely because the Ghanaian government did not have much faith in the OAU, its spokesman, Brigadier Ankrah, said the Joint Service Military Command Headquarters should be sited not at the OAU Secretariat, but somewhere close to it.[36] Furthermore, there were provisions for the formation of a Union Strike Force to serve as a deterrent to any possible aggressor and for a Joint Intelligence Organization.

Brigadier Barwah said the Supreme Command Headquarters would be responsible to the Defence Commission for the collective security of Africa; and that it was the Commission that should appoint the commanders for the Supreme Command Headquarters and the Regional Command Headquarters. The Commission was to give policy directives to the Union Joint Services Supreme Military Command Headquarters about plans for operations and training, and recommendations for equipment and weapon standardization. It was also to make recommendations about the siting of military bases and installations, methods of transportation, and movement of troops for the defence of Africa.[37] Brigadier Barwah said that although to implement all this might require all African countries to tax themselves the result would be a better tomorrow for all of them. He then went on to stress the need to establish the Supreme Command Headquarters 'here and now.'[38] He argued that a strategic reserve force to be raised by contributions from member states was necessary 'now',[39] for any delay would be disastrous to the whole concept of an African High Comand.

The Nigerian government's proposals, document DEFI/Memo.4 dated 31 October 1963, introduced by Mr M. T. Mbu, were more modest. Firstly, they provided for the establishment of a permanent body consisting of men from the three main branches of the armed forces in the OAU Secretariat to deal with defence problems.

Secondly, regional committees made up of Service Chiefs of Staff of the four regions into which Africa was usually divided for the sake of convenience, namely West, East, Central, and North Africa, were to be set up to formulate plans for possible military action in their respective regions.

Apart from all this, the document distinguished between two different types of High Command, and showed why Nigeria preferred one to the other. All these points were repeated and re-empahsized by Mr Mbu on 30 October 1963 while introducing his government's proposals. The first type was a unified command with some supra-national authority, which was being advocated by Ghana; and the second was a central military planning system. Mr Mbu argued that under the latter there would be no integration of forces nor any assignment of troops; each nation would retain control over its own forces, ordering them into action if necessary at the request of the central planning headquarters. He said Nigeria preferred this central planning system because it left the country fully in control of its own armed forces and their operation. But the unified type of command could not appeal to his government for three main reasons. First, it involved some loss of sovereignty, second, the cost of having such a command was prohibitive, and third, it was bedevilled by other problems such as manpower, equipment and weapon standardization, problems of logistics, unified training, deployment of troops, and the appointment of the Supreme Commander etc.[40]

During the discussion on 1 November 1963 Mr Mbu made a sweeping attack on the Ghanaian proposals. First he condemned them for calling for what he described as 'a substantial loss of sovereignty by member states'.[41] He went on to say that in view of the poverty of many African states the Ghanaian proposals which 'would cost millions of pounds'[42] were 'too lavish' and 'unrealistic'.[43] He blasted the Ghanaian proposal for a strike force which he mistakenly understood to mean a 'nuclear-equipped strike force'.[44]

Apart from Brigadier Ankrah's statement that 'we should not think too much of sovereignty but how to defend Africa against enemies within and without',[45] the Ghanaians played it cool. In order to achieve unanimity which Mr Asante, one of the Ghanaian delegates to the Defence Commission said was the hope of the Ghanaian government, a compromise arrangement acceptable to all was worked out by Ghana after consultation with all the heads of various delegates. The compromise agreement provided for the setting up of a small permanent military headquarters in the OAU Secretariat at

Addis Ababa, that the headquarters should be empowered to carry out the planning and liaison duties of the Defence Commission and to recommend to the Commission methods of raising troops in times of emergency, and that regional headquarters be established with only a small staff adequate for such functions as might be delegated to it by the main headquarters. Finally, it provided for the establishment of other military branches necessary for the effctive functioning of the defence organization.[46] Mr M. T. Mbu, the Nigerian spokesman at the Commission, applauded these revised Ghanaian proposals and said his delegation would join the Ghanaians in sponsoring them.[47]

All this was hardly more than papering over the cracks. Dr Nkrumah agreed to such drastic revision of his government's proposal partly so as not to scare off the majority of the OAU member states by being too intransigent on an issue of which he was the protagonist, and partly because he wanted the first meeting of the Defence Commission to leave Accra with something positive to work with. He remained unshaken in his belief in his original brand of an African High Command as the best for Africa. Soon the army mutinies in East Africa late in January 1964 and the swift despatch of the British troops to restore order there provided the opportunity for Nkrumah to renew his call for an African High Command. The *Ghanaian Times* said the incident showed clearly that security in Africa could not be maintained on individual state basis, and that an African High Command could have made it unnecessary for the East African countries to ask for British troops.[48] At the meeting of the OAU Council of Ministers that opened in Lagos on 24 February 1964, Mr Kojo Botsio, then the Ghanaian Foreign Minister, called for the immediate formation of a continental African army. He argued that only that type of force could intervene effectively in such issues as the recent border conflict between Somalia and Ethiopia, and the coups and mutinies elsewhere in Africa.[49] The Nigerian representative at the meeting, Jaja Wachuku, opposed this Ghanaian proposal. He asked who would finance such a force, what country would command it, and when would the force act?[50] When no agreement could be found, the Council merely referred the issue to the next OAU Summmit Conference in Cairo in July 1964.

At the Cairo Summit, the question of an African High Command was discussed, with Dr Nkrumah advocating it and Sir Abubakar opposing it.[51] On his return to Nigeria Balewa told the nation in a broadcast on 24 July 1964 that the majority of the OAU member states at Cairo had rejected the formation of a High Command as being 'premature'.[52]

With Ghana continuing to insist on an African High Command, the impatience of the Nigerian leaders grew with anything that looked like it. Thus the Nigerian representative at the second meeting of the Defence Commission of the OAU at Freetown in February 1965 criticized the Sierra Leonean proposal for an African Peace Force which had many features in common[53] with the central planning type of command recommended to other African countries by Nigeria at the first meeting of the Defence Commission in Accra late in 1963. The Nigerian representative said the Sierra Leonean proposal was designed to let 'the High Command in by the back door'.[54] He argued that bilateral agreements were the only practicable alternative to an African High Command,[55] and that his delegation wanted the question of an African High Command to be regarded as closed. Major-General (later Lt-General) J. A. Ankrah, the Ghanaian spokesman, argued that there was an urgent need to protect the sovereignty of African states, and to ward off 'dangers posed to Africa by South Africa, and Southern Rhodesia which were armed to the teeth'[56] by a continental military arrangement.[57] Although the Commission managed to work out finally a draft resolution[58] based on the Sierra Leonean proposal acceptable to the majority of the OAU member states, the meeting left Ghana and Nigeria as antagonistic as ever over the question of the High Command.

(c) *African Common Market: I*

In spite of the fact that the structure of the economy of the African states did not make an African Common Market a very attractive proposition,[59] both Ghana and Nigeria agreed on the need to establish one. Although the approaches of the Ghanaian and Nigerian leaders to the question were different in many ways, they all believed that an African Common Market would be of immense benefit to the continent.

To Dr Nkrumah an African Common Market using a common currency and operating a common external trade policy would be in the best interests of the whole of the African people. First he said it would eliminate competition among the African states in the bid to sell their primary products in the world market. In his book *Africa Must Unite* Dr Nkrumah specifically referred to the fact that although Ghana and Nigeria had been producing over fifty per cent of the world's cocoa, they could not influence the world prices of cocoa because they had been selling 'against each other'.[60] He then went on to say that under a united trade policy both countries would be able 'to undercut the tactics of the buyers who set us against the other'.[61] Under an African Common Market system therefore, the Africans would obtain better prices for their products. Furthermore, it would eliminate the difficulties of exchange, and what Dr Nkrumah called 'illegitimate trade dealings'[62] in Africa. An African Common Market would also attract into the continent more foreign investment, and would also promote the growth of great industrial complexes[63] in Africa. Finally Nkrumah believed that it would turn Africa into an economic giant as powerful as any of the existing economic giants such as the United States, the Soviet Union, West Germany or Britain.

At the inaugural Conference of the OAU in Addis Ababa in May 1963, Sir Abubakar gave four reasons why his government was in favour of an African Common Market. The first was that it would boost inter-African trade; the second was that it would help Africa to overcome many economic difficulties; the third was that it would enable Africa to stand on its own economically as did other parts of the world; and the fourth was that it would prevent the danger of being 'colonized' economically.[64]

In spite of this broad agreement between Ghana and Nigeria on the objectives of an African Common Market their approach to it was different. While Ghana had taken some bilateral steps to improve trade with other African countries, such as the customs abolition agreement with Upper Volta in June 1961, and the trade and payment agreement reached in principle with Dahomey on 25 June 1961,[65] Dr Nkrumah believed that the question had to be tackled on a Pan-African basis, as contained in the joint communique issued at the end of the meeting of the leaders of Ghana, Guinea and Mali at Bamako on 26 June 1961[66] and the Charter of their Union called the Union of African States (UAS).

To Dr Nkrumah the African Common Market had to be considered along with the formation of a Union African Government. Indeed, he believed that only the latter could genuinely establish the former. Thus in May 1963 at the OAU Inaugural Conference at Addis Ababa, where he strongly advocated the formation of a Union Government of Africa, he also proposed that a commission of such a Union Government should work out a continent-wide plan for a unified, or common, economic and industrial programme for Africa.[67] The plan should contain proposals for the establishment of a common market for Africa, African currency, an African monetary zone, an African Central Bank, and a continental communication system.[68]

In contrast to this, Nigeria believed that the only practical way to establish an African common market was through bilateral and multilateral economic and commercial arrangements between states. Thus Sir Abubakar told the Assembly of African Heads of State and Government at Addis Ababa in May 1963 that it was unrealistic to try to establish an African Common Market 'by taking the continent as a whole'.[69] He said it must be based on regional groupings such as North, West, East and Central African grouping.[70]

In furtherance of this policy Alhaji Usman Angulu Ahmed, then the Federal Parliamentary Secretary to the Ministry of Commerce and Industry, said in March 1964 that the Government had taken the following steps. The first was the establishment of a common customs post between Nigerian and Dahomey by the Customs Conventions of 1962.[71] The second was the agreement of 1963 for the establishment of joint customs posts between Nigeria, Dahomey and Togo. The third was the Nigeria-Cameroons trade agreement of 1963. The fourth was the agreement with the riparian states of the Niger and Lake Chad for joint development purposes. Finally, he said the government had been establishing telecommunications links with the neighbouring countries to facilitate contacts between them and Nigeria.[72]

Although the different approaches of Ghana and Nigeria to the question of an African Common Market caused some suspicion and mistrust between them, they did not result in any major antagonism. This was partly because neither of them took an extreme position at the meetings of the OAU Economic and Social Commission at Niamey in 1964 and at Cairo in January 1965, where the question of economic integration in Africa was discussed, and partly because the majority of the OAU member states believed that the regional and continental approaches were complementary.[73] In fact, the usual title given to the question of economic integration in Africa by the OAU Economic and Social Commission was the 'possibility of creating continental and regional unions'[74] thereby combining the Ghanaian and the Nigerian approaches.

But the meeting of the OAU Council of Ministers in Accra in October 1965 saw some friction between Ghana and Nigeria over the discussion of the resolution[75] of the Economic and Social Commission on economic integration in Africa. This resolution adopted by the Economic and Social Commission in its meeting at Cairo in January 1965 merely called *inter alia* for efforts to create a free trade area in Africa, a joint external tariff, an African payments union, an African trade union and the harmonization of national development schemes.[76] The Nigerian representative told the Council of Ministers not to adopt the resolution, but to ask the Commission to give it further consideration.[77] Immediately he was opposed by the Ghanaian spokesman who said that the Council should adopt it, and that the resolution had been earlier discussed and approved by the Economic and Social Commission at Cairo in January 1965 where Nigeria was represented. He then called on the Ministers to adopt the resolution because it did not require the establishment of a Union Government as some (referring to Nigeria) feared.[78]

But this was more or less a tactical manoeuvre to disarm the Nigerian representative. For in his impassioned address to the OAU Assembly of Heads of State and Government a few days later in Accra, Dr Nkrumah reiterated his usual call for an African Common Market on a pan-African basis, and that this could only come about with the establishment of a Continental Union Government. He went on to say that although 'some half-hearted attempts at economic co-operation had been made', they would not go much further 'without a political machinery'.[79] He then added that with courage on the part of all the African leaders all this was possible. Although there was an element of truth in this,[80] the Nigerian government's attitude to it was to dismiss it as one of the unrealistic proposals of Nkrumah.

(ii) (a) **LIBERATION COMMITTEE: II**

As earlier indicated, after the coup of 24 February 1966 Ghana changed its attitude to the Organization of African Unity. Instead of the past contemptuous attitude to the Organization, Ghana accepted it as the best possible form of association for African countries. The Progress Government, like its predecessor the NLC, had faith in the Charter of the OAU and its institutions. Indeed, in many ways Ghana's attitudes to the OAU after the unseating of the Nkrumah regime were, as pointed out earlier, similar to those of Balewa's Nigeria to the Organization. Although while, as earlier stated, Nigeria since the overthrow of the Balewa Government did not change its basic attitudes to the OAU, it nonetheless tried to look at the Organization more critically than ever before, with a view to making some minor changes that would make it work better. The former attitude of Nigeria under the Balewa Administration that the OAU as set up at Addis Ababa in May 1963 should not be tampered with, on the moot assumption that if things were left on their own they would work themselves out, was jettisoned. Furthermore, the restrained approach of Sir Abubakar to such African issues as colonialism and racism in Africa was replaced by a more radical style while Ghana's approach to them moderated after the coup of February 1966. It was this kind of minor difference that could be said to have been responsible for the disagreements in their attitudes to the OAU between early 1966 and 1970.

Shortly after the seizure of power by the army and the police in Ghana in February 1966, the NLC government announced its faith in the OAU Charter, and it promised to pay the country's contributions to the special fund of the Liberation Committee, part of which was only grudgingly paid by the CPP regime shortly before the OAU Summit in Accra in October 1965. Unlike the Nkrumah regime, contributions to the liberation fund became the only concrete support given to freedom fighters by Ghana. Although largely because of financial difficulties, the Ghanaian government had been unable to make its contributions on time,[81] it had continued to make efforts to pay up its arrears. In the 1971-2 estimates, the government made a provision of about N₵260,000[82] or just about £65,000 sterling to the special fund of the Liberation Committee which represented 4.73 per cent of the total budget of the Committee allocated to Ghana.

Not only had Nigeria been paying her contributions of £N84,000,[83] or about 6.99 per cent of the total budget of the Liberation Committee, thereby making Nigeria the third largest contributor after Egypt and Libya,[84] she had been advocating an increase in the volume of financial assistance given to the Liberation Committee.[85] In February 1969, the Nigerian delegate told the meeting of the Council of Ministers that his country was prepared to grant more money to the Liberation Committee if requested.[86] Likewise at the OAU Council of Ministers in June 1971, Dr Okoi Arikpo made a strong appeal for an increase in the budget of the Liberation Committee. He described its budget of about £1 million approved a few days earlier as 'a pathetically paltry budget' which 'would not cover more than a day's expenditure for a moderate army.'[87] On the other hand, Ghana who only managed with difficulty to make her contribution could hardly be expected to favour an increase in the budget.

Shortly after the coup, the NLC Government recognized all the liberation movements, including the Angolan Revolutionary Government of Holden Roberto (GRAE)[88] recognized by the majority of the OAU. But Nigeria which had since late 1963 recognized Holden Roberto's GRAE began from late 1968 to be critical of it. At the meeting of the Council of Ministers held in Addis Ababa in February 1969, the Nigerian representative spoke against the GRAE for lack of effectiveness, and said that the funds given to it by the

Executive Secretariat of the Liberation Committee ought not to have been given.[89] It was perhaps this type of criticism that led the OAU Council of Ministers at its seventeenth session in Addis Ababa in June 1971 to withdraw its recognition from the GRAE.[90]

Another point of disagreement between Ghana and Nigeria was the question of how to improve the work of the Liberation Committee. Ghana believed that this could only be done if more and more states were directly associated with the Committee.[91] But Nigeria said this was a wrong approach, and that the way to improve the Committee's work lay in increasing the level of efficiency of its Executive Secretariat.[92] Furthermore, Nigeria felt that the Committee's work could be more properly done if its administration were decentralized. Thus the Nigerian representative at the OAU Council of Ministers, Dr Arikpo, proposed at the seventeenth session of the Council in Addis Ababa in June 1971 that a Regional Office of the Executive Secretariat should be opened in Conakry in order to co-ordinate its aid to the PAIGC of Guinea-Bissau.[93]

(b) African High Command: II

With the dismissal of the Nkrumah regime the question of an African High Command disappeared as an important factor in Ghanaian and African politics. Since then the question of an African High Command had become anathema in Ghana. Neither the Ghanaian press nor her leaders, including Lt.-General Ankrah who became the NLC chairman from the coup in February 1966 till April 1969 and who under the Nkrumah regime had been one of the most important Ghanaian spokesmen on the subject, would have anything to do with it. To the newspapers any talk of a Pan-African military command was an indulgence in wishful thinking.[94] To the Progress Government leaders the question of a High Command was one of the quixotic ideas of the ex-President, Dr Kwame Nkrumah, and it should be, with him, forgotten.[95]

Likewise, at the various OAU Summit Conferences, the question of an African High Command was for some time after the overthrow of Dr Nkrumah's government relegated to the background. Indeed, the Defence Commission which provided the main focus for the discussion of African defence problems was not revived after its second session in 1965 at Freetown, Sierra Leone, until September 1970 in Addis Ababa[96] in order to meet the growing menace posed to Africa by the white supremacist regimes in Southern Africa.[97]

At its meeting in December 1970 in Lagos, held simultaneously with the extraordinary session of the OAU Council of Ministers on the invasion of Guinea, the Defence Commission discussed the proposal for an African High Command. The Ghanaian delegate on the Commission spoke strongly against it in view of the political, administrative and technical difficulties in the way of such a Command. On the other hand, the Nigerian representative while not being rigid on an African High Command insisted that the Commission should take immediate practical measures to set up some form of defence arrangement that would be sufficiently viable to deter future aggressors such as the Portuguese.[98]

Although the Defence Commission rejected the formation of a High Command and instead recommended 'the creation of Regional Defence Units which will consist of national armed forces within the various Regions in Africa and which could be placed at the disposal of the OAU for use whenever the need arises,'[99] Nigeria after the end of the civil war turned round to accept the idea of an African High Command. Thus in March 1970 Brigadier (later Major-General) Hassan Usman Katsina, then the Chief of Staff of the Nigerian Army, said that Nigeria was in favour of setting up an African High Command to speed up the collapse of the white minority ruled regimes in Africa.[100] The same view was accepted in principle by General Gowon though he was always careful to point out the difficulties facing the formation of such a continental Command.[101] In his address to the seminar organized for top army officers in July 1971, Dr Arikpo said the Government accepted in principle the formation of an African High Command.[102] All the Nigerian newspapers were unanimous in their call for the formation of an African High Command. The *Daily Times*, the leading advocate of the High Command, on the eve of the OAU Summit Conference in Addis Ababa in September 1970 called on the African leaders to accept 'now' the idea of an African High Command which they had cold shouldered when proposed by Dr Nkrumah in 1964.[103]

But while the Nigeria leaders accepted the Nkrumah idea of an African High Command, they were, unlike him, realistic enough to know that such a Command could not be set up immediately because of the enormous political, administrative, financial and technical problems that had to be tackled before its formation. Thus Brigadier Olufemi Olutoye, the leader of the Nigerian delegation to the recent OAU Defence Commission meeting in Mogadishu, Somalia, told reporters in Lagos on his return that the African High Command could not be established until the near future.[104] But the Nigerian leaders after the end of of the civil war stressed that the absence of the High Command was due to the unco-operative attitude of other

African countries. Thus, Alhaji Baba Gana, then the Permanent Secretary of the Ministry of External Affairs, told the seminar of top army officers that 'unless all the leaders of African nations become real Africans, the question of setting up of an African High Command will be difficult.[105] In the same vein, Brigadier Olufemi Olutoye later said that if there was the political will on the part of other African countries, an African High Command could easily be formed.[106]

Among the African countries hostile to the idea and who would not therefore co-operate was seen to be Ghana. Because of this the editor of the *Nigerian Observer* in September 1971 went to interview General Aferi, then the Ghanaian High Commissioner in Nigeria, about his country's attitude to the question of an African High Command. General Aferi said, among other things, that there were several pre-conditions to the formation of an African High Command. There should be a clear charter for command procedure, location and standardization of weapons and equipment.[107] He then added that other major problems such as language, finance and sovereignty[108] would have to be resolved before the formation of such a Command.

(c) *African Common Market: II*

After the coup of 24 February 1966, Ghana's approach to an African Common Market changed. Instead of the continental approach of Dr Nkrumah, a sub-regional[109] approach was preferred. So Ghana began to concentrate on fostering economic integration in West Africa. In spite of the various trade agreements between Nigeria and many non-West African states such as Egypt, Algeria, the Sudan, Ethiopia, Kenya and the Central African Republic, most of which were signed mainly for political reasons during General Gowon's visit to these countries between mid-1970 and mid-1971, Nigeria still believed that only a sub-regional approach to the question of an African Common Market was realistic, as stated in the joint communique[110] by President Ould Daddah and General Gowon issued at the end of the latter's visit to Mauritania late in February 1971.[111]

It was expected that this common approach by Ghana and Nigeria to the question of an African Common Market would make it easy for them to co-operate. Another factor making for their co-operation in this field was the fact that both countries wanted the West African associates of the European Economic Community (EEC) to abolish the reverse preferences[112] they had granted to the EEC countries, and to abolish their tariff and non-tariff barriers in order to promote intra-West African trade.[113]

Apart from signing bilateral trade agreements with their immediate neighbours, both Ghana and Nigeria worked together at the various conferences on economic integration in West Africa between late 1966 and early 1968. It is important to note that these conferences were sponsored by the Economic Commission for Africa (ECA)[114] rather than by the OAU Economic and Social Commission. This was partly because the latter was paralysed for nearly three years following the political bitterness and frustration arising from the series of coups that swept away many African regimes between late 1965 and early 1966. Other contributory causes to this paralysis were their inability to do anything about the Rhodesian question, and the division of the African states over the Nigerian civil war between July 1967 and January 1970. In addition the ECA was part of the United Nations, their work was largely technical rather than political in nature and they were found more acceptable to the majority of the African states.

The first of these conferences, which were intended to lead to what the ECA called a West African Community consisting of fourteen countries, namely, Dahomey, Gambia, Ghana, Guinea, Ivory Coast, Liberia, Mali, Mauritania, Niger, Nigeria, Senegal, Sierra Leone, Togo and Upper Volta, took place at official level in Niamey, Niger, in November 1966.[115] This was followed up in April 1967 with another meeting in Accra where they signed Articles of Association of a West African Common Market described by the ECA as 'a transitional agreement governing the means of co-operation between the member states prior to the formal establishment of a West African Community'.[116] By signing these Articles, Ghana and Nigeria as well as other signatory states committed themselves to 'endeavour to formulate and adopt common policies, including specific branches of industry and agriculture, the joint operation of specific transport and communication services, the development and use in common of sources of energy, joint research, training of manpower and the joint implementation of all other projects designed to promote the objectives of the (West African) Community, as well as of common trade and payment arrangements'.[117]

Likewise, at the West African meeting in Dakar in November 1967, there was not much difference between the Ghanaian and the Nigerian proposals. This was the case, too, at the first West African Summit Conference[118] at Monrovia between 23 and 24 April 1968, which was preceded by a preliminary ministerial meeting in the

Liberian capital from 17 to 21 April 1968. At the end of their meeting the Heads of State and Government signed on 24 April 1968 a Protocol establishing the West African Regional Group.[119] According to Article 2 of its Treaty, the West African Regional Group was to establish a common market. It, therefore, made provision for the abolition of tariffs and quantitative restrictions among member countries, for establishing a common external tariff against other countries and for ensuring factor movements in the sub-region.[120] Article 25 of the Treaty provided for the immediate establishment of a customs union to be followed by free factor movements for the purpose of the common market arrangement.[121]

Both Ghana and Nigeria were signatories to this Treaty. In spite of this, Ghana barely twenty months later took drastic measures through her Business Promotion Act and the Aliens Compliance Order to expel aliens, mainly Africans, most of whom had settled in Ghana for over fifty years, who were without residence and work permits. The worst hit West African country was Nigeria where over 140,000 of her nationals had been forcibly ejected from Ghana by early 1970, according to Mr Victor Adegoroye, then the Nigerian High Commissioner in Ghana,[122] without being given sufficient time to sell their immovable property, or being allowed to bring with them their movable possessions. The value of the Nigerian assets abandoned in Ghana was difficult to estimate. Some put it at more than £6 million. Mr Ladosu Ladapo, then the Western State Commissioner for Economic Planning and Reconstruction, put the value of the properties which those from the Western State alone were forced to abandon in Ghana as about £2.5 million.[123] The fact that most of the Nigerians expelled from Ghana were molested and man-handled by the police and Ghanaian civilians alike made the matter worse. What made the whole exercise look more hostile was that it took place early in December 1969 when the Nigerian civil war was entering its critical stage. It was perhaps this more than anything else that sharpened the anger generated in Nigeria at the wholesale expulsion of Nigerians from Ghana.[124]

These Ghanaian measures convinced the Nigerians that Ghana was not really serious about any common market either for West Africa or for the whole of Africa. All the Nigerian newspapers were unanimous in their judgement that the expulsion of the African aliens was a deliberate attempt by Ghana to frustrate efforts at economic integration in West Africa.[125] This view was largely shared by the Nigerian leaders. Thus General Gowon warned at the OAU Summit Conference in Addis Ababa in September 1970 that the idea of

African unity and African economic co-operation would be worse
than useless if Africans from some states were not to be allowed to live
and work in other African countries and to compete with their
nationals.[126]

Thus we see that some attempts made between late 1966 and early
1968 by Ghana and Nigeria to co-operate in fostering economic links
and establishing a common market in West Africa had by December
1969 come to nothing because of the Ghanaian expulsion of a large
number of Nigerians. It was partly because of this, and partly
because of political difficulties between such countries as Guinea and
Ghana, Guinea and Senegal, and Sierra Leone and Ghana, together
with other factors such as the association of all the Francophone West
African countries except Guinea with the EEC, and the existence of
at least four different currency zones[127] in the area, that it was
virtually impossible for the West African Regional Group to advance
beyond the agreements reached in Monrovia in April 1968, which in
any case had hardly been implemented by any of them.

1. *H. R. Deb.*, 1 August 1963, col. 2455.

2. *MR PRIME MINISTER*, op. cit. p. 103.

3. *Africa Research Bulletin*, October 1965, p. 378.

4. *West Africa*, 9 July 1971.

5. Ibid.

6. Although the four main institutions of the OAU as laid down in the Charter were
   the Assembly of Heads of State and Government, the Council of Ministers, the
   General Secretariat and the Commission of Mediation, Conciliation and
   Arbitration, nothing very useful could be said about any of them in this study.
   Indeed, no action was taken to set up the Commission of Mediation,
   Conciliation, and Arbitration until October 1965. Even then the Commission
   did not meet until over two years later in December 1967 at Addis Ababa, See
   Africa Research Bulletin, December 1967, p. 924. Likewise, little could be said
   of the five commissions, namely economic and social; educational and cultural;
   health, sanitation, and nutrition; defence; and scientific, technical, and
   research set up under the OAU Charter. Some of them had not been able to
   meet for years for lack of a quorum. The frustration was so much that at the
   OAU Summit Conference of November 1966 it was suggested by many member
   states that the number of the commissions should be reduced to three, namely
   economic and social; education, cultural, and health; and defence. It was
   further said that even these should meet only once in two years. See *Africa
   Research Bulletin*, November 1966, p. 654. For further details about the
   failures of the OAU Commissions, see Catherine Hoskyns, 'Trends and
   Development in the Organization of African Unity' in *The Year Book of World
   Affairs*, London 1967, pp. 164-78.

7. At the Accra Summit of the OAU in October 1965 two other African countries,
   Somalia and Zambia, were appointed to serve on the liberation committee. See
   Africa Research Bulletin, October 1965, p. 379. At the Rabat Summit of June
   1972 the membership of the committee was increased to seventeen.

8. *H. R. Deb.*, 1 August 1963, col. 2459.

9. Kwame Nkrumah *United We Stand*, op. cit.

10. Since its establishment no national from any state but Tanzania has been
    appointed the executive secretary of the Liberation Committee.

11. *Africa Diary*, 27 July-2 August 1963, p. 1366.

12. *H. R. Deb.*, 1 August 1963, col. 2459.

13. Ibid.

14. Nigeria was followed by Egypt with £100,000, then Algeria with £70,000; £30,000 from Tanganyika; £21,430 from Ethiopia; and £10,000 from Uganda *Africa Diary*, September 7-13 1963, p. 1338.

15. *Africa Diary*, 22-8 August 1964, p. 915.

16. *Committee B—OAU Summary Records of the Fifth Ordinary Session of the Council of Ministers, October 1965*, Addis Ababa 1965, p. 6.

17. *Africa Diary*, 27 July-2 August 1963, p. 1268.

18. *Spark*, 25 October 1963. See also *Africa Diary*, 14-20 December 1963, p. 1492.

19. Ibid.

20. *Africa's Finest Hour, Text of the speech delivered by Osagyefo Dr Kwame Nkrumah, President of the Republic of Ghana at the Conference of African Heads of State and Government in Cairo on 19 July 1964*, Supplement to *Ghana Today*, 29 July 1964.

21. President Nyerere misunderstood Dr Nkrumah by attributing his attacks solely to Ghana's exclusion from the Liberation Committee. See *The Times*, London 21 July 1964.

22. D. C. Watt, 'America and Russia: The Rise of The Super Powers' in *International Affairs*, London November 1971, p. 33.

23. *Africa Diary*, 27 July-2 August 1963, p. 1268.

24. Ibid.

25. *Committee B—OAU Summary Records of the Fifth Ordinary Session of the Council of Ministers at Accra, October 1965*, Addis Ababa 1965, p. 2.

26. Ibid. p. 6.

27. *The Ghanaian Times*, Accra 18 October 1965.

28. See *Africa Diary*, 14-20 December 1963, p. 1492.

29. There was substance in some of Nkrumah's charges against the Liberation Committee, especially that of ultra vires. Thus at the OAU Summit Conference in Addis Ababa in November 1966 the functions of the Committee were specifically laid down by the Assemby of Heads of State and Government as follows: (a) The Liberation Committee's terms of reference were limited to action and administration, and did not extend to policy-making;(b) The OAU Secretariat at Addis Ababa would have an overall control over the Committee's activities; and (c) every member state of the OAU had the right to attend the Committee's meeting though without the right to vote. See *Africa Research Bulletin*, November 1966, p. 652.

30. *West Africa*, 20 December 1958.

31. *OAU—Proceedings and Reports of the Defence Commission, held in Accra in October-November 1963*, Addis Ababa 1964, p. 2.

32. Kwame Nkrumah *United We Stand*, op. cit.

33. Early in 1962, one Opposition MP, Mr Joseph Tarka, criticized the Government for not promoting the formation of an African High Command. See *H. R. Deb.*, 3 April 1962, col. 766.

34. See *Doc. DEF1/Comm II./SR.1*, Accra 1 November 1963, p. 5 in OAU-Proceedings and Report of the Defence Commission at Accra, 29 October-2 November 1963, Addis Ababa, 1964.

35. Ibid. pp. 5-6.

36. *OAU Committee II—Summary Report DEF1/Comm II./SR2*, p. 6.

37. *OAU Doc. DEF1/Comm II./SR.1*, p. 2.

38. Ibid.

39. Ibid.

40. *OAU, Committee II—Summary Report DEF1/Comm II./SR2*, p. 5.

41. *OAU, DEF1/Comm. II./SR1,* p. 5.

42. Ibid. pp. 4-5.

43. Ibid.
44. Brigadier Ankrah denied that the strike force was to be equipped with nuclear weapons.
45. *OAU Committee II—Summary Report DEF1/Comm II. /SR2*, p. 6.
46. OAU—DEF1/Comm II./SR1, p. 8.
47. Ibid. p. 8.
48. *The Ghanaian Times*, Accra, 4 February 1964.
49. *Africa Diary*, 4-10 April 1964, p. 1692.
50. Ibid.
51. *Africa Research Bulletin*, February 1964, p. 21.
52. *Africa Research Bulletin*, July 1964, p. 108.
53. For details about the Sierra Leonean proposal see *OAU, DEF/PRO6 (II) 3 February 1965.*
54. *OAU, DEF/SR 3 II*, February 1965, p. 6.
55. Ibid.
56. Ibid. p. 3.
57. Ibid. p. 8.
58. See 'Recommendation to Create An African Peace-keeping Defence Organization', *Document DEF/Res 3(II)*, 4 February 1965. This resolution provided into alia for the creation of an African Defence Organization to ensure and to maintain Peace; each member state shall, according to its possibilities, voluntarily earmark one or more units of its national Armed Forces to be placed at the disposal of the OAU for specific operations. The forces would remain stationed in their own countries and employed in the normal way at the expense of their state. Such forces when mobilized shall be used only at the express request of one or more member states who have been victims of extra-African aggression, or who suffer serious internal troubles; the resolution also called for the strengthening of the Defence Department in the General Secretariat of the OAU:
59. Geral K. Helleiner has argued that on purely economic calculation Nigeria has little to gain from an African Common Market; and that its appeal to the Nigerian leaders stemmed from political considerations. See his article on 'Nigeria and the African Common Market' in *The Nigerian Journal of Economic and Social Studies*, Vol. 4 No. 3 November 1962, pp. 283–98.
60. Kwame Nkrumah *Africa Must Unite*, London 1963, p. 163.
61. Ibid.
62. Ibid.
63. Kwame Nkrumah *United We Stand*, op. cit.
64. *MR PRIME MINISTER*, op. cit. p. 9?.
65. *N. A. Deb.*, Vol. 24, 4 July 1961, col. ?.
66. Kwame Nkrumah *Africa Must Unite*, op. cit. p. 19.
67. Kwame Nkrumah *United We Stand*, op. cit.
68. Ibid.
69. *MR PRIME MINISTER*, op. cit. p. 97.
70. Ibid. p. 98.
71. Chief Okotie-Eboh said the Federal Government regarded customs union as the nucleus of a common market. See *Africa Research Bulletin*, June 1964, p. 89.
72. *H. R. Deb.*, 23 March 1964, col. 578.
73. See *OAU—Ecos/Res. 13 II 22 January 1965.*
74. *OAU—Economic and Social Commission, Second Session, Cairo*, January 1965, *Doc. Ecos/P.2.*
75. *OAU, Ecos/Res 16 (II) 22 January 1965.*
76. Ibid.
77. *OAU Committee B, Fifth Ordinary Session of the Council of Ministers, Accra, 16-20 October 1965.*

78. Ibid.

79. *OAU—Verbatim Records of the Plenary Meeting of the Second Ordinary Session of the Assembly of Heads of State and Government*, Accra, 21-6 October 1965, p. 8.

80. While the problems facing the formation of an African Common Market have been staggering, one of them has been the lack of the political will among the African leaders. See P. N. C. Okigbo, *Africa and the Common Market*, London 1967, p. 157.

81. See *OAU, Summary Records of the Proceedings of the 12th Session of the Council of Ministers, Committee B, Addis Ababa, February 1969*, p. 2.

82. *West Africa*, 17 September 1971.

83. This was in Nigerian pounds and so higher than sterling.

84. The percentages paid by Egypt and Libya were 9.28 and 7.40 respectively.

85. Because in 1968 Nigeria suspected the Tanzanian Government of assisting the Biafran secessionists with part of the money from the Liberation Fund, Nigeria between that year and 1970 made her own contributions direct to the freedom fighters with a top official of the OAU Secretariat assessing the value of aid given in kind. With the reconciliation with Tanzania in September 1970, Nigeria promised to pay her own contributions to the special fund; but she also said she would continue, as she had been doing since 1968, to give the freedom fighters assistance outside what was levied by the Liberation Committee.

86. *OAU, Summary Records of the Proceedings of the 12th Session of the Council of Ministers at Addis Ababa, Doc. CM/SR 10 (XII)*, p. 10.

87. See Text of Dr Okoi Arikpo's Statement to the meeting of the OAU Council of Ministers on 17 June 1971, in *Nigeria: Bulletin of Foreign Affairs*, p. 39.

88. *OAU—Summary Records of the Proceedings of the Ninth Ordinary Session of the Council of Ministers, Kinshasa, 4-10 September 1967, Doc. CM/SR.3 (IX)*, p. 5.

89. *OAU—Summary Records of the Proceedings of the 12th Session of the Council of Ministers, Committee Report, Report of the Liberation Committee, CM/251*, pp. 5-6.

90. *West Africa*, 9 July 1971.

91. *OAU, Summary Records of the Proceedings of the 12th Session of the Council of Ministers, Committee B, Doc. CM/251*, p. 2.

92. Ibid. pp. 6-7.

93. *Morning Post*, Lagos 26 June 1971.

94. See, for example the *Daily Graphic*, Accra 25 June 1970, and *The Ghanaian Times*, Accra 6 September 1967, and 22 June 1970.

95. No important figure in Ghana since the coup has ever made any call for the formation of an African High Command.

96. *West Africa*, 19 December 1970.

97. The decision was prompted by the dire warning of Mr John Vorster to President Kaunda that if his government continued to back guerrilla fighters against South Africa he would hit Zambia so hard that she would never forget.

99. A similar call was made by General Gowon in his opening address to the OAU Council of Ministers' meeting in Lagos. See *West Africa*, 12-18 December 1970.

99. *Nigeria: Bulletin on foreign affairs*, Vol. 1, No. 2, Lagos, Nigerian Institute of International Affairs, October 1971, p. 54.

100. *Daily Times*, Lagos, 24 March 1970.

101. See for example his speech at Maiduguri the capital of the North Eastern State of Nigeria on the African High Command in July 1970 in the *Daily Sketch*, Ibadan 31 July 1970.

102. *Daily Times*, Lagos 15 July 1971.

103. *Daily* Lagos 24 August 1970.

104. *Daily Times*, Lagos 1 November 1971.

105. *Morning Post*, Lagos 16 July 1971.

106. *Daily Times*, Lagos 1 November 1971.

107. For further details about the interview, See *West Africa*, 17 September 1971.

108. It is interesting to note that unlike the Balewa era Nigeria no longer raised the question of her sovereignty as an obstacle to the formation of an African High Command.

109. For purposes of better economic co-operation in Africa, the Economic Commission for Africa divided Africa into four sub-regions, namely, North, West, Central, and East.

110. For the text of the communique see *Morning Post*, Lagos 2 March 1971.

111. A similar view is contained in the *Second National Development Plan 1970-4*, p. 79.

112. For Nigeria's view on this Ibid. pp. 80-1.

113. For the Ghanaian view, see the complaint of Mr J. H. Mensha, then the Finance Minister, against the obstacles to intra-West African trade as a result of the association of some West African states with the EEC in *West Africa*, 13 August 1971.

114. The various conferences were a follow-up to the ECA Resolution 142 (VII). See also the *Second National Development Plan 1970-4*, p. 81.

115. Apart from the Gambia and Guinea all the other states were represented at this first conference.

116. *ECA, Doc. E/CN 14/366*.

117. See *Articles of Association of a West African Common Market*, Accra, Government Printer 1967.

118. This Summit Conference was, however, boycotted by all the 'Entente' states except Upper Volta. See *Africa Research Bulletin*, Vol. 5, No. 4, 15 April-14 May 1968.

119. The Articles of Association signed in Accra on 4 May 1967 formed an integral part of the protocol. See Z. Cervenka *The Organization of African Unity*, London 1969, p. 157.

120. *Second National Development Plan 1970-4*, p. 79.

121. Ibid.

122. *West Africa*, 11 July 1970.

123. *West Africa*, 19 November 1971.

124. For further details about this, see chapter VII.

125. See for example, *Daily Sketch*, Ibadan 23 November 1970; *Sunday Times*, Lagos 15 November 1970. Sunday Post, Lagos 23 May 1971.

126. *Long Live African Unity—Text of Speech by His Excellency Major-General Yakubu Gowon to the Seventh OAU Assembly of Heads of State and Government*, Addis Ababa 1-4 September 1970.

127. These are the sterling zone, the CFA franc zone, the Guinea franc, and the US dollar, to which the Liberian currency is closely tied.

CHAPTER V

Conflict over the Congo Crisis

A major source of discord between Ghana and Nigeria during the first half of the sixties lay in their different attitudes to the Congo (later Zaire)[1] crisis.[2] The crisis which started with the mutiny of the 'Force Publique' during the first week of independence in July 1960 and which continued in different forms till the sacking of the Kasavubu government by General Mobutu on 23 November 1965, soured the Ghanaian-Nigerian relationship. Why was this so? The main explanation could be found in the fact that their national interests conflicted in the Congo.

Ghana's interest in the future of an independent Congo went back to the first All-African People's Conference in Accra in December 1958 where Dr Nkrumah met Patrice Lumumba, then the leader of the Congolese nationalist party, the 'Mouvement National Congolais' (MNC), which was seen by Nkrumah as a replica of his CPP. From then until the country's independence on 30 June 1960, Ghana took a special interest in its affairs. Nkrumah was in constant contact with Patrice Lumumba. He used his personal influence to bring together Lumumba and Joseph Kasavubu to form the first government of an independent Congo, for which he said his government had earned 'the special commendation and gratitude of the Belgian Government.'[3] All these efforts were made so that after independence the Congo and Ghana might work together, in Nkrumah's words, 'for the total liberation of Africa, and for the establishment of a really effective political union of all the independent African states.'[4] To achieve one of these objectives, Nkrumah and Lumumba on 8 August 1960 signed in Accra a secret agreement providing for the union of Ghana and the Congo on the pattern of the Ghana-Guinea-Mali Union.[5] The task of liberating the whole of Africa, Nkrumah thought, could more easily be accomplished by building up an anti-imperialist regime in Leopóldville (later Kinshasa) because of the strategic position of the country, which in 1960 was a sort of a buffer state between independent and colonial Africa. Such an anti-imperialist regime could only from Nkrumah's point of view be built around Patrice

Lumumba and his close associates in the MNC. Under such a regime, Nkrumah believed that the Congo would serve as 'a corridor and a base for all possible aid to the peoples of Angola and Southern Africa fighting for their liberation'.[6] Furthermore, Ghana wanted an important ally in the crusade against neo-colonial forces in Africa; and the Congo under Lumumba's leadership would serve this purpose. It has to be remembered that Lumumba shared most of the Nkrumah ideas about the Union African government, the total liberation of Africa, and the elimination of neo-colonialism in Africa.[7]

It was all this that determined most of the Ghanaian attitude to the Congo crisis. So the Ghanaian government tried to give full support to the Lumumba government to ensure its survival. And after the dismissal, and murder, of Lumumba, Dr Nkrumah offered assistance to the Lumumbist group, led by Mr Antoine Gizenga, who stood for the ideals of the late Patrice Lumumba.

On the other hand, Nigeria saw the tragedy in the Congo as providing an opportunity for her to demonstrate the sterility of Nkrumah's concept of Union African Government, and to win for herself a significant ally in the contest for the best approach[8] to African unity, especially during the period between late 1960 and early 1963, when the African states were split into various groups as the Brazzaville states, the Casablanca bloc, the Monrovia Powers and the 'Union Africaine et Malgache' (UAM). Although Sir Abubakar told the Parliament in November 1960 that Nigeria had no special interest in the Congo,[9] this attitude immediately changed once Nigeria, through Mr Jaja Wachuku, intervened in a big way as the Chairman of the UN Congo Conciliation Commission. It is interesting to note that Jaja Wachuku regarded the appointment of Nigeria rather than Ghana as the Chairman of the Commission as a defeat for Nkrumah's policies in Africa.[10]

As the chairman of the commission, Mr Wachuku quickly had access to all the confidential letters between Dr Nkrumah and Lumumba, and also to the text of the secret union agreement between Ghana and the Congo. Wachuku came to the conclusion that Ghana had signed the agreement because Nkrumah was envious of Nigeria, and because Ghana was too small for him, and so he wanted an alliance with the Congo in order to realize his dream of 'a United States of Africa.'[11] He added that Nigeria would have nothing to do with this. He said he was horrified to note that it was Dr Nkrumah who had been conducting Lumumba's foreign policy for him.[12] Partly because of Lumumba's close collaboration with Dr Nkrumah, and partly because the Nigerian government leaders were very suspicious of any militancy[13] such as that displayed by Lumumba, the Nigerian Government was intensely anti-Lumumba. As far back as October 1960, Sir Abubakar had said that any pro-Lumumba policy would bring Communisum back to the Congo, and he added that Nkrumah could not speak for Africa on the Congo.[14] Jaja Wachuku said Lumumba was in too much of a hurry to assert his country's independence,[15] and that he had evil plans to murder and imprison all his political rivals,[16] and that if Lumumba had succeeded in destroying Kasavubu the Congo would have been torn into pieces. Furthermore, he stressed that it was not the responsibility of his Commission to safeguard Lumumba's life.[17]

The preliminary report of the Congo Conciliation Commission was published on 18 February 1961. Its main message was to confirm the dismissal of Lumumba by Kasavubu on 5 September 1960 though it called for the widening of the base of the Ileo Government[18] which Dr Nkrumah regarded as illegal. The final report[19] of the Commission published on 20 March 1961 contained the same conclusions as the first one. By the time of its publication it had been overtaken by events, especially the death of Lumumba, thereby reducing the value of its usefulness.

Nonetheless, Mr Wachuku claimed that the formation of the Adoula Government in August 1961 was the result of the work of his Commission.[20] Beginning effectively with the Adoula Government, Nigeria began to woo the Congo through the provision of technical assistance and the exchange of visits between the leaders of the two countries. Thus late in 1961 at a time when all the Ghanaian envoys had been declared 'persona non grata' in Leopoldville (later Kinshasa), their Nigerian counterparts negotiated and signed a technical assistance agreement with the Adoula Government, under which Nigeria was to provide the Congo with the services of legal and financial experts. In December 1962 one of these experts was said by Alhaji Muhammadu Ribadu, then the Nigerian Defence Minister, to have had a year of 'meritorious service' as a legal adviser in the Congolese Ministry of Defence.[21] But a more comprehensive agreement on technical, trade, transport, telecommunication, financial, cultural, and educational co-operation between Nigeria and the Congo was signed in Leopoldville (later Kinshasa) early in March 1963.[22] Through this type of agreement Nigeria hoped that the Congo would join her in forming a West African Common Market which Sir Abubakar said at Addis Ababa in May 1963 must extend to the Congo River.[23] As a result of this agreement, direct telex and telephone links between Lagos and Leopoldville (later Kinshasa) were formally inaugurated in February and August 1964 respectively.[24]

Furthermore, Nigeria under another agreement in September 1963 undertook to help train the Congolese police.[25] By the end of 1964, two sets of Congolese policemen had undergone training at the Southern Police College, Ikeja, near Lagos. Indeed, early in April 1963, the possibility of training the Congolese military personnel in Nigeria[26] was discussed during the visit to Nigeria of a seven-man Congolese military mission headed by General Mobutu.

Apart from this visit, Mr Cyrille Adoula, then the Congolese Prime Minister, visited Nigeria early in May 1963 at the invitation of the Nigerian government. During his stay in Nigeria, Cyrille Adoula visited all the former Regional capitals. Before he left, the former Western and Eastern Regional governments announced the offer to the Congolese government of ten scholarships each tenable in Nigerian secondary schools or Universities.[27] The joint communiqué issued at the end of the visit said that Mr Cyrille Adoula and Sir Abubakar Tafawa Balewa discussed the forthcoming conference of African Heads of States and Government at Addis Ababa, and that they were satisfied with 'the complete identity of views and common attitude of their governments on important problems in Africa.[28] problems in Africa.[28]

About mid-September 1963, Sir Abubakar paid a four-day official visit to the Congo. At the end of the visit, Sir Abubakar and Mr Adoula in a joint communiqué spoke of their determination to strengthen the close relationship existing between their two countries, and to further their practical co-operation especially in commerce, telecommunications, and transport, and technical, cultural and educational fields.[29]

Given all this interest in the Congo the Nigerian Government was determined to support as far as possible the Central Government in Leopoldville (later Kinshasa) after Lumumba's dismissal regardless of how such a government was established. Thus at a press conference in Leopoldville (later Kinshasa) on 15 September 1963, Sir Abubakar promised to keep the Nigerian troops in the Congo if so requested by the Congolese Government after the withdrawal of the UN forces.[30] Indeed, late in 1963, the two countries signed an agreement under which the Nigerian Government was to provide 400 policemen to the Congo after the withdrawal of the UN troops on 30 June 1964.[31]

In these circumstances, a clash between Nigeria and Ghana was inevitable. To Dr Nkrumah all the Congolese Prime Ministers after

Lumumba, namely, Joseph Ileo, Cyrille Adoula, Moise Tshombe and Evariste Kimba, were puppets put in power by the imperialists and the neo-colonialists. Any co-operation with them was a betrayal of the true interests of the Congolese people and of Africa. The Ghanaian-Nigerian clashes occurred over basic issues[32] which split the African countries on the Congo crisis, up to the time of the withdrawal of the UN forces in June 1964. The major issues were the question of identifying the real 'enemy' in the Congo, the role of the UN forces or the 'Organisation des Nations Unies au Congo' (ONUC), and the structure of the Congo. After June, 1964[33] the main issues over which Ghana and Nigeria were sharply divided were the return of Moise Tshombe to power in Leopoldville (later Kinshasa), the armed rebellion in the country, and the American-Belgian rescue operation of November 1964.

(i) IDENTIFICATION OF THE 'ENEMY'

The rapidity with which the Democratic Republic of the Congo slipped into chaos barely a week after independence following the mutiny of the Congolese army, 'Armee Nationale Congolaise' (ANC), the landing of the Belgian paratroopers in the country on 10 July 1960, the secession of Katanga led by Moise Tshombe on 11 July 1960, the secession of South Kasai under Albert Kalonji shortly after, the introduction of the ONUC, and the continuing disorder in the country for over five years after independence, raised questions about who was the 'enemy'. Which forces were behind them? And what were their motives? These were important questions, and the 'right' answers to them would provide a useful guide towards solving the crisis. But various countries had different answers according to their national objectives.

Although some Ghanaian leaders were able to see that the chronic disunity among the various political leaders of the Congo was one of the factors making for the instability of the country,[34] the dominant view of the Ghanaian government was that the whole chaos and confusion were a result of what Nkrumah called the 'colonialist machinations'.[35] It was the imperialists, the neo-colonialists and their lackeys, namely, Kasavubu, Moise Tshombe, Albert Kalonji, and General Mobutu who were the moving force behind the whole unrest in the country. It was the Belgian officers commanding the Congolese troops who in the first place goaded them into rioting because of their insistence that despite independence the control of the forces would continue to be in Belgian hands.[36] The despatch of the Belgian paratroopers to the Congo on 10 July 1960 precipitated on the following day the Katanga secession which was maintained by arms and men from Europe, South Africa and Rhodesia, and by funds from the *Union Miniere*.

With the reluctance of the United States, the United Kingdom and France to criticize the Belgian action against the Congolese government at the UN General Assembly and Security Council debates on the crisis, and with their increasing anti-Lumbumbist action, Dr Nkrumah lumped all of them together with the Belgians as aggressors in the Congo. Another 'enemy' were the UN top officials in the Congo. Not only did they not support the Lumumba Government, but they also frustrated the Ghanaian government attempt to reconcile Lumumba and Kasavubu, by successfully preventing the latter from signing a reconciliation agreement to which he and Lumumba had earlier agreed before Mr Andrew Djin, then the Ghanaian Ambassador in Leopoldville (later Kinshasa).[37] To Dr Nkrumah their action was designed to serve the colonialist interests and not those of the Congolese people.[38]

The motives behind the actions of the imperialists, their allies and their lackeys were, according to Nkrumah, fourfold. The first and most important was the desire to continue, through a policy of balkanization and divide-and-rule tactics, the economic and mineral exploitation of the country in 'complete disregard to the interests of the people of the Congo'.[39] This was how Nkrumah saw the United States' massive support for anti-Lumumbist forces; and he tried to substantiate this by the fact that since 1964 the American financial and economic interests had started to rival if not to displace those of the Blegians.[40] Another explanation offered by Nkrumah was that the control of the Congo by a regime friendly to the West was essential from the point of view of Western strategy in Africa.[41] The main motives for the support of South Africa and Rhodesia for Tshombe's secession was to prevent the emergence of a strong anti-imperialist regime in Leopoldville (later Kinshasa) which in Nkrumah's words could 'present a deadly threat'[42] to their survival. The explanation for the action of the imperialist 'stooges', Kasavubu, Tshombe, Kalonji and General Mobutu, could be found in selfishness and their lust for personal aggrandisement at the expense of the masses. To cope with these problems, Ghana believed that effective military measures had to be taken by the whole of Africa and the UN forces.[43]

Nigeria saw the root causes of the agony in the Congo differently. Although the Nigerian leaders saw external pressures originating from inside and outside Africa as a contributing factor, the main causes of the confusion and the disorder could be found in the unhealthy rivalry[44] among the Congolese leaders, and their lack of experience in government as a result of inadequate preparation for independence. Another source of trouble was, according to Sir Abubakar, the break-up of the ANC into local fighting units, owing allegiance to different local chieftains instead of to a single national leader.[45] In spite of the fact that Jaja Wachuku said in September 1961 that the Western Powers were determined not to allow 'the Congo through the leadership of Lumumba to choose her own international friends',[46] he did not regard their action as a major obstacle to peace and concord in the Congo. On the other hand, he regarded Nkrumah's letters of warning and advice to Lumumba as a grave interference in the internal affairs of the Congo. Indeed, he regarded them as being as poisonous to peace and understanding in that country as they were fatal to Lumumba's life.[47]

While the Nigerian leaders recognized the deadly rivalry between the Congolese leaders, they did not go to the extent of accusing them of being agents of the imperialists. In fact, there were occasions when in spite of the Federal Government policy of supporting the territorial integrity of the Congo, Mr Wachuku would refer to Tshombe as President of the Katanga state.[48] Indeed, it was Lumumba whom the former Nigerian Foreign Minister, Mr Wachuku, saw as the single greatest threat to harmony in the Congo.[49]

Another source of instability from the point of view of Sir Abubakar was the fact that in the pre-independence election no single party won over a quarter[50] of the total seats in the Chamber of Representatives. This was why in his maiden address to the UN General Assembly on 7 October 1960 Sir Abubakar called for fresh elections in the Congo.[51] To make up for the lack of adequate preparation for full self-government and their educational backwardness, he suggested the need to set up a massive programme of technical assistance to help the Congo.[52]

(ii) THE ROLE OF THE ONUC

It was to tackle what the Congolese leaders saw initially as the main source of disorder in the country, namely, the Belgian aggression against 'the national territory of the Congo', that made them request, on the advice of the Ghanaian government, military aid from the United Nations on 12 July 1960.[53] But because of pressure from Belgium and from her NATO allies, notably the United States, the

United Kingdom and France, the Security Council had to modify this request so that the functions of the United Nations forces in the Congo, the ONUC, could include securing the withdrawal of the Belgian troops and the restoration and maintenance of law and order in the country. These were the functions given to the ONUC under the Security Council resolutions of 14 July and 22 July 1960. But all these were to be carried out 'in consultation with the Government of the Republic of the Congo' to which such 'military assistance may . . . be made necessary'.

But on 9 August 1960, the Security Council passed another resolution[54] on the Congo crisis which, together with the interpretation given to it by the then UN Secretary-General, Mr Dag Hammarskjold, created ambiguity about the role of the ONUC. One of the consequences of this, as we shall soon see, was to intensify hostilities among the African countries over the Congo crisis. Although this resolution of 9 August 1960 confirmed the earlier ones by the Security Council of 14 July and 22 July 1960, the operative paragraph 4 stated 'that the United Nations Force in the Congo will not be a party to or in any way intervene in or be used to influence the outcome of any internal conflict, constitutional or otherwise'. Citing the precedents of Lebanon, Mr Hammarskjold gave this operative paragraph 4 an interpretation which in effect meant that the ONUC would be neutral between the Central Congolese Government, and the Katangese authorities, and that it would only act in self-defence. Part of this interpretation stated that 'the United Nations Force cannot be used on behalf of the Central Government to subdue or to force the provincial government to a specific line of action . . . UN facilities cannot be used, for example, to transport civilian or military representatives under the authority of the Central Government to Katanga against the decision of the Katanga provincial government . . .'[55]

To the Ghanaian government Mr Hammarskjold's interpretation was unacceptable as it was a perversion of the whole purpose of the ONUC. If the ONUC was to assist in maintaining law and order then it could not be neutral. As put by Dr Nkrumah 'it is impossible for the United Nations at one and the same time to preserve law and order and to be neutral between the legal authorities and the law breakers'.[56] Mr Alex Quaison-Sackey, then the Ghanaian Permanent Representative at the UN, criticized Hammarskjold's interpretation for laying too much emphasis on Article 2(7) of the UN Charter, which precluded the UN from interfering in the internal affairs of member states.[57] He went on to say that in any case the Security

Council action on the Congo fell 'under Chapter VII of the UN Charter which overrides Article 2(7) . . .'.[58]

On the other hand, Nigeria accepted the interpretation of Mr Hammarskjold as valid. Thus Sir Abubakar told the UN General Assembly on 7 October 1960 that the ONUC had to be neutral, and that there was no question of reducing the Congo Republic to a sort of a UN 'trusteeship territory', or of 'infringing the sovereignty' of the country.[59] Early in 1961, Alhaji Muhammudu Ribadu, then the defence Minister, summed up the Nigerian government view about the role of the ONUC as follows:

> The overall mission of the UN Military Forces is to assist the Congolese authorities in the maintenance of law and order and this is done by peaceful means wherever possible. Where it is sometimes not possible then the minimum force has to be employed.[60]

One of the results of this divergent interpretation of the role of the ONUC was the worsening of the Ghanaian-Nigerian relations over the UN operation in the Congo. In keeping with Dag Hammarskjold's interpretation, the ONUC did not assist the Lumumba government, who had initially invited it to the country. Not only that, it succumbed to being used as an agent of the Western Powers in the country. For example, Andrew Cordier, then the American Executive Assistant to the UN Secretary General used the Ghanaian troops under UN Command to carry out what Conor Cruise O'Brien described as an 'anti-Communist coup'[61] in the Congo on 6 September 1960, by preventing Lumumba from addressing the nation in a radio broadcast in Leopoldville (later Kinshasa) when his rival, Joseph Kasavubu, could be heard by the Congolese broadcasting from Brazzaville radio.[62] It was this action by Andrew Cordier that, according to Dr O'Brien, decisively turned the tables against Lumumba in the Congo.[63] Not only this, the ONUC did not prevent Lumumba's arrest on 7 December 1960 by the Mobutu troops, nor did it take any action to save his life once arrested. Even after the death of Lumumba, the vacillating attitude of the ONUC to the Katanga secession and to Moise Tshombe, regarded in Ghana as the murderer of Lumumba, did not inspire confidence in Ghana in the UN operation mainly because Dr Nkrumah believed that the ONUC should employ force not only to back up the Lumumba government, but also to suppress the secessionist leader, the mutinous Congolese troops, and other forces opposed to the establishment of a strong centralized regime in Leopoldville (later Kinshasa).

After the anti-Lumumba action of the UN Command on 6

September 1960, Dr Nkrumah, though remarkably he did not withdraw his forces till the end,[64] became suspicious and critical of the whole UN involvement in the Congo. Criticism of the UN action in the Congo was widespread in the Ghanaian press and radio. The Government, too, issued statements from time to time to decry what it called 'the persistent blundering'[65] of the UN in the Congo. Beginning with his letter to Mr Hammarskjold on 12 September 1960,[66] Dr Nkrumah threatened on several occasions to withdraw his forces from the ONUC and to place them in the service of the legitimate Lumumba Government. But because Dr Nkrumah believed that it was on balance better to leave his forces under the UN, he did not carry out these threats even after the Casablanca Conference of early January 1961, which called on all its member states to withdraw their troops from the ONUC. Instead he strove, at least for a brief period, to make the UN Command effective by putting forward a number of proposals.

Shortly after the murder of Lumumba, for which Nkrumah held the UN and the imperialists responsible,[67] he went to address the UN General Assembly on the Congo. The essence of his speech was the re-organization of the ONUC and the re-definition of its functions.[68] He demanded that the UN Command should be primarily African, and should take over complete responsibility for law and order and for reasserting the territorial integrity of the State.[69] All airfields and sea ports should come under the ONUC to stop the flow of arms and ammunition into the country from the outside. Furthermore, Nkrumah said the UN Command should disarm the Congolese army, and should reorganize and retrain them, and that the civil side of the Command should assist the Congolese Government to formulate 'a banking and foreign exchange policy' to free the government 'from outside pressure of all kinds.'[70]

Mainly because of the rejection of these proposals by the majority of the UN member states, the Ghanaian government began to give direct bilateral assistance outside the UN framework to pro-Lumumba forces in the Congo. This assistance took the form largely of the supply of doctors and other civilian specialists.[71] Late in March 1961, however, Dr Nkrumah wrote to the Gizenga government in Stanleyville, which he had recognized on 15 February 1961, that he was considering how he could send food, medicine, arms and fuel to it.[72] Dr Willard Scott Thompson said that because of the hostile attitude of the Government of Sudan through whose territory Dr Nkrumah wanted to send the arms, he was unable to do so, and only managed to get some financial aid through to Stanleyville.[73]

This policy was soon abandoned partly because it had no chance of ever subverting the ONUC, and partly because, with the adoption of the U Thant Plan[74] by the Security Council late in 1962, the ONUC began to take tougher action against Katanga.[75] Although Dr Nkrumah welcomed the ONUC action which formally ended Katanga's secession on 16 January 1963, he soon started to demand the termination of its services in the Congo and its replacement by a joint African High Command. Dr Nkrumah's argument was that if the ONUC remained longer in the country, it would help to perpetuate the imperialist exploitation of the country, and that it would continue to be a barrier to the task of liberating the white redoubt of Southern Africa with the Congo as a base. Furthermore, he believed that the reorganization and the re-training of the Congolese soldiers should be entrusted to Africans, to give them a proper African outlook and orientation which they would lack if left in the hands of any of the NATO Powers. In a series of letters between early 1963 and early 1964 U Thant, then the UN Secretary-General, and to Cyrille Adoula, then the Congolese Prime Minister, Dr Nkrumah advocated a speedy end to the work of the ONUC, and the introduction of an African High Command to maintain law and order and to see to the training of the Congolese army.[76]

All these Ghanaian attacks on and criticism of the ONUC were regarded as unjustified by the Nigerian Government. To Sir Abubakar the ONUC had been doing very useful work in extremely difficult circumstances. Thus early in 1961 his government rejected a motion by some of its own back benchers condeming the ONUC for not preventing Lumumba's murder which Dr Kalu Ezera, the seconder of the motion, described as 'the blackest record of United Nations in the Congo.'[77] Instead Sir Abubakar got the Parliament to approve an amended version of the motion which said that the Government noted with satisfaction the work of the UN in the Congo.[78] He said that apart from the fact that the ONUC could not interfere in the internal affairs of the Congo the problems in that country could only be solved by political rather than military action.[79]

Nkrumah proposals on the Congo put forward at the UN General Assembly on 7 March 1961, which he summarized in his address to the Prime Ministers' Conference in London later that month, were bitterly opposed by Sir Abubakar at the Conference. He said that the suggestions to replace the ONUC Command by an African Command and to retain only African troops in the Congo were difficult for him to understand, and that in any case the call was unjustified.[80] At a time when Dr Nkrumah was energetically calling for the termination of the ONUC operation in 1963, Sir Abubakar and Cyrille Adoula stated in a joint communique in September 1963 that they were satisfied with the role of the UN forces in the country.[81]

(iii) STRUCTURE OF THE CONGO

At the very beginning, the question of the structure of the Congo was not a subject of controversy.[82] However, as the crisis deepened and as the hopes of ending the secession of Tshombe's Katanga and Kalonji's South Kasai by any peaceful means began to fade,[83] there began to emerge different opinions among various governments[84] and the other Congolese parties in favour of a federal form of government.[85] Beause those parties, the National Liberation Movement and the Northern People's Party, who had advocated a federal form of government for the Gold Coast before independence, were tribally based and supported, according to Nkrumah by 'alien interests',[86] he became suspicious and contemptuous of any person championing federalism. So irrespective of the difference in size, population and communication between Ghana and the Congo, Nkrumah passionately believed that the form of government that worked in the former country must also be good for the latter.

Following the Tananarive Conference of March 1961 where all non-Lumumbist leaders in the Congo agreed on a confederal form of government for the country, Dr Nkrumah made a scathing attack on 'Kasavubu, Tshombe and a number of other persons interested in splitting up the Congo into tribal units.'[87] In particular, he attacked Kasavubu who 'by agreeing to the proposals of this Conference' had 'in the view of the Government of Ghana abdicated his position as President of the Republic in a very similar way to that in which the Belgian King abdicated his position as the constitutional ruler when he surrendered to the Nazis and acknowledged, in effect, that Belgium had become annexed to Germany.'[88] He went further to say that the Congolese electorate had voted for a unitary government and that any suggestion of federalism or confederalism was to perpetuate what he called Belgian 'absolutism'[89] in the country. His argument was that a federal system would require more skilled civil servants, and, in the face of the acute shortage of trained and highly educated men in the Congo, the Belgians would naturally be invited to fill all the vacant posts, thereby putting the Congo more under the Belgian Government than ever before.

As the constitutional deadlock continued because the Tananarive agreements were not implemented, partly as a result of the Afro-Asian pressure at the UN and partly as a result of the American pressure,[90] Cyrille Adoula, then the Congolese Prime Minister, announced on 29 July 1962 proposals for a federal form of government to be worked out with UN assistance. Dr Nkrumah opposed these proposals which he described as 'a significant concession to Tshombe'.[91] Apart from the press campaign in Ghana against the proposed federation, Nkrumah himself wrote Cyrille Adoula on 17 August 1962 warning him that a federal form of government would 'constitute a backward move for the Republic of the Congo', and would make it very difficult for the country to 'free itself from neo-colonialism and . . . collective imperialism'.[92]

The Nigerian attitude was different. From their own experience the Nigerian leaders could not understand how a country twice as big as theirs, which was a federation, could be effectively run as a unitary state. This was why Sir Abubakar said in October 1960 that he did not understand how the 'Loi Fondamentale' was drawn up.[93] Was it a document imposed from above or was it a product of proper consultation at the grass roots?[94] However, Sir Abubakar said irrespective of how it was drawn up he did not think a unitary form of government was suitable for the country in view of its size, its diversity and the communication difficulties in the country. He, therefore, demanded that considerable powers should be given to local and provincial authorities while preserving the essential unity of the country.[95]

The Nigerian Government did not condemn the Tananarive agreements on confederation. Its stand was that any arrangement however loose and tenuous was better than a unitary system as long as it preserved the territorial unity of the country. In this connection it is important to note that while the government back-benchers critical of its policy in the Congo were opposed to a confederal structure they favoured a federal rather than a unitary system of government for the country.[96] When Cyrille Adoula announced his decision to work out a federal constitution for the country Nigeria welcomed this. And she was one of the four countries[97] appointed by U Thant, then the Acting UN Secretary-General, to assist the Congolese government in working out the details of such a constitution.

(iv) RETURN OF TSHOMBE TO POWER AND ARMED REBELLION IN EASTERN CONGO

The return of Moshe Tschombe to power in Leopoldville (later

Kinshasa) as the prime Minister on 10 July 1964, after nearly eighteen months of self-exile in Europe, was regarded in Ghana as the worst disaster in the Congo since the murder of Lumumba early in 1961. Tshombe's return could not but be very galling to Dr Nkrumah who between early 1963 and early 1964 had put forward proposals to the Adoula Government and to other African governments for an all-African force to replace the ONUC in order to prevent this from happening.[98] In Ghana, Tshombe was regarded not only as the murderer of Lumumba but also as a traitor to African independence and African revolution. Nkrumah had feared that his return would 'turn the Congo back into a colony in all but name'.[99]

But once the worst had happened, Dr Nkrumah decided not to deal with Tshombe, whom he described as 'the puppet of the Union Minière',[100] placed in power by the imperialists for their own ends. He tried first to isolate him from other African leaders, and then to neutralize his administration by whatever means he could, including aid to the Congolese rebels in Stanleyville (later Kisingani). It must be remembered that on the eve of the OAU Summit Conference in Cairo late in July 1964, Dr Nkrumah sent an urgent telegram to President Nasser that Tshombe should not be allowed to participate in the Conference.[101]

Although Nigeria did not vote against the decision of the OAU Council of Ministers in Cairo in July 1964 to exclude Tshombe from the Summit Conference,[102] she accepted that his appointment as the Congolese Prime Minister was constitutional and that she must treat with him. Indeed, this decision to exclude Tshombe was later described as 'unfortunate' by the Federal Government-controlled Radio Nigeria.[103] On 29 August 1964, Sir Abubakar and Tshombe spoke to each other by telephone to inaugurate the establishment of the direct telephone link between Lagos and Leopoldville (later Kinshasa).[104] The mutual trust and sympathy between Nigeria and Tshombe's Congo were so great that Nigeria was one of the five African countries[105] to which Tshombe in August 1964 appealed for military aid to suppress the armed rebellion in the eastern part of the country.

Although the Nigerian government was unable to provide Tshombe with military aid because it said on 21 August 1964 that it would require all its troops for internal security until after the Federal elections of December, 1964[106] it did its best to give the Tshombe Government moral and non-military material aid in its fight against the Congolese rebels. This was to cause friction and antagonism between Ghana and Nigeria.

At the OAU Council of Ministers' emergency meeting in Addis Ababa early in Septemoer 1964 on the Congo, and at the meetings later of the OAU ad hoc Commission on the Congo, of which both Ghana and Nigeria were members,[107] the two countries took conflicting stands. For instance, at the Addis Ababa meeting of the OAU Council of Ministers referred to above, the then Ghananain Foreign Minister, Mr Kojo Botsio, put forward far-reaching proposals that would have neutralized the Tshombe Government if they had been accepted. The proposals which said only a political and not a military solution to the Congo problem was possible, called for, firstly the immediate proclamation of a cease-fire; secondly the neutralization of all armies in the country; thirdly, the summoning of a round-table conference of all the leaders of the main political parties and the revoutionary factions in the Eastern part of the country under the auspices of the OAU at Addis Ababa. The task of the meeting would be to set up a provisional government whose sole aim would be to organize fair and peaceful elections under the OAU auspices. The fourth proposal was the introduction of an 'African peace force' into the Congo until after the elections.[108]

These proposals, which were rejected by Tshombe, were also criticized by the Nigerian representative at the meeting as constituting interference in the internal affairs of the Congo forbidden under the OAU Charter.[109] Later Nigeria joined the Congo in abstaining on a vote on a watered-down nine-point draft resolution which essentially called for an end to hostilities, to foreign interference in the Congo and to the recruitment of mercenaries, and which was adopted by twenty-seven members of the thirty-three member-states present.[110]

Similarly at the meeting of the OAU ad hoc Commission held in Nairobi, Kenya, under the chairmanship of President Jomo Kenyatta during the second half of September 1964, and the subsequent meetings held early in 1965,[111] Ghana and Nigeria took opposite stands. So bitter was their disagreement on the situation in the Congo that Ghana in February 1965 refused on two occasions to attend the meeting of the sub-committee — consisting of Nigeria, Ghana, and Guinea — of the ad hoc Commission on the Congo formed to plan how to mediate between the Congo and her two neighbours, Congo (Brazzaville) and Burundi, accused by the Tshombe government of assisting the rebels.[112] When eventually the sub-committee met without Ghana on 18 February 1965 in Lagos and decided to send a delegation under the chairmanship of Mr Osakwe, then the Nigerian Ambassador to the Congo, first to Leopoldville (later Kinshasa) and then to Brazzaville on 23 February 1965,[113] the *Ghanaian Times* ridiculed this move as a waste of time; and added that it was 'futile' to embark on the mission since not all the three states concerned had indicated their readiness to welcome it.[114]

(v) US-BELGIUM RESCUE OPERATION

Another area of discord between Ghana and Nigeria in the Congo was the United States-Belgium rescue operation that took place in Stanleyville between 24 and 28 November 1964. This operation, carried out by Belgian paratroopers from giant American transport aircraft, was designed to save the lives of all the whites, especially the Americans and the Belgians who had previously been held hostages by the rebel government of Christopher Gbenye in Stanleyville. The action was said to have been carried out at the express request of the Tshombe Government.

To Ghana this was a blatant act of aggression especially since it was carried out at a time when discussions were still going on in Nairobi between the American Ambassador in Kenya, Mr William Attwood, the OAU representatives headed by President Kenyatta, and the representatives of the Gbenye Government in Stanleyville led by its Foreign Minister, Mr Thomas Kanza, on how best to safeguard the lives of the white hostages.[115] The criticism of this operation in Ghana was severe and widespread. This was understandable because the military operation served to boost the position of Tshombe while breaking the back of the Congolese rebels who were regarded in Ghana as the true nationalists, representing the aspirations of the Congolese masses. The first to move to the attack was the *Ghanian Times*, which in a fiery front-page editorial condemned what it called 'American brutalities and inhumanities,[116] and disgraceful aggression against Stanleyville'.[117] Two days later, Dr Nkrumah in an after-dinner speech to mark the fifth anniversary of the Ghana Academy of Sciences condemned the rescue operation as 'a flagrant act of aggression against Africa.'[118] He said he doubted whether the consent of the Tshombe government was given, as the Americans and the Belgians claimed, and that if it was, it must have been 'extracted under duress' from Tshombe.[119] Later Dr Nkrumah stated that the operation was carried out to protect 'the Belgian and the American interests' in the Congo, and to frustrate 'the legitimate and rightful aspirations of Africans in Angola, Mozambique, Southern Rhodesia and South Africa'.[120] The CPP overseas journal, *The Dawn*, described the operation as 'a mission of death planned and executed with cold-blooded calculation that is truly savage.'[121]

Early in December 1964, Ghana joined twenty-one other Afro-Asian states in presenting a memorandum[122] to the UN Security Council calling for a debate on the rescue operation, and explaining why they saw it as an interference in African affairs, a violation of the UN Charter, and a threat to peace and security in Africa. When the issue was debated at the Security Council, Kojo Botsio, then the Ghanaian Foreign Minister, condemned it as a breach of international law and accused the United States of 'inhumanitarianism', 'racism' and 'genocide'.[123]

The Nigerian Government saw the rescue operation in a different way. Mr Jaja Wachukwu, then the Nigerian Foreign Minister, said in a press statement on 28 November 1964 that the US-Belgium operation was carried out 'to perform an act of mercy to save human beings from being massacred.'[124] He said the act was carried out at the request of the Tshombe Government, and so the question of aggression did not arise. He added that if faced with a similar situation, he would have acted as Tshombe. He said he did not see anything wrong in making use of military aid as the Congolese Government was doing, and that in any case all African countries relied to varying degrees on military aid from the developed countries. He went on to say that, while he was opposed to the use of mercenaries, those in the Congo came at the request of the legal government of the country.[125] Furthermore, he added that the Nigerian government recognized the right of any state to subdue rebellion by whatever means possible including the use of foreign troops.[126]

After this he came down specifically to fire a broadside at Ghana without mentioning it by name. He said the main trouble in the Congo was caused by those African countries who wanted to dictate who should be premier in Leopoldville (later Kinshasa). He added that such countries refused to accept the Congo as a sovereign independent state. He then condemned a number of African states for interfering in the Congo, and for using their Embassies in Lagos to plan subversion. 'What we are now seeing,' he said, 'is an attempt to replace foreign imperialism by African imperialism'. He added 'today their target is the Congo, the next is Nigeria.'[127]

During the Security Council debate[128] of the episode, Wachuku spoke strongly in support of the stand of the Tshombe government, which had earlier submitted a memorandum[129] to the Council that the action was taken at its request for humanitarian purposes. Furthermore, Wachuku again condemned those African countries who had interfered in the Congo by giving assistance to the rebels.

This attitude of Jaja Wachuku at the Security Council was roundly condemned by Radio Ghana on 16 December 1964. It said: 'Wachuku has not only missed a golden opportunity to defend the rights of his people and the principles for which the UN stands, but he has committed an act which amounts to a betrayal of the aspiration of the Africans for justice and fair play. By his defence of the imperialist cause, he has let down the whole of Africa.'[130]

In the meantime, as fighting continued on an increasing scale, Ghana stepped up her material and military aid, which she had started late in 1964 to the Congolese rebels in Stanleyville through Juba in Sudan.[131] On 9 December 1964, when the Security Council began to debate the US-Belgium rescue operation Dr Nkrumah wrote a lengthy letter to President Nasser calling for military and other assistance to the Congolese insurgents.[132] In contrast to this, Nigeria gave her unflinching support to the Tshombe government, to whom she provided 400 of her policemen to assist in the maintenance of law and order under an agreement signed late in 1963 with the Adoula Government. Although all the Nigerian troops had been withdrawn from the country on 30 June 1964, along with other troops under the UN Command, it was believed in Ghana, though without any concrete evidence, that Nigeria after that date still maintained in the Congo a battalion of 900 men[133] financed by the American Government to assist the Congolese government forces in their campaign against the rebels.[134]

One of the main consequences of all this was the further straining of Ghanaian-Nigerian relations. Ghana's aid to the rebels was seen in Nigeria as a grave act of interference in the internal affairs of a sovereign independent state.[135] On the other hand, Nigeria's support for the Tshombe Government was regarded in Ghana as a betrayal of Africa and support for the imperialists and the neo-colonialists.

But the worst was still to occur over the Congo. On 5 March 1965, Captain Kissonga of the Congolese rebel forces said in a press statement in Dar es Salam, Tanzania, that six Nigerian soldiers had been captured in the town of Lulemba in Northern Katanga during a clash with the Central Government troops.[136] He went on to say that the soldiers had confessed that they were part of a Nigerian battalion sent by their government to fight for Tshombe.[137] Although the then Nigerian High Commissioner in Kenya, Mr Ade Martins, immediately on 6 March 1965 denied the story and called on the rebel forces to produce the captured soldiers and to prove by documents that they were Nigerians, and added that Nigeria was prepared to welcome any investigation into the charges either under the auspices of the OAU or the UN,[138] the story was believed in Ghana, where it raised a furore.

So on 12 March 1965, about 400 Ghanaian students joined by workers took to the streets to demonstrate in front of the Nigerian High Commission in Accra against what they called 'the presence of Nigerian mercenaries in the Congo.'[139] After smashing the windows and the doors of the High Commission, they called on the Nigerian Government to accept the challenge of the Sudanese government for an investigation into the matter; and they demanded an end to any act that might be prejudicial to the efforts of the OAU in the Congo.[140]

This anti-Nigerian demonstration in Accra provoked anger among the Nigerians. This was understandable since the Nigerians knew that their troops were no longer in the Congo. The Nigerian students at the Lovanium University near Leopoldville (later Kinshasa) staged a counter-demonstration against Ghana on 15 March 1965 in front of her Embassy in Leopoldville (later Kinshasa), and they issued a statement condemning the violent attacks on the Nigerian High Commission in Accra by the Ghanaian students.[141] After returning from Accra where he had gone to investigate the nature of the demonstration, the President of the Students Union of the University of Ibadan issued a statement on 16 March 1965 condemning it as something organized not by the Ghanaian Students Union, but by those he called the 'brain-washed CPP students' of the Ideological Institute at Winneba.[142] He then called on the Nigerian Government to take retaliatory measures against Ghana including breaking off diplomatic relations. On 17 March 1965 a small anti-Ghana demonstration in Lagos occurred, organized mainly by the members of the United Labour Congress (ULC). The demonstrators marched to the Ghanaian High Commission in Lagos carrying placards such as 'Down with Nkrumah', 'Up Balewa'.[143] Addressing the demonstrators later, Alhaji Adebola, then the President of the ULC, said the press statement of the Congolese rebels about the Nigerian military intervention on the side of Tshombe was drafted in Accra by the Ghanaian government and only carried to East Africa to be read.[144]

The reaction of the Nigerian leaders was equally severe. Several members of Parliament called for the breaking off of diplomatic relations with Ghana.[145] Sir Abubakar reacted in a tough way. On 16 March 1965, he described the anti-Nigerian demonstration in Accra as 'madness'.[146] He added that he was not surprised because Ghana had become 'the headquarters of all wanted persons', and of 'every undesirable person, and anyone wanted for crime in his country of origin'.[147] Although Mr Owusu-Ansah, then the Ghanaian High Commissioner in Nigeria, issued a statement the following day dissociating his government from the anti-Nigerian demonstration,[148] the Nigerian Government did not accept this. Thus on 21 April 1965, Sir Abubakar made what was perhaps his worst and most savage criticism of Ghana since independence. He said it was 'a lie'[149] that there was a single Nigerian soldier in the Congo. He said that under the system of government in Nigeria his government could not secretly send troops outside the country without Parliamentary approval, although he realized that under the Nkrumah dictatorship Ghana could secretly despatch some of her forces abroad. He then went on to accuse the Ghanaian government of a campaign of calumny and hatred against Nigeria.[150] After referring to Accra again as 'the headquarters of subversive elements in Africa,' Sir Abubakar said that matters would not be pushed to the extreme with Ghana, mainly because she was too small in comparison with Nigeria.[151]

1. Although the Congo's name has now been changed to Zaïre, we shall for purposes of convenience use the former name, Congo, throughout this study, since this is what that country was called during the period covered.

2. The Congo crisis is dealt with here only in so far as it affected the Ghanaian-Nigerian relations. No attempt is made to tell the story of the causes and course of the events of those dark days which have been ably dealt with in a spate of works. To name a few, see C. Hoskyns *The Congo since Independence, January 1960 to December 1961*, London 1965; C. Legum *The Congo Disaster*, London 1961; C. C. O'Brien, *To Katanga and Back*, London 1962; C. Young *Politics in the Congo*, Princeton 1965; E. W. Lefever *Uncertain Mandate*, 1968.

3. Kwame Nkrumah *Challenge of the Congo*, op. cit. p. 113.

4. *Ghana Today*, 6 July 1960.

5. For the text of this agreement see Kwame Nkrumah *Challenge of the Congo*, op. cit. pp. 30-1.

6. Ibid. p. 237.

7. The communique issued at the end of Lumumba's visit to Ghana early in August 1960 called inter alia for the complete evacuation of the Belgian military bases in Kitona and Kamina in the Katanga Province of the Congo.

8. The main approaches were the continental political union approach led by Nkrumah; the functional approach led by Nigeria and Liberia; and the linguistic approach of the Brazzaville group of states.

9. *H. R. Deb.*, 25 November 1960, col. 477.

10. *H. R. Deb.*, 4 September 1961, col. 2799.

11. *Drum*, Lagos October 1971.

12. Wachuku was perhaps unaware of the fact that between independence on 30 June 1960 and November 1960, it was Lumumba and Kasavubu who jointly entrusted the conduct of their country's diplomatic business to Ghana.

13. Frederick Schwarz said that Sir Abubakar regarded any militancy as immoral. See F. Schwarz op. cit. p. 233.

14. *US News-week*, 10 October 1960, pp. 27-8.

15. *Drum*, September 1961, p. 26.

16. The text of the confidential letter dated 15 September 1960 purported to have been written by Lumumba to the Provincial Presidents, asking them to liquidate all his political enemies in order to establish dictatorship, published by the Wachuku Commission early in 1961 (see *UN Doc A/4711/Add.2*) and certified by experts as forgeries (see Catherine Hoskyns *The Congo Since Independence*, op. cit. p. 216n), were still published in *Drum* of November 1971 by Mr Wachuku as being proof of Lumumba's plans for a full-scale 'progrom'.

17. *Drum*, Lagos September 1961, p. 26.

18. *UN Doc. A/4696.*

19. *UN Doc. A/4711*, 20 March 1961.

20. *H. R. Deb.*, 4 September 1961, col. 2800.

21. *H. R. Deb.*, 11 December 1962, col. 116 (Written Answers).

22. *Africa Diary*, 16-22 March 1963, p. 1051.

23. *MR PRIME MINISTER*, op. cit. p. 98.

24. *Africa Diary*, 21-7 March 1964, p. 1664; 19-25, September 1964, p. 1951.

25. *Africa Diary*, 7-13 September 1963, pp. 1329-30.

26. *Africa Diary*, 13-19 April 1963, p. 1102.

27. *Africa Diary*, 25-31 May 1963, p. 1167.

28. Ibid.

29. *Africa Diary*, 28 September–October 1963, pp. 1363-5.

30. Ibid.

31. *Africa Diary*, 18-24 January 1964, p. 1557.

32. For further details about these basic issues, see Robert C. Good, 'The Congo Crisis in Laurence' W. Martin (ed.) *Neutralism and Nonalignment*, New York 1962, p. 62.

33. For the sake of convenience some writers such as Catherine Hoskyns have divided the tragic Congo drama into two acts, the first beginning with the introduction of the ONUC into the Congo and ending with its withdrawal, and the second from the rise to power in Leopoldville (later Kinshasa) by Moise Tshombe to General Mobutu's coup d'etat of November 1965.

34. See Alex Quaison-Sackey *Africa Unbound*, New York 1963, p. 86.

35. Kwame Nkrumah *Challenge of the Congo*, op. cit. p. 19.

36. *Alex Quaison-Sackey*, op. cit. p. 84.

37. For Andrew Djin's account of this episode see Kwame Nkrumah *Challenge of the Congo*, op. cit. pp. 58-61. See also *C. Hoskyns* op. cit. p. 221.

38. *GAOR 869th Pl. meeting*, paragraph 28, 15th session, 23 September 1960.

39. *N. A. Deb.*, Vol. 20, 8 August 1960, col. 641.

40. Kwame Nkrumah *Challenge of the Congo*, op. cit. p. 250.

41. Dr Nkrumah referred to certain Western writers who had stated that the domination of Africa could be more easily secured through the control of the Congo Ibid. p. 236.

42. *N. A. Deb.*, Vol. 24 4 July 1961, col. 6.

43. More on this will be said in the next section.

44. *Drum*, Lagos September 1961, p. 26.

45. *H. R. Deb.*, 18 April 1961, col. 1862.

46. *Drum*, Lagos September 1961, p. 28.

47. Very late in 1971, over ten years after Lumumba's death, Jaja Wachuku continued to say that if Lumumba had not listened to Nkrumah's advice he would not have been killed by his political enemies. See *Drum*, Lagos, of October and November 1971.

48. *Drum*, September 1961, p. 26.

49. Wachuku described Lumumba as a heady young man with dangerous plans to carry out a 'large-scale pogrom' in the Congo. Ibid.

50. But if the eight seats won by an ally of Lumumba's party were taken into

consideration, then his MNC were sure of 41 seats which would be more than one-quarter of the total seats of 137 in the Chamber.

51. *Text of the Speech of Sir Abubakar Tafawa Balewa to the UN General Assembly*, 7 October 1960.

52. Ibid.

53. See the joint telegrams from President Kasavubu and Prime Minister Lumumba to the UN Secretary-General, Mr Hammarskjold, on 12 and 13 July 1960 in *Documents on International Affairs 1960*, London 1964, pp. 270-71.

54. *SCOR 15th Year, Supplement for July, August and September 1960*, pp. 91-2.

55. *Doc. S/4417/Add 6—SCOR 15th Year, Supplement for July, August and September 1960*, pp. 64-5, 70-1.

56. *GAOR 869th Parliamentary meeting*, 23 September 1960, paragraph 17.

57. *GAOR 950th pl. meeting*, 16 December 1960, paragraph 1320.

58. Rosalyn Higgins has, however, argued that although the basis of the UN operation in the Congo was Article 40 under Chapter VII of the charter the emphasis placed by the Secretary-General and the UN on the ONUC operation was one of a 'preventive' action rather than an 'enforcement action' under Chapter VII, and that in this sense, the ONUC operation was still subject to Artical 2(7). See Rosalyn Higgins *The Development of International Law through the Political Organs of the United Nations*, London 1963, pp. 88-9.

59. *Text of the Speech by Sir Abubakar Tafawa Balewa to the UN General Assembly on 7 October 1960*.

60. *H. R. Deb.*, 18 April 1961, col. 1868.

61. Conor Cruise O'Brien *To Katanga and Back*, London 1962, p. 60.

62. Ibid. p. 93.

63. Ibid. p. 60.

64. Dr Nkrumah later explained his government's decision not to withdraw his forces as follows: 'The reason why we did not withdraw our troops . . . was because we felt that by doing so we would weaken the authority of the UN and leave the way open for the intensification of, and intervention from, just those forces we are anxious to oust'. See Kwame Nkrumah *Africa Must Unite*, op. cit. p. 195.

65. *Ghana Today*, 20 February 1961.

66. For the text of the letter, see Kwame Nkrumah *Challenge of the Congo*, op. cit. p. 42.

67. See text of President Nkrumah's radio broadcast immediately the news of the murder of Lumumba and his two colleagues, Joseph Okito and Maurice Mpolo, became known in *Ghana Today*, 1 March 1961.

68. This came to be known as the eight-point programme of Dr Nkrumah for peace and order in the Congo.

69. For details see *GAOR, 961st Plenary meeting 15th Session*, 7 March 1961, paras. 1-112.

70. Other important points made by Dr Nkrumah included the closing down of all foreign missions in the Congo and the expulsion of all non-African personnel in the Congolese army.

71. Henry T. Alexander *African Tight-rope*, London 1965, p. 50.

72. Kwame Nkrumah *Challenge of the Congo*, op. cit. p. 153.

73. Willard Scott Thompson *Ghana's Foreign Policy 1957-66*, Princeton 1969, p. 157.

74. The U Thant Plan was designed to bring Katanga back into a federation of the Congo, and was backed up with economic sanctions against Katanga if it failed to accept the proposals.

75. Kwame Nkrumah *Challenge of the Congo*, op. cit. pp. 207-9.

76. For further details about these letters see Kwame Nkrumah *Challenge of the Congo*. 'Proposals for an All-African Force'. See also *Ghana Today*, 1 January 1964.

77. *H. R. Deb.*, 18 April 1961, col. 1856.

78. Ibid. col. 1859.

79. Ibid. col. 1863.

80. *Minutes of the meeting of the Prime Ministers March 1961*, London 1961.

81. *Africa Diary*, 28 September–4 October 1963, pp. 1363–4.

82. *US Newsweek*, 10 October 1960, p. 28.

83. *Drum*, (Lagos) September 1961, p. 26.

84. For example, Britain favoured the confederal arrangement agreed upon by the non-Lumumbist Congolese leaders at Tananarive in March 1961; the US wanted a loose federation; and the USSR favoured a highly centralized unitary form of government.

85. Kwame Nkrumah *Challenge of the Congo*, op. cit. pp. 17, 199.

86. Ibid.

87. *N. A. Deb.*, Vol. 23, 18 April 1961, Col. 15.

88. Ibid.

89. Ibid. col. 14.

90. Shortly after the Tananarive Conference, Mr Adlai Stevenson, then the US Permanent Representative at the UN, said his government was opposed to the confederal structure, but would work instead for a federal form of government in the Congo. See *GAOR 983rd parliamentary meeting*, 14 April 1961, paragraphs 44–5.

91. Kwame Nkrumah *Challenge of the Congo*, op. cit. p. 198.

92. For the text of the letter see Kwame Nkrumah *Challenge of the Congo*, op. cit. pp. 200–1.

93. Text of the Speech by Sir Abubakar Tafwa Balewa to the UN General Assembly on 7 October 1960.

94. Ibid.

95. Ibid.

96. See *H. R. Deb.*, 18 April 1961, col. 1854.

97. The others were Canada, India and Switzerland.

98. Kwame Nkrumah *Challenge of the Congo*, op. cit. p. 238.

99. Ibid.

100. Ibid.

101. *Africa Diary*, 22–8 August 1964, p. 916.

102. Immanuel Wallerstein *Africa, The Politics of Unity*, London 1968, p. 84.

103. *Africa Research Bulletin*, December 1964, p. 201.

104. *Africa Diary*, 19–25 September 1964, p. 1951.

105. The others were: Ethiopia, Senegal, Liberia, Madagascar. *Africa Diary*, 26 September–2 October 1964, p. 1961.

106. Ibid.

107. Other members of the Commission were Ethiopia, Tunisia, Kenya, Cameroons, Upper Volta, the UAR, Somalia and Guinea.

108. *Africa Diary*, 17–23 October 1964, p. 1992.

109. Ibid.

110. There was no negative vote. There were four other abstentions, namely, Togo, Senegal, Sierra Leone, and Liberia. Ibid. p. 1991.

111. For details about the OAU involvement in the Congo crisis from July 1964 till 1965 see Immanuel Wallerstein op. cit. p. 82–4 and 86–91; and C. Hoskyns, 'Pan-Africanism and Integration' in Arthur Hazlewood (ed.) *African Integration and Disintegration*, London 1967, pp. 381–2.

112. *Africa Research Bulletin*, February 1965, p. 237.

113. *Morning Post*, Lagos, 19 February 1965.

114. *Ghanaian Times*, Accra 25 February 1965.

115. Immanuel Wallerstein op. cit. p. 89.

116. We shall refer to how the Congo crisis affected Ghanaian-American relations in the next chapter.

117. *Ghanaian Times*, Accra 25 November 1964.

118. *Ghana Roday*, 2 December 1964.

119. Ibid.

120. *N. A. Deb.*, Vol. 38, 12 January 1965, cols. 5-6.

121. *The Dawn*, London 2 December 1964.

122. See *Doc. S/6076 and Add. 1-5*, eighteen of the twenty-two countries that presented this memorandum were from Africa.

123. *SCOR 1170th meeting*, 9 December 1964, paras. 123-219.

124. *Daily Times*, Lagos 29 November 1964.

125. Ibid.

126. Ibid.

127. Ibid.

128. It has to be noted that Radio Nigeria came out strongly on 7 December and 14 December 1964 against this Security Council debate. See *Africa Research Bulletin*, December 1964, p. 201.

129. *Doc. 6062*, and *S/6063*.

130. *Africa Research Bulletin*, December 1964, p. 201.

131. For further details see Adlai Stevenson's charge against Ghana at the Security Council for supporting the rebels militarily in *SCOR 1174th meeting*, 14 December 1964, paragraph 49.

132. For the text of the letter see Kwame Nkrumah *Challenge of the Congo*, op. cit. pp. 265-7.

133. Ibid. p. 248.

134. So widespread was this view in Ghana that Mr Jitendra Mohan, an Indian lecturer at the University of Ghana, still wrote in 1969, again without substantiation, that some Nigerian troops remained in the Congo after the withdrawal of the ONUC to assist the Tshombe Government against the rebels. See his article, 'Ghana, The Congo, and the United Nations' in *The Journal of Modern African Studies*, October 1969, pp. 369-406.

135. From the point of view of the CPP leaders this was nonsense because only the involvement of an extra-African Power could be regarded as interference in the internal affairs of the Congo. This was one of the main ideas behind most of the Nkrumah government's actions in Africa, the concept that 'We Africans are one, and we are our brothers' keepers'. See *Kwesi Armah*, op. cit. p. 136.

136. *Africa Research Bulletin*, March 1965, p. 255.

137. Ibid.

138. *Africa Diary*, 10-16 April 1965, p. 2274.

139. *Africa Research Bulletin*, March 1965, p. 255.

140. Ibid.

141. Ibid.

142. Ibid.

143. Ibid.

144. Ibid.

145. *H. R. Deb.*, 29 March 1965, cols. 236-8; and *H. R. Deb.*, 21 April 1965, cols. 1127-36.

146. *Africa Research Bulletin*, March 1965, p. 255.

147. Ibid.

148. Ibid.

149. *H. R. Deb.*, 21 April 1965, col. 1140.

150. Ibid. col. 1138.

151. Ibid. He said Ghana was to Nigeria as an ant to an elephant.

CHAPTER VI
Attitude to the Great Powers

The attitude of Ghana and Nigeria to the Great Powers, especially those in North America and Western Europe, were of paramount importance. There were the historical links with some of them, especially Britain. These developed countries were the main sources of foreign aid and investment for both countries. Furthermore, the bulk of their external trade was with them. Instead of co-operating to tap the capital and the technical resources of these countries for their own development, Ghana and Nigeria competed for them. Not only that, they also competed for the sale of their commodities in the markets of these developed countries.

Again, one of the consequences of this was to strain their relations. Before late 1960, Ghana had caught the attention of the Great Powers and had been given some pre-eminence by them. Indeed until Nigeria's independence in October 1960, Ghana was regarded in many world capitals as the spokesman for Africa, and as such the advanced countries were ready to assist her with aid and technical assistance.[1] But shortly before, and after, Nigeria's independence, the Ghanaian Government was said to have launched a campaign of calumny against her in almost all the capitals of the developed countries in order to prevent them from diverting aid and investment from Ghana to Nigeria.[2] Thus in 1961 when Chief Festus Okotie-Eboh, then the Federal Finance Minister, led a trade delegation to North America and Europe he said they were met everywhere with anti-Nigerian propaganda financed by Ghana that Nigeria was 'big for nothing' and so not deserving of any serious attention.[3] Though difficult to corroborate from Ghanaian sources, this did poison the Ghanaian-Nigerian relationship almost from the time of independence till the end of the Nkrumah era. Thus early in 1965, Chief Okotie-Eboh,[4] and several other MPs,[5] still referred to this anti-Nigerian campaign in Europe and North America as a proof of Ghana's hostility to Nigeria.

But a greater source of conflict between them was what should be the 'correct' attitude to the Great Powers. Broadly speaking both

Ghana and Nigeria adopted the policy of 'positive neutralism', 'non-alignment',[6] and at times 'neutrality'[7] towards the Great Powers.

As indicated earlier in chapter one, the different interpretation[8] given to 'non-alignment' by each country was to sour their relations. As was the case among most Afro-Asian countries, each country's leaders interpreted the term in the light of the national interest taking into account security, political, ideological, economic and cultural considerations. Thus the Anglo-Nigerian defence pact signed on independence in October 1960[9] was seen by the Nigerian leaders as compatible with their policy of non-alignment.[10] But this was seen in Ghana as having drawn Nigeria into the cold war conflict on the side of Britain and NATO. Therefore Nigeria from the point of Dr Nkrumah was not non-aligned. It was because of this that his government tried successfully to exclude Nigeria from the First Conference of the Non-aligned Powers[11] in Belgrade in September 1961.[12] On the other hand, Dr Nkrumah believed that his government was pursuing a policy of non-alignment when towards the end of his regime he was increasingly leaning more and more on the Communist countries, especially the Soviet Union. Although not publicly expressed by the Nigerian government leaders, this was seen in some official circles in Lagos as an attempt to turn Ghana into a sort of a Soviet satellite in Africa. Indeed, one of the Nigerian Senators, Chief S. T. Hunponu-Wusu, early in 1965 said that since Ghana would always take advice from the Soviet Union she should be expelled from the Commonwealth.[13]

For reasons of space, we cannot deal with their attitudes to all the Great Powers. We will confine ourselves here to a consideration of their attitudes to their common ex-colonial Power, the United Kingdom, to the Super Powers, and to the EEC. This will have to be dealt with in two sections since the year 1966, as earlier shown, was a watershed in the internal and external policies of both countries. This means that the first section will cover the period from 1957 till early 1966, and the second from that time till 1970.

(i) (a) Attitudes to Britain: I

Ghana's attitude to Britain between her independence in March 1957 and the coup of February 1966 could be described in two phases. The first period was from independence till late 1960, while the second was from then till February 1966. Partly because of the understanding between Dr Nkrumah and Sir Charles Arden-Clarke, the last colonial Governor in the Gold Coast, and partly because of the absence of any major issue to drive a wedge between Accra and

London, Ghana's attitude to Britain during the first period was very friendly. Dr Nkrumah rarely took any position on major international issues without first consulting the British Government and the British officials[14] in Ghana. For instance, Dr Nkrumah forwarded a copy of the text of the Ghana-Guinea Union agreement of 23 November 1958 to Mr Harold Macmillan, then the British Prime Minister, before its publication, with a note that the agreement would not affect Ghana's friendship with Britain.[15] The British Government in turn replied warmly to Ghana's friendly attitude. Apart from providing her with technical assistance, the United Kingdom sent a Parliamentary delegation headed by Mr R. H. Turton to present to the Ghanaian National Assembly a Speaker's chair which Dr Nkrumah described as a symbol of 'the special relationship between the British people and the people of Ghana — the Commonwealth'.[16] On his return to Accra from the Prime Ministers' Conference held in London in May 1960, Dr Nkrumah described the Commonwealth as 'a unique association of free, independent sovereign states, irrespective of their racial origins working for world peace'.[17]

Given this attitude, the number of the British experts in the Ghanaian public service was considerable, according to Mr E. N. Omaboe, until July 1960 when the government took far-reaching measures to 'Ghanaianize' the top posts of the service.[18] Similarly, there were a large number of British officers in the Ghanaian army till 22 September 1961. Until that date, when Dr Nkrumah dismissed all the British officers in the country's army,[19] the Chief of Defence Staff was British.

However, radical changes in the Ghanaian attitude to Britain began late in 1960, mainly as a result of sharp disagreement with her over the Congo crisis and the colonial and racial issues in Southern Africa.[20] From that time onwards till the coup in February 1966, the Ghanaian attitude to the United Kingdom ranged from one of love-hate through antagonism to near-hostility.

Criticisms of Britain neo-colonialist manoeuvres in Africa were incessant and widespread in the Ghanaian press and radio. The situation was so bad that in October 1961 Mr Duncan Sandys, then the Commonwealth Secretary, had to say in the Commons that it appeared as if Ghana was becoming increasingly hostile to the United Kingdom and that she was supporting Soviet attacks against Britain.[21] So much had the attitude of Ghana changed that on 16 December 1965 Dr Nkrumah, who in mid-1960 had spoken of the uniqueness of the Commonwealth, said his government was giving serious thought to withdrawing from the Commonwealth.[22]

One of the important effects of this apparent Ghanaian hostility to Britain was the worsening of Ghanaian-Nigerian relations. For the Nkrumah regime believed strongly that its attitude since late 1960 to Britain was a 'correct' one which should be adopted by all other African countries. But Balewa's Nigeria would have nothing to do with this kind of policy. Indeed, Nigeria's attitude to Britain from independence in October 1960 till the coup of January 1966 was more friendly than Ghana's attitude to the United Kingdom between March 1957 and late 1960. Even before independence the admiration for Britain in Nigeria was great. Thus in August 1958, Sir Abubakar announced that his government had granted free a piece of land in Lagos to the British government to build a house for its High Commission; and that in addition the government had granted the UK the sum of £40,000[23] towards the cost of the building.[24] Furthermore, the government later allocated twenty residential houses at Ikoyi at a nominal rent of 8.3 per cent for the staff of the British High Commission in Nigeria.[25]

As a result of the goodwill among the Nigerian leaders towards the United Kingdom they did not hesitate to sign a military pact[26] with her on independence. Just as Dr Nkrumah during the first three years of Ghana's independence, Sir Abubakar till late 1962 could hardly take any decision on any important international problem without first visiting London, or consulting the British government or its representatives in Lagos.[27]

The Nigerian leaders trusted the British government so much that for a couple of years after independence they gave it exclusive right to operate radio frequencies in the country.[28] Furthermore, Nigeria for some years after independence relied on the British diplomatic Missions in countries such as India, Japan, Gabon, Canada and most of the East European countries including the Soviet Union to transact diplomatic, consular and commercial business.[29] It was mainly because of this trust that the Nigerian leaders continued to request from Britain technical experts, doctors and teachers to fill vacant posts in the country's public services. This was also why Nigeria continued till nearly five years after independence to retain a large number of British officers in the army and navy. Indeed, till early 1965, the General Officer Commanding the Nigeria army was British, Major-General Welby-Everard. Furthermore, unlike Ghana where loose talk of nationalizing British interests was frequently voiced at party rallies especially from early 1961 onwards, there was nothing like this in Nigeria, at least not among the ruling class. Nor was there any talk of reducing the predominance of the British firms in the Nigerian economy. Thus until early 1965, it was the British firm, Shell-BP, that was the sole producer and exporter of crude oil from Nigeria.[30]

At a time when Ghana's criticism of British imperialism and neo-colonialism was at its height late in 1962, Chief Okotie-Eboh on 5 November 1962, in the presence of a British Parliamentary delegation led by Sir John Vaughan-Morgan to present a Speaker's chair to the Nigerian Parliament,[31] spoke glowingly of 'the many enduring and abiding ties' between Nigeria and the United Kingdom. Similarly, on 18 July 1963, when the Anglo-Ghanaian relationship was at its worst because of the Ghanaian government's attitude to the question of Southern Rhodesia, Mr Harold Macmillan spoke in London at an annual dinner of the Britain-Nigeria Association of 'the very special ties of friendship between Britain and Nigeria'.[32] Finally, at a time when the Ghanaian government was contemplating withdrawing from the Commonwealth over the Rhodesian question, Sir Abubakar was exploring how best to strengthen it by ensuring through his sponsored Prime Ministers' Conference in Lagos early in January 1966 that the difficulties over Rhodesia did not wreck the Commonwealth.[33]

Several factors were responsible for these differing attitudes to Britain. The most important were the differences in outlook between Dr Nkrumah and Sir Abubakar, and their different assessment of the contribution of British colonial rule to their countries at independence; the need for aid and investment from the United Kingdom; their divergent views about the British involvement in the Congo crisis and British colonialism in Southern Africa. Another factor was the criticism in the United Kingdom, especially by the press, of Dr Nkrumah's internal policies.

As shown in an earlier chapter Dr Nkrumah and Sir Abubakar, who both until early 1966 had a profound impact on their countries' foreign policies, were totally different men in outlook, experience and background. Dr Nkrumah was a revolutionary deeply imbued with the Marxist-Leninist theory of imperialism, whereas Sir Abubakar was a conservative who, more than most of his colleagues, was very pro-Britain.[34] This meant that while Ghana could easily criticize Britain for any of her colonial actions seen as unacceptable, Nigeria could not. Indeed, from independence until the end of the Balewa regime, it was difficult to find any public criticism of the United Kingdom by any of the members of the Federal cabinet. This was chiefly because Sir Abubakar till the end of his regime did not regard Britain as 'a foreign country', but as a member of the same Commonwealth family[35] criticisms of whom, if any, should be confined within it.

Another contributing factor was their differing assessment of the contribution of British rule to their countries' progress at independence. Although until early 1960 Dr Nkrumah used to refer to the positive contribution of British private and public interests to the development of his country,[36] the central element of his view from that time onwards was that the British despoiled the country during the colonial period. Thus in July 1961, he condemned the British colonial educational policy which had resulted in 'an acute shortage of trained manpower for managerial, and educational tasks'[37] after independence. After criticizing the British policy of exploitation of the Gold Coast he condemned the British government's fiscal policy during the colonial days which, he claimed, led to a reduction on independence of about £15 million[38] in the country's foreign reserves invested in Britain. Henceforth Nkrumah used to speak of reconstructing the economy of a country that had been badly damaged during colonial rule.

In contrast to this Sir Abubakar's view was that it was the British officers who served in the country during the colonial period that in his own words 'helped us to catch up with the twentieth century'.[39] Because of this it was right that Nigeria should always be grateful to Britain, as he made clear in his speech[40] at the celebrations to mark the atainment of independence on 1 October 1960.

Another important factor influencing their attitude to the UK was the need for aid and investments. But the significance of this should not be exaggerated. Apart from aid to develop the Volta River Project, Ghana did not require other capital aid from abroad during the first three years of independence, partly because the economy was relatively buoyant then and partly because the country lacked the necessary absorptive capacity for it. But even when the country's finances were in chaos early in 1965 and when it needed all the financial assistance it could get, Dr Nkrumah blasted the British neo-colonialist manouevres in the Congo at a time when his application for a capital loan of £188 million was being considered by the British government.[41] One important factor contributing to his attitude was Dr Nkrumah's awareness that he could easily turn to the Soviet Union and other communist countries if the United Kingdom turned down his request.

The case of Nigeria was a little different. On independence, as we have shown in an earlier chapter, her economy was not as good as that of Ghana. Therefore the Nigerian leaders wanted to attract as much foreign aid and investment as they· could into the country for development. It has to be remembered that one of the two main reasons given by Sir Abubakar in 1960 for joining the Commonwealth was to secure aid and foreign investments.[42] Although Sir Abubakar realized that there were other sources of aid he believed that aid should be received from 'real genuine friends', meaning Britain and other Western Powers, and not from 'self-interested countries with ulterior motives',[43] that is, the Communist countries. Although the United Kingdom was a little more generous with aid to Nigeria than to Ghana with the sum of over £32 million within a little over two years of her independence as compared with only £7.16 million to Ghana after over six years of independence,[44] this was only a contributory rather than a decisive factor influencing Nigeria's attitude to Britain.[45]

The divergent views of Ghana and Nigeria about the British involvement in the Congo were part of the explanation for their different attitudes to her. For instance, Ghana saw the British government's anti-Lumumba stance, and its opposition to the use of force to end Katanga's secession, as a calculated attempt to balkanize the Congo in order to perpetuate colonialist and neo-colonialist privileges and to halt the march to freedom in Southern Africa.[46] It has to be remembered that the major reason given by Dr Nkrumah for the wholesale dismissal of all the British officers in the Ghanaian army including Major-General Henry Alexander in September 1961 was the British government's attitude to Katanga's secession.[47] But Nigeria took an anti-Lumumba stand in the Congo like the United Kingdom, and so there was no conflict between them. Similarly, Nigeria and Britain broadly agreed that Katanga's secession should be ended through peaceful and political means rather than through the use of force as Ghana wanted.

Another important factor that accounted for different attitudes in Ghana and Nigeria to the United Kingdom was the question of the Portuguese and British colonialism in Southern Africa. As earlier indicated in chapter one,[48] Dr Nkrumah was violently anti-colonial, and from independence he had committed his country to the task of eliminating colonialism in Africa. Because of this he was extremely impatient of anything that tended to support colonialism in Africa. Thus the speech[49] of Lord Home, then the British Foreign Secretary, in Lisbon in May 1961 on the riots in Angola in which he said that it was entirely the business of the Portuguese to solve their colonial problems was severely criticized by Dr Nkrumah for giving 'assistance to Portuguese colonialism'.[50] Dr Nkrumah described as 'grave' the alleged statement of Lord Home promising 'to despatch British troops to Portugal'[51] to assist her.[52] The British government's sympathy for Portugal later in the Security Council, during the debate of the Angola riots, and its subsequent abstention on the draft resolution which essentially demanded an end to Portuguese military action against the insurgents were bitterly criticized in Ghana. Dr Nkrumah later in 1962 explained Britain's support for Portugal as being due to 'her special trading and concessionary rights in both Portugal and the Portuguese territories'.[53]

But the worst antagonism was to come over the British colonialism in Southern Africa. By late 1961, Dr Nkrumah had asked the British government to fix a target date for ending its colonialism in Africa.[54] But Mr Duncan Sandys told him in October 1961 that the British government could not do this because the pace of decolonization in each territory would be largely dependent on its particular circumstances.[55] But Nkrumah would not accept this. From late 1961 until the overthrow of his government in February 1966, Dr Nkrumah and his lieutenants pressed the British Government hard for the immediate establishment of African majority rule in Southern Rhodesia.[56] But the British Government resisted this. The upshot was to harden Ghana's attitude to the United Kingdom. For instance, the 1961 Constitution which gave the Africans a quarter of the seats in the Legislature and the remaining to the white minority, which was acclaimed by the British government in October 1961 as 'a remarkable progress unthinkable a year ago',[57] was described by Mr Alex Quaison-Sackey at the UN General Assembly as an attempt to turn Southern Rhodesia[58] into another South Africa.[59]

Dr Nkrumah in 1962 condemned the British government's talk of partnership, and of what he described as 'the perversions of multi-racial societies' in Central Africa as platitudes designed 'to keep the Africans at the hewer-of-wood and drawer-of-water level'.[60] Similarly the British government's veto on 13 September 1963 of the three-Power[61] draft resolution which *inter alia* called on Britain not to transfer to Southern Rhodesia as at present governed any powers or attributes of sovereignty until the establishment of government fully representative of all the inhabitants of the colony, and 'not to transfer to its colony of Southern Rhodesia the armed forces and aircraft as envisaged by the Central Africa Conference of 1963',[62] was roundly condemned by Dr Nkrumah as 'a clumsy substitute for convincing arguments at the world forum'.[63]

Later in 1965, the Labour government's handling of the Rhodesian

question was bitterly criticized in Ghana. For instance, the advance
commitment by Mr Harold Wilson that his government would not use
force in case of a unilateral declaration of independence (UDI) by the
white minority regime in Salisbury was condemned as an attempt to
apply double standards, because Britain had used force in similar
situations in the past such as Aden. Dr Nkrumah also condemned the
proposal of Mr Wilson to set up a Royal Commission in October 1965
under the chairmanship of Sir Hugh Beadle, whom he considered a
racialist, to test the opinion of the whole population about an
independence constitution for the territory, as 'a betrayal of the
African majority'.[64] Shortly after UDI, Dr Nkrumah declared that the
Wilson government's prior announcement that it would not use force
against the Ian Smith regime in case of a UDI was a direct invitation
to the rebellion in Salisbury on 11 November 1965.[65] The British
government's request to the Security Council for limited economic
sanctions against Rhodesia after UDI was ridiculed by Dr Nkrumah
as useless, since he thought only force could bring down the rebellion.
On 26 November 1965, when the National Assembly debated the
Africa Defence (Ghana) Bill which was to empower the Government
to make all necessary preparations, including military, along with
other African countries to meet any emergencies arising out of UDI,
saw the worst and most vituperative attacks by almost all the
MPs against the British handling of the Rhodesian problem.[66] Finally
Ghana broke off diplomatic relations with the United Kingdom over
Rhodesia on 15 December 1965 in accordance with the unanimous
resolution of the OAU Council of Ministers at Addis Ababa on 5
December 1965.

Nigeria's reaction to all this was different mainly because, as
pointed out earlier, the Balewa Government did not see colonial
questions as being central to its major preoccupations. Consequently
its attitudes to them were different from those of the Nkrumah
government. For instance, the British government's sympathy with
Portugal at the Security Council over the Angolan riots did not
provoke any criticism of the United Kingdom from the Nigerian
government leaders. Indeed, Jaja Wachuku defended Britain by
saying that she was independent, and so she was free to express her
sympathy and support and to cast her vote at the Security Council as
she saw fit in her national interest.[67]

On the Rhodesian problem, the Nigerian Government was ready to
show sympathy and understanding of the British Government's
handling of it. The British Government, too, realized this, and its
leaders were prepared to consult the Nigerian leaders on the

problems of that territory as Sir Alex Douglas-Home, then the British Prime Minister, did when he visited Lagos in March 1964 to seek, according to him, the counsel of Sir Abubakar.[68] Till the end of his regime, Sir Abubakar continued to co-operate with Britain to solve the Rhodesian problem. Thus the Wilson proposal to set up a Royal Commission to test the opinion of all the Rhodesians on an independence constitution, which Dr Nkrumah had condemned as shown above, was supported by Sir Abubakar, who said the success of the Commission should not be prejudged.[69] After UDI he said he would not agree that Britain had let down the Africans over the Rhodesian question.[70]

Although his representative to the OAU Council of Ministers' meeting in Addis Ababa early in December 1965, Alhaji Nuhu Bamali, had voted along with others on 5 December 1965 that all African countries should break off diplomatic relations with Britain if by 15 December 1965 she did not supress the rebellion in Salisbury, Sir Abubakar refused to implement this resolution, saying it was too grave a step to be taken.[71] Instead, he tried to assist Britain in solving the problem. It was his initiative that led to the Commonwealth Prime Ministers Conference that took place in Lagos early in January 1966 in order to assist the United Kingdom in tackling the Rhodesian problem and to preserve Commonwealth solidarity.

Another important factor that contributed to the differing attitudes between Ghana and Nigeria to Britain was the frequent cirticism of internal developments in Ghana. The British were very unhappy about the series of measures taken by Dr Nkrumah to establish a sort of dictatorship in Ghana. Thus in May 1960 some British MPs had referred with disdain to what they called 'the quirks of the dictatorship in Ghana.'[72] But the British press criticism of the trends towards dictatorship in Ghana was so severe as to provoke counter-attack by the Ghanaian press. By late 1961 one could talk of a sort of press war between Ghana and Britain. Although both Dr Nkrumah and Mr Sandys appealed to the news media in their respective countries for a truce[73] in October 1961, this was not heeded by either side. The establishment by the Ghanaian government of a Special Criminal Division of the High Court, from which there would be no appeal, in October 1961 was bitterly criticized by some sections of the British press,[74] especially the London *Times* which the Ghanaian government accused of conducting a 'hostile campaign' against Ghana which it said 'can be compared to the similar campaign conducted by the London *Times* in 1938 against Czechoslovakia which had as its object the dismemberment of that country in the interest of Hitler'.[75]

As Dr Nkrumah continued his drive towards establishing personal rule through the arbitrary detention of his political enemies, by the unscrupulous use of the Preventive Detention Act and other repressive masures, the British newspapers also continued their criticism of his regime. For instance, his dismissal of the country's Chief Justice, Sir Arku Korsah, on 11 December 1963 was condemned by almost all the British newspapers. The *Times* criticized Dr Nkrumah for being 'so careless of his country's reputation'.[76] The *Guardian* said by this act Ghana had become 'second in infamy only to South Africa.'[77] Similarly, the turning of Ghana into a formal single party state through the referendum of January 1964 was widely criticized in the United Kingdom. The consequence of all this was to provoke hostile reaction from the Ghanaian press and radio. And this continued with some brief intervals from 1961 until the coup in February 1966.

On the other hand, the British leaders and the press were full of praise for Nigeria's multi-party system of government. In fact until the overthrow of the Balewa government, in spite of some obvious repressive acts by both the Federal and the Regional Governments, the British press continued to put Nigeria up as an example of the success of parliamentary democracy in Africa.

(b) Attitudes to the Super Powers: I
Like Ghana's attitudes to the United Kingdom, those to the Super Powers fell into two parts. The first part was from the time of independence in 1957 till mid-1960, and the second from that time till the coup of February 1966. During the 1957–60 period, Ghana's attitude to the United States was cordial, while that to the Soviet Union was indifferent and suspicious. For instance, Washington was one of the first four capitals in which Ghana established her diplomatic Mission immediately after independence. The United States diplomatic staff and technical experts in Ghana were trusted and treated with respect. Although the American experts were responsible to the United States Mission in Accra, they had their offices in the various Ministries and Departments of the Government in line with the terms of the technical aid agreement of 3 June 1957 between Ghana and the United States.[78]

Appreciation of the United States contribution to Ghana's development through the provision of technical assistance was publicly expressed by the Ghanaian leaders. Thus in 1958 Dr Nkrumah expressed his government's gratitude to the United States for her aid.[79] In August 1959 the whole National Assembly unanimously passed a resolution thanking the United States for her assistance to the country through the International Co-operation Administration (ICA), and the International Development Service (IDS).[80] Similarly during his visit to the United States in summer 1958 Dr Nkrumah was happy at President Eisenhower's promise to assist Ghana to develop the Volta River Project.[81] The Ghanaian attitude was so friendly to the United States that by mid-1960 President Eisenhower was able to write to Dr Nkrumah to inform him of his country's readiness to participate in bringing to life the Volta River Project.[82]

During this period there was hardly any criticism of the United States in Ghana. Indeed, during his visit to the United States in 1958, Dr Nkrumah said that while he abhorred racialism he believed that racial problems in the United States were being exaggerated by people who wanted to bring the country into 'disrepute'.[83] On major international issues such as the Lebanon crisis and the Hungarian question Ghana's stand was essentially similar to that of the United States.

On the other hand, Ghana's attitude to the Soviet Union before mid-1960 was, as earlier indicated, one of suspicion. Although Dr Nkrumah had told the National Assembly in July 1958 that agreement had been reached in principle to set up a diplomatic Mission in Moscow,[84] this was not actually done until early in 1960. The Soviet Union was not allowed to establish her Mission in Accra until mid-1959. And when it was set up, the Ghanaian government limited the number of its staff to eighteen because the government said it did 'not want to allow the proliferation of hangers-on through which in some countries Soviet policies are pursued by other means.'[85]

Although a Ghanaian Parliamentary delegation led by Mr Kojo Botsio had visited the Soviet Union at the latter's request between late April and early May 1960, the Ghanaian government still wanted to keep its distance from Moscow. Thus at the Prime Ministers' Conference of May 1960, Dr Nkrumah suggested the establishment of a Colombo-type Commonwealth assistance programme for Africa so that the African countries might not take Soviet aid.[86] It is interesting to note that Sir Robert Menzies, then the Australian Prime Minister, told Dr Nkrumah at this Conference that he as Ghana's leader had a 'historic mission' to resist Communist expansion in Africa.[87] Shortly after Dr Nkrumah's return to Ghana, he was pressed in vain by several MPs to request aid from the USSR.[88]

But things were to change rapidly from late 1960 onwards and in such a way as to reverse Ghana's earlier attitude to the Super Powers. Largely because of the differences with the United States over the Congo crisis and the ideological differences between them and other factors which we shall consider briefly later, Ghana's attitude to Washington changed almost completely. From late 1960 until the coup in 1966, the central element in Ghana's attitude to the United States was one of resentment, resistance, suspicion and outright hostility though there were brief periods when attitudes to Washington could be a little relaxed, as during mid-1962 when President Kennedy decided to back strong United Nations action to end Katanga's secession.

From late 1960 onwards Dr Nkrumah became so mistrustful of the American experts that he did not allow them to have their offices in the Government Departments and Ministries as before.[89] Not only this, they were subjected to vitriolic attacks and frequent detention and deportation for alleged subversion.[90] The peace corps volunteers who were regarded in Ghana as the agents of the United States Central Intelligence Agency (CIA) working for the overthrow of the Nkrumah regime were usually the target of press attack from almost the beginning of their work in Ghana in August 1961. One of the worst of these attacks was the one of the *Ghanaian Times* of 23 July 1963. In a front-page fiery editorial entitled 'Let the Peace Corps Pack Out of Africa' the newspaper condemned them as 'spies and meddlers.' It then went on to say that the other NATO countries were known to be considering sending volunteers to Africa like the United States, and added:

. . . it is hard to isolate the role of the peace corps from the cold war aims of its organizer and financier. No one knows what will be happening in Africa when the Russians, the Chinese, and the Bulgarians also start sending peace corps volunteers to our continent. The cold war arena will have been firmly erected in Africa . . . let the peace corps pack out of Africa.[91]

Apart from the incessant attacks on American technical experts, the Ghanaian government became hostile to American scholarships. For instance from mid-1964 until the coup in February 1966 it refused to take up any scholarships offered by the United States Agency for International Development (USAID) in spite of the efforts of some MPs to make the government use them.[92]

The Kennedy decision in December 1961 to provide capital aid amounting to $147 million for the Volta River Project did not appreciably alter Ghana's basic attitude to the United States. This was partly because of the laborious and protracted negotiations that preceded this, and partly because all the loans except the AID one of $27 million carried a high rate of interest.[93] Dr Nkrumah said that the Volta loans were commercial 'loans', and not 'free grants' or 'gifts', and so did not entitle the donor countries to any political influence.[94] Indeed, once the arrangements for financing the Volta River Project[95] had been finally completed in December 1961 Dr Nkrumah was no longer happy to ask the United States for capital aid even when Ghana was desperately in need of it. Thus from 1961 until 1965, Ghana did not request capital aid from Washington; and when she did in March 1965 it was as part of an aid package of about £1,500 million[96] requested from the leading OECD countries; and even then according to the London *Times* it was the American government that was the last to be contacted by Accra.[97]

On diplomatic and political levels the attitude to Washington was not good. In April 1961, Dr Nkrumah condemned Washington as an aggressor over the Bay of Pigs episode.[98] Racial conflicts in the United States which Dr Nkrumah tried to play down in 1958 were now constantly criticized by the Ghanaian press and radio. In June 1963, Dr Nkrumah made a ringing denunciation of racial discrimination in the United States.[99] The hostility to Washington was so great that the Nkrumah government[100] organized a massive anti-American demonstration in Accra very early in 1964. This anti-American demonstration which was said to be about 1,000 strong and which was led by two cabinet Ministers,[101] Mr A. E. Inkusah, then the Minister of Information and Broadcasting, and Mr Krobo Edusei, then the Minister of Agriculture, and by some party members such as Mr Thomas Baffoe, then the editor of the *Ghanaian Times*, took place on 4 and 5 February 1964.[102] The demonstrators stormed the American Embassy and pulled down the flag there. The main reason for all this seemed to be what the CPP activists called the 'rumour-mongering' about the relationship between the Osagyefo Dr Nkrumah and the army.[103]

Henceforth till the coup the Ghanaian press and radio stepped up their criticism of the United States, especially after Tshmobe's return to Leopoldville (later Kinshasa) as the Prime Minister in July 1964. We have earlier referred to the charges of 'genocide', 'racism', 'brutalities' and 'inhumanitarianism' levied by Kojo Botsio against the United States during the debate of the US-Belgian rescue operation at the Security Council in December 1964. In May 1965 Dr Nkrumah in his opening address to the meeting of the Afro-Asian Solidarity Conference in Winneba accused the United States of aggression in the Congo, Cuba, Vietnam, Korea and the Dominican Republic.[104]

He said the United States was the sole cause of trouble all over the world. Finally in October 1965, Dr Nkrumah launched his book, *Neo-colonialism, The Last Stage of Imperialism* in which he described the United States as 'the citadel of neo-colonialism',[105] and in which he repeated his charges referred to above that Washington was the source of misery and disaster in all the trouble spots of the world.

In contrast to all this, however, Ghana's attitude to the Soviet Union began to be warm from late 1960 onwards. In fact the trend continued in such a way that by February 1966 some people in, and outside, Ghana thought that the country had virtually become a Soviet satellite.[106] Though we shall soon deal with the reasons for this type of development, it is relevant to note here that the most important ones were the ideological affinity between Accra and Moscow, especially from 1961 onwards, and the similarity of their views on major international issues.

Although no aid agreement was signed with the Soviet Union until August 1960, and although Soviet aid projects till the coup were in no way as impressive as those of the United States, the Ghanaian press and radio were full of praise for them. Indeed the total value of Soviet aid to Ghana till the coup, amounting to $82 million,[107] was considerably less than that of the United States, amounting to about $165.6 million by February 1966. In spite of this, however, the Nkrumah government was more appreciative of the Soviet aid. Even before the Soviet Union began to disburse her aid commitments in 1961 Dr Nkrumah had started to thank the Soviet leaders for their interest in Ghana's economic progress.[108] As Fritz Schatten has rightly noted the mere mention of the possibility of securing Soviet aid was sufficient to send the Ghanaian press and radio into 'ecstacies of admiration and gratitude'.[109] This was partly because to secure Soviet aid did not require prolonged negotiations, and partly because the terms of such aid were better and 'more impressive' than those of the West, as Dr Nkrumah himself said.[110] Furthermore, Soviet aid fitted in well with the 'socialist' ideology of the CPP government.

The Soviet experts in Ghana were trusted by the government. The trust in them was so great that when Dr Nkrumah dismissed all the British officers in his army in September 1961, he transferred the training and the control of the Presidential Guard[111] at Flagstaff House to them. The following month, October 1961, the first batch of Ghanaian cadet army officers numbering seventy-one left for the Soviet Union for training.[112] Till the coup Ghana continued to send her young men and women to the Soviet Union at a time when she refused to allow them to take up United States scholarships. Furthermore, by 1963 the Soviet geologists working in the Department of Water Supplies Division of the Ministry of Communication and Works had been fully integrated with the Department, whereas during the same period the United States peace corps geologists working with the Geological Survey Department of the Government were not similarly treated.[113]

The Ghanaian attitude to the Russians was so cordial that Dr Nkrumah had to invite Mr Brezhnev, then the President of the Praesidium of the Supreme Soviet, who was then visiting Guinea, to Ghana in February 1961. Henceforth till the coup there was a frequent exchange of visits between the officials of the political parties and governments of both countries. For instance Dr Nkrumah, accompanied by a party of twenty-seven, paid an official visit to the Soviet Union between 10 and 25 July 1961. He so much enjoyed his stay in the Soviet Union that after he had completed his official visit to the other Eastern European countries and China he and his family returned on 19 August 1961 for a brief holiday in the Crimea.[114] Later in October of the same year, the CPP sent a powerful delegation to attend the 22nd Congress of the Communist Party of the Soviet Union (CPSU).[115] Again in 1962, the CPP was represented at the conference of eighty-one Communist countries in the USSR.[116] In 1964, Kofi Baako, then the Defence Minister, led a government delegation to attend the celebrations to mark the seventieth birthday[117] of Nikita Khrushchev, then the Soviet Premier. Early in 1965, Kojo Botsio, then the Minister of External Affairs, headed a Ghanaian delegation to Moscow, while shortly before the end of the same year, Mr Amoako-Atta, then the Finance Minister, visited Moscow at the head of a Ghanaian government delegation.[118] Among the important Soviet figures who visited Ghana apart from Mr Brezhnev were Mr Mikoyan, then the First Deputy Premier, early in 1962, and Major Yuri Gagarin.

Apart from all this, the limitation placed on the staff of the Soviet Embassy in 1959 was discarded by 1961. As a result of this it was said that there were about 100 men and women in the Embassy when the coup occurred in 1966. Furthermore, there were frequent consultations between Dr Nkrumah and Mr Georgi Rodionov, the Soviet Ambassador in Ghana from 1962 until 1966, on major international issues. This stimulated co-operation between the Ghanaian and the Russian representatives at international conferences.

Apart from strengthening Moscow-Accra relations while straining those with Washington, one of the by-products of Ghana's attitude to the Super Powers especially from late 1960 till the coup was to cause disharmony in the Ghanaian-Nigerian relationship. Just as the Ghanaian leaders thought of their attitude to the United Kingdom from late 1960 as the 'correct' one to be followed by all other truly independent African states, so also did they think of their attitude to the Super Powers during the same period. To the CPP leaders any African country that did not adopt a similar attitude was a stooge of the imperialist Powers.[119]

Although the Balewa government's attitude to the Super Powers was different from that of Ghana between late 1960 and February 1966, it was in many ways similar to that country's attitude to them from its independence in March 1957 until the second half of 1960. Like Ghana till mid-1960, the Nigerian government from independence in October 1960 till January 1966 gave preferential treatment to the United States and the United Kingdom over the USSR. For instance, while it did not place any limit on the number of diplomatic staff of the American and the British Diplomatic Missions in Lagos, it put a limit on the number of Soviet diplomatic staff. While 100 diplomatic car plates each were given to the American Embassy and the British High Commission in Lagos, only ten were given to the Russians.[120] Furthermore, while the government made all possible efforts to ensure that the staff of the American and British Missions were well housed, it refused, even in the face of pressure by some MPs, to assist the Russian diplomats in solving their accommodation problems in Lagos.[121]

Like Ghana till mid-1960, the Balewa government did not ask Moscow for and did not receive any capital aid from it till the coup. Indeed, in April 1965, when the government was being pressed to balance its non-alignment by taking capital aid from the Russians, Chief Okotie-Eboh, then the Finance Minister, accused those making such demands of 'making friends with the socialists'.[122] Nor was the government enthusiastic about Russian scholarships. For instance, in 1963, of the forty-five scholarships offered by Moscow, only eleven were taken up by the government.[123] In short, it could be said that the government was rigidly anti-Communist. Although Sir Abubakar announced a partial lifting of the ban on Communist literature[124] in Nigeria in 1962, this was not strictly observed. For in October, 1965, Mr Michael Ogon, then an MP in the Eastern House of Assembly, had to appeal to the Federal government to lift its ban on Communist books and literature.[125]

On the other hand the government attitude to Washington was very warm and cordial. It allowed the United States to set up a satellite tracking station at Kano, which was regarded in Ghana as more or less a military base for the imperialists.[126] Capital aid from the United States was welcome and was solicited with energy. Similarly, the American experts were trusted as friends in Nigeria at a time when they were considered as fiends in Ghana. The trust was so great that the drawing up of the country's First National Development Plan 1962-8 was left largely in the hands of economic and financial experts provided, and financed, by the United States Government,[127] and the Ford Foundation.[128] Till the coup the government leaders were full of praise for and gratitude to the United States for all her economic and technical assistance and for what Chief Okotie-Eboh in 1965 called her 'contribution to the economic growth of Nigeria'.[129]

The attitude of the Balewa administration was so friendly to Washington that it was almost impossible for it to see anything wrong in the American involvement or its actions in different parts of the world. In this connection, it is interesting to note that while Dr Nkrumah was visiting the USSR in July 1961 and condemning all the imperialist Powers for their actions in Africa, especially in the Congo and Cuba Sir Abubakar was visiting the United States and was full of praise for the American role in the world. Indeed, on such issues as the American breach of the nuclear test ban in April 1962, the US-Belgian rescue operation in November 1964, and the war in Vietnam,[130] Sir Abubakar had actually come out in defence of the United States.[131]

A number of things were responsible for the differences in the Ghanaian and Nigerian attitudes to the Super Powers prior to the coups in the two countries early in 1966. Broadly speaking the most important were the following. The first was the need for aid and investment, the second was their ideological affinity with or differences from the two Super Powers; and the third was the identity or conflict of views on international problems. The fourth was the criticism of internal developments in Ghana by some American leaders and the press. None of these could be said to be sufficient explanation in itself.

However, because of the use of English as the *lingua franca* in both Ghana and Nigeria as well as in the United States, and because of some past links, however tenuous, during the colonial era with the United States, Washington was better placed for aid to these two countries than Moscow. And up till late 1960, apart from the United Kingdom, the United States was the next important Western donor country to which both of them could turn for aid. Thus when the

Nkrumah government was finding it difficult to secure firm British
financial aid for the Volta Project shortly after independence, it was
to Washington it turned in October 1957. The early interest shown by
the American government in the Project and 'the future development'
of Ghana, as contained in President Eisenhower's reply to Dr
Nkrumah,[132] and later President Kennedy's sustained interest in the
development of the Volta River Project went a long way towards
strengthening[133] Accra-Washington links until early in 1961.[134] This
was partly because of the importance placed by Dr Nkrumah on the
Project, through which he believed Ghana could attain what he
called 'economic independence',[135] and partly because until early
1961 Ghana was ideologically oriented more to the West than to the
East. The importance of aid in determining Ghana's attitude to the
Super Powers should not however be exaggerated. For instance, early
in 1965 while the Government's request for aid amounting to about
£220 million was being considered in Washington, Dr Nkrumah was
busy condemning the Anglo-American neo-colonialist manoeuvres in
the Congo.[136] Similarly, in October 1965, while Ghana's request for
commodity aid under the PL 480 was receiving attention in the State
Department, and when a World Bank Mission was visiting Ghana to
review the economy and to make recommendations for aid for which
the American support was needed,[137] Dr Nkrumah launched his
book, *Neo-colonialism: The Last Stage of Imperialism*, which was a
Marxist-Leninist indictment of the United States described as
'foremost among the neo-colonialists'.[138] Indeed, one could say that
although the economy needed external aid to help it to become self-
sustaining, it was doubtful whether the Nkrumah regime seriously
wanted aid from Washington after Kennedy's final decision in
December 1961 to support the Volta River Project, partly because of
the prolonged negotiations that preceded the Kennedy decision,[139]
and partly because for political reasons Ghana wanted to reduce its
dependence on the United States. In this regard, it is pertinent to note
that Dr Nkrumah's government in 1961 chose to pay the salaries of all
the American peace corps volunteers working in Ghana as if they
were its employees.

Likewise, Ghana's need for Soviet aid was not decisive in her
attitude to Moscow. Nonetheless, aid from the Soviet Union and her
readiness to understand and to assist in solving Ghana's economic
problems, as seen in the agreement of November 1965, under which
she was to buy 150,000 tons of cocoa per year from Accra for the
following five years,[140] and her agreement at the same time to
reschedule the debts owed her by Ghana[141] when the Western Powers

declined to do this until after a World Bank report on the economy, contributed substantially towards the Soviet-Ghanaian friendship. The increasing rate at which the USSR started to buy Ghana's cocoa especially from 1964 until the coup, done deliberately in order to force up the price of cocoa in the world market, earned her the praise of many Ghanaian MPs, including even those critical of the USSR such as Mr B. F. Kusi.[142] Barely forty eight hours before the coup, Mr Kwasi Amoako-Atta, then the Finance Minister, praised the Soviet Union for her 'keen sympathy towards our aspirations.'[143]

The extent to which the need for aid from the United States affected the attitude of the Balewa government is difficult to determine precisely. During the Balewa era, although the US apart from the World Bank was the single largest provider of aid, the value of her aid, amounting to about $200 million[144] by January 1966, was not considered impressive in Nigeria. However, aid from the American-led World Bank had been more substantial and significiant. Several important development projects such as the Bornu railway extension and the Niger Dam hydro-elecctric project, regarded by the government as the corner-stone of the 1962-8 Development Plan, were largely financed from loans provided by the World Bank and the United States. Besides this, the United States used to spend an annual average of about £8.5 million on technical assistance in Nigeria, apart from another annual sum of about £1,250,000[145] on the United States peace corps volunteers in the country. While the government leaders continued till the coup to express their gratitude to Washington for all its aid, it is not easy to say that it was the need for American aid that was decisive in influencing Nigeria's attitude. As indicated earlier, aid was merely a contributory factor.[146] However, since Sir Abubakar set his face firmly against capital aid from the Soviet Union or any other Communist country, it was possible for his government's actions to have been more influenced by the need for aid from the United States and other major Western donor countries than those of Ghana after 1961.

Another important factor making for the differences in attitude to the Super Powers was their different ideological orientation. While Dr Nkrumah had announced in June 1959 that the organization of his party was based on the principle of democratic centralism, socialism did not emerge as the dominant ideology of the CPP until early 1961.[147] Prior to that time, the CPP was ideologically closer to the West. It could be said that this somehow contributed to Ghana's friendly attitude to the West till late 1960. But by mid-1961 socialism had triumphed, following the dismissal and the disgrace of some right wing party leaders such Mr Krobo Edusei and Mr Kojo Botsio after the Dawn Broadcast of 8 April 1961,[148] and later the removal of perhaps the most important right wing figure in the party, Mr. K. A. Gbedemah, from the Ministry of Finance in May 1961, a post which he had held since 1955.

From 1961 till the coup the Nkrumah regime emphasized with vigour its socialist nature, and that of the party. The organization of the party was in many ways patterned after that of the Communist party of the Soviet Union (CPSU). Authority was to come from above as in Moscow. Likewise, there were some similarities in the roles of the CPP, its central committee and its General Secretary[149] and those of the CPSU, its central committee and its General Secretary. Furthermore, as earlier stated, by 1962 a police state apparatus had been established in Ghana and was followed by the formal introduction of a one-party socialist state in 1964. From 1961 until February 1966, the Nkrumah government took a number of steps to develop the country along the socialist line. It did its best to stifle the emergence of indigenous private enterprise, and in this it succeeded to such a degree that when the coup occurred in 1966 there was hardly any Ghanaian businessman who could be described as a tycoon. As previously indicated the government set up a number of state enterprises and state farms, some of them actually with Russian assistance. It has to be said that from 1961 onwards Dr Nkrumah and a number of his colleagues believed strongly that the pattern of development that turned Russia from a near-peasant country in 1917 to a World Power within a generation should be copied if Ghana and Africa were to catch up with Europe in technologicial advancement and economic power.[150]

Flowing from the adoption of a socialist philosophy at home was the emergence of a view of the international scene in Ghana similar to that of Moscow. This is the simplistic view of the world which says that only the socialist countries are peace-loving while all the imperialist powers are by their very nature aggressive. Although Dr Nkrumah had expressed this view before 1960, it was not until after 1960 that he and those described as 'socialist puritans'[151] by David Apter gave constant expression to this view even more so after the establishment of the *Spark* in December 1962. To the Ghanaian socialist leaders the United States was an imperialist Power and so must be prone to aggression, while the Soviet Union was as a socialist Power peace-loving. This view, which they usually tried to substantiate by the actions of the United States in many parts of the world after the end of the Second World War while conveniently ignoring instances of Soviet aggression in Eastern Europe, condititioned the thinking of the CPP leaders to Washington and Moscow between 1961 and the coup in 1966.

Although to the Ghanaian leaders Britain, too, was an imperialist Power like the United States, the hostility to the latter was more intense. This was mainly because Ghana believed that the United States was working for the overthrow of the Ghanaian government because of its socialist policies.[152] They believed that the United States Government were trying to achieve this by using the CIA, the peace corps volunteers in Ghana and dissident top Ghanaian officials, by support for the opposition leaders, and by depressing the world prices of cocoa. Thus the Ghanaian government accused the CIA and the US peace corps volunteers in connection with the series of bomb outrages in Accra shortly before and after the Queen's visit to Ghana in November 1961.[153] Similarly the United States and West Germany were charged with complicity in the Kulungugu bomb episode of 1 August 1962,[154] and the abortive attempt on Dr Nkrumah's life on 2 January 1964 was believed to have been engineered by the Americans.[155]

Although the Ghanaian leaders did not produce concrete evidence of the United States government's plan to overthrow their regime, it was possible that there was some element of truth in their allegations. Willard Scott Thompson referred to the presence of CIA agents in Ghana, and how they were in contact with Nkrumah's opponents in exile.[156] He even went as far as to say that the 'Americans were calculating carefully what might be the odds for a coup'[157] in Ghana.[158] Apart from all this, the CPP leaders could point to anti-Nkrumah actions by the United States. The most notable of these included the testimony of Dr K. A. Busia, then the opposition leader in exile, against the Nkrumah regime on 3 December 1962[159] before the sub-committee to investigate the Administration of Internal Security Laws of the Committee on the Judiciary of the United States Senate. Another was the testimony of two dissident Ghanaian students, Mr K. A. Akwawuah and Mr W. K. Biddier, before the same sub-committee on 29 August 1963 and on 11 January 1964,[160] calling for the termination of American aid to Ghana.

From 1963 onwards the CPP leaders had been accusing the imperialists, especially the United States, the largest single importer of cocoa beans, of manipulating world cocoa prices in order to overturn their government, which was heavily dependent on cocoa. During the Prime Minister's Conference in June 1965, Nkrumah declared that the American chocolate manufacturers were only interested in lowering the world price of cocoa to the detriment of the producing countries. Two days before the coup, Mr Amoako-Atta, then the Finance Minister, talked of the imperialist design to topple the CPP government through all forms of pressure, including low cocoa prices, because of its socialist policies which the imperialist Powers considered a dangerous threat to their 'powerful vested interests' in Africa.[161] In spite of the attractiveness of this argument for the CPP leaders it is difficult to prove. Although it is easy to point out that cocoa prices in the world market shot up immediately after the overthrow of the Nkrumah regime, this would be inadequate as proof. For since then the price of cocoa has continued to fluctuate under the NLC and the Busia Administration, just as it did under the Nkrumah government. Like the situation under Nkrumah, Ghana had failed to secure an international agreement on cocoa nearly six years after the coup. The price of cocoa in the world market, like that of other primary commodities, is subject to the economic rule of supply and demand. In fact, the increase in price shortly after the coup was largely due to the disclosure in the Western capitals that large quantities of Ghana's cocoa beans had been previously shipped to the USSR under the agreement of November 1965.

But between Washington and Lagos there was nothing like this kind of suspicion, which arose chiefly out of ideological differences. Like the United States, the Balewa government was frankly anti-Communist.[162] In spite of some difficulties, the Balewa government managed to maintain a multi-party state system and to preserve the rule of law perhaps better than any other part of Africa. There was nothing in Nigeria like the police state apparatus in Ghana from 1962 till the coup. In 1963, the Nigerian leaders succeeded in resisting a move to enact a Preventive Detention Act.

While the government practised what might be called a mixed form of economic organization, it tried as much as possible to put a very heavy emphasis on free enterprise economy. Shortly after independence when some radical elements were demanding the nationalization of foreign concerns in Nigeria, Dr Michael Okpara, then the Premier of the former Eastern Region and the National President of the NCNC, a junior partner in the Federal coalition, dubbed those people 'communists'.[163] Till the coup all the governments in Nigeria maintained their opposition to nationalization. It is interesting to note in this regard that, while Dr Nkrumah after 1961 felt that he had much to copy from the development of the USSR, Sir Abubakar believed that it was the

American model of development that his government must copy.[164]

On the international scene, Sir Abubakar shared the Western and especially the American simplistic view that the greatest threat to world peace arose from the desire of the Communist Powers to impose their ideologies on others.[165] In spite of the anti-Soviet stance of Nigeria this did not invoke press and radio criticism of her government in Moscow. And largely because of this, attack and counter-attack between Ghana and Washington were avoided.

Another important factor making for a difference of attitude in Accra and Lagos to the Super Powers could be found in the fact that while one of them had common interests with one or other of the Super Powers the other had conflicting ones with the same Super Power. For example, Ghana and the USSR had, broadly speaking, similar objectives in the Congo crisis.[166] They shared the same views on the dangers of colonialism, neo-colonialism and apartheid, and also on the way to solve major international problems such as the Berlin problem, the Cuban missile crisis, and Vietnam and China's representation at the UN. They also agreed to a great extent on how to tackle the question of disarmament.[167]

On the other hand, Nigeria's objectives in the Congo were totally different from those of the Soviet Union, but similar to those of the United States. While Nigeria believed in the need to eliminate colonialism, racism and apartheid from Africa, her approach was unlike that of Moscow but like that of Washington which preferred gradual, non-violent and non-revolutionary methods. Likewise, the views of the Balewa government on how to tackle major international problems such as Berlin, Cuba, Vietnam and disarmament were similar to those of Washington but entirely different from those of Moscow.[168] On the question of China's representation at the United Nations, Nigeria took the same position as the United States which by early 1966 favoured a two-China approach.

Finally, the criticism in the United States, especially from late 1960, of internal development in Ghana and to some extent her external policy contributed to her hostile attitude to Washington. For instance, in mid-September 1960, Christian Herter, then the US Secretary of State, because of Nkrumah's pro-Lumumba pronouncements on the Congo crisis accused him of taking Ghana into the Soviet orbit.[169] Early in 1961, the United States Ambassador in Ghana had in an *aide memoire* to the government protested at the delivery in the country of Soviet arms and ammunition.[170] All this caused some anger in Ghana.[171]

But it was the criticism of the dictatorial measures of Dr Nkrumah's regime that bred the worst anger and led to a sort of press war between Ghana and the United States. For example, the renewal of the Preventive Detention Act late in 1963 and the enactment, in November of that year, of a new Security Service Act to establish a secret political police to carry on espionage for the government under the direct control of Dr Nkrumah[172] invoked criticism from the United States.[173] Similarly the dismissal of the Chief Justice by Dr Nkrumah on 11 December 1963, the enactment of the Law of Criminal Procedure (Amendment No. 2) Act on 23 December 1963, empowering Dr Nkrumah to quash any court's decision he found unacceptable in the national interest,[174] and the referendum of late January 1964 to turn Ghana formally into a one-party state, and to empower the President to sack any High Court Judge for 'reasons which appear to him sufficient', provoked a barrage of criticism of Nkrumah from the United States. For instance, the *Washington Post* condemned all these measures as tantamount to introducing into Ghana the worst type of personal despotism in Africa.[175] The *New York Times* deplored the measures, and denounced them as barbarous, jungle justice and a complete negation of democracy.[176] In a blistering attack on Dr Nkrumah early in 1964, Senator Thomas Dodd said 'no other modern Communist leader had patterned his apparatus so slavishly after the model established by Lenin'.[177] The effect of all this was to stiffen Ghana's resistance to the United States.

On the other hand, the attitude to the USSR was relaxed because she was full of praise for the internal 'socialist' measures of Dr Nkrumah. Even before Accra and Moscow became closer late in 1960, the Soviet press and radio avoided making any criticism of Ghana.

Nigeria's attitude to the Super Powers could hardly be said to have been influenced by criticism from either Washington or Moscow. The United States had very little to criticize in Nigeria because both countries had many things in common, and although the Balewa government was clearly anti-Communist, Moscow, apart from probably lumping Nigeria with other client-states of the West, did not single her out for attack.[178]

(c) *Attitudes to the European Economic Community: I*
There was very little difference between Ghana's attitude to the European Economic Community (EEC) and that of Nigeria. The representatives of both countries joined together early in 1959 to persuade the six Common Market countries to lower their tariffs on tropical products and to liberalize their trade policies.[179] Apart from

their common anxieties about the adverse effects of the Rome Treaty on their major exports, their attitude to the EEC up to the middle of 1961 when the United Kingdom applied to join it was largely one of indifference. But this indifference soon turned to hostility once the British government formally applied in 1961 to join the Community and undertook to negotiate with the Six on behalf of its former colonies.

Both Ghana and Nigeria were opposed to the British application between mid-1961 and January 1963, when General de Gaulle vetoed it. Furthermore, they were implacably hostile to being linked with the EEC under Part IV, Article 131, of the Rome Treaty as were the eighteen African associates.[180] But while Sir Abubakar announced in Parliament on 24 September 1962 his government's decision to negotiate a trade agreement[181] with the EEC without necessarily acceding to Part IV, Article 131, of the Rome Treaty[182] in order to protect Nigeria's commodities that would be adversely affected by tariffs and quotas,[183] Dr Nkrumah till the end of his regime set his face firmly against any type of formal link with the Community.

Not content with this, Dr Nkrumah launched himself into a campaign against the EEC with a view to dissuading other African non-associates from joining the Community and the associated African countries from continuing their associateship. Thus in his address to the All-African Conference on Positive Action and Security in Africa, in April 1960, Dr Nkrumah declared that he hoped on independence the Congo (Leopoldville) and the other African territories associated with the EEC would sever their former links with it on the attainment of their independence.[184]

When after independence these countries maintained their links with the Common Market Dr Nkrumah brought greater energy to his denunciation of the EEC. In July 1961 he warned the African associates that the financial gains they were getting through their association with the EEC would be very small when compared with 'the losses they would suffer from perpetuating their colonial status — losses in terms of retarded economic and cultural development, and harm to African unity'.[185] During his visit to the Eastern European countries during the second half of 1961, Dr Nkrumah and his host in each of the state capitals he visited joined to denounce the EEC as 'a scheme to attach African countries to European imperialism'.[186] At the All-African Conference on Positive Action in Accra in June 1962[187] and other subsequent meetings of African nationalists, Dr Nkrumah attacked the EEC and the African countries associated with it.

A number of reasons could be given for the attitude of Ghana and Nigeria to the EEC. To both countries, especially to Ghana, the EEC was not merely an attempt to effect the political, military and economic union of Western Europe but was also an economic arm of NATO. This was why Chief Okotie-Eboh stated during the meeting of the Commonwealth Finance Ministers in Accra in September 1961 that the Community had 'political, social, economic, and even emotional features' that made it unsuitable for African countries.[188] This was also why Sir Abubakar said that to associate with the EEC under Part IV, Article 131, of the Rome Treaty would be contrary to Nigeria's policy of non-alignment.[189] This was part of the reason for Ghana's rejection of any formal link with the Community. This view was reinforced by the attempt of West Germany during the early sixties to use association with the EEC as a weapon against the recognition of East Germany.[190]

Furthermore, both countries believed that association with the Six under Article 131 of the Rome Treaty would hamper their industrialization programme. This was mainly because association under that Article was meant exclusively for countries predominantly dependent on the export of primary products as were the eighteen African associates, while countries at an advanced stage of industrialization could only seek association under a different Article of the Rome Treaty, Article 238.

The fear of losing the warm and informal atmosphere of the Commonwealth, with its historical and familiar links, in an enlarged European Community was an important factor in the opposition of both Ghana and Nigeria to the British application between 1961 and January 1963. To prevent this Mr Goka, then the Ghanaian Finance Minister, appealed to Britain during the Prime Ministers' Conference in London in September 1962 not to sacrifice 'Commonwealth values' to 'new loyalties'.[191] On another occasion, Ghana tried to use some sort of threat to prevent the United Kingdom from joining the Community. Dr Nkrumah said if the United Kingdom joined the EEC in a way disadvantageous to Ghana then she would withdraw from the sterling area 'to safeguard our trading position'.[192] Sir Abubakar told reporters at London airport on his arrival for the Prime Ministers' Conference in September 1962 that the Commonwealth should be developed into an economic unit, and that this would make Britain's application to join the Common Market unnecessary.[193]

Apart from all this, however, there was some difference in the attitude of Accra and Lagos to the EEC. Most importantly, Dr Nkrumah believed that any association with the Community would be detrimental to African unity. His view was that any formal link between African countries and the Common Market would involve commercial, financial and other discriminatory action between those associated and those not associated; and that the effect of this would be to preserve the artificial boundaries and other barriers of the colonial era which he had committed himself towards eliminating. Furthermore, he believed that it would make it almost impossible to establish an African Common Market, which was very dear to him. Thus in July 1961 he said '. . . it is on account of its retrograde effect to the cause of African unity that the Government of Ghana is so completely opposed to the European Economic Community'.[194] He therefore called on all African states to unite to build an African Common Market 'rather than serve as appendages to the European Common Market'.[195]

Still another reason for Dr Nkrumah's opposition to any association with the EEC was that it would frustrate the struggle for liberation in Africa. He believed that since the Community was an imperialist club most of its financial aid through the European Development Fund would be used to prop up in Africa regimes whose commitment to the liberation struggle was nil or at best minimal. Thus he told the All-African Conference on Positive Action in Accra in June 1962 that 'the desperate efforts of the neo-colonialists to associate African countries with the EEC' were designed 'to stay the advance of African liberation and the march to unity'.[196]

The threat posed by the EEC to African unity and liberation, which Dr Nkrumah believed really existed, was doubted by the Balewa government. Instead after an initial outright rejection of any link with the Community, it took a less emotional attitude by setting up towards the end of 1961 two study groups[197] to study and report on the British government's application to join the EEC and the implications of this for Nigeria. It was largely the report[198] of these study groups which essentially recommended that for economic reasons Nigeria should seek an accommodation with the EEC[199] along with the assumption in Lagos by late 1962 that Britain's membership of the Common Market was a foregone conclusion, that finally led the government to announce on 24 September 1962 that it was to open negotiations with the EEC for a trade agreement to protect her main products.

(ii)(a) Attitudes to Britain: II
The period between early 1966, when the coups occurred in both Ghana and Nigeria, and the end of 1970 saw considerable changes in

the attitudes of Ghana and Nigeria to Britain. Immediately after the overthrow of the Nkrumah regime, Ghana resumed diplomatic relations with the United Kingdom broken off on 15 December 1965 over the British handling of Rhodesian UDI. The attitude to the United Kingdom became relaxed and warm. Unlike the CPP government the NLC and the Progress Government did not encourage press criticism of Britain.

Ghana's attitude to London was so cordial that late in 1967 Ghana and the United Kingdom signed an agreement under which they were to exchange detachments of their troops for exercise in each other's country for six weeks every year. During 1971 6000 British soldiers of the third battalion of the Parachute Regiment came to Ghana under this troop exchange programme.[200]

Unlike the later period of the Nkrumah regime, the Ghanaian leaders had since the coup, especially since the Progress Party came into power in October 1969, been paying friendly visits to London. General J. A. Ankrah as the Chairman of the NLC visited Britain in October 1967 at the invitation of the British government. Similarly, shortly after Dr K. A. Busia came to office in October 1969, he paid an official visit to the UK. After that he continued, till the overthrow of his government, to frequent London for public and personal matters at least twice a year. After his return from one of these visits in August 1971, at which he succeeded in persuading the Heath Government to take back the £5 million frigate ordered by the Nkrumah government in 1965, Dr Busia spoke in Parliament of what he called 'the new and refresing atmosphere'[201] between Accra and London.

After the first coup, the Ghanaian leaders had been showing considerable understanding of problems facing the United Kingdom over Rhodesia and South Africa. They did not allow the British government's policy to Salisbury after UDI or its links with Pretoria to upset their friendly attitude to London. Thus. while some African Commonwealth leaders late in 1970 were threatening to quit the Commonwealth if the United Kingdom resumed arms sales to South Africa, Dr Busia said his country would remain within the Commonwealth.[202]

On the other hand, Nigeria's attitude to Britain was different in many ways. Frequent criticism of the British government over its policy to Rhodesia and South Africa was not only made by Nigeria's press and radio but also by her leaders. For instance, the British government's decision to sell seven Wasp helicopters to South Africa in February 1971 led to widespread criticism of Britain in Nigeria,[203] and led directly to the Federal Government's withdrawal from the eight-nation Commonwealth Committee on the security of the Indian ocean, set up at the Singapore Conference of the Commonwealth leaders in January 1971. Announcing the withdrawal, General Gowon accused Britain of 'total disregard of the African opinion.'[204] Likewise all the British attempts to solve the Rhodesian problem after 1966 short of majority rule before independence, such as the *Tiger* and the *Fearless* proposals of 1966 and 1968 respectively, were decried in Nigeria as surrender to the racists in Salisbury. The despatch of British troops to quell the rebellion in Anguilla in March 1969 while at the same time refusing to send troops to put down the one in Rhodesia was bitterly attacked in Nigeria as an evidence of British hypocrisy and double standards over UDI[205] The proposed Anglo-Rhodesian settlement of November 1971 was condemned by General Gowon as 'totally unacceptable'.[206] A few days later on 22 December 1971 the Federal Government issued a statement deploring the settlement with a stern warning that any settlement short of majority rule before indepenence would be resisted by Nigeria, and that if the United Kingdom went ahead to implement the Home-Smith accord, Nigeria would 're-examine her obligations as a member of the Commonwealth and would take other appropriate measures to safeguard Nigerian and African interests and security.[207] However, this kind of attitude did not lead to action against British experts serving in different parts of Nigeria.

Unlike the Ghanaian leaders only a few important figures in Nigeria had visited London since 1966. Indeed, no Nigerian head of government or state visited the United Kingdom between 1966 and mid-1973. Although it was reported in mid-1970 that General Gowon accepted the Heath government's invitation to visit the United Kingdom in 1971,[208] this did not take place until June 1973 largely because of the Conservative government's attitude to colonial and racial issues in Southern Africa,[209] and to race relations in the United Kingdom.

In the middle of 1971, the Federal Government announced that it would review all land and house allocations to foreign Missions in Nigeria, to ensure that they were based on the principle of reciprocity. It further said that where this principle was not applied all such land and houses would be taken over by the government. Of all the foreign Missions in Nigeria it was the British one which would be the hardest hit. It had a large area of land and about fifty houses[211] in Lagos allocated to it at a nominal rate, some indeed free on independence, at a time when the government was unable to find any suitable house in London for its High Commission.[212]

All these measures could not have been envisaged under the Balewa government. Thus we see that the period between early 1966 and the end of 1970 witnessed some profound changes in Nigeria's attitude to London just as the same period saw considerable changes in Ghana's attitude though in the opposite direction.

There were a number of reasons for these differing attitudes in Accra and Lagos to the United Kingdom. But only the important ones are briefly considered here. In the case of Ghana, the explanation could be found in the outlook, the experiences and the ideological orientation of the post-coup leaders of the country, the economic difficulties, and the mood of retreat from extensive involvement in world affairs.

The army and the police officers who seized power in Accra on 24 February 1966 were, as earlier indicated, pro-West, and pro-Commonwealth in particular. Thus Colonel (later Lt.-General) A. A. Afrifa soon after the coup wrote about his affection towards 'the British way of life, its legal system, and its democratic ideas'.[213]

The same was true of the leaders of the Progress Party that succeeded the NLC on 1 October 1969. In a speech at the luncheon party with diplomatic and Commonwealth writers of Britain in London in October 1969, Dr K. A. Busia spoke glowingly of the importance of the Commonwealth links to Ghana. He said *inter alia:*

> Our visit to Britain so soon after assuming office is a sign of the importance we attach to this (Commonwealth) happy association of free peoples linked by historical ties and by common ideals and values. We share the common ideals of the democratic life, respect for the dignity of the human person and ordered society ruled by law . . .[214]

This commitment to preserving Commonwealth ideals of democracy and the rule of law was important in influencing Ghana's attitude to London.

The economic difficulties of the country and its need for the injection of massive aid from abroad went a long way towards shaping Ghana's attitude to the United Kingdom. As earlier stated in chapter one, the NLC inherited a decadent economy, a large amount of external debt, an acute shortage of foreign exchange and galloping inflation, and to all this was added later the problem of high unemployment. The NLC leaders and the Progress Government regarded the solving of these problems and preserving national security as 'the supreme law'[215] of their Administrations. Since the threat to national security was not great, it was the task of improving the standard of living of the Ghanaians on which the Government placed a premium. Thus in a press statement in London in October 1970 Dr Busia said that although he discussed the question of the proposed resumption of arms sales to South Africa with Mr Edward Heath, his government's main pre-occupation was how to settle its debts.[216]

To do this required the British government's support, for over forty per cent of Ghana's short-term debts, owed to twelve Western countries, was owed to British firms.[217] Because of her cordial attitude to the United Kingdom, Ghana succeeded in securing the British government's support to re-schedule her debts to the Western countries, which had been done in 1966 and again in 1968. On coming to office in October 1969, Dr Busia asked the British government to help in re-scheduling the country's debts. The British government agreed to this, and so a meeting of the representatives of the creditor countries and Ghana was held in London under the auspices of the World Bank in July and in December 1970, to arrange another relief for Ghana.[218]

Apart from this, Ghana wanted long-term loan and grants from Britain. Although Britain increased her bilateral aid to Accra after the coup,[219] the Ghanaian government wanted London to assist in forming an international aid consortium for the country. Thus during Dr Busia's visit to London in August 1971, he appealed to the British government to assist in setting up such a consortium to arrange for Ghana a long-term loan of £108 million 'to give us enough time to improve our economic growth'.[220]

Finally the mood of retreat in the country from foreign adventures to which we earlier referred in chapter one favoured warm attitude to the United Kingdom. Because of the economic and the financial difficulties of the country, especially between 1964 and the coup in 1966, which many Ghanaians attributed to Dr Nkrumah's over-extended commitment abroad, the mood of the country after the coup favoured 'a low profile' in foreign affairs. In fact, many Ghanaians believed that Dr Nkrumah's antagonism to the Western Powers over colonial and racial issues contributed substantially to their reluctance to come to the rescue of the country during the difficult years between 1964 and the coup. Largely as a result of this, many Ghanaians lost interest in the anti-colonial and anti-imperialist crusade in order not to scare off the Western countries who might be interested in helping the country out of its economic throes.

The reasons for Nigeria's change of attitude to the United Kingdom were many. But broadly speaking they could be grouped into three. The first was the coup and the civil war, the second was domestic pressure, and the third was the obsolescence of some interests previously valued.

The coup of January 1966 swept from office political leaders and parties who were very pro-British. Indeed, the first open criticism of the British government by the Nigerian Government did not occur until after the coup, when the Ironsi government accused the British government of inciting the Northerners into rioting against the Ibos, following Decree 34 of May 1966 which turned Nigeria into a unitary state.[221] Although the Sandhurst-trained men who seized power in a counter-coup on 29 July 1966 were as conservative as the former Nigerian civilian leaders, events soon took things out of their hands. The most important of these events was the civil war that began on 6 July 1967.[222]

There were two main ways in which the civil war affected Nigeria's attitude to the United Kingdom. The first was the initial attitude of London to Nigeria, and the second was the support given to the secessionists by the white supremacist regimes in Southern Africa. The British government's decision to remain neutral at the outset of the war was regarded in Lagos as the betrayal of a former friend. But more agonising to the Nigerian leaders was the British government's refusal to grant a licence for the purchase of jet fighters and bombs, and even to allow the shipments of large quantities of light arms and ammunition to Nigeria until after a military aid agreement had been concluded with the Soviet Union on 2 August 1967. The denunciation in July 1967 of the oil blockade of the former Eastern Nigerian coast as a breach of 'international law' by Mr George Thomas, then a Minister of State in the Commonwealth Relations Office, worsened matters.[223] The furore caused by Mr George Thomas's denunciation could be imagined if it is remembered that earlier, on 30 June 1967 the British government had informed the Federal government to its chagrin that the British oil companies, Shell and BP, would make a token payment of royalties to the secessionists because of the serious damage they could do to the companies' assets around Port Harcourt.[224]

All this led to disillusionment with the past close links with Britain. The Federal government issued a statement rejecting Mr George Thomas's denunciation of the blockade as a violation of international law.[225] The *Morning Post* summed up the general impression in Nigeria by saying that the statement of Mr George Thomas was evidence that the United Kingdom was not interested in the survival of Nigeria as a unit, but only in the flow of oil, and that it showed the bankruptcy of the previous pro-British stance of Nigeria's foreign policy.[226] The *New Nigerian* declared that the statement of Mr George Thomas showed that the British government was involved in the war on the side of the rebels.[227]Writing in 1968, Mr Walter Schwarz said that as a result of the civil war Britain had 'lost ground, perhaps irretrievably in Nigeria.'[228] Though this contained some truth, it was a little too harsh, and too rash.[229] For through patient and skilful diplomacy Sir David Hunt, who until late in 1969 was the British High Commissioner in Nigeria, succeeded in regaining some of the ground lost for his government. The unflagging support and defence of the federal cause, amidst a barrage of criticisms from both sides of the Commons, by Mr Michael Stewart, then the Foreign Secretary, especially from late 1968 onwards was appreciated in Nigeria. Similarly, Mr Wilson's visit to Nigeria in March 1969 was reassuring in Lagos.

But if the difficulties over the initial hesitation of the British government to back the Federal government against the secessionist rebellion were almost overcome by the time the war ended in January 1970, the problems created by the support of South Africa, Rhodesia and Portugal for the secessionists could not easily be solved. Because of their moral and material aid to the rebel regime, the Nigerian leaders saw the existence of these white minority regimes in Africa as a direct threat to the independence, sovereignty and territorial integrity of their country. And, therefore, they wanted a speedy elimination of all these regimes from Africa. Any attempt to prop up colonialism and racism in Africa was seen in Lagos as a hostile act. Consequently the Conservative government's policy of selling arms to South Africa and of negotiating a settlement with the Ian Smith regime that did not ensure majority rule before independence provoked criticism and hostility to the United Kingdom in Nigeria.

Another important reason for Nigeria's change of attitude to London was the influence of various radical groups in Nigeria. Since independence there had always existed radical elements in the country which held the view that Nigeria's independence could only be genuine by maintaining a tough attitude to Britain. But partly because of the unorganized nature of these groups and partly because of the overwhelming majority of the Balewa government in the Parliament, the government was able to disregard them. But since 1968, more and more radical groups and associations had been formed with the tacit encouragement of the government. For instance, in 1968, the Nigerian Trade Union Congress (NTUC) was allowed to affiliate with the Prague-based World Federation of Trade Unions, something prevented by the Balewa government. The other important militant groups included the Nigerian Youth Council and the Nigerian Afro-Asian Solidarity Organization whose patron was Aminu Kano, later the Federal Commissioner for Health. Still others included the Nigeria-Soviet Friendship Association and the Black Renaissance. All these various groups held seminars and public lectures on anti-imperialist struggles in Africa. They also issued statements on major international issues. For instance, the National Youth Council in September 1970 called on General Gowon not to visit the United Kingdom if the Heath government sold arms to South Africa.[230] After the civil war, all the Nigerian newspapers became more vocal and violent in their campaign against colonialism and racism in Africa. The influence of these radical groups and the press was, however, derived more from the fact that their campaign was in line with the Government's commitment to a speedy end to colonialism ·and racism in Africa than from their own intrinsic strength.

The fact that some interests hitherto valued in Nigeria had become obsolete was important in influencing Nigeria's attitude to the United Kingdom. The two main reasons given by Sir Abubakar shortly before independence as to why Nigeria's attachment to the United Kingdom would continue to be strong after independence were the following. The first was the need for aid and investments; and the second was the need to rely on British diplomatic Missions to transact commercial and diplomatic matters in areas where Nigeria had no Embassies.[231] These two interests were greatly valued by Nigeria during the first years of her independence. Although Sir Abubakar knew that other sources of aid existed, his view was that this must be taken from 'genuine friends', that is, the Western Powers, and not from the Communists. As earlier stated, the UK was a little more generous with aid to Nigeria than to Ghana. For instance British aid commitments to Nigeria within a little over two years of her independence was over £32 million as against only £7.16 million to Ghana nearly six years after independence.[232]

But all this changed. First the British government's suspension of the £10 million aid commitment to telecommunication development at the beginning of the civil war meant that Nigeria had to turn elsewhere for development aid as Alhaji Aminu Kano, then the Federal Commissioner for Communications, made clear late in 1967.[233] The confidence and self-assurance arising from victory over the secessionist forces, backed by some freign interests, assured the

Nigerian leaders that they could raise development loans from any source without any fear. Furthermore, the government decided to reduce the country's reliance on foreign aid, partly because of the resilience of the economy during the civil war and partly because of the oil boom which put Nigeria among the ten largest oil producing countries in the world. For instance, only about twenty per cent of the capital required for investment in the public sector during the Four-Year Plan 1970–4 was expected from abroad as against the corresponding percentage of fifty per cent under the 1962-8 Development Plan.[234]

Although Nigeria still welcomed aid from the United Kingdom which had already promised to grant Nigeria the sum of £39 million[235] for capital development during the Four-Year period, apart from her grants and technical assistance running at an annual average of over £6 million,[236] Nigeria merely regarded this as part of aid required for development from both the West and the East, and as such it did not justify any special attitude to the United Kingdom.

The other factor, which was the reliance on British Embassies in some parts of the world for commercial, consular and diplomatic activities, was valuable up till 1963 when Nigeria had only about thirteen diplomatic posts overseas. But this number rose to thirty-nine in January 1966, and to over sixty at the end of 1970,[237] and the transaction of business through the British diplomatic Missions abroad became a thing of the past.

(b) *Attitudes to the Super Powers: II*
After the coup in February 1966, Ghana reversed her previous attitude to the Super Powers. She became extremely friendly with the United States while becoming hostile to the Soviet Union, especially during the first two to three years after the coup. An end was put to criticism of United States experts in Ghana. Unlike the previous suspicion of the United States peace corps volunteers in Ghana, the NLC government trusted them, and got the United States Government to agree to finance them, as it had been the case in many other African countries. After the coup there was nothing but praise for the assistance received from America.[238] Indeed, in December 1967, the NLC government dismissed all the four editors of its own two newspapers, the *Ghanaian Times* and the *Daily Graphic,* for daring to criticize as unfavourable to Ghana an agreement between the government and an American firm, the Abbott Laboratories.[239]

Terms like 'imperialism', and 'neo-colonialism' disappeared from the pages of the Ghanaian newspapers except where they were ridiculed as a fantasy coined by certain leaders to maintain a vicious type of dictatorship. Likewise, other terms such as 'Uncle Sam', used during the Nkrumah period in an abusive way against the United States, ceased to find expression among the Ghanaian leaders and the press.

Just as in the case of the United Kingdom, all the leaders of government in Ghana after the coup paid official visits to Washington. General J. A. Ankrah went there late in 1967 and Dr Busia late in 1969, and again in 1970 and 1971. In May 1970, the then Deputy Speaker of the National Assembly, Mr Isaac Amissah-Aidoo, went to Washington for two weeks to acquaint himself with Congressional life and procedure.[240] In return, some important American figures visited Ghana after 1966. These included Mr Humphrey, then the Vice-President, in January 1968, and Mr William Rogers, the then Secretary of State, in February 1970.

On major international issues Ghana's position became close to that of the United States. For instance, during 1967, when public opinion in Western Europe was very critical of the United States bombing of North Vietnam the *Ghanaian Times* praised the American President for his 'restraint so far on the bombing'.[241] It added that it should continue until the Soviet Union and China stopped their assistance to North Vietnam, and until the North Vietnamese ended their movements of troops and materials to the South.[242] On the question of China's representation at the United Nations, Ghana's position was close to that of the United States.[243] Although she abstained on the vote at the United Nations General Assembly to seat Mainland China and to expel Formosa in October 1971,[244] the government-owned newspaper, the *Daily Graphic* decried the expulsion of Formosa as senseless and dangerous for the future of the United Nations.[245]

On the other hand, Ghana's attitude to the Soviet Union since the coup varied between outright hostility and indifference. Immediately after the coup, the NLC reduced the number of staff at the Soviet Embassy to the original level of eighteen allowed in 1959. Apart from this, all the Soviet technical experts were sent back to Moscow shortly after the coup. It was not until September 1967 that the Government indicated that it would allow some Soviet experts to return to complete potentially viable projects, such as the fishing complex at Tema on which they had been working before 24 February 1966.[246] But because of the continuing hostility towards Moscow in the country, the Soviet Union did not respond to this. And a new technical aid agreement under which Soviet experts were to be sent to

Ghana was not signed until July 1970.[247] Even then, suspicion of the
Soviet Union remained in Ghana and this till early 1972 made it very
difficult to implement the agreement.

Indeed, the anti-Communist hysteria which gripped Ghana
immediately after the coup but which by the end of 1968 was dying
out surfaced again in mid-1971, and between June and August 1971
two members of the Soviet diplomatic staff, Mr Valter Vinigradov
and Mr G. P. Potemkin, were deported from Ghana on charges of
espionage.[248]

Furthermore, there was hostility to Ghanaians trained in the USSR.
All doctors who received their training in the Soviet Union were
required to be retrained for another eighteen months in Ghana
before they were allowed to practise. Indeed, after the coup it became
difficult for Soviet-trained Ghanaians to find jobs in their own
country.

On international problems, the Ghanaian government from
February 1966 to 13 January 1972 took an anti-Soviet stance. In 1967
it was the Soviet Union that was condemned by the *Ghanaian Times*
which said that her aid to the North Vietnamese was unbecoming to
her as the co-chairman of the Geneva Agreement.[249] In August 1968,
it condemned Moscow for the Warsaw pact invasion of
Czechoslovakia.

Just as the period between early 1966 and the end of 1970 saw
considerable changes in Ghana's attitude to the Super Powers so it
was in Nigeria's attitude to them. Instead of the previous pro-
American stance of Nigeria she became from 15 January 1966
onwards increasingly critical of the United States. Although the
Federal government was not antagonistic to the American diplomats
in the country, its attitude to them was far from the warm one of the
Balewa era. Although the government in mid-1969 brusquely
dismissed as uncalled for the 'aide memoire' from the American
Ambassador demanding whether it had lifted its previous restriction
on the Soviet Embassy, which then had thirteen men instead of the
original ten on its staff,[250] it refrained from pursuing direct hostile
policy to Washington.

While the American experts were not directly attacked by the
government, it strongly criticized the way in which they carried out
their work in the country, especially the publicity aspect and the type
of aid provided by America. Referring to the past activities of the
USAID, and USIS, though not mentioned by name, General Gowon
in his budget statement in April 1970 said:

We are no longer interested in external donors who spend all their time on publicizing their aid activities in Nigeria without really doing anything concrete to really assist our development effort[251] on the ground.[252]

Furthermore, in an indirect attack on the American practice of providing separate assistance for each project and the prolonged negotiations that usually preceded it, General Gowon added that '. . . we shall welcome only the external assistance that can be promptly utilized . . . Assistance in the form of programme support or generaly commodity loan will be more valuable than protracted and endless negotiations over individual projects as in the past.'[253]

On international issues Nigeria became critical of Washington. On the increasing bombing of North Vietnam during 1966 and 1967, the Nigerian press and radio bitterly criticized the United States.[254] Likewise, the American invasion of Cambodia early in 1970 was widely condemned in Nigeria as barbarous and indefensible.

The American decision to start importing chrome from Rhodesia was bitterly attacked by the Nigerian press and Government as a subversion of the United Nations sanctions and as support for the racists in Southern Africa.[255] On China's representation at the UN, Dr Okoi Arikpo on 18 October 1971 made a powerful speech in favour of seating Mainland China, and expelling Formosa.[256] At the voting later at the General Assembly, Nigeria voted against the American stand of a 'two China' policy.

Nigeria's attitude to Moscow has also undergone some changes. Although the restriction on the number of Soviet diplomats was not formally lifted, the attitude to those of them in the country became relaxed and cordial. Indeed, between late 1968 and the end of the civil war in January 1970, there were frequent meetings and consultations between General Gowon and Mr Romanov, then the Soviet Ambassador in Nigeria.

Capital and military aid from Moscow which was never contemplated under the Balewa regime, let alone requested, was sought and warmly received after the coup. When the British government suspended its aid to the telecommunication development at the outset of the war, it was to the Soviet Union to which Nigeria turned.[257] Furthermore, after all the Western Powers had refused to allow the Federal government to buy military aircraft and bombs and heavy arms for its campaign gainst Biafra, it was to Moscow to which it turned, and negotiated a military aid agreement, signed on 2 August 1967. Although the number of Russian experts in Nigeria was still small compared to that of the United Kingdom, the attitude to them was on the whole friendly. There was no question of suspecting them of sabotage, let alone of deporting them, as was the case in Ghana after the coup. On international issues except in the Warsaw pact invasion of Czechoslovakia in August 1968, which was widely condemned by the Nigerian press[258] though not by the Government, Nigeria and the USSR were in broad agreement, and so the question of Nigeria criticizing Moscow did not arise.

A number of reasons were responsible for the differences in attitude of Accra and of Lagos to the Super Powers between early 1966 and the end of 1970. Most of them were similar to those already mentioned earlier. In the case of Ghana the important factors were the outlook of the NLC and Progress Party leaders, their suspicion of Soviet intentions, the economic difficulties of the country, and the mood of the country. Much of what we have discussed under the section dealing with attitude to the United Kingdom applies here, and so we shall only refer to what is of particular relevance to the Super Powers.

The NLC and the PP leaders were anti-Communist[259] and pro-West. Dr K. A. Busia in an address to the African-American Chamber of Commerce in New York late in 1969 spoke of 'the common . . . fundamental philosophies about life and politics'[260] between Ghana and the United States. To some extent this contained some truth because the Progress Government like the United States Administration placed great emphasis on the role of private free enterprise in the economy, and the role and the value of the individual within the society. All this contributed to the warm attitude of Accra to Washington while its attitude remained one of suspicion and hostility to Moscow.

Another important reason for the wave of anti-Soviet hysteria in Ghana was that Moscow was closely identified in Ghanaian eyes with the Nkrumah regime. The troops and the police that stormed the Flagstaff House during the early hours of 24 February 1966 had to fight against the Presidential Guard trained and equipped by the Russians. Furthermore, the fact that some Russian and East German experts were closely connected with the intelligence service under the Nkrumah regime further drew the ire of the Ghanaians towards the Russians. Apart from this, the NLC and even the Progress Government suspected, though without producing any concrete evidence, that the USSR was planning to assist Dr Nkrumah to return to power by force from Conakry in Guinea. For instance, the NLC issued a statement late in 1966 in which it said that in June of that year a Soviet ship loaded with arms and ammunition docked at Conakry in order to help the deposed President to seize power in

Accra.[261] Though not really well substantiated, the suspicion and the fear of Dr Nkrumah returning to power under the Soviet arms persisted in Ghana.[262] While this suspicion subsided after late 1968, it could surface any time. Thus as we said earlier, in mid-1971 the Ghanaian government deported two members of the staff in the Soviet Embassy suspected of espionage for Dr Nkrumah.

The economic difficulties of Ghana further brought her closer to Washington. Although the short-term debt owed to the United States by Ghana was relatively small, the government needed all the assistance she could get from Washington to surmount her economic difficulties. The prompt American offer of food and commodity aid to Ghana immediately after the coup was greatly appreciated in the country. After that Washington continued to be generous with aid to Ghana more than to many other African countries. For instance, during the visit of Mr William Rogers to Ghana in February 1970 he announced a further loan of $15 million[263] to the country at a time when Washington had been cutting down its aid commitments in different parts of the world. As a result of this, within just over five years after the coup Ghana received the sum of N₵184 million[264] in aid from Washington, which was more than the total value of its aid to Ghana during the first nine years of her independence. Furthermore, the Ghanaian government wanted American government support for an international cocoa agreement, as Dr K. A. Busia made clear during his visit to the United States late in 1969.[265] The effect of all this was to strengthen the links between Accra and Washington.

On the other hand, the Ghanaian government after the coup, like the Balewa government, did not request nor take any capital aid from Moscow. And as we pointed out earlier, the technical aid agreement between them in 1970 was not implemented by the Progress Government. However, the Busia government tried to promote its trade with Moscow. In pursuit of this, it opened a trade mission[266] in Moscow late in 1971.

The reasons for Nigeria's attitude to the Super Powers during the 1966–70 period were similar to those mentioned earlier while dealing with her attitude to London. These were the coup and the civil war, and the problem of colonialism and racism in Africa. We shall only consider all these briefly in so far as they directly affected Nigeria's attitudes to Washington and Moscow.

The coup in January 1966 swept from office leaders who were extremely pro-West and anti-Communist. The Ironsi government was not as pro-West as the former civilian government. In this regard it should be remembered that the first open protest to Washington by the Nigerian government after independence was made under the Ironsi administration over the opening of an information office in Washington by the Rhodesian rebel regime early in 1966. Furthermore, it should be noted that the first request for Soviet capital aid[267] by Nigeria was made and accepted in April 1966.

The different reaction of Washington and Moscow to the civil war considerably influenced Nigeria's attitude to them. The neutrality of the United States in the war and its refusal to grant a licence to Nigeria to buy arms and ammunition to suppress the Biafran secession was seen in Nigeria, as Colonel (later Brigadier) Ikwue, the then Chief of Air Staff, told the American Ambassador in Lagos, as an 'indirect support for the secessionists.'[268] Apart from the pro-Biafran propaganda by the American press, the Nigerian Government noted with anxiety and anger that neither President Johnson nor President Nixon ever made any unequivocal statement in favour of one Nigeria throughout the dark days of the civil war. Likewise, and more irritating to the Nigerian leaders, was the American government's criticism of the alleged bombing of the civilian population in Biafra.[269] This reached such a point that the Federal Government had to issue a series of statements decrying the American government's attitude, and asking it to respect the sovereignty and the territorial integrity of the country.[270]

On the other hand, the speed with which the Soviet Union came to support the federal cause with arms, bombs and military aircraft after the Western Powers had turned down Nigeria's request was highly appreciated throughout the country. Moscow's continuing support till the end through the supply of such weapons as the 122mm guns, which were said to have been decisive in the war, gave the Nigerians a good impression of the USSR as a true friend of the country. Shortly after the end of hostilities on 12 January 1970, General Gowon specially called in Mr Romanov, then the Soviet Ambassador in Lagos, to Dodan Barracks to offer the country's gratitude for his government's unflinching support for the federal cause.[271]

Another reason for the differing attitude of Nigeria to Washington and Moscow was that after the civil war, during which the white supremacist regimes in Africa assisted the secessionist forces, the total elimination of these regimes had become urgent in Nigeria. While the United States favoured a gradual process to achieve this, she was on the whole in favour of the *status quo* in Africa. She continued to trade with South Africa, while her investments there were fairly substantial. Later she decided to be buying chrome from Rhodesia. Furthermore, after UDI, the Anglo-American Corporation continued to operate in Rhodesia.

Furthermore, she was an ally of Portugal through NATO, and to her the Azores islands were still of strategic value. Because of all this Washington was not anxious to see the *status quo* in Southern Africa suddenly disrupted as Nigeria wanted. Thus in a series of statements after 1968 the Nigerian spokesmen demanded the speedy end to colonialism and racism in Africa. In his opening address to the third African-American Dialogue early in March 1971, General Gowon said *inter alia* that '. . . Africans are generally more concerned about the important moral question regarding their personal dignity, and self-respect.'[272] He then warned all the Powers supporting, even if indirectly, colonialism, racism and oppression, which he described as 'potentially explosive issues in the continent', to 're-examine the basis of their relations with Africa.'[273]

On the other hand Nigeria and the Soviet Union had what Dr Arikpo called 'an identity of views'[274] on issues of colonialism, racism and oppression. Moscow like Lagos favoured a speedy change in the *status quo* in Southern Africa. The Soviet interests in the area were minimal, and so she had little or nothing to fear from a sudden change. Because of this 'identity of views' over colonialism and racism, Nigeria's attitude to Moscow became warm. For instance, late in 1970, when Mr Edwin Ogbu, then the Nigerian Permanent Representative at the United Nations, was at the General Assembly lambasting the Western Powers for supporting colonialism and racism in Africa, he had only praise for the Soviet Union for 'assiduously observing' all UN Security Council and General Assembly resolutions on the situation in Southern Africa.[275]

Another factor influencing Nigeria's attitude to the Super Powers was their attitude to the question of poverty in the developing countries. Here again Dr Arikpo spoke of 'identity of views' between Lagos and Moscow.[276] It was believed by the Nigerian leaders that the USSR was genuinely interested in raising the standard of living in the developing world. To substantiate this they frequently pointed to the fact that there were no Soviet firms exploiting the developing countries. On the other hand, it was believed that the Western Powers led by the United States would always do their utmost to depress the price of the primary products of the developing countries. For instance, in his review of his nine-month period in office, Brigadier O. Rotimi said in December 1971 that owing to the manipulation of world cocoa prices by some powerful (imperialist) forces his government's revenue fell by about £5 million.[277] In General Gowon's speech at the third African-American Dialogue referred to above he condemned the exploitation of Africa by foreign investors, and said that foreign investments to be meaningful in Africa must serve the true interests of the indigenous population.[278]

(c) Attitudes to the European Economic Community: II

Shortly after the coup of 24 February 1966, the NLC government looked at the problems posed for Ghana by the EEC with fresh eyes. After an initial study of the situation, it accredited early in 1968 its Ambassador at the Hague and Brussels, who was then Professor de Graft Johnson, to the European Commission in Brussels to study how Ghana could be linked with the EEC either through a formal trade agreement, or by acceding to Part IV Article 131 of the Rome Treaty as had the eighteen African associates.[279] With the change of government in Accra in October 1969, Ghana did not change her attitude to the EEC. Thus in the middle of 1970, Mr C. O. Nyanor, then the Ministerial Secretary to the Ministry of Finance and Economic Planning, said the Progress Government had been studying the EEC to know what type of formal association it would have with it.[280]

But with the agreement on the British membership of the Community as from 1 January 1973 being reached by late 1971, the Ghanaian government started more frequently than ever before to express its readiness to come into some form of formal association with it. Indeed, Dr K. A. Busia said in September 1971, before a team of British army officers visiting Ghana, that his country might seek an association with the Common Market once the United Kingdom became a member.[281]

Nigeria's attitude to the EEC also changed though in a different direction. As we indicated earlier, Nigeria and the EEC signed an association agreement under Article 238 of the Rome Treaty in Lagos on 16 July 1966. This agreement which was more of a trade one[282] was ratified in January 1968 by Nigeria[283] but never by France or Luxembourg before its expiry on 30 June 1969. When the flow of oil was severely curtailed in mid-1968, the then Federal Commissioner of Trade and Industry, Alahji Ali Monguno, summoned a meeting of all the Ambassadors of the Common Market countries in Lagos, and appealed to them to ratify the agreement urgently to protect the country's exports to the Community.[284] But as earlier indicated only four of the Six actually did.

But with the recapture of most of the oil producing areas from Biafra late in 1968, Nigeria began to lose interest in any formal link with the EEC. After 1969, the Federal Government virtually set its face against the EEC, particularly after the end of the war when there was no longer any hindrance to the export of crude oil, which by mid-1971 was providing over fifty-five per cent of the total export earnings of the country. Because of this Nigeria lost interest in having any formal link with the Common Market. Late in 1971, Alhaji Shettima Ali Monguno, then the Federal Commissioner for Trade and Industry, said that if the United Kingdom joined the EEC Nigeria would set up an export promotion council to ensure the expansion of the country's trade with the Community.[285] In December 1971 after the British Parliament had overwhelmingly voted in favour of joining the EEC, Alhaji Shehu Shagari, then the Federal Commissioner for Finance, said that in spite of this Nigeria would not seek an associate membership of the Common Market.[286] He added, however, that Nigeria might negotiate special bilateral trade agreements with member countries of the Community.[287]

The main reasons for the divergent attitudes between Accra and Lagos to the EEC were the following. In the case of Ghana, these included the economic difficulties which would be compounded if the United Kingdom joined the Community; and the second was the outlook or the ideologicial orientation of the Ghanaian leaders.

For economic reasons, Ghana whose economic backbone was still cocoa would benefit from associating with the EEC. Through reduced tariffs and non-tariff barriers, her exports would be competitive with those from the other African associates. This would help in solving the economic malaise of the country. The need for Ghana to seek an accommodation with the Community had become urgent in view of the fact that the United kingdom would join it in January 1973. It has to be remembered that unlike the trade of many other Commonwealth African countries, Ghana's trade with the United Kingdom since 1966 had been expanding.[288] Apart from this, Mr Richard Quarshie, the then Minister of Trade, said that because over fifty-three per cent of Ghana's external debt would be owed to an enlarged EEC if the UK joined it, it was imperative that the country should seek an association with it.[289]

Another reason was the outlook of the leaders of the NLC and the Progress Government. As previously stated, they were pro-West. So unlike Dr Nkrumah they did not consider the EEC as an imperialist or neo-colonialist organization halting the economic progress of Africa. Indeed, the government-owned newspaper, the *Daily Graphic*, said in October 1971 that the Progress Government could not afford to regard the Common Market as an imperialist and neo-colonialist organization designed to suppress the poor countries.[290]

The reasons for the changed attitude of Nigeria to the EEC were three-fold. The first was the government's belief that association with the Community would hinder the establishment of a West African Common Market.[291] The second was the fact that the oil boom in the country made it almost unnecessary for the country to seek an association with the EEC since crude oil did not face any external tariff or quota system under the Treaty of Rome. Furthermore, Britain's membership of the Community would mean less to Nigeria than to Ghana, since already the bulk of Nigeria's trade was with the EEC as Alhaji Shehu Shagari made clear.[292] The final reason was the hostility in the country to association with the Community. Early in 1971 when the Conservative Government's negotiation with the EEC was almost successfully completed, the *New Nigerian* warned that Nigeria must not have anything to do with the Common Market, and called on the Federal Government to withdraw Nigeria from the Commonwealth if Britain joined the Six. Shortly after the Six had finally agreed to British membership of the Community, the *New Nigerian* came out again in a powerful front-page editorial warning the Federal Government against joining 'the host of client states (that is the eighteen African associates) in a scarcely-veiled neo-colonialist division of labour between Europe and Africa.'[294] It added that Britain's membership of the Community 'makes the NATO and the Common Market ominously co-terminous'[295] and therefore Nigeria should avoid it like a plague.

1. However, mainly because of technical bottlenecks Ghana did not exploit the goodwill existing towards her between 1957 and 1960 in the developed countries, especially in North America and Western Europe, to attract large aid resources. See *W. Birmingham, E. N. Omaboe and I. Neustadt*, Vol. 1 op. cit. p. 21.

2. *H. R. Deb.*, 26 April 1965, col. 1493.

3. Ibid.

4. Ibid.

5. *H. R. Deb.*, 29 March 1965, col. 236.

6. The Nigerian Government did not use the term 'non-alignment' until late 1961 to describe its policy to the Great Powers.

7. Lt.-General J. A. Ankrah, then the Chairman of the NLC, described Ghana's extra-African policy as one of 'balanced neutrality'.

8. It is difficult to find any universally accepted interpretation of 'non-alignment'. Some say it means merely non-participation in any of the Super Power-led multilateral defence organizations. See Anthony Enahro. op. cit. p. 253.

9. But some still feel that the term is in reality 'an informal unstated unilateral alignment with unnamed Powers.' See Raj Krishna's article on Non-alignment in *India Quarterly*, April-June 1965, p. 122. The pact was abrogated in January 1962.

10. For the government defence of this view see *H. R. Deb.*, 3 April 1962, cols. 759-60.

11. Colin legum *Pan-Africanism*, op. cit. pp. 60–1.

12. After the intervention of Ethiopia and some other countries an invitation was sent to Nigeria, but the Government turned this down as being too late and so unacceptable.

13. *Senate Debates*, 25 March 1965, col. 36.

14. The CPP government was severely criticized by some of its own back-benchers for relying too much on British officials in Accra for advice on foreign policy matters. See *N. A. Deb.*, Vol. 16, 28 July 1959, col. 1087.

15. N. Mansergh (ed.) *Documents and Speeches on Commonwealth Affairs, 1952-62*, London 1963, p. 605.

16. *N. A. Deb.*, Vol. 14, 20 February 1959, col. 24.

17. *Ghana Today*, 22 June 1960.

18. *W. Birmingham, E. N. Omaboe and I. Neustadt*, (ed.), Vol. op. cit. p. 452.

19. *Henry T. Alexander*, op. cit. p. 93.

20. More will be said of this later in this chapter.

21. *H. C. Deb.*, Vol. 646, 19 october 1961, Col. 646.

22. *N. A. Deb.*, Vol. 42, 16 December 1965, col. 151.

23. *H. R. Deb.*, 5 August 1958, col. 2083.

24. The fact that the building was to be put up at a place very close to the Prime Minister's residence caused much criticism in Nigeria. In 1958 Jaja Wachuku even called it 'a spy house' Ibid. col. 2082.

25. *H. R. Deb.*, 4 September 1961, col. 2827.

26. Till its abrogation in January 1962, this pact was regarded by radical elements at home and abroad as tying Nigeria to Britain's apron-strings.

27. For this the Balewa government was frequently castigated by several Opposition MPs. See for instance, Chief Awolowo's 'Philosophy for Independent Nigeria' — Text of a lecture to Nigerian students in London on 3 September 1961; and *H. R. Deb.*, 30 November 1961, cols. 3651-2 — for Chief Enahoro's attack on the attitude of Balewa's government to the United Kingdom.

28. *H. R. Deb.*, 3 April 1962, cols. 806-7

29. *H. R. Deb.*, 28 March 1962, col. 413.

30. See Chief Okotie-Eboh's statement to the Parliament on 31 March 1965 — *H. R. Deb.*, 31 March 1965, cols. 324-5.

31. *H. R. Deb.*, 5 November 1962, col. iii.

32. *Africa Diary*, 3-9 August 1963, p. 1271.

33. Dr Nkrumah who did not attend the Lagos Conference because his government had broken diplomatic relations with the United Kingdom on 15 December, 1965 ridiculed it as having served 'no useful purpose'. — *N. A. Deb.*, Vol. 43, 1 February 1966, col. 5.

34. *Walter Schwarz*, op. cit. p. 120.

35. *H. R. Deb.*, 5 August 1958, col. 2083.

36. Kwame Nkrumah *Hands Off Africa*, op. cit. p. 56.

37. *N. A. Deb.*, Vol. 24, 4 July 1961, col. 16.

38. Ibid.

39. *H. R. Deb.*, 14 January 1960, col. 34.

40. *MR PRIME MINISTER*, op. cit. p. 49.

41. *The Guardian*, London 27 March 1965.

42. The other was for purposes of representation overseas where because of financial constraint Nigeria could not establish her own diplomatic Missions. See *H. R. Deb.*, 14 January 1960, cols. 35-6.

43. Ibid.

44. *British Aid to Developing Countries*, Cmnd. 2147, p. 24.

45. Douglas G. Anglin has shown that the decisive factors influencing Nigeria's foreign policy were personal and political conviction rather than economic

factors. See his article, 'Nigeria and Political Non-alignment' in *The Journal of Modern African Studies*, July 1964, p. 263.

46. See *Ghanaian Times*, Accra 12 November 1960, and 18 December 1960; and Kwame Nkrumah *The Challenge of the Congo*, op. cit. p. 111; see also the *Evening News*, Accra 30 November 1961.

47. Henry T. Alexander op. cit. pp. 93, 149.

48. See also chapter three.

49. *The Times*, London 26 May 1961.

50. *N. A. Deb.*, Vol. 23, 30 May 1961, col. 1021.

51. Ibid.

52. There was nothing in Lord Home's statement in Lisbon as reported in *The Times* of 26 May 1961 to say that British troops would be sent to assist the Portuguese. However, during that particular time, there was some criticism by Labour MPs of the proposed visit of British warships to the Portuguese port of Luanda in Angola.

53. Kwame Nkrumah *Step to Freedom*, p. 7.

54. As earlier shown in chapter three Dr Nkrumah wanted colonialism to end in Africa by December 1962.

55. See the joint communique issued at the end of Mr Sandys' visit to Accra in October 1961, *H. C. Deb.*, Vol. 646, 19 October 1961, cols. 1-12 Written Answer.

56. The author carefully examined Ghana's efforts between 1961 and February 1966 to secure majority rule for the Africans in Southern Rhodesia, and how these had poisoned the Anglo-Ghanaian relations during this period in an article entitled 'The Role of Ghana in the Rhodesian Question 1961-66', *Quarterly Journal of Administration*, April 1972.

57. *H. C. Deb.*, Vol. 646, 19 October 1961, col. 478.

58. For the purpose of convenience, we shall use 'Southern Rhodesia' here to refer to the territory before UDI on 11 November 1965, and 'Rhodesia' for the same territory after that date.

59. Sir Hugh Foot, then the UK representative at the UN, denied Quaison-Sackey's charge, and regarded it as 'fantastic' *GAOR 1964th Pl. meeting*, 24 November 1961, p. 834.

60. *Step to Freedom*, op. cit. p.

61. The sponsors were Ghana, Morocco and the Philippines.

62. This draft resolution was the culmination of a four-day debate in the Security Council of the Rhodesian question at the request of Ghana which had supplied the Council with an eighty-four-page memorandum (S/5403 and corr. 1) on 2 August 1963 on the history and the political, economic and racial developments in the territory since 1890.

63. *N. A. Deb.*, Vol. 34, 25 September 1963, col. 202.

64. *Ghana Today*, 17 November 1965.

65. *Ghana Today*, 26 November 1965.

66. For details see *N. A. Deb.*, Vol. 41, 26 Novamber 1965, cols. 21-74.

67. *H. R. Deb.*, 30 August 1961, col. 2593.

68. *H. R. Deb.*, 20 March 1964, col. 483.

69. *Morning Post*, Lagos 1 November 1965.

70. *Africa Research Bulletin*, November 1965, p. 409.

71. *Africa Research Bulletin*, December 1965, p. 424.

72. *H. C. Deb.*, Vol. 623, 17 May 1960, col. 1133.

73. See the joint communiqué issued at the end of Mr Sandys' visit to Accra in October 1961 *H. C. Deb.*, Vol. 646, 19 October 1961, cols. 1-12; and *Ghana Today*, 25 October 1961.

74. Mr Sandys expressed misgivings about this Ghanaian action, which was taken shortly after his return from Accra. See *H. C. Deb.*, Vol. 646, 19 October 1961, col. 477.

75. *Statement by the Government on the Recent Conspiracy*, 11 December 1961, WP No. 7/61, p. 28.

76. *The Times*, London 12 December 1963.

77. *The Guardian*, London 2 January 1964.

78. For the text of this agreement see UN Treaty Series, Vol. 284.

79. *N. A. Deb.*, Vol. 10, 20 February 1958, col. 78.

80. *N. A. Deb.*, Vol. 16, 5 August 1959, col. 1358.

81. President Eisenhower was so impressed by Dr Nkrumah during his visit to the United States that he agreed to finance the services of a consultant to report on the Project.

82. As a result of this, on 16 December 1960 an agreement called 'Principles of Agreement' was signed in accra by Dr Nkrumah and Mr D. A. Rhoades of the Kaiser Aluminium and Chemical Corporation. See *Volta River Project—Statement of the Government of Ghana*, 20 February 1961, p. 6.

83. Kwame Nkrumah *I speak of Freedom*, op. cit. p. 140.

84. *N. A. Deb.*, Vol. II, 15 July 1958, col. 470.

85. *Ghana Today*, 13 May 1960.

86. *Minutes of the Meeting of Prime Ministers*, held in London May 1960.

87. Ibid.

88. *N. A. Deb.*, Vol. 19, 29 June 1960, col. 233.

89. Dr Nkrumah simply disregarded the section of the 1957 technical aid agreement which provided for this.

90. For instance, early in 1964, six American experts were summarily deported after being detained for about a week. Again in 1965, some American experts were expelled from Ghana for subversive activities, see the *Guardian*, London 29 March 1965, and the *Ghanaian Times*, Accra 28 March 1965. Early in January 1966 an American lecturer in the University of Ghana, Legon, Dr Martin, was accused of operating under the false name of Gordon Mills, and acting as the chief of a spy ring for the USA CIA, the Ivory Coast Intelligence Agency and the French Intelligence Service. After being detained for ten days, he was asked to keep on reporting to the Special Branch at least once a week. He continued this till the coup. See the *Guardian*, London 21 March 1966.

91. *Ghanaian Times*, Accra 23 July 1963.

92. *N. A. Deb.*, Vol. 38, 29 January 1965, col. 500.

93. *Seven-Year Plan*, op. cit. p. 204.

94. *Achievements in 1961*, Text of Osagyefo Christmas Message, 22 December 1961.

95. For financing this project, the US was to provide $147 million (of this amount $110 million was for the American company, Valco at Tema); the World Bank $47 million; the UK $14 million; and the Accra Government $98 million. See the *Volta River Project—The Volta River Authority*, and *the VALCO*, Vols. I & II especially Doc. 16.03g; Doc. 12 oz; Doc. 13.01; Doc. 14.01; and Doc. 15.01.

96. Ghana's request from the United States was put at £220 million. See the *Guardian*, London 27 march 1965.

97. *Times*, London 14 April 1965.

98. See the text of his congratulatory message to Fidel Castro in *Ghana Today*, 26 April 1961.

99. *N. A. Deb.*, Vol. 32, 21 June 1963, cols. 85–6.

100. The demonstration which began on 4 February 1964 was preceded the day before by a nationwide broadcast by Dr Nkrumah in which he called on the people to expose and disgrace all rumour-mongers and liars in the country. See the *Ghanaian Times*, Accra 4 February 1964.

101. *Ghanaian Times*, Accra 5 February 1964, and the issue of 6 February 1964. See also *Spark*, 5 February 1964.

102. *Washington Post*, 5 and 6 February 1964.

103. *Spark*, 5 February 1964.

104. *Ghana Today,* 19 May 1965.

105. Kwame Nkrumah *Neocolonialism,* op. cit. p. 241.

106. Colonel (later Lt.-General) A. A. Afrifa accused Nkrumah shortly after the coup of having 'sold his country to the Russians'. See *The Ghana Coup, 24 February 1966,* op. cit. p. 15. Indeed in 1963, Senator Thomas Dodd of Connecticut had stated that 'Nkrumah's Ghana has become the first Soviet satellite in Africa'—See *Is US Money Aiding Another Communist State?,* p. 1.

107. *The USSR and Developing Countries—Economic Cooperation,* Moscow 1966, p. 7.

108. *Soviet News,* 21 February 1961.

109. Fritz Schatten *Communism in Africa,* London 1966, p. 161.

110. Kwame Nkrumah *Neocolonialism,* op. cit. p. 243.

111. However, the training of the three arms of the regular armed forces was later given to the British under an agreement of 1 May 1962, under which Britsin established a joint training mission of about 200 men in Ghana.

112. *Ghanaian Times,* Accra 13 October 1961.

113. *N. A. Deb.,* Vol. 34, 7 November 1963, col. 645.

114. For further details about Nkrumah's visit to the USSR and other Eastern European countries and China in 1961 see Senator Thomas Dodd op. cit. pp. 52–70.

115. *Ghanaian Times,* Accra 18 October 1961.

116. Colin Legum, Socialism in Ghana in W. H. Friedland & Carl G. Rosberg (ed.) op. cit. p. 153.

117. *Ghana Today,* 22 April 1964.

118. *Ghana Today,* 1 December 1965.

119. For instance, in December 1962 after criticizing Mr Mennen Williams, then the US Assistant Secretary of State for African Affairs, for saying that Ghana was becoming hostile to Washington while becoming friendly with Moscow, the *Ghanaian Times* fired a broadside at Nigeria, whom it described as the 'favourite' and the 'lackey' of the imperialist Powers, for leaning more and more towards NATO and the EEC. See *Ghanaian Times,* Accra 8 December 1962.

120. Claude S. Phillips, op. cit. p. 58.

121. *H. R. Deb.,* 10 April 1963, col. 982.

122. *H. R. Deb.,* 1 April 1965, col. 418.

123. *H. R. Deb.,* 19 September 1963, cols. 3044–5.

124. Claude S. Phillips, op. cit. p. 102.

125. *Morning Post,* Lagos 16 October 1965.

126. *Ghanaian Times,* Accra 19 May 1965.

127. *MR PRIME MINISTER,* op. cit. p. 59.

128. *H. R. Deb.,* 2 April 1962, col. 667.

129. *Africa Diary,* 9–15 October 1965, p. 2551.

130. In spite of the pressure of some MPs on the government to condemn the American involvement in Vietnam early in 1965 it refused to do so. See *H. R. Deb.,* 26 April 1965, cols. 1480–1 and 1487.

131. See *Claude S. Phillips,* op. cit. p. 102; and also *African Research Bulletin,* October 1965, p. 388.

132. *N. A. Deb.,* Vol. 10, 20 February 1958, col. 81.

133. Dr Nkrumah promised that his government would co-operate with any government and any agency that assisted in bringing the Volta River Project to life; and it tried to keep this promise as far as possible, at least till early 1961.

134. Up till mid-1961 when Dr Nkrumah announced that he had received what seemed to be the final decision of President Kennedy and Mr Macmillan, the attacks on the US in Ghana, even on the Congo, were not as severe as during the following period up to the time of the coup. For instance, Dr Nkrumah's speech to the UN General Assembly on 7 March 1961 shortly after the death of Lumumba was said to be 'moderate' and 'well received' by the Assembly,

according to General Alexander. See Henry T. Alexander op. cit. p. 26. On 4 July 1961, while announcing the decision of Kennedy to back the Volta River Project financially, Dr Nkrumah eulogized the US for her interest in the development of Ghana and other developing nations. See *N. A. Deb.*, Vol. 24, 4 July 1961, cols. 3, 11.

135. *N. A. Deb.*, Vol. 22, 21 February 1961, col. 1371

136. The *Guardian*, London 27 March 1965.

137. For any favourable recommendation for aid from the World Bank the support of the US was necessary. For she had the largest single voting bloc in the Bank which still on 30 June 1967 represented 25.98 per cent of the total. See *IBRD and IDA—Annual Report 1966/67*, Washington DC 1967, p. 61.

138. Kwame Nkrumah *Neo-colonialism*, op. cit. p. 239.

139. Dr Nkrumah said on 22 December 1961 that the lesson of the Volta River Project was that 'we must in the future depend upon our own resources in order to build industries we shall require'. See *Achievements*, 1961.

140. *N. A. Deb.*, Vol. 43, 22 February 1966, col. 664.

141. Ibid.

142. *N. A. Deb.*, Vol. 38, 28 January 1965, col. 425.

143. *N. A. Deb.*, Vol. 43, 22 February 1966, col. 664.

144. Even by June 1971 the total value of American aid to Nigeria was about $250 million. See USAID. *Assistance to Nigeria*, Lagos 1971 mimeo.

145. *Africa Diary*, 23-9 November 1963, p. 1458.

146. On his return from the United States Sir Abubakar said in a nationwide broadcast on 2 August 1961 that he had not gone there to seek aid, but to discuss important world problems with President Kennedy. See *MR PRIME MINISTER*, op. cit. p. 65.

147. See Colin Legum, 'Socialism in Ghana' in W. H. Friedland, and Carl G. Rosberg (ed.) op. cit. p.

148. This broadcast was a clarion call for the purge of the government and the party of corrupt and anti-socialist leaders.

149. As indicated earlier, Dr Nkrumah held this post himself from 1962 until the coup, just as Khrushchev did till 1964 in Moscow.

150. *Ghanaian Times*, Accra 7 November 1964.

151. David Apter, 'The Politics of Solidarity in Ghana' in J. S. Coleman and Carl G. Rosberg (ed.) op. cit. pp. 296-7.

152. Commenting on the Kulungugu bomb attack on him later, Dr Nkrumah said 'the attempt on my life was surely engineered in a desperate attempt to arrest our progress and halt our fight against imperialism . . . colonialism, and neo-colonialism. Without doubt, our government's declared policy of socialism at home, and non-alignment and support of total African independence and unity abroad has (sic) drawn hatred of those who regard these attitudes as inimical to their vital interests.'—*N. A. Deb.*, Vol. 29, 2 October 1962, cols. 3-4.

153. *Government Statement on the Recent Conspiracy*, Accra December 1961, WP No. 7/61, pp. 26-33.

154. *Ghanaian Times*, 31 December 1961.

155. *Spark*, Accra 5 February 1964.

156. W. Scott Thompson op. cit. p. 394.

157. Ibid. p. 397.

158. Dr Nkrumah, strongly believed that the US Government was from 1961 onwards planning a coup against his regime, to such a degree that when it occurred in February 1966 he said it was organized and financed by the United States with the sum of $13 million. See Kwame Nkrumah *Dark Days in Ghana*, op. cit. p. 49.

159. The report was not published until 14 July 1963 under the title 'Is US Money Aiding Another Communist State?' op. cit. Senator Thomas Dodd's remark in the introduction that Ghana had become the first Soviet satellite in africa as Cuba in Latin America was severely criticized by the New York Times as

damaging to the American position in Ghana. See*New York Times*, 15 July 1963.

160. This testimony was not published until 24 February 1964 under the title 'Ghana Students Oppose US Aid to Nkrumah'. See *Staff Conferences of the subcommittee to investigate the Administration of the Internal Security Laws of the Committee on the Judiciary of the United States Senate, 88th Congress, 2nd Session.*

161. *N. A. Deb.*, Vol. 43, 22 February 1966, col. 647.

162. This was understandable. The basis of the NPC, whose Vice-President Sir Abubakar was till his death, was the traditional élite in the North. He could not be pro-Communist without undermining the basis of his power. Furthermore, most of the other Nigerian leaders, especially those from the South, were men with wealth and a high level of education, who had something to lose by being pro-Communist.

163. *West Africa*, 12 November 1960.

164. *MR PRIME MINISTER*, op. cit. pp. 62-3.

165. Sir Abubakar expressed this view in his address to the UN General Assembly in October 1960. See *MR PRIME MINISTER*, op. cit. p. 57.

166. Because both Ghana and the Soviet Union were pro-Lumumba in the Congo crisis they became, according to General Alexander, allies 'in the fight against the wicked colonialists'. See H. T. Alexander, op. cit. p. 113.

167. See Nkrumah's proposals for disarmament at the Second Conference of the Non-aligned Powers in Cairo on 7 October 1964 in 'Africa and World Peace' supplement with *Ghana Today*, 21 October 1964.

168. On almost all cold war issues Nigeria sided with the United States against the USSR. For example in 1962, Sir Ahmadu Bello, while on an official visit to West Germany, did not merely deplore the Berlin wall but also bitterly attacked Moscow for it. See *Daily Times*, Lagos 28 September 1962.

169. *Ghana Today*, 7 December 1960.

170. *Ghana Today*, 24 May 1961.

171. Ibid.

172. It is interesting to note that one of the reasons given by Mr Kofi Baako to justify the new Security Service Bill was the threat posed by Busia's testimony against Ghana before the US Senate. See *N. A. Deb.*, Vol. 34, 25 November 1963, col. 1006.

173. *Washington Evening Star*, 15 November 1963.

174. On 25 December 1963, Dr Nkrumah employed this law to nullify the judgement of the dismissed Chief Justice, Sir Arku Korsah, in which on 9 December 1963 he had acquitted Tawia Adamafio, Ako Adjei and Coffie Crabble of complicity in the Kulungugu bomb episode.

175. *Washington Post*, 4 January 1964.

176. *New York Times*, 9 January 1964.

177. *Ghana Students Oppose United States Aid to Nkrumah*, op. cit. p. v.

178. The fact that the information and the news media in the USSR were rigidly controlled made it easy for the Soviet leaders to prevent the reckless criticism of any country they did not like.

179. Through this joint effort Ghana and Nigeria won concessions from West Germany who agreed to relax the imports of cocoa from all sources. See *H. R. Deb.*, 9 February 1959, col. 111.

180. The eighteen associates were former colonies of France, Belgium and Italy in Africa who became associate members of the EEC under Part IV, Article 131, of the Rome Treaty on 1 January 1958 when they were still under colonial rule.

181. For further details about how the Balewa Government reached this decision, see *MR PRIME MINISTER*, op. cit. pp. 66-73.

182. On 1 February 1963, Dr P. N. C. Okigbo was appointed as Nigeria's Ambassador to the European Commission in Brussels, to negotiate a trade agreement under Article 238 of the Treaty of Rome. See P. N. C. Okigbo op.

cit. pp. 130-1, 164, 167.

183. The negotiations with the EEC were tortuous and protracted and an agreement was not signed until 16 July 1966. For details about the agreement, see *Agreement Establishing an Association between the EEC, and the Republic of Nigeria*, Lagos Government Printer 1966.

184. *Ghana Today*, 27 April 1960.

185. *N. A. Deb.*, Vol. 24, 4 July 1961, col. 8.

186. See the joint communique of Nkrumah and Khrushchev on 24 July 1961; and that between him and Novotny on 2 August 1961 in Thomas Dodd op. cit. pp. 10, 70.

187. Kwame Nkrumah *Step to Freedom*, op. cit.

188. *West African Pilot*, Lagos 13 September 1961.

189. *MR PRIME MINISTER*, op. cit. pp. 69-70.

190. Ali Mazrui: 'African Attitudes to the European Economic Community' in *International Affairs*, London January 1963, p. 34.

191. *Minutes of the Prime Ministers' Conference, 1962*, London 1962.

192. *N. A. Deb.*, Vol. 24, 4 July 1961, col. 10.

193. *Daily Times*, Lagos 6 September 1962.

194. *N. A. Deb.*, Vol. 24, 4 July 1961, col. 9.

195. Ibid.

196. Kwame Nkrumah *Step to Freedom*, op. cit. p. 7.

197. One was to be carried out at home by the Ministry of Commerce and Industry in collaboration with the Cabinet office, the Ministries of External Affairs, of Economic Development, and of Finance. The other was to be carried out abroad by a team of British and American experts.

198. For a summary of the conclusions of these reports, see *MR PRIME MINISTER*, op. cit. pp. 68-9.

199. *The European Common Market and the Nigerian Economy—A report to the Federal Ministry of Commerce and Industry of Nigeria*, by Arthur D. Little, 1962.

200. *West Africa*, 13 August 1971.

201. *West Africa*, 10 September 1971.

202. *West Africa*, 24 october 1970.

203. See *Daily Times*, Lagos 26 February 1971; the *Renaissance*, Enugu 7 March 1971; and the *Daily Sketch*, Ibadan 26 February 1971 — all demanding 'positive action now' against the United Kingdom, including the nationalization of her business concerns in Nigeria.

204. *New Nigerian*, Kaduna 25 February 1971.

205. *New Nigerian*, Kaduna 21 March 1969.

206. *Morning Post*, Lagos 7 December 1971.

207. *Daily Times*, Lagos 23 December 1971.

208. *West Africa*, 5 December 1970.

209. *The Daily Sketch*, Ibadan 11 November 1971.

210. *Daily Times*, Lagos 26 June 1971.

211. Ibid.

212. Dr Kalu Ezera, then a government backbencher, complained bitterly in 1961 about the Government's excessive generosity with houses to the staff of the British High Commission in Lagos while Nigerian foreign service officers found it difficult to get good accommodation in London, and while the Nigerian national flag was not flown on top of the country's High Commission in London. See *H. R. Deb.*, 4 September 1961, cols. 2826-7.

213. *A. A. Afrifa*, op. cit. p. 29.

214. *Dr Busia in Europe and America*, Accra, Government Printer 1969, p. 55.

215. Lt.-General Ankrah's Broadcast, 6 March 1966 (mimeographed).

216. *West Africa*, 24 October 1970.

217. *West Africa*, 27 June 1970.

218. *West Africa*, 5 December 1970.

219. For instance British bilateral aid disbursed in Ghana in 1965 amounted to £575,000 and the equivalent value in 1968 was £5,728,000. See *British Aid Statistics 1965-9*, London, HMSO, pp. 26-7.

220. *West Africa*, 8 October 1971.

221. Walter Schwarz op. cit. p. 119.

222. For the effect of the civil war on Nigeria's foreign policy see Olajide Aluko, 'The Civil War and Nigerian Foreign Policy' in the *Political Quarterly*, April 1971.

223. *West Africa*, 15 July 1967.

224. Ibid.

225. *Morning Post*, Lagos 11 July 1967.

226. *Morning Post*, Lagos 1 November 1967.

227. *New Nigerian*, Kaduna 12 July 1967.

228. Walter Schwarz op. cit. p. XV.

229. However, when Walter Schwarz was writing his book in 1968 it was difficult to forecast the future pattern of Anglo-Nigerian relations.

230. *West Africa* 26 September 1970.

231. *H. R. Deb.* 14 January 1960 cols. 35-6.

232. *British Aid to Developing Countries*, 1963 Comnd. 2147 p. 24.

233. *West Africa* 18 November 1967.

234. *The Second National Development Plan 1970/74* op. cit. p. 299.

235. *West Africa* 2 July 1971.

236. *Ibid*.

237. For further details about the growth of the Nigerian Foreign Service, see Olajide Aluko, 'Nigerian Foreign Service' in *the Quarterly Journal of Administration*, October 1970.

238. See praise of the United States during a debate on a resolution approving a loan of $9,792,200 from the United States in mid-1970 — *N. A. Deb.*, Vol. 3, 17 June 1970, col. 869-72.

239. *West Africa*, 6 January 1968.

240. Mr Isaac Amissah-Aidoo also visited Canada and the United Kingdom for a similar purpose. See *N. A. Deb.*, Vol. 3, 12 May 1970, col 1.

241. *Ghanaian Times*, Accra 6 September 1967.

242. Ibid.

243. Since the middle of 1966 Ghana had been receiving technical assistance from Formosa in form of experts and equipment for the development of paddy rice in the country. See *West Africa*, 15 June 1968.

244. *West Africa*, 15 October 1971.

245. Ibid.

246. *Ghana Today*, 6 September 1967.

247. *West Africa*, 25 July 1970.

248. *West Africa*, 6 August 1971.

249. *Ghanaian Times*, Accra 6 September 1967.

250. We shall soon refer to this below. But what is important to note is that the government did not formally lift its restriction on the number of the Soviet diplomats in Nigeria. The additional three men thattemporarily joined the Embassy in 1969 were on special assignment and they left for Moscow after the end of the civil war.

251. There was great disappointment in Lagos at the United States aid towards the 1962/68 Plan which had been drawn up with the American assistance in the expectation that she would provide the bulk of the foreign aid requirement.

Instead of the fifty per cent of the total capital investment in the public sector under the Plan expected from abroad only about twenty per cent did actually get through to Nigeria. See *The Second National Development Plan 1970/74*, op. cit. p. 299.

252. General Gowon's Statement on 1970-71 Budget in *Federal Government Estimates 1970/71*, p. 385.

253. Ibid.

254. *Africa Research Bulletin*, October 1966, p. 644.

255. *Daily Times*, Lagos 20 November 1971; *Daily Express*, Lagos 20 November 1971; *Nigerian Tribune*, Ibadan 19 November 1971.

256. *Statement on China By His Excellency Dr Okoi Arikpo to the 26th Session of theUnited Nations General Assembly on 18 October 1971*, New York, permanent Mission of Nigeria To the UN, 1971.

257. *West Africa*, 18 November 1967.

258. See *New Nigerian*, Kaduna 22 August 1968; and *West Africa*, 7 September 1968 for criticism in the *Nigerian Observer*; and *Daily Times*, Lagos 23 August 1968.

259. We have earlier referred to Colonel (later Lt.-General) A. A. Afrifa's accusation to Nkrumah of having 'sold his country to the Russians'. Lt.-General J. A. Ankrah spoke with disdain of the 'democratic centralism' of the CPP. See the text of the *Press Statement by the Chairman of the NLC*, Lt.-Gerneral J. A. Ankrah, on 21 March 1966.

260. See *Dr Busia in Europe and America*, op. cit. p. 4.

261. NLC — *Nkrumah's Deception of Africa*, p. 25.

262. *The Times*, London 23 February 1967.

263. *West Africa*, 28 February 1970.

264. *West Africa*, 1 October 1971.

265. *Dr Busia in Europe and America*, op. cit. p. 20.

266. This trade mission was also to foster Ghana's trade with the other Eastern European countries. See *West Africa*, 1 October 1971.

267. This aid was for establishing a teaching hospital in the former Eastern Nigeria. See *Africa Research Bulletin*, April 1966, p. 502.

268. *West Africa*, 22 August 1970.

269. *West Africa*, 12 April 1969.

270. *Daily Times*, Lagos 7 June 1969.

271. *The Economist*, 31 January 1971.

272. See text of General Gowon's Speech to the Opening Session of the Third African-American Dialogues in the *Morning Post*, Lagos 10 March 1971.

273. Ibid.

274. *West Africa*, 26 September 1970.

275. *Daily Sketch*, Ibadan 2 November 1970.

276. *West Africa*, 26 September 1970.

277. *Daily Times*, Lagos 30 December 1971.

278. *Morning Post*, Lagos 10 March 1971.

279. *Ghana Today*, 1 May 1968.

280. *N. A. Deb.*, Vol. 3, 11 June 1970.

281. *West Africa*, 8 October 1971.

282. The essence of the agreement was that the Community extended to all Nigerian exports except four commodities — cocoa, plywood, groundnut, and palm products — the same privileged position as it offered to the eighteen African associates. But Nigeria would not receive aid from the European Development Fund because she did not want this. Finally, the number of institutions between Nigeria and the EEC was much smaller than between the eighteen and the Community. For further details see *The Agreement Establishing an Association between the EEC and the Republic of Nigeria*.

283. *West Africa*, 3 February 1968.

284. *West Africa*, 15 June 1968.

285. *West Africa*, 8 October 1971.

286. *West Africa*, 31 December 1971.

287. Ibid.

288. See *West Africa*, 30 Januray-5 February 1971. For instance in 1965, 25.8 per cent of Ghana's imports came from the United Kingdom while 20.8 per cent of her exports during the same year went to London. But in 1969, the corresponding percentages were 26.8 and 28.6 per cent respectively. See *Economic Survey 1966*, Accra, Government Printer 1967, p. 36; and *Economic Survey 1969*, Accra, Government Printer 1970, p. 46.

289. *West Africa*, 19 November 1971.

290. See *West Africa*, 29 October 1971.

291. For further details about this, see the *Second National Development Plan 1970/74*, pp. 79-81.

292. *West Africa*, 31 December 1971.

293. *West Africa*, 11 June 1971.

294. *West Africa*, 30 July 1971.

295. Ibid.

CHAPTER VII

Ghana and The Nigerian Civil War

A major source of conflict between Ghana and Nigeria, especially during the late sixties, was the former's attitude to the Nigerian civil war.[1] Although the enforced and the sudden expulsion of about 140,000 Nigerians[2] from Ghana between December 1969 and early 1970 did contribute to the worsening of their relations during this period, the furore and indignation in Nigeria over the expulsion owed much to the existing pent-up anger at Ghana's role during the civil war. Indeed, many Nigerian newspapers saw the expulsion order as a deliberate attempt on the part of the Ghanaian government to frustrate the government's attempt to rush the secessionist rebellion.[3]

What role exactly did Ghana play? and why did it choose that role? These are the questions we shall attempt to consider here. But with the diplomatic despatches and other important documents dealing with this subject remaining classified, the account given here cannot be more than tentative. No attempt will be made to give the details about the crisis, the war and the various peace efforts, except in so far as they have a direct bearing on the Ghanaian-Nigerian relations.

To place in a proper perspective Ghana's role in the civil war and in the constitutional crisis that preceded it, it is pertinent to say something about the initial partnership between the military leaders who came to power in each country early in 1966. For it was this partnership that made it possible for Ghana to play a very significant role in the crisis and the civil war, especially during the immediate months before and after the outbreak of hostilities in Nigeria.

(i) INITIAL PARTNERSHIP

The overthrow of the civilian governments in the two countries early in 1966 brought an improvement in their relations which had hitherto not been totally free from mutual suspicion, jealousy, antagonism and abuse. The factors making for this were not far to seek. Firstly, most of the army officers that came to power in both countries early in 1966 had up till 1956 belonged to the Royal West African Frontier Force, and they were under the same West African Command Headquarters in Accra. Furthermore, some of them had been contemporaries in British military training institutions. For instance, Major-General E. Kotoka who led the coup in Accra received part of his training in Eaton Hall , Chester, England, which was attended by General Ironsi, Colonel (later Lt.-General) A. A. Afrifa who was second in command in the coup was General Gowon's contemporary at Sandhurst. Apart from this, there was very little ideological difference between them. Not only this, the NLC made the policy of good neighbourliness, of accommodation and of freindship the cornerstone of its African policy,[4] partly to improve Ghana's relations with other African countries, and thereby to demonstrate the bankruptcy of Nkrumah's policy, and partly to be able to concentrate most of its resources on solving the economic difficulties facing the country.

The improvement in their relations could be seen from the support they gave each other, in the exchange of visits and letters between the leaders of the two countries, and in the attitudes of the people in the two countries to each other. The Nigerian Military Government of General Ironsi was one of the first African countries to recognize the new government of the NLC under General Ankrah. At the meeting of the OAU Ministerial Council held in Adis Ababa between 28 February 1966 and 5 March 1966, the Nigerian delegates supported the acceptance of the credentials of the NLC's delegation led by Mr E. T. K. Seddoh, whereas the representatives of some other African countries not only opposed the seating of the NLC's delegation, but also refused to participate in the meeting once the credentials of the Ghanaian delegation were accepted by the majority of the African Ministers attending the meeting.

As if this was not enough, General Ironsi went out of his way to decry the attitude of the African countries that withdrew from the meeting of the OAU Ministerial Council because of the majority decision to accept the credentials of the NLC's delegation, and who were secretly 'preparing to mount a military expedition against a sister African country'.[5] This was an indirect reference to Guinea's threat to use force to restore Nkrumah to power in Ghana, a threat which Radio Nigeria condemned as illogical and unreasonable.[6] On 3 March 1966, the Nigerian Ministry of External Affairs put out a statement in which it described the coup in Ghana as an internal matter, and warned that any refusal not to see it as such would be an interference in the internal affairs of that country, and so a violation of one of the basic principles of the OAU Charter.[7]

The NLC government was very much impressed by this demonstration of support and friendship by the Nigerian military government. On 18 March 1966, a high-powered delegation of the NLC came to Lagos on a goodwill visit. The leader of the delegation delivered a letter from General Ankrah to General Ironsi. At the end of the visit, a communique was issued which said that the two governments agreed to 're-establish and strengthen the traditional bond of friendship' between their countries.[8] It also said that the representatives of the two governments discussed a wide range of subjects, including matters concerning their nationals residing in each other's country with a view to effecting a free flow of persons and goods between the two countries.[9] Later too a Nigerian delegation visited Ghana with a message from General Ironsi to General Ankrah. It thus appeared as if this would mark the beginning of a real close partnership between the two countries.

This was the state of their relationship when the second coup occurred in Nigeria on 29 July 1966. Although the news of this second coup was received with some misgivings in Ghana,[10] the NLC government regarded it as an internal affair of Nigeria in which it would not interfere. However, the NLC watched with close interest the constitutional crisis that began to develop in Nigeria as a result of the coup. The efforts of Lt-Colonel (later General) Gowon to resolve the crisis by setting up an all-Nigeria Constitutional Committee, and by announcing early in September 1966 the programme of restoring the government to the civilians in 1969, were recognized by General Ankrah, who praised Gowon for what he called his 'peculiar grasp and understanding of the difficulties afflicting your great country'.[11]

In spite of the sympathy among the Ghanaians for the Ibos following the massacre that occurred in the North between the latter part of September and early October 1966, the NLC government did not allow this to affect its friendly attitude to the Nigerian government. Thus early in October 1966, General Ankrah referred to Ghana's 'cordial relations' with Nigeria.[12] As a result of this the Nigerian government was able to intervene early in November 1966 to secure the release of some Guinean diplomats and fifteen other Guinean nationals detained in Ghana by the Ghanaian authorities.[13] Towards the end of December 1966, Ghana and Nigeria announced their agreement in principle to pool their airways in their operation in West Africa.[14]

It was this spirit of mutual understanding that made it possible for General Ankrah to take the initiative in the Nigerian crisis late in December 1966. As a result of his personal initiative, all the Nigerian military governors met, for the first time since the second coup of July 1966, at Aburi, Ghana, on 4 and 5 January 1967, to resolve the country's constitutional crisis. This Aburi conference was opened with an address by General Ankrah who appealed to the military governors to resolve their difficulties in a most brotherly and peaceful way. He urged them not to behave as politicians but as statesmen. He added that Ghana regarded the crisis as an internal matter which the military leaders should settle amicably.[15]

What effect General Ankrah's speech had on the Nigerian military governors could not be established. What was certain was that all the Nigerian military leaders were grateful to him for providing them with such an excellent opportunity to resolve their problems. At the end of the meeting on 5 January 1967, the military governors issued a communique in which they expressed their gratitude to the Ghanaian people, the NLC and its Chairman, General Ankrah, for his 'constructive initiative, and assistance'. To mark the end of the meeting some members of the NLC and the Nigerian military governors drank a toast to the continuing solidarity between Nigeria and Ghana.[16]

No sooner had the military governors returned to Nigeria than controversy arose between them about the interpretation of the Aburi agreements.[17] This controversy soon degenerated into mutual rancour and recrimination between Lagos and Enugu. On 28 February 1967, Colonel Ojukwu said he would implement the Aburi agreements unilaterally if by 31 March 1967 they were not implemented by the Federal Military Government; and Colonel (later General) Gowon replied that if the threat was carried out he would be compelled to use any means to bring the Ojukwu government back to order.

As a mark of respect for General Ankrah, Gowon flew to Accra on 5 March 1967 to brief him about the controversy in the country.[18] Although what Gowon told Ankrah is difficult to ascertain, it was probable that he must have repeated what he told the Heads of diplomatic Missions in Lagos the previous day, that if Ojukwu carried out his threat the Federal Military Government would no longer be bound by the Aburi agreement not to use force to settle the crisis, and that his government would certainly use force to prevent the dismemberment of the federation.[19]

Within a few days of his return on 17 March 1967 Gowon issued Decree 8 of 1967 on the Aburi agreements. This Decree No. 8

represented a compromise between the original extreme position of Ojukwu and his own on the interpretation of the Aburi agreements.[20] What this decree owed to General Ankrah cannot perhaps be known. However, the very day the compromise solution was announced it was rejected out of hand by Ojukwu as being dictatorial and defective. Thus the crisis continued.

To avert disaster, General Ankrah despatched a three-man delegation to confer with Ojukwu in Enugu on 23 March 1967.[21] The details of their discussion were not known. But it was most probable that it was focussed mainly on the disagreements over the Aburi decisions. For according to the weekly journal *West Africa* the main purpose of the Ghanaian delegation was to persuade Ojukwu to modify his stand on the Aburi agreements and not to carry out his ultimatum to implement the agreements unilaterally on 31 March 1967, and to agree to meet his other military governors for further talks.[22]

It did not appear as if the delegation got much from Colonel Ojukwu. However, they persuaded him to meet General Ankrah in Accra, and on 26 March 1967 he, accompanied by a few of his officials, went to Accra. Again what passed between Ojukwu and Ankrah was not known. It appeared most probable that they must have concentrated on the disagreement over the Aburi decisions, with Ojukwu explaining his government's stand on the controversy and Ankrah trying to make him compromise a little. Although General Ankrah's talks had little influence on Ojukwu, as we shall soon see, the NLC government was determined to make another desperate attempt to getting a solution to the Nigerian crisis. Towards the end of March 1967, it invited all the senior law and finance officers of all the governments in Nigeria to Accra to work out how they could translate into action the Aburi constitutional and financial proposals.[23] This was certainly helpful. For by this time the senior officials of the Ojukwu government were reluctant to participate in any such discussion within Nigeria because of their personal safety, which they thought insecure outside the former Eastern Region. On 30 March 1967, the meeting of all the senior law and finance officers of the governments in the federation was held in Accra.

Whatever they had agreed upon became totally irrelevant with the Ojukwu Revenue Collection Edict of 31 March 1967. Under this edict the Ojukwu government took possession and control of all Federal government establishments such as the railways, airfields, ports etc in the former Eastern Region. This meant that General Ankrah's efforts to persuade Ojukwu against carrying out his threat on 31 March had come to nought. He became frustrated and perhaps sullen, and began to watch helplessly the deterioration of the situation in Nigeria. In the meantime, Gowon on 1 April 1967 declared Ojukwu's revenue edict illegal, and ordered the diplomatic and economic blockade of the Region. From that moment to secession and to the outbreak of hostilities was but a short distance.

(ii) SECESSION, OUTBREAK OF WAR, AND REACTION IN GHANA

When secession occurred on 30 May 1967, Ghana was one of the six African countries which the Ojukwu government claimed had accorded the new republic of Biafra diplomatic recognition. The Ghanaian government did not deny this publicly until 9 June 1967,[24] although it was possible for it to have informed the Nigerian Federal government privately earlier that it did not support the secession. However, the fact that it took ten days before Ghana could make its stand clear publicly caused some doubts among the Nigerian public, especially when it is remembered that Ethiopia, which was one of the countries claimed by the secessionists to have recognized their regime, denied the claim the very day it was reported in the world press on 31 May 1967.[25]

Ghana's reaction to the war could be judged from the opinions in the Ghanaian newspapers. At a very early stage, Ghana's attitude to the secession and the war was one of scepticism. For instance, the *Daily Graphic*, the government-owned newspaper, described the secession as 'foolhardy'. But within a month of the war, and for a variety of complex reasons which we shall soon discuss, a pro-Biafran tide swept the country. In the forefront was the *Daily Graphic* which called for a halt in the war, and called on the Nigerian government to use negotiation to settle the country's problems.[26] The *Ashanti Pioneer* called on all African leaders to intervene to end the war, and condemned Britain for 'sending arms to one side in the war'.[27]

With the intensification of the war following the secessionist occupation of the Mid-West between 9 August and 20 September 1967, the Ghanaian press brought greater energy and vigour into their pro-Biafran campaign. The *Ghanaian Times*, another government-owned newspaper, said that with the escalation of the war it had ceased to be an internal affair, and that foreign Powers should now intervene to stop the war.[28] The *Daily Graphic* called on the OAU, the Commonwealth leaders and the UN to intervene to restore peace in Nigeria through mediation. Radio Ghana in a news talk called for a ceasefire, and urged the next OAU Summit at Kinshasa to take up the Nigerian war.[29] Added to all this was the practice of these nwspapers to refer to the territory under the secessionists as 'Biafra'.

Early in September 1967, twenty-four leading Ghanaians, including the then Chief Justice, Akufo-Addo, later Ghana's President till 13 January 1972, issued a joint statement in which they decried the war and affirmed that it had ceased to be an internal affair, and therefore, the Nigerian Federal Military Government should submit it to a sort of international adjudication.[30] The fortnightly journal, the *Legon Observer*,[31] published in the University of Ghana, came out early in September 1967 with its editorial on the Nigerian war, and called on all the African leaders to discuss it during the coming Summit in Kinshasa. For the first time, the *Legon Observer* carried a pro-Biafran article by Mr Onyemaeke Ogum, who later became the Secretary of the Biafran Union in Ghana.[32] On the eve of the OAU Kinshasa Summit of 13–15 September 1967 the *Daily Graphic* called for the revision of the OAU Charter to make secession compatible with the principles of the Charter.[33]

These Ghanaian attitudes brought trenchant protests and caustic comments from Nigeria. The Nigerian *Morning Post* condemned the *Daily Graphic* of 29 July 1967 for calling for a halt to the war, and described its suggestion for negotiation with the rebels as 'unhelpful'.[34] A news talk broadcast on Radio Nigeria towards the end of August 1967, entitled 'Pray, what are the Ghanaians up to', criticized all the Ghanaian papers including the *Legon Observer* for their pro-Biafran stance, and said they were anti-Nigeria out of selfish motives.[35]

Nigeria's government officials were not slow to react to the Ghanaian attitude. In a press statement in Lagos directed against Ghana, though she was not specifically mentioned by name, Mr A. A. Haastrup, then the Nigerian Ambassador in Addis Ababa, declared that some African countries pretending to support Nigeria actually hated her, that they disliked Nigeria being called the giant of Africa, and that they wanted Nigeria's disintegration so that they could lead Africa.[36] Shortly before the meeting of the OAU heads of state and government in Kinshasa in September 1967, the Nigerian Acting High Commissioner in Ghana, Mr O. Adeniji, gave a hard-hitting press conference in which he replied to all the Ghanaian comments on the Nigerian war. After explaining the case of the

Federal Military Government, he declared that the war was an internal affair, and that any attempt to raise it at the next OAU Summit would be an unwarranted interference in the internal affairs of Nigeria, a breach of one of the basic principles of the OAU Charter, and that such a step might lead to the disintegration of the OAU.[37] It was against this atmosphere of mutual suspicion and recrimination between Ghana and Nigeria that the African leaders met in Kinshasa between 13 and 15 September 1967.

(iii) GHANA, OAU, AND PEACE MOVES

As a result of the stiff resistance of the Nigerian Military Government, the Nigerian war was not discussed during the meeting of the Council of Ministers that preceded the Summit of heads of state and government in mid-September 1967. However, the Summit discussed the war with the agreement of the Federal Government. What individual heads of state or government said at the Summit is difficult to ascertain, so we cannot say much about the role of Ghana. However, Ghana was one of the seven African countries[38] that sponsored an eight-point draft resolution[39] adopted by the Summit on the war. The main features of the resolution were the condemnation of secession, the acceptance of the crisis as an internal affair of Nigeria, and the despatch of a consultative mission of six heads of state to Nigeria 'to assure' General Gowon of the OAU assembly's 'desire for the territorial integrity and unity, and peace of Nigeria'.[40]

Ghana was a member of the consultative committee set up by the OAU.[41] When General Ankrah returned to Accra, he did not make any positive pronouncement on the OAU Kinshasa resolution on Nigeria. The *Daily Graphic* welcomed the setting up of the committee, but expressed doubts whether General Gowon would allow it 'to mediate' in the war especially since he was still firm on his conditions for peace, which were the renunciation of secession and the acceptance of the twelve-state structure of the country.[42] The *Daily Graphic* was just being mischievous. For its comment totally ignored the terms of reference given to the Consultative Committee.

(a) Lagos Peace Conference
The OAU Mission did not visit Lagos until late in November 1967. But before then, the Ghanaian government's reference to the Nigerian civil war at the General Assembly of the UN on 25

September 1967 brought further complications into the Ghanaian-Nigerian relations.[43] The Nigerian Permanent Representative at the UN, who was then Chief S. Adebo, protested immediately to the Ghanaian delegate on the floor of the General Assembly. The Ghanaian delegate explained his government's stand with which Chief Adebo said he was satisfied.[44] But the Nigerian newspapers picked on this reference to the situation in Nigeria by Ghana at the UN General Assembly as another evidence of Ghana's support for the rebels. On 28 September 1967, there was a news commentary on the Radio Nigeria which not only criticized Ghana for the reference to Nigeria before the world body, but also castigated her for her concealed support for the secessionists. The following day, 29 September, the Ghanaian government issued a statement regretting the commentary, and said that it had been sincere in its support for the Federal government.[45] In actual fact, the Nigerian news media did over-react in this case. Indeed, it was doubtful whether they had actually seen the text of the Ghanaian address[46] to the UN before they jumped in to the attack. The whole incident showed lack of trust and confidence on both sides. This attitude did not change much when the OAU Consultative Committee met in Lagos in November 1967.

At this first peace meeting of the Consultative Committee held in Lagos on 22 and 23 November 1967, General Ankrah, partly because of his past personal involvement in the Nigerian crisis and partly because of the historical ties between Ghana and Nigeria, was mandated by the Committee to convey to the secessionist members the text of the OAU Kinshasa resolution on Nigeria, and the conclusions and discussions of its first meeting in Lagos which re-affirmed the OAU support for the territorial integrity of Nigeria. He was expected to report urgently to the Committee about the results of his contacts with Colonel Ojukwu.[47] The then OAU Secretary-General, Diallo Telli, said in Lagos at the end of the meeting that the main task of General Ankrah was 'to convince the secessionist to abandon secession, and to return to take part with other Nigerians in the building of their nation'.[48]

It was doubtful whether Ankrah saw his role in the same way as Diallo Telli. For on returning to Accra, he merely told the newsmen at the airport that if the proposals of the Lagos peace meeting were accepted by the Ojukwu government considerable progress would be made towards restoring peace to Nigeria. This perhaps indicated his dissatisfaction with the conclusions of the Lagos meeting. All the Ghanaian newspapers seemed unhappy at the decisions of the meeting, and so they merely reported the communique issued at the end of the meeting without any comment.

With this attitude Ankrah's role became clumsy. For instance, the Ghanaian High Commissioner in London said General Ankrah had been in contact with Colonel Ojukwu by telephone after his return to Accra,[49] but General Ankrah himself said later that he had not succeeded in getting in contact with Ojukwu at all.[50] What really happened may never be known. Ankrah was unable to report on time to the OAU Consultative Committee about the result of his contact with Ojukwu. Anxious to know precisely what was happening, General Mobutu, one of the six heads of state forming the OAU Consultative Committee, flew to Accra late in April 1968 to see General Ankrah.

The Communique issued at the end of his visit, apart from stressing their commitment to the principles of the OAU Charter, did not refer specifically to the Nigerian war.[51] This would suggest lack of agreement between the two leaders on the war, and on his way home, General Mobutu at Accra airport condemned secession in Africa. He said it should not be encouraged and that secession should not be seen as a moral issue, but as a matter of high principle.[52]

In the meantime, the pro-Biafran campaign continued unabated in Ghana. On 29 May 1968, the two government-owned newspapers, the *Ghanaian Times* and the *Daily Graphic*, carried advertisements in memory of '30,000 civilians who were murdered during the pogrom of 1966 in Northern Nigeria'. The advertisements, which were paid for by the 'Biafra Union of Ghana,' also announced that there would be a memorial service on that same day at the Holy Spirit Roman Catholic Cathedral in Accra. The Nigerian High Commission in Accra protested at the advertisements which must have received the tacit support of the Accra government.[53] The Ghanaian government replied that it did not recognize the so-called Biafran state, or 'the residence in Ghana of any citizens of such a state'.[54] It added that in the interests of religious freedom it could not prevent the memorial service from being held.

(b) Niamey Peace Talks

After a period of nearly eight months General Ankrah reported to the OAU Consultative Committee meeting in Niamey, Niger, in mid-July 1968. The details of his report were unknown. But he gave a press statement on 16 July 1968, at Niamey, in which he said that he had succeeded only in part in the assignment given to him by the Lagos meeting of the Consultative Committee, and that he had not succeeded in getting through to Ojukwu, whom he referred to as the

'Head of State',[55] to the annoyance of the Nigerian delegates.

General Ankrah further infuriated them by his proposals at Niamey on relief supplies to the rebels. These proposals, which were essentially similar to those put forward by Ojukwu earlier in Aba,[56] called *inter alia* for a limited truce with a demilitarized zone up to ten miles wide, to be patrolled by neutral troops.[57] They were rejected by the Federal delegates not only because they were similar to those of the rebels but also because the Ghanaian proposals side-tracked the issue of ending the secession which was basic to the conflict. The Nigerian delegates were said to have been extremely bitter about General Ankrah's private talk with General Gowon at Niamey, in which he said that the latter must admit that there was a danger of widespread starvation in Nigeria.[58] President Ahidjo of the Cameroons was said to have been so annoyed at this statement by Ankrah that he was compelled to ask him whether people were not starving in Ghana where there was no war,[59] and where it was no secret that Ghana had been devoting a significant part of its dwindling foreign exchange to food imports. The extent to which this contributed to the unexpected return of President Ahidjo to the Cameroons two days before the end of the meeting is difficult to say.[60]

The effect of the Niamey peace conference on the Ghanaian-Nigerian relations was bad. Henceforth the Nigerian government leaders, who had previously avoided antagonizing the Accra government despite its known sympathy for the rebels, began to criticize its role in private and in public, though often without necessarily mentioning its name. A full stop was put to the Nigerian government's previous practice of informing the Ghanaian government of its peace proposals and about the progress of the war.[61] On the Ghanaian side, the pro-Biafran campaign in the press and the radio continued with greater force than ever. In march 1969 the *Evening Standard,* the newspaper of the National Alliance of Liberals (NAL), expressed misgivings about the visit of Mr Harold Wilson, then the British Prime Minister, to Nigeria in that it could not bring peace nearer since Britain had been supplying arms to one side in the conflict.[62] The same newspaper ridiculed the role of the OAU in the war as being bogus, and said that the OAU could only make any breakthrough in the war if it made a 'serious readjustment' to its views on it.

Although in mid-April 1969 Mr Victor Owusu, the newly appointed Commissioner of External Affairs, came to Lagos on a private visit[63] during which he met Dr Arikpo, his Nigerian counterpart, for informal talks on the war, relations between Nigeria and Ghana did not show any improvement. In fact, it was said that Dr Arikpo agreed to meet Mr Owusu partly out of mere courtesy, and partly because he was not in Nigeria in his official capacity. This was the state of the Ghanaian-Nigerian relations on the eve of the Monrovia peace meeting, which incidentally came to be the last effort to resolve the Nigerian conflict under the aupices of the OAU Consultative Committee before the end of the war in January 1970.

(c) *Monrovia Peace Conference*
Another meeting of the OAU Consultative Committee on Nigeria met in Monrovia between 18 and 20 April 1969.[64] Unlike the Niamey peace conference, Ghana was unable to play any active role in the work of the Committee at Monrovia for three main reasons. First, there was no Nigerian support and co-operation for Ghana's peace efforts. Secondly, when the meeting was held, Ghana was reeling from a major government crisis which led to the sudden dismissal of General Ankrah on 2 April 1969 from the Chairmanship of the NLC, and his replacement by Brigadier A. A. Afrifa. Afrifa was unable to lead the Ghana delegation to the conference and it was led by the Vice-Chairman of the NLC, Mr J. W. Harlley. Furthermore, Victor Owusu, who had visited Lagos only a few days earlier, resigned his post as Commissioner for External Affairs three days before the start of the meeting.[65] Thirdly, the involvement of Mr Francis Nzeribe, a powerful Biafran propagandist working in Ghana for a foreign firm, Jeaffan and Company Limited, in the sordid episode that led to General Ankrah's removal weakened Ghana's moral standing at the peace meeting. This incident did more than anything else to confirm Nigeria's worst fears about Ghana's support for the rebels.

As it turned out, the leader of the Ghanaian delegation, Mr J. W. K. Harlley, did not take any active part in the discussions of the committee. He did not even participate in the series of private talks that took place between the leaders of the Consultative Committee and the representatives of both sides in the war.[66] And for some months after the Monrovia peace conference, the Ghanaian government was so preoccupied at home with intricate political issues relating to the preparation for the general election of 29 August 1969, and the handing over of the administration to civilian leaders, that it did not take any active interest in the Nigerian war until after the Progress Party of Dr Busia came to office on 1 October 1969.[67]

However, the Ghanaian newspapers still maintained their hostile attitude to the Federal cause. On 31 May 1969, the report of an enquiry said to have been conducted under the auspices of the so-called International Committee for the Investigation of Crimes of Genocide by a Ghanaian, Dr Mensah, and financed by the Ojukwu regime was published in London; and it concluded that there was *prima facie* evidence of genocide, and that genocidal intent existed among the Nigerians against the Biafrans.[68] It was not, however, until after the general elections of 29 August 1969 that the Ghanaian papers were able to give more and more prominence to Biafran propaganda, and to bring greater energy into their anti-Nigerian campaign. Till the end of the war, the Ghanaian press and radio maintained this emotional and hostile attitude towards Nigeria.[69] Three days before the formal surrender of the rebels, the *Evening Standard,* owned by the opposition NAL party criticized U Thant, then the UN Secretary-General, who was visiting Ghana, for calling on the rebel leaders to give up secession, and it called on him to reconsider the situation properly, and to take steps to stop 'genocide against Biafrans'.[70]

The attitude of the government party of Dr Busia who came to power on 1 October 1969 was not much different from that of the NLC government, except that it was less glamorous. The first major public pronouncement of Dr Busia on the war was made in the Ivory Coast in an interview with the *Fraternité Matin,* the PDCI party newspaper. Throughout this interview, Dr Busia declined to mention anything about the basic issue of secession in Nigeria, but merely stressed the urgency of getting a cease-fire at all costs.[71] This was unhelpful and perhaps mischievous. For to press solely for an immediate and unconditional cease-fire was to ignore, and deliberately too, the basic 'issues involved in the war, and to do violence to the facts of the Nigerian government's case. A few days after his interview in the Ivory Coast, Dr Busia returned to Ghana to launch his country into participating actively in the peace efforts begun by Emperor Haile Selassie at the end of September 1969.

Thus on 10 October 1969 he sent his Foreign Minister, who was then Mr Victor Owusu, first to Lagos with a message to General Gowon and then with a similar message to ex-Emperor Haile Selassie. Later in November 1969,[72] Dr Busia sent a message on the Nigerian war to Mr Harold Wilson, then the British Prime Minister.[73] The contents of these messages are difficult to fathom. Certainly they contained something about ending the war, but although Victor Owusu told newsmen at Lagos airport that his government was in support of the Federal Government's effort to achieve lasting peace and unity in the country,[74] this was not convincing to the Nigerian leaders who had only a few days previously read Dr Busia's views on the war in the interview to which we have already referred. Dr Busia's interview a few days later in France with the Paris weekly, *Jeune Afrique*,[75] in which he spoke of his efforts to promote peace in Nigeria, without mentioning the need to preserve the country's territorial integrity, further confirmed Nigeria's doubts about Ghana's sincerity in its professed support for the Federal Government. But it was the decision of the Busia government to offer special refugee status to the Ibos in December 1969, while treating all other Nigerians as aliens who were subject to expulsion under the new Aliens Compliance Laws, that proved more than anything else to the Nigerians that the Ghana government was in support of the secessionists. This decision was rightly translated by Dr Eke, then the Biafran Commissioner for Information to mean the acceptance by the Ghanaian government of the view that the Ibos were no longer Nigerians.[76] This decision of the Ghana government was interesting and revealing. For it brought into the open the hypocrisy of the government which had in May 1968 denied its recognition of Biafra[77] or 'the residence in Ghana of any citizens of such a state'.[78]

Although the Accra government did not accord diplomatic recognition to the rebel regime, any more than did France, the Ghanaian government throughout the civil was was on the whole in support of and in sympathy with the secessionists. And diplomatic recognition is not in any case the only way to approve the existence of another regime. Why did Ghana, in spite of its earlier efforts at Aburi and a few months subsequently to help in resolving the Nigerian crisis, choose to adopt a pro-Biafran stance during the war? This is a very difficult question to answer with precision. Nonetheless, on the basis of evidence available we can try to offer some tentative explanation.

(iv) GHANA'S STAND: AN EXPLANATION

The *Legon Observer* which was the most consistent and outspoken advocate of the Biafran cause in Ghana gave four reasons for Ghana's stand.[79] The first was the Russian military involvement and presence in Nigeria which the Ghanaians regarded as 'worrying', and a security threat. After the overthrow of Nkrumah, there had been, as indicated in an earlier chapter, an anti-Communist hysteria in Ghana; and by the time the Nigerian Government signed an agreement with Moscow for the supply of military aircraft and spare parts on 2 August 1967, Ghana was rife with rumours of an imminent subversion of the government, or even invasion of the country, to be masterminded by the Russians to place Nkrumah back into power. This fear of Soviet-led invasion or subversion was so strong about the time the Nigerian war began that the Ghanaian government and the Ivory Coast government were forced to sign an agreement, on 10 July 1967, to strengthen further their joint security measures, which were based on the Defence Agreement of May 1966.[80]

In these circumstances the Ghanaians became unnecessarily uneasy at the Soviet presence in Nigeria. In fact it was believed in Ghana, though wrongly, that as a result of the Soviet military and moral support for the Federal Government Nigeria would soon become a bridge-head for the Soviet penetration of Africa,[81] and especially for launching an attack on Ghana for the restoration of Nkrumah to power. This thought which would appear bizarre to many Nigerians was accepted by many Ghanaians as valid. This was the main reason why the Ghanaians wanted from the beginning to internationalize the war, in order to neutralize the Soviet military presence and thereby ensure their own security. To attain this end, the Ghanaians called loudly on their government to 'give the lead if only to guard itself against such nearness to Nkrumah's comrades'.[82] In this regard it should be noted that the vigorous pro-Biafran campaign did not begin in Ghana until after Nigeria had started to receive Soviet military aid.

The second reason was the view of many Ghanaians that 'in the light of Africa's concern for progress', the Ojukwu regime was more impressive than the Gowon government in Lagos which they described as representing the interests of 'the feudal North'.[83] By this they meant that the Ojukwu government was more devoted to the African cause of unity and freedom than was that of Gowon, and therefore deserved greater support.[84] It is interesting that many Ghanaians who had been condemning Nkrumah for his extensive commitment to Africa's problems and progress should in the same breath turn round to condemn another regime for supposedly not showing such concern for Africa's 'progress'.[85] Whatever might have been the validity of this view at the beginning, it became untenable with the Ojukwu government allying itself with the 'imperialists' and the racist regimes of Southern Africa to back up the rebellion.

The third reason was what the *Legon Observer* called 'the Federal government's clumsiness over the Aburi agreement'. The Ghanaians, including a few who showed some understanding of the Federal government's case, could simply not understand why the Aburi decisions were not quickly translated into action by the Federal government. Many Ghanaians genuinely felt that the failure of the Federal government to implement the Aburi agreements made secession inevitable,[86] and justified their suport for it. They were not concerned with the complexity or the implications of the agreements; nor were they prepared to appreciate the subsequent efforts at mediation between Lagos and Enugu during the period mid-January to late May 1967. Thus Chief Anthony Enahoro's reply to a reporter's question at Accra airport in December 1967 on the failure to implement the Aburi agreement that 'it was not for a group of military leaders to impose a constitution on the Federation'[87] was to Ghanaians inadequate and unsatisfactory.

The fourth reason was the effectiveness of the rebel propaganda in Ghana. Throughout the length and breadth of Ghana there were few homes without copies of the rebels' propaganda publications such as *Crisis 1966, Pogrom, the Problem of Nigerian Unity* etc. some of which had been widely distributed in Ghana early in 1967. The lurid and distorted account of events leading to the war was passionately believed by many Ghanaians, who were quick to jump to the conclusion that the 'events in Nigeria had to a large extent destroyed the basis of a federation'.[88] Indeed, some Ghanaians went to the ludicrous extent of believing the rebel propaganda that the war was unwinnable, and that if the Federal government persisted in the struggle the whole federation would surely disintegrate.[89]

Two more reasons could be added. The first was the external pressure on Ghana. The friendly relationship and close co-operation that developed between the Ivory Coast and Ghana after the coup which resulted in the Defence Agreement of May 1966 made the Ghana government susceptible to Ivory Coast pressure. It has to be remembered that the Ivory Coast government moved its troops to its border with Guinea immediately after the coup to prevent Guinean troops from marching across its territory in their supposed bid to restore Nkrumah to power by force. Furthermore, since late 1966, the Ghana government had been seeking to join the 'Entente' group of states, partly for more profitable trade relations with its neighbours and partly to benefit from the 'Entente' Council Fund; and to gain admission the Ghana government needed the support of the Ivory Coast, the leader of the 'Entente' group of states. Because of all this the Ghana government could not but view with sympathy the Ivory Coast's view on foreign issues.[90] So Ivory Coast's support for the rebels must have influenced the Accra government towards adopting a more determined pro-Biafran stance. It was more than a coincidence that the first public pronouncement of Dr Busia on the Nigerian war should have been made in the Ivory Coast.

Similarly the close relationship between France and Ghana since the coup must have gone some way towards encouraging a pro-Biafran feeling among the Ghanaian leaders. French aid to Ghana since 24 February 1966 had been steadily rising. Although it was not as great as that of the British government it was nonetheless given better and wider publicity in Ghana than British aid.[91] The NLC inherited a country that was economically sick, and so it needed all the financial help it could get to keep the economy going. So French aid might have been used to influence the attitude of the Ghanaian leaders to the civil war.[92] Top officials of the Nigerian Ministry of External Affairs believed that towards the end of 1969 the French government went to the extent of urging the Ghanaian government to accord diplomatic recognition to the secessionist regime in return for substantial economic and financial aid.[93] Though difficult to check, this might be true; and the French aid to Ghana of 30 million francs announced by President Pompidou during Dr Busia's visit to Paris late in October 1969 might be the aid in question. For it seems reasonable to suggest that it was the failure of the Busia government to fulfil its own part of the bargain that, over four years after the announcement, prevented the French government from disbursing any part of the promised aid. The top Ghanaian leaders involved in 'the deal' understood the French stand, and so they did not press for the utilization of the aid. Indeed, it was not until ten months[94] after Pompidou's announcement that the Accra government put out a feeble statement that it would send a delegation to Paris before the end of 1970 to discuss with the French government leaders how the aid promised to Dr Busia in October 1969 would be spent.[95] This account may not be the whole story, but on the basis of available evidence it does not seem too far away from the truth. For it is difficult to see precisely what had been holding back utilization of the aid. Franco-Ghanaian relations remained very cordial as can be seen from the fact that Dr Busia was one of the few African leaders who attended General de Gaulle's funeral. The need for foreign aid in Ghana was desparately urgent if the government was to continue to enjoy the confidence of its people.

The last reason for Ghana's attitude to the Nigerian civil war was perhaps its attempt to further its 'traditional' desire or dream of leading Africa. This was the most popular explanation among many Nigerians, including top government officials, for Ghana's pro-Biafran stance. Many Nigerians believed, rightly or wrongly, that the Ghanaians had since the time of Nkrumah been ambitious to lead Africa, that it was the emergence of Nigeria as the largest and most

populous independent African country in October 1969 that had
thwarted this Ghanaian ambition, and that since then the Ghanaians
had been trying to work against Nigeria. Early in 1965, Chief Festus
Okotie Eboh said in Parliament that the Ghanaian government had
expected the constitutional crisis that followed the federal elections of
December 1964 to lead to Nigeria's disintegration so that Ghana
could easily assume the leadership of Africa.[96] Many Nigerians in this
frame of mind quickly jumped to the conclusion from the very
beginning of the hostilities that the Ghanaians were happy to take
advantage of the opportunity created by the disaster in the country to
further their ambition of leading Africa, which they could only do
through the weakening or disintegration of Nigeria. This view might
contain some truth, but it is difficult to substantiate. Although there
was some loose and irresponsible talk among Ghanaians during the
war about Nigeria's size, which they said was too big for a single
African country, this was not a widespread view in Ghana. Despite
the subsequent attitude of the Accra government, there can be no
doubt that its efforts to achieve peace between Enugu and Lagos at
Aburi in January 1967, and for a few months after, were genuine.
However, this is not saying that the Ghanaian 'ambition' to lead
Africa did not play any role in shaping Ghana's attitude to the war.[97]
All that is being stressed is that this must have been a minimal factor
in determining the Ghanaian response to the war.

More reasons for Ghana's stand during the civil war may be added
to those given above as more and more documents relating to the war
are published. Whatever might have been responsible for Ghana's
hostile attitude to Nigeria during the war, there can be little doubt
that the Ghanaian stand did serious damage to political and
diplomatic relations between the two countries.

For instance, so sour was their relationship that there was a strong
rumour in diplomatic circles in Lagos in September 1970 that the
Nigerian government was contemplating giving political asylum to Dr
Nkrumah.[98] Though denied by General Gowon, it showed the exent
to which Ghana's relations with Nigeria had deteriorated.[99] Similarly,
because of the strained relationship between the two countries, the
Airways Pool Agreement which was signed with fanfares in May
1967, and which was then seen as a bold attempt to revive the defunct
West African Airways Corporation (WAAC), was terminated on 15
December 1970. Furthermore, the Nigerian government declined to
indicate until 25 January 1971 that it would participate in the
Ghanaian Second International Trade Fair of February 1971, in spite
of the fact that it had received the Government invitation to the Fair

as far back as February 1970.[100] And when it accepted, its delegation to the Fair was led by a relatively junior Military Governor, Colonel Mobolaji Johnson.[101] Likewise, after the end of March 1971 when Mr Victor Adegoroye, then the Nigerian High Commissioner in Ghana, left the country for good no attempt was made to appoint a successor until the middle of 1973. In fact, it is said that for nearly two and a half years the Government did not give any serious thought to appointing one. During this period the Nigerian High Commission in Accra was headed by a relatively junior external affairs officer. This was nothing but a show of diplomatic displeasure.

Even in trade matters there was marked deterioration. The total value of Nigeria's exports to Ghana in 1964 was £3,595,000 and the corresponding value for 1969 declined to £1,344,000.[102] In 1964 and 1969, the total value of imports from Ghana was £208,000 and £320,000 respectively. On the other hand, Nigeria's trade with her immediate neighbours increased.[103] The value of Nigeria's exports to Dahomey which was about £0.5 million in 1964 rose to about £2 million in 1969.[104] while the value of imports from Dahomey rose from about £200,000 to £500,000 during the same period.[105] It is interesting to note that General Aferi, then the Ghanaian High Commissioner in Nigeria, should describe the decline in Ghanaian-Nigerian trade as 'regrettable.'[106]

From all this, we can see that Ghanaian-Nigerian relations sank to their lowest point, especially between 1967 and 1970 as a result of Ghana's attitude to the civil war. What are the prospects for an improvement in their relations during the seventies? This is the question which we shall deal with in the next chapter.

1. Much of what is said here is a modified version of the author's article titled 'Ghana and The Nigerian Civil War' published in *The Nigerian Journal of Economic and Social Studies*, Vol. 12, No. 3, November 1970.

2. *West Africa*, 11 July 1970.

3. For a summary of the opinions of the Nigerian newspapers on Ghana's Aliens Laws and Compliance Order see *West Africa*, 3 January 1970.

4. For further details about the African policy of the NLC, see Olajide Aluko, 'Ghana's Foreign Policy under the NLC', *African Quarterly*, January 1971.

5. *Africa Research Bulletin*, March 1966, p. 487.

6. Ibid.

7. Ibid.

8. Ibid., p. 486.

9. This statement is interesting in the light of subsequent developments in their relationship. Freedom of persons and goods between the two countries was later severely curtailed by Ghana, and after December 1969 it became impossible for Nigerians without residence and work permits to stay in Ghana.

10. Some Ghanaian radical intellectuals viewed the government Lt.-Colonel Gowon

set up as a result of the second coup with suspicion because they saw it as a 'feudal' government. We shall say more of this later.

11. *West Africa*, 10 September 1966.

12. *Ghana Today*, 19 October 1966.

13. *West Africa*, 5 November 1966.

14. *Ghana Today*, 28 December 1966.

15. See A. H. M. Kirk-Green *Crisis and Conflict in Nigeria*, Vol. I, January 1966 – July 1967, London, OUP 1971, p. 321.

16. *Ghana Today*, 11 January 1967.

17. For the verbatim report of the Aburi meeting see *Morning Post*, Lagos 3 March 1967.

18. *Morning Post*, 6 March 1967.

19. *Africa Research Bulletin*, March 1967, pp. 735-6.

20. The *Daily Times* described Decree 8 as 'the most suitable broad constitutional framework within which Nigeria's military leaders find it possible to carry on their legislative and executive work'. *The Daily Times*, Lagos 23 March 1967.

21. *Africa Research Bulletin*, March 1967, p. 737.

22. *West Africa*, 1 April 1967.

23. One of the main reasons why Gowon said the Aburi agreements could not easily be implemented as quickly as demanded by Ojukwu was the fact that it would take some time before the relevant governments' officials could work out the details on how to implement them.

24. *Africa Research Bulletin*, June 1967, p. 798.

25. Ibid.

26. *Daily Graphic*, Accra 29 July 1967.

27. *Ashanti Pioneer*, Kumasi 11 August 1967.

28. *West Africa*, 26 August 1967.

29. Ibid.

30. *West Africa*, 16 September 1967.

31. *Legon Observer*, 1-14 September 1967.

32. Till the end of the war, the *Legon Observer* maintained its pro-Biafran policy. We shall refer to this later.

33. The fact that the Ghana Government, unlike other African countries such as Juxon-Smith's Sierra Leone, Somalia and the UAR, did not declare publicly its support for Nigeria during the dark days of August and September 1967 made it suspect in Nigeria.

34. *Morning Post*, Lagos 30 July 1967.

35. For details of the newstalk see *Morning Post*, Lagos 31 August 1967.

36. *Morning Post*, Lagos 31 August 1967.

37. The anger in Nigeria at the Ghanaian call for a cease-fire and negotiation could be imagined if it is remembered that by early September 1967, Nigeria was determined not to allow any foreign organization, including the OAU, to have any say in the war. In fact, by 2 September 1967, General Gowon added another stiff condition that his government would not negotiate with Ojukwu.

38. Other members were Zambia, Congo (Kinshasa), Uganda, Cameroons, Liberia and Sierra Leone.

39. For the text of the resolution see A. H. M. Kirk-Green, op. cit. Vol. 2, July 1967-January 1970, pp. 172-3.

40. For further details see *Report on the OAU Consultative Mission to Nigeria*, Lagos, Government Printer 1967.

41. The others were Ethiopia, Liberia, Niger, Cameroons and Congo (Kinshasa).

42. *Daily Graphic*, 19 September 1967.

43. For the exact statement on the Nigerian civil war see the text of the address of Mr J. W. K. Harlley to the UN General Assembly on 25 September 1967 in *Ghana Today*, 4 October 1967.

44. *Ghana Today*, 4 October 1967.

45. Ibid.

46. All Mr Harlley, the Ghanaian delegate who read Ghana's address to the UN General Assembly, said in passing was that the OAU was doing its best 'to end this most regrettable fratricidal war' in Nigeria.

47. A. H. M. Kirk-Green, Vol. 2, op. cit., pp. 173-4.

48. *Africa Research Bulletin*, November 1967, p. 901.

49. Ibid.

50. *West Africa*, 27 July 1968.

51. For the text of the communique see *Ghana Today*, 1 May 1968.

52. Ibid.

53. The Ghanaian government could not reasonably claim that the papers were entirely free. For in December 1967, it dismissed four editors of the two papers for criticizing its agreement with the Abbott Laboratories of the United States.

54. *West Africa*, 8 June 1968.

55. *West Africa*, 27 July 1968.

56. For Ojukwu's proposals at Aba see *West Africa*, 27 July 1968.

57. Ibid.

58. Interview.

59. Interview.

60. President Ahidjo left Niamey for home the day following the discussions by the Consultative Committee on Ghanaian proposals for relief supplies see, *West Africa*, 27 July 1968.

61. In December 1967 Chief Enahoro had visited Ghana to brief the Accra government about the details of the war and Nigeria's stand on peace.

62. *Evening Standard*, Accra 14 March 1969.

63. *Morning Post*, Lagos 14 April 1969.

64. For a summary of the proceedings of the meeting see *Africa Research Bulletin*, April 1969, pp. 1382-3.

65. *Morning Post*, Lagos 16 April 1969.

66. It was this virtual withdrawal of Ghana that made it easy for the conference to blame the secessionist leaders for the first time for the failure of the peace efforts, while it praised the Nigerian government for its co-operation and conciliatory attitude. See *Africa Research Bulletin*, April 1969, p. 1383. See also A. H. M. Kirk-Green, Vol. 2, op. cit., pp. 375-6.

67. The replacement of Ankrah by Afrifa early in April 1969 brought about some improvement in Ghanaian-Nigerian relations, as could be seen from Afrifa's visit to Lagos in July 1969. This was mainly because Afrifa and Gowon had been contemporaries at Sandhurst, and unlike Ankrah showed little interest in foreign adventures.

68. A. Waugh and S. Cronje: *Biafra: Britain's Shame*, London 1969, p. 113.

69. See, for instance, the *Legon Observer* of 5 December 1969, 7 November 1969, and that of 2 January 1970 which carried a long pro-Biafran article by Dr A. O. Chukwurah, said to be a lecturer in Law in the University of Biafra.

70. *Evening Standard*, Accra 9 January 1970.

71. *West Africa*, 4 October 1969.

72. *West Africa*, 26 November 1969.

73. *West Africa*, 6 December 1969.

74. *Daily Times*, Lagos 11 October 1969.

75. *West Africa*, 6 December 1969. See also *Dr Busia in Europe and America*, op. cit. p. 65.

76. *West Africa*, 20 December 1969.

77. *West Africa*, 8 June 1968.

78. Any visitor to Ghana during the war would feel the intensity of pro-Biafran

feelings among Ghanaians. From the beginning till the end, the *Legon Observer*, a paper published by a group of academics of the Ghana University, refused to publish anything about the Nigerian case and gave only the one-sided story of the rebels.

79. For the details see the *Legon Observer*, 1 September 1967, pp. 10-11.

80. Till the end of the NLC rule in october 1969, and even after, the Ghanaian leaders continued to be haunted by the fear of a Soviet-inspired subversion. But on the basis of facts, this was but a mirage.

81. The author has discussed this Ghanaian view further in an article titled 'The Civil War and Nigerian Foreign Policy' in *The Political Quarterly*, April 1971.

82. The *Legon Observer*, 1-14 September 1967, p. 11.

83. Ibid.

84. The memory of the nationalist campaign of Dr Azikiwe in Ghana between 1934 and 1937 boosted the Ojukwu government's image as a nationalist government.

85. It is, however, fair to say that many Ghanaians in spite of their dislike for Nkrumah's government still wanted their country to follow his radical vigorous African policy. For instance, Mr Victor Owusu, though with some exaggeration, told an Afro-American group in New York late in 1969 that 'we do not oppose Nkrumah's foreign policy, but his domestic policy'. *Legon Observer*, 2 January 1970.

86. Many Ghanaians did not know anything about Decreee 8 of 17 march 1967, and the few who did saw it as a poor substitute for the original agreements at Aburi.

87. *Daily Graphic*, Accra 18 December 1967.

88. *The Legon Observer*, 1 September 1967.

89. *The Legon Observer*, 30 January 1970.

90. Indeed by the Treaty of Friendship and Understanding of May 1970 between Ghana and Ivory Coast the two countries agreed to co-ordinate their foreign policies.

91. A writer, Mr Jonathan Lamptey, in the *Legon Observer*, of 5 December 1969, criticized the Ghanaian newspapers for giving undue publicity to French aid.

92. Although the US government has been the largest single source of aid to Ghana since the coup, it seemed that it did not use this to influence Ghana in favour of Biafra largely because it, at least in principle, supported the concept of a united Nigeria.

93. Interview.

94. *West Africa*, 15 August 1970.

95. If a delegation is eventually sent to Paris it will probably be for another aid commitment rather than this one.

96. *H. R. Deb.*, 31 March 1965, col. 302.

97. There were few Ghanaians who hoped that the war would result in the disintegration of Nigeria.

98. *West Africa*, 12 September 1970.

99. It is reasonable to argue that it was the fear of the possible presence of Nkrumah in Nigeria that persuaded Dr Busia's government to change its original stand of rejecting any dialogue over the property and assets of the Nigerians expelled from Ghana.

100. *Morning Post*, 3 March 1971.

101. As against this, the Nigerian delegation to the International Trade Fair in Egypt in March 1971 was headed by the Chief of Staff of the Nigerian Army, Brigadier Hassan Katsina; while the Head of State himself, General Gowon, visited Dahomey during that country's International Trade Fair in August 1970.

102. *Annual Abstract of Statistics 1969*, Lagos: Federal office of Statistics, p. 82.

103. Ghana, too, strengthened her trade with her Francophone neighbours, notably Mali and Upper Volta. For further details see *Economic Survey*, 1967, Accra: Central Bureau of Statistics 1968, pp. 41-2.

104. *West Africa*, 22 August 1970.

105. For further details about the growth of Nigeria's trade with her francophone
      neighbours, see *Review of External Trade*, Lagos: Federal Officer of Statistics
      1968, p. 23.
106. *Daily Times*, 29 December 1970.

CHAPTER VIII

Future Prospects

It is now difficult to write about the future of Ghanaian-Nigerian relations in view of the recent coup d'etat of 13 January 1972 that unseated the Busia government. Although the new National Redemption Council Government of Colonel Ignatius Acheampong has made some important changes in Ghana's foreign policy which have already resulted in improved relations with Nigeria, it is too early to say whether the change of government in Accra will radically affect the relationship between the two countries.[1]

As can be seen from the earlier chapters, the sources of discord between the two countries are more basic than mere differences between their governing élites.[2] The vast differences in size, population, and material resources between the two countries which led to jealousy on the part of Ghana and arrogance on the part of Nigeria still remain. In actual fact, the differences in material resources have increased largely as a result of the oil boom in Nigeria which made it possible for Nigeria late in December 1971 to revalue her currency by over eight per cent against the American dollar, while Ghana followed the United States by devaluing her currency by about 48.6 per cent.[3] Although the National Redemption Council (NRC) Government revalued the cedi by about forty-one per cent[4] against the dollar late in February, 1972, this was no proof of the strength of the economy. For instance, when Britain decided to float the pound in June 1972, the exchange rate of the cedi moved down by 0.24 cedis[5] against the pound sterling, while that of the Nigerian pound moved up against the British pound by an extra £N6 on every £N100.[6]

Likewise, the differences in the structure of their governments — between a federal and a unitary system — remain. Although the fact that the two countries are now under army rule may lessen these differences, some of them will still persist. And this may affect their approach to international issues. As pointed out in chapter one, since the late sixties the two countries have been steadily moving in opposite directions in social, economic and military policies. For instance, late in 1971 while Nigeria was making every effort to expand her armed forces through the recruitment of different types of technical experts and to make them the best in Black Africa, Ghana was cutting down the size of her armed forces. Thus in October 1971, the seventh infantry battalion stationed at Takoradi was disbanded.[7]

True, the NRC government has begun to reverse the trend started under the NLC in social, economic and military matters. But its freedom for manoeuvre has been limited by the country's economic difficulties. In spite of this, however, the Acheampong Government has tried to make some changes in the economic sphere by increasing state participation in the economy of the country. Like the Nkrumah government, the government has started to set up state enterprises such as the newly created Food Production Corporation. And unlike the practice under the Busia regime, Colonel Acheampong has pledged to use state power, in his own words, 'to capture the commanding heights of the economy'.[8] Like the present Nigerian government, the Accra government has announced its intention to participate in all the foreign-owned mining and timber extraction companies in Ghana to the tune of about fifty-five per cent.[9] All these measures will surely narrow the gap between the two countries, and so may make for better understanding between them.

Competition for the leadership role in Black Africa in general, and in West Africa in particular, which was an abundant source of disharmony between the two countries in the sixties will not entirely disappear in the foreseeable future. As seen in chapter three the Nigerians have since independence believed that leadership in Black Africa is their 'birthright'. This belief has come to the fore with greater force than ever before since the end of the civil war. For instance, on the tenth independence aniversary of the country on 1st October 1970, all the Nigerian newspapers were unanimous in their call for Nigeria to take up the leadership of Africa.[10] Unlike the leaders of the Balewa Government, the present leaders are anxious that Nigeria should lead Black Africa in everything. For instance, on General Gowon's return from his state visits to the Gambia and Mauritania early in 1971, he told reporters at Ikeja airport that everywhere he and his entourage went since the end of the civil war other African governments had looked upon Nigeria as a great country with potential to lead the continent.[11] He added that his government would not disappoint their hopes.[12]

In spite of the economic woes of Ghana, she did not under the Busia regime give up the task of competing with Nigeria. Late in

1969, Dr Kofi Busia was quoted as saying that his government was determined 'to restore the lost pride, and dignity of Ghana in Africa.'[13]

Although the economic weakness of the country hamstrung Dr Busia's administration in this bid, it was believed in Nigeria, though denied late in 1970 by Dr Kofi Dsane-Selby, then the Ghanaian Ambassador in France, that the growing links between Ghana and France and between her and the 'Entente' countries were designed to set up an anti-Nigerian bloc in West Africa.[14]Given this situation, it is doubtful whether Ghana under the new military leaders, though still faced with grave economic problems, will abandon her competition with Nigeria. For one thing, most of the top civil servants who advised Dr Nkrumah, General Ankrah, General Afrifa and Dr Busia are the same people advising the National Redemption Council Government of Colonel Acheampong.

Apart from this, as indicated in an earlier chapter, the Ghanaians are a proud people who believe seriously that their country must play a leading role in Africa. In actual fact, Colonel Acheampong has said on several occasions that his government was determined to restore the country's 'dignity in Africa.' This was elaborated by Major General N. A. Aferi, then the Ghanaian Commissioner for External Affairs, who told a correspondent of the *West Africa* magazine at Rabat in June 1972, that since the overthrow of the Busia Government many other African countries including those larger than Ghana had approached her 'to resume the leadership of the continent'[15] as during the Nkrumah era. He further said that the people of his country were 'unhappy' that under the Busia regime their country was in 'obscurity' in Africa, and that the new Accra Government was bent on playing a leading role in Africa.[16]

The Nigerian government leaders seem to realize that Ghana cannot easily accept playing second fiddle to their country. So the two countries will continue to compete. But if, as General Gowon said when receiving the new Ghanaian High Commissioner, Colonel Samuel Asante in his Dodan Barracks on 13 July 1972,[17] an end can be put to 'any form of unhealthy rivalry'[18] between the two countries then the competition will be slightly different. It will allow co-operation to take place between the two countries, and differences to be resolved without an undue rise in blood pressure.

Other factors likely to affect the future pattern of their relationship include their respective views about the types of policies or attitudes to be adopted towards the Great Powers, and towards African problems such as African unity, colonialism and racism. Until the overthrow of the Progress Government, Ghana and Nigeria appeared to be pursuing diametrically opposed policies to the Great Powers, and to the colonial and racist problems in Southern Africa. For instance, while Nigeria after the civil war became more and more critical of the Western Powers for their links with South Africa, Portugal and Rhodesia, Ghana was from 24 February 1966 to 13 January 1972 pro-Western and anti-Communist. Indeed, the Busia Government was almost crudely so. Thus the troubles between his government and the Trade Union Congress (TUC) in August and September 1971 were blamed on the Communist Powers and their Ghanaian agents who wanted 'to exploit the economic problems to subvert the democratic institutions of the day.'[19]

On the other hand, Nigeria has become more accomodating to the Communist countries though she can still be critical of them if need be. These divergent policies and attitudes to the Great Powers soured the Ghanaian-Nigerian relationships. To many Nigerians, because of Dr Busia's pro-Western policy Ghana was nothing but, in the words of a Ghanaian journalist, Mr Cameron Duodu, 'a Western client-state.'[20] For instance, in December 1971, a correspondent of the *Sunday Times* wrote from Accra that since the unseating of the Nkrumah government Ghana had become 'the den of the imperialist, and the neo-colonialist intrigues.'[21]

But the Acheampong government has now modified the country's attitudes and policies to the Great Powers. Like the Federal Military Government, the National Redemption Council Government has become more critical of the Western Powers, and has improved relations with the Communist Powers. Diplomatic relations with China, broken off shortly after the 1966 coup had been re-established by June 1972. The Ghanaian government has sent powerful trade delegations to almost all the Communist countries. In May 1972, a government mission visited Moscow to recruit doctors for the services of the government, and the armed forces.[22] Technical aid agreements had by mid-1972 been signed between Ghana and several Eastern European countries such as Bulgaria, Czechoslovakia, and Poland.

The NRC government has repeatedly criticized the Western Powers for their links with Portugal and the white supremacist regimes in Southern Africa. Not only that, but by repudiating some £36 millions owed to four British firms, and by declaring unilaterally that Ghana would only talk to the creditor countries on bilateral rather than on a multi-lateral basis,[23] the Acheampong government has demonstrated that it could be tough with the Western Powers. All this has gone some way to improve the standing of the Acheampong government in Lagos. If the two countries can continue to pursue this type of similar policy and attitude to the Great Powers, their relationship will be closer and more cordial than ever before.

One of the main areas of discord between Lagos and Accra till the coup d'etat of 13 January 1972 was their different approach to the solution of colonial and racial issues in Africa. While Nigeria favoured a policy of total isolation of South Africa and an armed confrontation with the racist regimes in Southern Africa, Dr Busia's Ghana was in favour of dialogue and contact with them. Thus while Mr Edwin Ogbu, the Nigerian Permanent Representative at the United Nations, was in November 1971 calling for the expulsion of South Africa from the world body.[24] the Ghanaian government-owned newspaper, the *Daily Graphic* decried this call as unnecessary, and said it would worsen the plight of the oppressed peoples of South Africa.[25] Because of Dr Busia's continued advocacy of dialogue with South Africa after the OAU had overwhelmingly voted against it at the Addis Ababa Summit in June 1971, the *Nigerian Observer* said that Ghana had become 'traitorous'[26] to the African cause while the *Daily Times* said Ghana had become 'one of the lackeys of the imperialist' in Africa.[27]

These charges can no longer be levelled at Ghana, for the NRC Government has adopted a militant policy towards colonial and racial issues. It has rejected with disgust dialogue with South Africa, and has called for the adoption of armed struggle to complete the liberation of Africa. For the first time since February 1966, Ghana celebrated Africa Freedom Day on 25 May 1972 with a variety of activities including fund-raising campaign for African freedom fighters.[28] In his speech to mark the day, General N. A. Aferi called for the setting up of an African High Command of the Nkrumah type to accelerate the collapse of colonial and racist regimes in Africa.[29] The statement of Colonel Acheampong[30] to the OAU Summit at Rabat in June 1972, in which he called for the creation of an African High Command, was as tough and militant as that of Dr Okoi Arikpo, in which he demanded the immediate establishment of an African task force to speed up the liberation struggle in Africa.[31] One of the main consequences of this similarity of views on the approach to solving the colonial and racial issues in Africa is to remove them from the areas of friction between Accra and Lagos. If this trend continues, the two countries will inevitably be drawn closely together in the task of employing common tactics and strategy to combat colonialism and racism in Africa.

Another important factor that is likely to affect the Ghanaian-

Nigerian relationship in the future is the attitude of the public of both countries to each other. For most of the sixties, antagonisms between the two countries were usually found more at unofficial than official level. Mainly because of the rivalry and the suspicion between the Ghanaians and the Nigerians, differences between them have always tended to degenerate into a sort of press war. For example, shortly after the end of the civil war, the Nigerian press and radio began to criticize the Busia government for its role during the civil war and for its sudden expulsion of thousands of Nigerians from Ghana. In one of these radio broadcasts the Busia administration was accused of 'vicious political antagonism towards Nigeria', and of 'backing the secessionists during the civil war'.[32] The Ghanaian press replied in anger. The *Daily Graphic* deplored the radio broadcast and accused Nigeria of ingratitude.[33] For, the newspaper continued, 'the NLC ignored the feelings of many Ghanaians and supported the Federal government refusing to see the massacre of millions of Biafrans for what it was . . .'[34] The Progress Party newspaper, the *Star,* also condemned the Nigerian broadcast and added that the Nigerians were behaving like 'a child in tantrums'.[35]

Although for a variety of complex reasons the relationship between the press of both countries has rarely been cordial, there can be no doubt that until the overthrow of Dr Busia's government it was the massive expulsion of Nigerians that worsened the situation. For instance, following the return of 3,000 Nigerians expelled from Ghana to Lagos in May 1971, the *Morning Post* called on the Federal Government to take drastic retaliatory measures against Ghana.[36] Similarly late in 1971, the *New Nigerian* accused the Ghanaian government of cruelty to Nigerians, and of imprisoning over 1,000 Nigerians without residence permits in Ghana.[37] The *Daily Graphic* dismissed this as nonsense. The situation was so bad that many Nigerian newspapers and their correspondents called, between January 1970 and December 1971, for Dr Nkrumah's return to Ghana to spite Dr Busia's government.[38] In fact, the *Daily Sketch* called on the Federal government in January 1970 to grant political asylum to Dr Nkrumah because according to it the Nigerians in Ghana during the Nkrumah era did not suffer humiliation nor were they expelled.[39]

However, the difficulties caused by the expulsions and the maltreatment of the Nigerians have been removed by the new government in Accra. The release of about 1,000 Nigerian detainees without residence permits by the Acheampong government shortly after the coup was warmly received in Nigeria, and this has substantially defused the large-scale expulsions as a political issue between Accra and Lagos. Similarly the pledge of the National Redemption Council to review the Aliens Compliance Order and the Ghanaian Business Promotion Act under which non-Ghanaian Africans had been excluded from certain sectors of the economy has been welcomed in Nigeria as being truly in line with the spirit of African Unity.[40] Furthermore, the swift implementation of the agreement reached between the two countries under which two estate agents in Ghana, Messrs Frank Boret and Company and Messrs A. K. Boakye and Company,[41] were appointed to handle the assets of the Nigerians expelled from Ghana to the owners. Indeed, late in May 1972, Mr Peter Onu, then the Acting Nigerian High Commissioner in Ghana, announced that with the help of the NRC Government over seventy-five per cent of the Nigerian expelleess had recovered their property.[42] The effect of all this has been an improvement in the relationship between the two countries.

In spite of these improved relations, however, it is not easy to predict that the future pattern of their relationship, as earlier indicated, will be radically different from that of the sixties, which was characterized largely by suspicion, jealousy, apathy, and even outright hostility. Yet there is need for some radical change in their relationship in favour of closer co-operation and understanding between the two countries. This is essential in the interest of both countries and in the interest of African unity, as General Gowon in May 1971 told General N. A. Aferi, then the Ghanaian High Commissioner in Nigeria.[43] Even the *Legon Observer* the most consistent supporter of Biafra during the civil war, recognized after the end of the war the need for considerable improvement in Ghanaian-Nigerian relationships.[44] Late in April 1972, Ghana's External Affairs Commissioner, Major General Aferi, told an inaugural meeting of the Ghana-Nigeria Friendship Association in Accra that since the coup the NRC Government had made improving relations with Nigeria a cardinal policy in West Africa. In actual fact Colonel Acheampong said that Nigeria was the first country to be informed of the coup that overthrew the Busia government.[45] Since then Ghanaian-Nigerian relations have improved considerably. This made it easy for General Gowon to assist Ghana in recovering the body of Dr Nkrumah from Guinea in mid-1972.

Given all this, it can be said that all is not lost, and that the prospects for better relations between Accra and Lagos are bright. But the desire for improved relationships is one thing and its realization is another. Therefore, the big question that arises is how can the wish for major improvement in relations be translated into reality. This can be done in several ways. These can include the promotion of functional co-operation between the two countries, the exchange of information between the information media of the two countries, and the exchange of visits between the leaders and those who shape public opinion in both countries.

At the end of the visit of Brigadier (now Lt-General) A. A. Afrifa, then the Chairman of the NLC, to Lagos in July 1969, a joint communique was issued in which the leaders of the two countries expressed their commitment in principle to improve the economic, commercial and cultural relations between their countries.[46] But up till very recently, nothing concrete came out of this, largely as a result of the political difficulties between them. Because of their past links during the colonial era there is plenty of room for functional co-operation between them if the will is there. In this regard, the renewal of the airways agreement between the two countries late in 1971 which Mr Jatoe Kaleo, then the Ghanaian Minister of Transport and Communications, hoped would form the basis of co-operation between the two countries[47] was somehow encouraging.

But late in June 1972 this was followed by a more comprehensive airways agreement which was first initiated in 1964, but which was never ratified by either Government as a result of their poor poitical relationship.[48] Under the new agreement each will grant to the other's airways landing facilities that will enable them to operate services.[49] In the field of shipping and research there is ample room for co-operation which will yield greater dividends than working within a national framework.

Trade between the two countries which declined considerably during the late sixties, as shown in the last chapter, can be improved. Already the new government in Accra has taken important measures in this direction. In March 1972, Colonel Acheampong announced that his government had set aside £N80,000 to import cattle from Nigeria in order to start cattle rearing and dairy farming in Ghana.[50] During the following month, a Government trade delegation led by Professor S. Sey, the deputy director of the Bank of Ghana, visited Nigeria to explore the possibilities for increased trade between the two countries.[51] During the same month an agreement was signed between Nigeria and Ghana under which the former is to supply 20,000 tons of coal annually to the latter for the next four years.[52] And the first shipment of coal under the agreement took place early in June 1972 when 1,500 tons of coal from Nigeria were off-loaded at Takoradi.[53] This was very significant. For it was the first time Nigeria had exported coal to Ghana since 1965[54] when it was stopped as a result of strained relationships between the two countries.

Further commercial contacts can be promoted between the two countries. For instance, it is difficult to see the economic justification for Ghana's import of crude oil from the Soviet Union instead of from Nigeria. Ghana can also import more cheaply some local foodstuffs such as rice, yams and beans from Nigeria. In return Nigeria can import from Ghana some types of textiles, footwear, matches and other kinds of goods produced in Ghana which are not produced in sufficiently large quantities in Nigeria.

Since the two countries now share a common approach to the question of a West African Economic Community, it will be easier for them to work closely together for its realization. During General Gowon's state visit to Togo late in April 1972, he and President Eyadema signed an agreement which they said would form the embryo of a West African Economic Community. Later in June this was followed by a meeting of experts of both countries in Lagos to work out further details about the Community. At the end of the talks, a communiqué was issued saying *inter alia* that General Gowon had been mandated by the meeting to summon a Summit of all West African Heads of State and Government to discuss the question of an economic community in West Africa,[55] but that this Summit should be preceded by a Ministerial meeting of all the West African countries. On the other hand, Colonel Acheampong had also written to all the West African Governments about a Summit conference to discuss how to establish the West African Economic Community. He too wanted the Summit to be preceded by a Ministerial meeting. But both Ghana and Nigeria should pool their efforts together in their bid to establish an economic community in West Africa. This should not be very difficult. For the agreement between Nigeria and Togo is open to any other West African country to join. Ghana's relations with Togo are good. And in April 1972, Colonel Acheampong visited Togo to discuss with President Eyadema how their countries could work together for the establishment of a West African Economic Community.[56] All this should make it easy for Ghana either to accede to the Nigerian-Togolese agreement on the establishment of the economic community, or to join forces with Nigeria to get a West African Summit Conference held to discuss various proposals for the community.

Another way to foster the Ghanaian-Nigerian relations lies in the improvement of communication between the peoples of both countries. Most of the past sources of disharmony between the two countries can be attributed to plain differences, misunderstandings and prejudices bred out of sheer lack of familiarity. Indeed, the Ghanaians and the Nigerians are both blithely ignorant of the actual facts of each other's country. For instance, many Ghanaians, including even some pressmen, did not know that the banned Ibo-dominated NCNC was in coalition with the banned NPC at the federal level from December 1959 until the coup of January 1966. This ignorance contributed substantially to the pro-Biafran feeling in Ghana during the civil war. Similarly, many Nigerians, including some of them men behind the press, were totally ignorant of the sufferings and the deprivations of the Ghanaians which were a result of Nkrumah's tyranny and his disastrous economic policies, especially between 1964 and 24 February 1966. This type of bland ignorance contributed considerably to the pro-Nkrumah sentiment[57] in Nigeria, especially among the radical elements after the overthrow of the CPP government early in 1966.

Similarly the intensity of anger generated in Nigeria by the massive expulsions of Nigerians without residence permit in Ghana between early December 1969 and late 1971 was to some extent due to the fact that the Nigerian public was, and is still, totally unaware of the fact that in spite of the expulsions thousands of Nigerians continue to live in Ghana. Towards the end of January 1970, Mr S. Dombo, then the Minister of Interior, told reporters in Accra that over 250,000 Nigerians[58] had already been given residence permits. Although this figure might have been exaggerated there is little doubt that over 100,000 Nigerians[59] have continued to live and work in Ghana in spite of the enforcement of the Aliens Compliance Order and the Ghanaian Business Promotion Act. Likewise, the Nigerian public, including those that shape public opinion in the country, has been totally ignorant of the fact that the number of Ghanaians in the country has always been remarkably small if compared with that of Nigerians in Ghana.[60] It was this type of ignorance that made the Nigerian press and public call stridently and even violently, early in 1970, that the Federal Government should retaliate by sending home all the Ghanaians in the country.

To overcome this mutual ignorance about each other the governments, the press, the radio and members of the public of both countries must learn to know more about the facts of each other's country. This can be done in several ways. Firstly, frequent exchange of visits between leaders of both countries should be encouraged. Already this has started to happen with greater frequency since 13 January 1972. Both governments have exchanged more than five visits at official level within six months of the coming to power of the Acheampong government. In May 1972, while returning from the OAU Committee of Seven on the Senegal and Guinea dispute in Monrovia, General Gowon stopped briefly at Accra, for the first time since March 1967, to see Colonel Acheampong at Christianborg Castle.[61] Furthermore, General Gowon accepted a Ghanaian Government invitation to visit Ghana in the near future.[62] Unfortunately General Gowon could not make the visit before the overthrow of his regime in July 1975.

Secondly, some exchange of visits—not confined to the capitals—between the men behind the press and radio of both countries to each other's country will help in breaking down the communication barrier between them. Thirdly, an agreement can be signed under which there will be frequent exchange of radio and television programmes between the two countries, as suggested in Lagos late in 1967 by Mr K. G. Osei-Bonsu, then the Ghanaian Commissioner for Information and Broadcasting.[63] Finally, the members of the public of both countries should be encouraged by their respective governments to pay frequent visits to each other's country as suggested by the *Legon Observer*.[64]

Regular consultations between the two Governments on major international issues should be encouraged and intensified. This will surely improve their diplomatic co-operation and narrow areas of disagreement. Already this has started since the coup of 13 January 1972. In mid April 1972, the Ghanaian Head of State, Colonel I. K. Acheampong, wrote to the Nigerian leader, General Gowon, to sound out his opinion about the possibility of recognizing Bangladesh.[65] But the latter on the experience of his country advised against recognition for the meantime. Not to rock the boat, Colonel Acheampong agreed.[66] Furthermore, the two Governments have exchanged views on what attitudes they should adopt to the EEC in view of the British entry into the Community as from 1 January 1973. All this has served to oil the diplomatic mill, and to increase understanding and confidence between Accra and Lagos.

If all this is carried out, much will have been done to dispel the mutual ignorance and suspicion which have in no small measure bedevilled the Ghanaian-Nigerian relationship in the past. With the Busia government overturned and with the new National Redemption Council government installed in Accra, which has on the whole been welcomed by the Nigerian public and press,[67] the opportunities for improving the relationship between Lagos and Accra are now better, at least in the immediate future.

As earlier pointed out, the new Ghana coup of 13 January 1972 may not mean the end of the traditional jealousy, suspicion, competition and differences between the two countries. What can be said is that the worst of these may in the near future be discarded by both countries. Given all this and given wise leadership and statemanship on both sides, and mutual understanding, sympathy and tolerance among the peoples of the two countries, and barring all major accidents, the chances of considerable improvement in the Ghanaian-Nigerian relations for the foreseeable future are now better than at any other time since their independence.

1. Although it is beyond the scope of this study, it has to be said that in foreign policy matters the options left for government leaders are few. Indeed, in foreign policy many things are pre-determined and governments are almost powerless against them.
2. It has to be remembered that while the two countries were under the military after the coup against Dr Nkrumah, from 1966 till September 1969, their relationship as shown in the last chapter was not close except during the short period from February 1966 till mid-1967.
3. *West Africa*, 7 January 1972.
4. *West Africa*, 18 February 1972.
5. *West Africa*, 21 July 1972.
6. Prior to the floating of the pound sterling £N100 would exchange for £117.8 sterling, but now £N100 will exchange for about £122 sterling.
7. *West Africa*, 22 October 1971.
8. *West Africa*, 12 May 1972.
9. *West Africa*, 21 July 1972.
10. See *Daily Sketch*, Ibadan 1 October 1970; *Daily Times*, Lagos 1 October 1970; *Morning Post*, Lagos 1 October 1970; *New Nigerian*, Kaduna 1 October 1970.
11. *New Nigerian*, Kaduna 25 February 1971.
12. Ibid.
13. *N. A. Deb.*, 2 December 1969, col. 253.
14. *West Africa*, 15 August 1970.
15. *West Africa*, 7 July 1972.
16. Ibid.
17. *Morning Post*, Lagos 14 July 1972.
18. Ibid.
19. *West Africa*, 24 September 1971.
20. Cameron Duodu, 'Two Troubled Years for Dr Busia' in *The Observer Foreign News Service*, London 30 September 1971.
21. *Sunday Times*, Lagos 12 December 1971.
22. *West Africa*, 16 June 1972.
23. *West Africa*, 17 March 1972.
24. *West Africa*, 26 November 1971.
25. Ibid.
26. *The Nigerian Observer*, Benin City 23 October 1971.
27. *Daily Times*, Lagos 23 October 1971, and *Sunday Times*, Lagos 17 October 1971.

28. *West Africa*, 7 July 1972.
29. *West Africa*, 2 June 1972.
30. Colonel Acheampong's speech was read by Major Felli, the Commissioner for Trade and Industry.
31. *West Africa*, 7 July 1972.
32. For further details see *West Africa*, 13 June 1970.
33. *West Africa*, 2 May 1970.
34. Ibid.
35. *West Africa*, 13 June 1970.
36. *Morning Post*, Lagos 23 May 1971.
37. *West Africa*, 8 October 1971.
38. See for instance, The *Sunday Times*, Lagos 29 November 1970, and 12 December 1971; *Daily Times*, Lagos 12 May 1971.
39. *The Daily Sketch*, Ibadan 21 January 1970.
40. *Daily Times*, Lagos 14 January 1972.
41. *Morning Post*, Lagos 7 December 1971.
42. *West Africa*, 2 June 1972.
43. *Daily Times*, Lagos 12 May 1971.
44. *Legon Observer*, 8-12 May 1970.
45. *Speeches by Colonel I. K. Acheampong*, Series 3, Accra, Government Printer July 1972, p. 7.
46. *West Africa*, 2 August 1969.
47. *West Africa*, 10 December 1971.
48. *Morning Post*, Lagos 26 June 1972.
49. Ibid. See also *West Africa*, 14 July 1972.
50. *West Africa*, 7 April 1972.
51. *West Africa*, 5 May 1972.
52. *Morning Post*, Lagos 3 June 1972.
53. *West Africa*, 16 June 1972.
54. Ibid.
55. *West Africa*, 21 July 1972.
56. *West Africa*, 28 April 1972.
57. For instance, Mr Remi Ilori, who was then the editor of the *Sunday Post* recalled a few days after the overthrow of Dr Busia's government in January 1972 that he had in 1966 described the coup that unseated the CPP regime as 'an act of ingratitude' by the Ghanaians to Dr Nkrumah whom he described as the founder of Ghana, and who had through his progressive African policies put Ghana and Africa on the world map. Mr Ilori then went on to ask the new National Redemption Council government to arrange for the return of Dr Nkrumah from Canakry to Ghana because of what he regarded as his past contributions to the progress of Ghana and Africa. See *Sunday Post*, Lagos 16 January 1972.
58. *West Africa*, 31 January 1970.
59. The Nigerian High Commission in Accra confirmed that the number of Nigerians still residing in Ghana was greater.
60. As pointed out in chapter two, the total number of Ghanaians in Nigeria was under 8,000 according to the 1963 census figures, and this figure has since not shown any substantial increase.
61. *Morning Post*, 2 June 1972.
62. *West Africa*, 12 May 1972.
63. *Ghana Today*, 1 November 1967.
64. *Legon Observer*, 8-12 May 1970.
65. Information from the Ministry of External Affairs Lagos.

66. However after waiting for a year the NRC Government has decided to recognize the Dacca government.

67. See for instance, the *Daily Sketch*, Ibadan January 1972, and the issue of 15 January 1972; *The Daily Express*, Lagos 14 January 1972. The front page of the *Daily Express* headlined 'No Tears for Busia' could be said to convey the reaction of the general public to the coup. For further details see also *The Sunday Post*, Lagos 16 January 1971; *The Sunday Times*, Lagos 16 January 1972; and the *Daily Times*, Lagos 17 January 1972.

Select Bibliography

The list here includes only a small fraction of the various books and documentary materials used in the text. Further details will be found in the footnotes.

BOOKS I

1. Afrifa, A. A., *The Ghana Coup*, 24 February 1966, London, 1966.
2. Alexander, H. T., *African Tight-rope*, London, 1965.
3. Armah, K., *Africa's Golden Road*, London, 1965
4. Austin, D., *Politics in Ghana 1946-60*, London, 1964.
5. Austin, D., *Britain and South Africa*, London, 1966.
6. Awolowo, O., *Path To Nigerian Freedom*, London, 1947.
7. Awolowo, O., *Awo, The Autobiography*, London, 1960.
8. Awolowo, O., *People's Republic*, London, 1968.
9. Awolowo, O., *Strategy and Tactics of the People's Republic of Nigeria*, London, 1970.
10. Ayandele, E. A., *Holy Johnson*, London, 1970.
11. Azikiwe, N., *Zik—A Selection from the Speeches of Dr. Azikiwe*, London, 1971.
12. Balogun, K., *Mission to Ghana*, New York, 1963.
13. Bello, A., *My Life*, London, 1962.
14. Birmingham, W., Omaboe, E. N. and Neustadt, I., (ed.), *A Study of Contemporary Ghana* Vols. I and II, London, 1966 and 1967.
15. Black, J. E. and Thompson, K. W., ed., *Foreign Policies in a World of Change*, New York, 1963.
16. Bretton, H. L., *The Rise and Fall of Kwame Nkrumah*, London, 1967.
17. Burns, A., *History of Nigeria*, London, 1963.
18. Busia, K., *Africa in search of Democracy*, London, 1967.
19. Cervenka, Z., *The Organisation of African Unity*, London, 1969.
20. Coleman, J. S., *Nigeria, Background To Nationalism*, Berkeley, 1963.

21. Crowder, M., *West Africa Under Colonial Rule*, London, 1968.
22. Dei-Anang, M., *Ghana Resurgent*, Accra, 1964.
23. Dudley, B. J., *Politics, and Parties in Northern Nigeria*, London, 1968.
24. Duverger, M., *Political Parties*, London, 1961.
25. Enahoro, A., *Fugitive Offender*, London, 1965.
26. Foster, P. J., *Education and Social Change in Ghana*, London, 1965.
27. Gutteridge, W., *Armed Forces in New States*, London, 1962.
28. Hailey, Lord, *African Survey*, London, 1957.
29. Haywood, A. and Clarke, F. A. S., *History of the Royal West African Frontier Force*, Aldershot, 1964, London, 1965.
30. Hazlewood, A. (ed.), *African Integration and Disintegration*, London, 1967.
31. Higgins, R., *The Development of International Law Through the political Organs of the UN*, London, 1963.
32. Hodgkin, T., *Nationalism in Colonial Africa*, London, 1956.
33. Hoskyns, C., *The Congo since Independence January 1960–December 1961*, London, 1965.
34. Hovet, T., *Africa in the UN*, London, 1963.
35. Iketuonye, V. C., *Zik of New Africa*, London, 1961.
36. Kimble, D., *A Political History of Ghana 1850–1928*, London, 1963.
37. Kirk-Green, A. H. M. (ed.), *Crisis and Conflict in Nigeria* Vols. I and II, London, 1971.
38. Lefever, E. W., *Uncertain Mandate*, London, 1968.
39. Legum, C., *Pan-Africanism*, New York, 1962.
40. Lyon, P., *Neutralism*, Leicester, 1963.
41. Mackintosh, J. P., *Nigerian Government and Politics*, London, 1966.
42. Mansergh, N. (ed.), *Documents and Speeches on Commonwealth Affairs 1952-62*, London, 1963.
43. Martin, L. W. (ed.), *Neutralism and Non-alignment*, New York, 1962.
44. Martin, W., *The Gold Coast Legislative Council*, London, 1947.
45. Mazrui, A., *On Heroes and Uhuru Worship*, London, 1967.
46. Mazrui, A., *Towards Pax Africana*, London, 1967.
47. Menzies, R., *Afternoon Light*, London, 1967.
48. Miners, N. J., *The Nigerian Army 1956-66*, London, 1971.
49. Newlyn, W. T. and Rowan, D. C., *Money and British Colonial Africa*, Oxford, 1954.
50. Nicolson, I. F., *The Administration of Nigeria 1900-60*, London, 1969.
51. Nkrumah, K., *Ghana, The Autobiography*, London, 1957.

52. Nkrumah, K., *I Speak of Freedom*, London, 1961.
53. Nkrumah, K., *Towards Colonial Freedom*, London, 1962.
54. Nkrumah, K., *Africa Must Unite*, London, 1963.
55. Nkrumah, K., *Consciencism*, London, 1964.
56. Nkrumah, K., *Neo-colonialism, The Last Stage of Imperialism*, London, 1965.
57. Nkrumah, K., *Challenge of the Congo*, London, 1967.
58. Nkrumah, K., *Dark Days in Ghana*, London, 1968.
59. Northedge, F. S. (ed.), *The Foreign Policies of the Powers,* London, 1968.
60. O'Brien, C. C., *To Katanga and Back*, London, 1962.
61. Okigbo, P. N. C., *Africa and the Common Market*, London, 1967.
62. Omari, T. P., *Kwame Nkrumah: The Anatomy of an African Dictatorship*, London, 1970.
63. Panter-Brick, S. K. (ed.), *Nigerian Politics and Military Rule*, London, 1970.
64. Perham, M., *Native Administration in Nigeria*, London, 1937.
65. Perham, M. (ed.), *Mining, Commerce and Finance in Nigeria*, London, 1948.
66. Phillips, C. S., *The Development of Nigerian Foreign Policy*, London, 1964.
67. Post, K. W., *The New States of West Africa*, London, 1964.
68. Post, K. W., *The Nigerian Federal Elections of 1959*, London, 1963.
69. Quaison-Sackey, A., *Africa Unbound*, New York, 1963.
70. Rivkin, A., *The African Presence in World Affairs*, London, 1963.
71. Rosberg, C. and Friedland, W. H. (ed.), *African Socialism*, London, 1964.
72. Schatten, F., *Communism in Africa*, London, 1966.
73. Schwarz, F., *Nigeria, The Tribe, The Nation, The Race*, Massachussetts, 1965.
74. Schwarz, W., *Nigeria*, London, 1968.
75. Smith, Sharwood B., *But Always As Friends*, London, 1969.
76. Thompson, W. S., *Ghana's Foreign Policy 1957-66*, Princeton, 1969.
77. Wallerstein, I., *Africa, The Politics of Unity*, London, 1968.
78. Waugh, A. and Cronje, S., *Biafra: Britain's Shame*, London, 1969.
79. Wheare, J., *The Nigerian Legislative Council*, London, 1950.
80. Zartman, I. W., *International Relations in New Africa*, London, 1966.

II OFFICIAL PUBLICATIONS

1. Gold Coast/Ghana
— Legislative Assembly Debates 1954-7.
— National Assembly Debates 1957-66, and October 1969-December 1971. Visit of the Prime Minister, Dr Nkrumah to Nigeria, 1959. Statement by the Government on the Recent Conspiracy (Accra) December 1961.
— Ghana Treaty Series 1960-6.
— NLC—Nkrumah's Deception of Africa 1967.
  NLC—Nkrumah's Subversion in Africa, 1966.
  NLC—New Era in Ghana—1968.
— Apartheid and Its Elimination, 1971.
— Dr Kofi Busia in Europe and America, 1969.
— The Prime Minister in Singapore, 1971.
— Ghana-Ivory Coast Fraternity, 1970.

Volta River Project
— The Volta River Development Act (Act 42).
— Statement by the Government on the Volta River project on 20 February 1961.
— Volta River Project and Volta Aluminium Company Limited Vols. I and II, 1962.

Economy
— Economic Survey 1955-69.
— Census Report 1960.
— Bank of Ghana, Annual Reports 1960-70
— Report of Professor Arthur Lewis on Industrialization and the Gold Coast 1953.
— Quarterly Digest of Statistics.
— Annual Report on External Trade, 1958-69.
— NLC—Budget Statements 1966-9.
— Ghana Business Promotion Act.
  Rebuilding the National Economy.
  The State of the Economy and the External Debts Problem, 1970.

Development Plans
— The First Development Plan 1951-2 to 1956-7.
— The Second Development Plan 1959-64.
  The Seven-Year Plan 1963-4 to 1969-70.
  The One-Year Plan 1970-1.

2. Nigeria
— House of Representatives Debates 1955-66.

- Government Foreign Policy Statement on 20 August 1960.
- Anglo-Nigerian Defence Pact.
- Report of the (Willink) Commission to enquire into the allaying of the fears of the Minorities (London, 1958).
- Report of the Commission.
- Long Live African unity—Text of Speeches by His Excellency General Gowon to the OAU, 1969-71.

The Economy
- The first Ten-Year Development Plan 1945/46-55; the 1955-62 Plan.
- The first National Development Plan 1970-74.
- The Second National Development Plan 1970-74.
- Digest of Statistics 1951-71
  Annual Abstracts of Statistics 1960-9.
  Annual Reports of Central Bank 1960-70.
  Federal Government Estimates 1960-1 to 1971-2.
  Annual Report on External Trade 1960-9.
- Census Reports 1952-3; and 1963.

3. Common Inter-territorial Institutions
- Report of the Proceedings of the First West African Governors' Conference, Lagos, 1939.
- Regulations for the West African Frontier Force, London, 1953.
- Report of the West African Forces Conferences held in Lagos 1953; Cmnd 6577.
- Annual Reports of West African Airways Corporation 1947-56.
- Annual Report of the West African Currency Board.
- Annual Reports of the West African Institute for Trypanosomiasis 1951-63.
- Annual Report of the West African Institute of Social and Economic Research 1952-60.
- Annual Report of the West African Institute for Oil Palm Research 1952-63.
- Annual Reports of the West African Examinations Council 1954-64.
- Annual Reports of The West African Council for Medical Research 1954-63.
- Report of the Proceedings of the West African International Cocoa Research Conference, 1953.
- Report of the Proceedings of the Cacao Mirid Control Conference at Tafo, 1963.
- Minutes of the first meeting of the West African Inter-territorial Conference, 1952.

4. Organization of African Unity

— Verbatim Records of the Plenary meeting of the Ordinary Sessions of the Assembly of Heads of State and Government 1965-9.
— Committee B—Summary Records of the fifth Ordinary Session of the Council of Ministers, October 1965.
— Report and Proceedings of the Defence Commissions in 1963; and 1965 Doc.
  DEF1/Comm. II/SR 1-2, 1963.
— DEF/SR3 II, 1965.
— DEF/RO 6(II) 3 February 1965.

5. United Kingdom

— General Assembly Official Records 1960-9 Security Council Official Records 1962-9.
— UN Doc. A/4694, A/4711.
  UN Doc. S/4417, /Add. 6.
  UN Doc. S/6062; and S/6063.
  UN Doc. S/54003.
— ECA Doc. E/CN. 14/480/Rev.
  UN Treaty Series 1957-68.

6. Other

— House of Commons Debates, 1960-66.
— British Aid Statistics 1965, 69 (London), HMSO.
— The Reports of the Special Commonwealth African Assistance Plan 1961-5.
— US—Congressional Papers 1957-66.
— Is US Money Aiding Another Communist State? Staff Conference of the subcommittee to Investigate the Administration of the Internal Security Laws of the Committee on the Judiciary of the US Senate—87th Congress, 2nd session, December 1962.
— Ghana Students in US Oppose US Aid to Nkrumah. Staff Conference of the sub-committee to Investigate the Administration of the Internal Security Laws of the Committee on the Judiciary—88th Congress, 2nd session, February, 1964.
— The Conference of Heads of State or Government of Non-aligned countries, Belgrade, 1961; and Cairo, 1964.

III PERIODICALS, AND NEWSPAPERS

Foreign Affairs.
International Affairs (London).
The Year Book of World Affairs.

The Political Quarterly
Quarterly Journal of Administration.
The World Today.
The Journal of Modern African Studies.
The Economist.
African Research Bulletin.
Africa Diary.
West Africa.
The Times (London).
The Guardian (London).
The New York Times
The Washington Post.
The Ghanaian Times (Accra).
The Evening News (Accra).
The Evening Standard (Accra).
The Daily Graphic (Accra).
The Ashanti Pioneer (Kumasi).
The Daily Times (Lagos).
The Morning Post (Lagos).
The Daily Sketch (Ibadan).
The New Nigerian (Kaduna).
The Daily Express (Lagos).

*Index

*This book is indexed by Mr Dokun Fadiran, University of Ife Library, Ile-Ife, Nigeria.